Market-Based Banking and the International Financial Crisis

Market-Based Banking and the International Financial Crisis

Edited by
Iain Hardie and David Howarth

OXFORD
UNIVERSITY PRESS

OXFORD
UNIVERSITY PRESS

Great Clarendon Street, Oxford, OX2 6DP,
United Kingdom

Oxford University Press is a department of the University of Oxford. It furthers the University's objective of excellence in research, scholarship, and education by publishing worldwide. Oxford is a registered trade mark of Oxford University Press in the UK and in certain other countries

First Edition published in 2013

British Library Cataloguing in Publication Data
Data available

Library of Congress Cataloging in Publication Data
Data available

ISBN 978–0–19–966228–9

In memory of Jinty Hackett and Keir Howarth

Preface

The financial crisis which began in 2007 caught nearly everyone by surprise. Queen Elizabeth may have been directing her question 'Why did no one see it coming?' at economists (or at least the economists assumed she was), but a lack of prescience was widespread both inside academia and outside. There is room for debate as to the extent to which particular academic disciplines should be expected to predict crisis. International Political Economy has had such a debate. However, in one area the lack of foresight is particularly striking: the study of banks and banking. With very few exceptions, such as James Crotty, academics were not looking closely at banks, far less seeing the build-up of problems.

As we survey the wreckage and ongoing destruction in national banking systems, that lacuna appears more and more striking. 'What were the bankers doing?' cannot only be a legitimate cry of exasperation, but must also be the subject of serious study across a range of academic disciplines. This volume is, we hope, part of a start to that process. It is the result of three workshops, two in Edinburgh (December 2009 and June 2012) and one in Victoria, British Columbia (October 2010). Participants came from a range of disciplines and geographic specialisms, but the authors of chapters included in this volume see themselves as primarily political economists. Our main focus therefore has been comparative political economy, although we believe this book will be of interest to international political economists and economists, as well as policy makers seeking to stabilize national and international banking systems.

We concluded in those workshops that much political economy, and indeed economics, lacked a focus on banks and banking, and largely accepted that banks, as actors within the financial system, are different in important and fundamental ways. Underpinning the varieties of capitalism distinction between Liberal Market Economies and Coordinated Market Economies is the conception of banks as the suppliers of 'patient' capital to non-financial corporations (NFCs). Banks are able to act for NFCs as bulwarks against pressures from financial markets because banks themselves are able to resist such pressures. In a world of 'market-based banking', we believe that this assumption must be challenged.

Banks, to varying extents across the eleven advanced economies we examine in this volume, are themselves subject to market pressures. Increasingly, market-based assets mean that profit and loss, and capital, are determined not by correct decisions as to corporate creditworthiness, but by market prices and banks' calculations as to future market conditions. Increased borrowing by banks from wholesale markets to finance their lending—market-based liabilities—means that the price of bank borrowing determines the interest rates of bank lending. Banks become another market intermediary and loans become another traded financial asset. Recognizing this is essential to any typology of national financial systems.

The changes we discuss in the chapters that follow accelerated in the years from 2000 to the start of the financial crisis. As our authors discuss, their specific nature and extent across different countries are essential to understanding the ongoing financial crisis, in terms of its timing, extent and impact, via lending to NFCs, on the real economy. The experience of crisis has been very different for the countries discussed in this book, and we seek to make sense of these differences through the design and application of a new framework of analysis.

A project of this length of gestation and involving this number of participants involves the accumulation of many debts. Support for the workshops came from the University of Edinburgh Europa Institute, the European Commission Representation to the United Kingdom, and the Social Sciences and Humanities Research Council of Canada Aid to Scholarly Conferences Programme. Both Michele Chang and Erik Jones benefited enormously from discussions with Ivo Maes. Iain Hardie gratefully acknowledges the support of the UK's Economic and Social Research Council (RES-062-23-1958) and David Howarth funding from the Carnegie Trust for the Universities of Scotland to conduct essential research and interviews in Paris. They both wish to thank Charlotte Rommerskirchen, PhD candidate in the Department of Politics and International Relations at the University of Edinburgh, for valuable support on German language material. George Pagoulatos wishes to acknowledge the valuable research assistance of Christos Triantopoulos, PhD candidate at the Department of International and European Economic Studies, Athens University of Economics and Business. Lucia Quaglia wishes to acknowledge financial support from the European Research Council (204398 FINGOVEU). Research for her chapter was undertaken while she was visiting fellow at the Max Planck Institute, the EUI, and the Hansewissenschaftkolleg. She also wishes to acknowledge the valuable research assistance of Nina Arbabzadeh. Particularly helpful comments at our workshops were provided by Henrik Enderlein of the Hertie School of Governance and David Mayes, of the University of Auckland. Detailed comments by over a dozen anonymous reviewers on most of the chapter drafts helped improve both their quality and the coherence of the volume.

Iain Hardie, Edinburgh and David Howarth, Luxembourg
2 November 2012

Contents

List of Figures

List of Tables

List of Abbreviations

ABCP	asset-backed commercial paper
ABS	asset-backed securities
CDO	collateralized debt obligation
CDS	credit default swap
CME	coordinated market economy
CPE	comparative political economy
EMU	European Monetary Union
FSA	Financial Services Agency
GDP	gross domestic product
HRE	Hypo Real Estate
IMPP	Insured Mortgate Purchase Programme
KfW	Kreditanstalt für Wiederaufbau
LB	Landesbank
LME	liberal market economy
LTRO	long-term refinancing operations
LTV	loan-to-value
MME	mixed market economy
NFC	non-financial company
RMBS	residential mortgage-backed securities
SIV	special investment vehicle
SMEs	small and medium-sized enterprises
VoC	varieties of capitalism
VoFC	varieties of financial capitalism

List of Contributors

Michele Chang is a Professor in the European Political and Administrative Studies Department at the College of Europe, Bruges. Michele Chang received her doctorate in political science at the University of California at San Diego. Her publications include *Monetary Integration in the European Union* (Palgrave Macmillan 2009) and *Realigning Interests: Crisis and Credibility in European Monetary Integration* (Palgrave Macmillan 2004). She previously held positions at Colgate University, Cornell University, and most recently the Centre for European Policy Studies in Brussels. She has received grants from the Institute of Global Conflict and Cooperation, the Deutscher Akademischer Austausch Dienst and the Picker Foundation and was a Fulbright Research Fellow in the European Union. Dr Chang's research interests include European monetary cooperation, European integration and legitimacy, and financial crises. She is currently the co-chair of the European Union Studies Association's Political Economy Section.

Iain Hardie is a Lecturer in the School of Social and Political Sciences at the University of Edinburgh. Iain completed his first degree in 1985 in History at Gonville and Caius College, Cambridge, before beginning an investment banking career in London and Hong Kong, specializing in emerging bond markets. He came to Edinburgh in 2001 to complete a part-time MSc in International and European Politics, before completing a PhD in 2003–07. His PhD and first book examines the links between the financialization of government bond markets and emerging market government policy autonomy, focusing on case studies of Brazil, Lebanon, and Turkey. He also works with Professor Donald Mackenzie on the sociology of financial markets. Among numerous other works, he has written 'How Much Can Governments Borrow? Financialization and Emerging Markets Government Borrowing Capacity' in *Review of International Political Economy* 2011. 'Die Krise but not La Crise? The Financial Crisis and the Transformation of German and French Banking Systems' in *Journal of Common Market Studies* 2009 (co-authored with David Howarth).

David Howarth is a Professor of European Political Economy at the University of Luxembourg and Honorary Fellow at the University of Edinburgh. Until

September 2012, he was a Jean Monnet Chair in the School of Social and Political Sciences at the University of Edinburgh. He has written widely on European political economy topics, specifically European Monetary Union, central banking, and national banking systems. In additional to over fifty journal articles and book chapters on these subjects, David has written *The French Road to European Monetary Union* (Macmillan 2001) and co-authored *The European Central Bank: The New European Leviathan?* (Macmillan 2003, second edition 2005). David has served as guest editor for five journal special editions, including the *Journal of European Public Policy*. Most recently he is the co-editor (with Tal Sadeh) of *At the Frontier of the Single European Market: The Political Economy of Market Integration in the Early Twenty-First Century*, Routledge, 2011. He also regularly contributes to the Economic Intelligence Unit on European Political Economy topics.

Erik Jones is Director of European Studies at the Paul H. Nitze School of Advanced International Studies and Director of the Bologna Institute for Policy Research of The Johns Hopkins University. He is also Head of Europe at Oxford Analytica, a Senior Research Fellow at Nuffield College in Oxford, United Kingdom, and a Non-Resident Fellow at Pázmány Péter Catholic University in Budapest, Hungary. Professor Jones is author of *The Politics of Economic and Monetary Union* (2002), *Economic Adjustment and Political Transformation in Small States* (2008), and, together with Dana Allin, *Weary Policeman: American Power in an Age of Austerity* (2012). He is editor or co-editor of more than twenty books or special issues of journals on topics related to European politics and political economy including *The Oxford Handbook of the European Union* (2012). He is a regular columnist with *E!Sharp*.

Ryunoshin Kamikawa is an Associate Professor in the Graduate School of Law and Politics at Osaka University. He holds a PhD from Kyoto University in 2002. In 2008–09, he was a Visiting Scholar in the Centre for Japanese Research at University of British Columbia, Canada, and in 2012–13, he is a Visiting Associate Professor in College of International Affairs at National Chengchi University, Taiwan. His research and publications focus on Japanese political economy, politics of financial crisis, and politics of central bank independence. He has written *Politics of Economic Policies: Clarification of Institutional Settings which Caused Japanese Economic Crisis in 1990s* (2005) and *Politics of the Koizumi Reforms: Was Jun'ichiro Koizumi really a 'strong Prime Minister'?* (2010) (in Japanese). He has also written 'Managing the Bank-System Crisis in Coordinated Market Economies: Institutions and Blame Avoidance Strategies in Sweden and Japan' in *Governance* 2006 (co-authored with Torsten Svensson and Masaru Mabuchi).

Patrick Leblond is Associate Professor in the Graduate School of Public and International Affairs at the University of Ottawa as well as Research Associate at CIRANO (Montreal). He is also Affiliated Professor of International Business at HEC Montreal and visiting professor at the World Trade Institute (Bern, Switzerland) and the University of Barcelona (IELPO LLM program me). He is a member of Statistics Canada's International Trade Advisory Committee and an advisor to the Canada-Europe Roundtable for Business. Dr Leblond has published extensively on financial and monetary integration, banking regulation, international trade and business–government relations, with a particular focus on Europe and North America. Prior to moving to Ottawa, he taught international business at HEC Montreal and worked in accounting and auditing (he holds the title of Chartered Accountant) as well as in corporate finance and strategy consulting for major international accounting and consulting firms.

Sylvia Maxfield is Dean of the Providence College School of Business. She is a specialist in the global economy, financial, crises and corporate social responsibility. Previously she was MBA Director and Professor of Management at Simmons College. In business, Dr Maxfield was Vice President and Senior Sovereign Credit Analyst at the Wall Street firm of Lehman Brothers. At Yale for ten years, Dr Maxfield held joint faculty appointments in Management and Political Science and directed the Master's program me in International Relations. She has published several dozen books and articles about the interface of politics, society, and financial markets and has translated her research for non-academic audiences through publication in venues including *The Wall Street Journal*. She is a graduate of Cornell's School of Arts and Sciences and earned her MA and PhD degrees at Harvard University.

George Pagoulatos is a Professor of European Politics and Economy at the Department of International & European Economic Studies, Athens University of Economics & Business; Visiting Professor at the College of Europe in Bruges; Senior Fellow at ELIAMEP. His research and publications focus on the EU and Southern European political economy, European integration, economic governance, the political economy of banking and finance, and politics of reform. He is a member of the High Council of the European University Institute in Florence, and has served in the past as member of the Greek government's Council of Economic Advisors and a board member of various academic and civic organizations. Since 2007 he has been a regular contributor to the Sunday edition of the main Greek centrist newspaper Kathimerini. He has edited, authored, and co-authored five books, and published in journals such as *West European Politics, European Journal of Political Research, Journal of Public Policy, Journal of Common Market Studies, Public Administration*.

Lucia Quaglia is a Professor in the Department of Politics at the University of York. Lucia's research interests include central banking governance in the EU; financial services governance in the EU; macroeconomic governance in the European Union and Comparative European Political Economy. Lucia has published extensively in: *Governance; European Journal of Political Research; New Political Economy; Journal of Common Market Studies; Journal of European Public Policy; West European Politics; Comparative European Politics*. Lucia's monographs on Central Banking Governance in the EU (2008) and Financial Services Governance in the EU (2010) were published by Routledge. With Professor Kenneth Dyson (University of Cardiff), she has co-edited two volumes on key documents on European Economic Governance with a commentary (2010). With Dermot Hodson (Birbeck College) he has been the guest editor of the special issue on the financial crisis for the *Journal of Common Market Studies*.

Sebastián Royo is Associate Dean and Professor of Government at Suffolk University in Boston, and director of the Suffolk University Madrid Campus. Royo's articles and reviews have appeared in *Governance, Comparative Political Studies, European Journal of Industrial Relations, PS: Political Science and Politics, West European Politics, South European Society and Politics, Democratization, Mediterranean Quarterly, SELA, FP,* and *Perspectives on Politics*. Books include *From Social Democracy to Neoliberalism* (2000), *A New Century of Corporatism?* (2002), *Spain and Portugal in the EU* (with P. Manuel, 2003), *Portugal, Espanha e a Integração Europeia* (2005), *Varieties of Capitalism in Spain* (2008), *Portugal in the 21st Century* (2011), and *Lesson from the Crisis in Spain* (forthcoming 2013).

Amy Verdun is a Professor and Chair of Political Science, Jean Monnet Chair Ad Personam and the Director of the Jean Monnet Centre of Excellence, at the University of Victoria, in Victoria BC, Canada. She holds a PhD in Political and Social Sciences from the European University Institute Florence Italy (1995). She is author or editor of fourteen books and has published in scholarly journals such as *Acta Politica, British Journal of Politics and International Relations, European Union Politics, International Studies Review, Journal of Common Market Studies, Journal of European Integration, Journal of European Public Policy, Journal of Public Policy and Review of International Political Economy*. Two of her recent books are *Globalization, Development and Integration*, Pompeo della Posta and Amy Verdun (eds) (2009) (Basingstoke: Palgrave Macmillan); and *Innovative Governance: The Politics of Multilevel Policymaking*, Ingeborg Toemmel and Amy Verdun (eds) (2009) (Boulder: Lynne Rienner). She has a book forthcoming with Cambridge University Press entitled *Ruling Europe: The Politics of the Stability and Growth Pact* co-authored with Martin Heipertz which was published in March 2010. Professor Verdun is the current co-editor of the *Journal of Common Market Studies*.

1

Introduction: Towards a Political Economy of Banking

Iain Hardie, David Howarth, Sylvia Maxfield, and Amy Verdun

Introduction

The dichotomy that underpins most contemporary examinations of national financial systems distinguishes between the two main components: bank credit and capital markets. Financial systems have been analysed in terms of the relative presence of these two components by economists, political economists, and scholars in a range of disciplines and sub-disciplines. Very few studies have queried the analytical usefulness of this dichotomy. The operation of the financial system in terms of the relative presence of bank credit versus capital markets is then seen as having implications for non-financial companies (NFCs) and other elements of the national economy.

We argue that this dichotomized understanding of financial systems has contributed to the widespread intellectual incapacity to grasp the nature of changes to national financial systems and to explain, much less predict, the differential impact of the recent financial crisis on advanced industrialized economies. The aim of this volume is to demonstrate why an appreciation of the new activities of banks is crucial to understand the development of financial systems. We propose market-based banking as a model and analytical tool that can be applied to explain the development of national financial systems over the decade prior to the international financial crisis that erupted in 2007. By focusing on banks' choices about their business activities, we are able to pinpoint important drivers for change in national financial systems and the activities that contributed to the international financial crisis. The eight country chapters of this volume examine market-based banking in eleven countries, examining banking and financial system change and the impact of the financial crisis. We have selected a range of wealthier countries, including all seven of the former G7 'advanced industrialized' economies, covering the different types of financial systems and economic models. We have included countries which have been affected very differently during the financial crisis.

In this introductory chapter, we first review the standard dichotomy and examine its influence in the comparative political economy (CPE) literature, which is the disciplinary focus of most of the contributors to this volume. We next explain how effectively scholars of the political economy of finance explain the phenomenon of change. The subsequent section briefly describes the market-based banking model in the context of the broader national financial systems. We present the details of the market-based banking framework in the second chapter of this volume (Hardie and Howarth). In the penultimate section, we consider the impact of market-based banking on the domestic political economy and the impact of the international financial crisis.

The Political Economy of Finance

Differences in national systems of finance have been the object of study in several academic disciplines: in financial economics (for example, Allen and Gale 2000; Hackethal 2001; Schmidt, Hackethal and Tyrell 2001); economic sociology (for example, Krippner 2005); business studies (for example, Davis 1996; Davis and Steil 2001; Useem 1996); legal studies (for example, La Porta et al. 1998); and International Political Economy (IPE) (for example, Helleiner 1996; Pauly 1995; Strange 1988, 1996). Nearly all these studies assume the bank credit–capital markets dichotomy and its perennity. There was, prior to 2008, surprisingly little examination of developments in banking and the impact of these developments on national financial systems. A small body of literature in the sub-field of financial economics is a partial exception. See, for example, Rajan (1998) on the decreasing importance of commercial banks in the US financial system. Rajan and Zingales (2003) predict a limit to the development of market-based systems in European financial systems but see political factors as most relevant, ignoring developments in banking. A handful of policy makers and practitioners also analysed changes in banking (Gerald Corrigan 1982; Feeney 1995).

Over the past thirty years, the literature on the political economy of finance has started from the premise that financial systems shape the availability of capital to actors through differential pricing. The resulting access and pricing structure has economic and political implications. Differences in national systems of finance, however, have rarely been the primary object of study in CPE. CPE studies on banks and banking systems are particularly lacking, with a very small number of important exceptions (notably Deeg 1999). Rather, most CPE studies assume that the financial sector fits a standard depiction and then construct an analysis about the interaction of the assumed financial system with other elements of the domestic political economy—including state and non-state actors—and then analyse the resulting economic outcomes.

For comparative political economists, Zysman's (1983) *Government, Markets and Growth: Financial Systems and the Politics of Industrial Change* is the work of reference on the political economy of national financial systems. In his study, Zysman outlines three main varieties of financial capitalism (VoFC): government-led credit based, bank credit based, and capital market based. Zysman's (1983) main contribution was to show how these three varieties, depicted as relatively static, shaped the scope for government action and industrial development. Zysman's contribution was institutionalist in that he placed emphasis upon long-standing institutional structures that determine the policy alternatives open to both government actors and financial market operators. Since the publication of Zysman's book, the government-led variety has been reformed largely out of existence in developed economies, leaving scholars with the standard dichotomy (Culpepper 2005; Clift 2007). In credit-based financial systems, bank institutions play a central role in the economy intermediating between household savers and entrepreneurs. This system is seen as a core element of the variety of capitalism (VoC) found in Japan and many West European economies, notably Germany, and frequently labelled as coordinated market economies (CMEs) (Hall and Soskice 2001a). The capital market-based financial system is similarly a core element of another VoC, referred to as the liberal market economy (LME) (Hall and Soskice 2001a) and typified by the UK and the US. Although there has been more nuanced categorization of the varieties of capitalism typologies by identifying new types, such as mixed market economies (MMEs), (see, for example, Amable 2003; Hancké, Rhodes and Thatcher 2007; Whitley 1999; Wood and Frynas 2006), there has been very little effort in unpackaging Zysman's understanding of national financial systems as such.

For Zysman and many comparative political economists, the contrast between market- and credit-based systems depends on a very specific role for banks as bulwarks against the influence of financial markets on NFCs. The banks' bulwark role is dependent on banks being suppliers of 'patient capital' to clients with which they have a relational, not arm's-length, interaction. Two economists, Rajan and Zingales (2003, 12), suggest that '[b]y its very nature, a relationship-based system does not pay much attention to market or price signals'. Crucially, in such a system, banks must be able to 'not pay much attention to market or price signals' (Rajan and Zingales (2003, 12). Banks 'draw their funds from deposits' (Zysman 1983, 61), depositors are loyal, and as a result banks have ready access to the funds they require for their lending. This is central to Zysman's typology and the more standard dichotomy. In contrasting 'a system based on capital markets with resources allocated by prices established in competitive markets' with 'a credit-based system dominated by financial institutions' (Zysman 1983, 55), Zysman is assuming, as many others implicitly have (for example, Rajan and Zingales 2003), that the capacity of banks in credit-based systems to themselves borrow would not change their dominant role. Zysman also does not consider the need for banks to have capital to support lending. The distinction Zysman makes is between financial agents and financial intermediaries (Zysman 1983, 57). Banks are agents in terms of their lending decisions, whose financial power allows them to influence the pricing of credit in an economy. Financial institutions that act as intermediaries in the provision of bond and equity financing merely reflect the relevant market's pricing of that financing.

Central to the bank-based system, and to the existing dichotomy, is therefore banks' 'financial power', derived from the fact that 'a limited number of financial institutions dominate the system' (Zysman 1983, 72).[1] Unless 'the movement of prices in the markets reflects [the] concentration of market power' (Zysman 1983, 72), the bank-based/capital market-based distinction is largely meaningless, because the movement of prices in bank lending would be determined by the market in the same way as the prices of other financial assets. We argue that this is now generally the case in bank lending, although to a different extent across the countries the following chapters analyse. In reality, banks acting as agents in terms of their business models have undermined their 'financial power' in lending to NFCs. Banks have increasingly turned themselves into market intermediaries in these lending activities.

Banks are seen as potentially supplying two kinds of patient capital: long-term holdings of equity or long-term bank loans. Importantly, Zysman emphasizes both, and the interaction between the two. When Hall and Soskice (2001b) published their book, CME banks were already selling down their shareholdings (Hall and Soskice 2001b, 23) and expanding their business activities (Hall and Soskice 2001b, 62). Yet CPE scholars writing on NFC finance in CMEs have largely insisted on the persistence of bank lending as 'patient'. They emphasize the continued importance of relational banking in CMEs, allowing 'access to capital independent of current profitability' (Hall and Soskice 2001b, 16), most notably in the archetypal bank-based financial system, Germany (Hall and Soskice 2001b, 62; Vitols 2004; Deeg 2010).[2] Such systems have persistently high aggregate bank lending in NFC finance (Vitols 2004; Deeg 2010). We argue that this claim of continued patient lending is problematic. It implies that the changing activities of banks do not have an impact upon their role as patient lender

[1] A further pillar of banks' 'financial power' is therefore a lack of competition between banks (see Byrne and Davis 2003; Rajan and Zingales 2003; Lall 2006).

[2] This view of the continued importance of the Hausbank to German NFCs is also challenged by some academics, e.g. Beyer and Höpner (2003).

to NFCs. The argument depends on banks being able to lend long term and to continue to support their NFC clients regardless of market pressures on the banks themselves. We argue that this view of banks as bulwarks against market pressures has become inaccurate, and relies—in contrast to extensive analysis of the changing nature of equity financing—on a static conception of banks and loans and an unwillingness to consider in detail this area of financial markets.

Our focus on banks and lending, and on the rise of market-based banking, highlights a crucial source of change which undermines 'patient capital'. Market-based banking inherently undermines the central position of 'relational' house banking by increasing the position of market considerations relative to long-term investment considerations in bank business decisions. Of further importance is that the rise of market-based banking potentially affects corporate governance in small and medium-sized enterprises (SMEs), which depend more heavily on bank financing than larger firms that tend to have more diversified funding, including equity. Examples of such SMEs would include the German *Mittelstand*, whose unchanged financing sources are emphasized in the debate on CME change (Deeg 2010).

The VoC literature rests on the importance and nature of equity financing, and often untested assumptions that the discipline imposed through dispersed equity ownership and take-over threats in capital market-based financial systems squeezes out labour protections, social welfare policies, and a host of other social, political, and economic characteristics. The key causal mechanism in this literature stems from the concentration or dispersion of share ownership, which is examined closely (Gourevitch and Shinn 2005), revealing significant cross-national variation. Patient equity capital (whether held by banks or other long-term investors) is a core observable feature of CMEs and it allows national political economies to maintain their distinctive VoC rather than converging on the liberal market model (Schmidt 2002; Culpepper 2005). The continued viability of this institutional diversity hinges on the ability of coordinated financial systems, such as those in Germany and Japan, to shield company managers from the short-term imperatives characteristic of liberal market economies (Culpepper 2005). Generally, the examination of national financial systems was not in the mainstream of the VoC literature, which has maintained a more narrow focus on the welfare state component of national systems of capitalism or labour relations within the state (see Hicks 1988; Hall and Soskice 2001a; Hancké, Rhodes, and Thatcher 2007).

Crucially, when we consider the recent financial crisis, the depiction of national financial systems originating with Zysman and the 'dichotomous framing' employed in the VoC literature does not fit the character of national financial systems in the 2000s. Banks (measured in terms of assets) increased their presence in national financial systems at the expense of equity in the large majority of advanced industrialized economies—including the LMEs. Trends in NFC financing further question existing depictions. The rise in both bank lending and bank assets to gross domestic product (GDP) were most marked in the supposedly model LME, the UK.[3] Indeed, the result left the Bank of England highlighting 'the potential benefits of lowering the economy's reliance on bank finance' (Bank of England 2009a: 11). Furthermore, in a range of other countries that had seen a previous shift towards capital market-based capitalism—notably France and the Netherlands—the direction was reversed in the 2000s. An examination of NFC external funding is provided in Figure 1.1 and Table 1.1. Here, we see the increased reliance of NFCs on bank lending in both real and relative terms in the seven years preceding the financial crisis in six of the eleven countries studied in this volume.

The data in Figure 1.2 and Table 1.2 provide the second principal method of distinguishing between national financial systems by focusing upon the

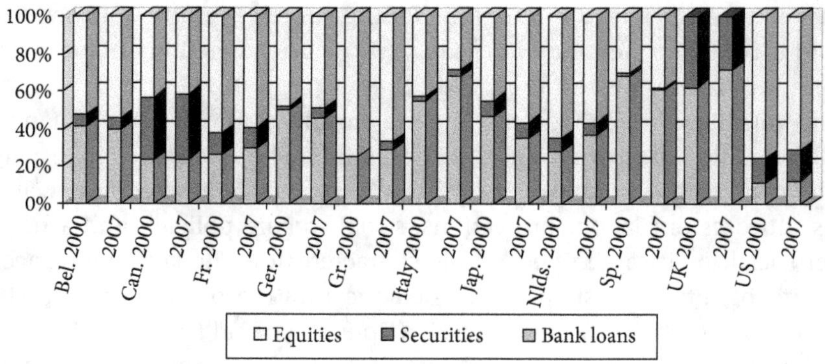

Figure 1.1. Non-financial company finance (bank loans, securities, equities) as a percentage of total (2000 and 2007)

Sources: EU member state figures are drawn from the ECB statistics data warehouse except where noted, accessed 22 November 2010; Federal Reserve Flow of Funds, December 2010 and December 2004 releases; Ministry of Internal Affairs and Communications, Statistical Research and Training Institute (2001, 2008), *Japan Statistical Yearbook*, Ministry of Internal Affairs and Communications, Statistics Bureau; Bank of Japan. Banque de France figures. Banque de France, Endettement des enterprise, <http://www.banque-france.fr/fr/statistiques/titres/titres-endettement-snf.htm>, accessed 22 January 2011. Bundesbank figures. Non-financial corporations/stocks/liabilities. <http://www.bundesbank.de/statistik/statistik_zeitreihen.en.php?lang=en&open=&func=list&tr=www_v39_nuverb>; accessed 2 November 2010. Japan (Bank of Japan) figures are for the end of the fiscal year (thus end-March). Banco de Espana figures. See <http://www.bde.es/webbde/es/estadis/ccff/0203.pdf>, accessed 12 January 2011. De Nederlandsche Bank, Security issues, Issues of securities other than shares by Dutch residents, <http://www.statistics.dnb.nl/index.cgi?lang=uk&todo=Emissie>, accessed 12 October 2010. US lending figures include bank loans, loans from other financial institutions and corporate mortgages with corresponding amounts as follows: (for 2000) 861, 651, 370; (for 2007) 609, 1350, 882. The Bank of England/Treasury does not collect data on outstanding equity issued (only new equity issues and growth). The figures for the UK thus only demonstrate the growth of bank lending in relation to securities

[3] Table 1.1 does not include figures for outstanding equity issuance by British NFCs because these data are not collected. Rather Bank of England and London Stock Exchange data cover annual flows (rise in equity issuance on an annual basis).

Table 1.1. Non-financial company finance (bank loans, securities, equities) 2000–7 (per cent increase/decrease, end of year)

	Lending Increase %	Securities Increase %	Equity Increase %
Belgium	20.7	25	32
Canada	26	38.5	27.4
France	45.6	18	21.5
Germany	5.2	123	17.9
Greece	63.1	325	29.6
Italy	62.8	190	−12.8
Japan	−28	2.5	21
Netherlands	45	6.3	3.5
Spain	42.3	−2.2	201.6
UK	74.9	40.3	N/A
US	51	59.6	24

Sources: See Figure 1.1.

Figure 1.2. National financial systems (2000 and 2007): bank assets, private debt market, equity market capitalization as a percentage of total financial system assets

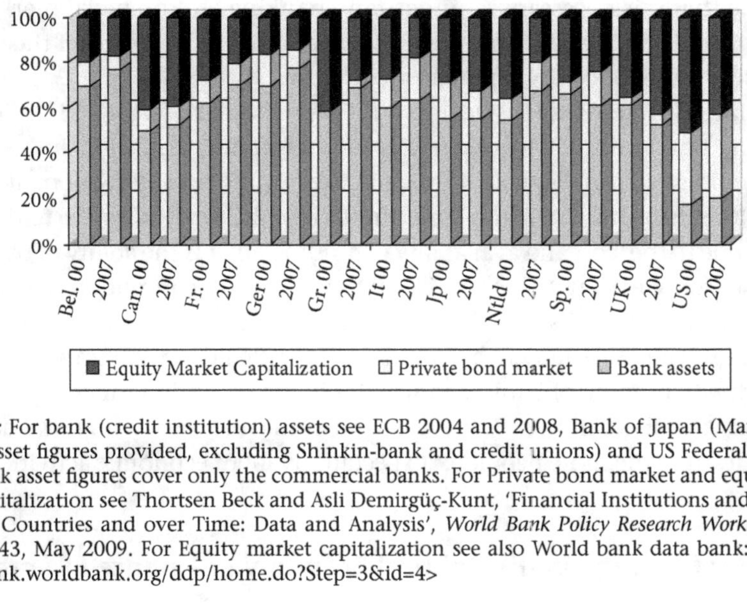

Sources: For bank (credit institution) assets see ECB 2004 and 2008, Bank of Japan (March 2001 bank asset figures provided, excluding Shinkin-bank and credit unions) and US Federal Reserve. US bank asset figures cover only the commercial banks. For Private bond market and equity market capitalization see Thortsen Beck and Asli Demirgüç-Kunt, 'Financial Institutions and Markets Across Countries and over Time: Data and Analysis', *World Bank Policy Research Working Paper* No. 4943, May 2009. For Equity market capitalization see also World bank data bank: <http://databank.worldbank.org/ddp/home.do?Step=3&id=4>

relative amounts of bank assets, private sector securities, and equity markets (as in Allen and Gale 2000). Here the increased real *and* relative size and importance of banks in national financial systems is indicated in *all* the countries except one (Japan[4]). However, rather than interpreting these data in terms of a return to the more bank-based financial systems of the past,

[4] The Japanese exception (where NFCs have relied increasingly on equity issues and a significant drop in borrowing from banks) reflects in part the limited engagement with market-based banking by Japanese banks (see Kamikawa, this volume). Total bank lending also dropped in Japan.

Table 1.2. National financial systems, bank assets, private debt market, equity market capitalization to gross domestic product, 2000–7, percentage increase

	Bank assets increase	Private bond market increase	Equity market capitalization increase
Belgium	39.1	–29	10.4
Canada	43.4	15.4	29.4
France	43.2	23.7	–7.7
Germany	4.5	–43.9	–20.5
Greece	2.7	3400	–40.2
Italy	17.3	68.6	–26.8
Japan	10.3	–18.7	27
Netherlands	48	57.4	–33.7
Spain	52.1	295.9	35.6
UK	49.2	19.4	–26.5
US	17.9*	23.3	–12.2

*Commercial banks' lending figures only.

Sources: see Figure 1.2.

we argue that it is necessary to understand banking and financial markets as intertwined. It is precisely this intertwining that lies at the heart of the financial crisis, as the following chapters make clear.

This intertwining is discussed more fully in the next chapter (Hardie and Howarth), but we make here one observation regarding the factors influencing bank lending to NFCs. Figure 1.3 shows figures for the tightening of bank lending to NFCs from mid-2007 (the intensification of the financial crisis) to the end of 2011 due to the 'cost and availability of funding', that is the ability of banks to borrow to fund lending.[5] This is a reason that Zysman's conception of banks as funded by stable deposits, and therefore as bulwarks against market pressures on NFCs, cannot envisage (absent a deposit run), yet it made a significant contribution to the tightening of bank lending conditions—a credit crunch—in all the countries examined. In the UK the 'cost and availability of funding' was almost as significant as the more nebulous 'expectations about economic activities'.[6]

Sources of Change in the Political Economy of Finance Literature

Most of the CPE literature that invokes a role for financial systems in advanced industrial economies does not pay attention to differences among national

[5] These data are not available for the Netherlands, Belgium, Canada, and Greece. Japanese banks reported no tightening of bank lending conditions for reasons linked to cost and availability of funding.

[6] UK credit conditions survey data show that cumulative tightening due to the 'cost and availability of funding' over the six quarters from mid-2007 to end 2008 was 233.4, while cumulative tightening due to 'expectations about economic activities' reached 235.8 (Bank of England 2009b).

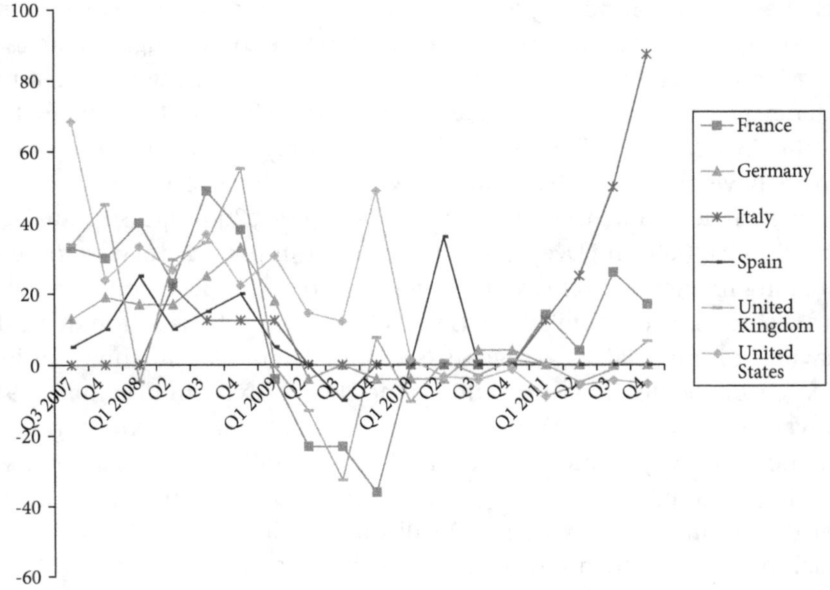

Figure 1.3. Tightening of bank lending due to 'cost and availability' of funding

banking systems. Recently, the institutionalist literature on capitalism has begun to explore sources of change in domestic political economies, but none focus, as this volume does, on banks' choices about business activities. In contrast, banking business has been construed as a source of change in the IPE literature to a much greater extent than in the CPE literature. In particular, as the nature of international financial markets changed after the 1970s with significant growth in global markets, IPE scholars made these changes an object of study and explored the way change in international financial markets shaped domestic political economy (Andrews 1994; Pauly 1988; Abdelal 2007). Political economy studies of financial market integration also focus on the actions and responses by individual states to these challenges (see, for example, Deeg (1999) on Germany; Katz (1998) on Japan; Loriaux (1991) on France, and Verdun (2000) on Britain, France, and Germany).

While dichotomous positioning is still characteristic of the CPE of capitalism, the literature includes a recent turn to exploring sources of change. Streeck (2004) focuses upon the role of governments, and Hall and Thelen (2009) theorize about the role of both governments and firms. A longstanding research stream at the intersection of CPE and management studies explores the way that NFC preferences and operations explain shifts in national capitalism and associated institutional characteristics (Whitley 1992, 1999; Guillén 2001; Aguilera and Jackson 2003; Crouch 2005; Hancké and Goyer 2005).

As the CPE literature begins to theorize sources of change in national capitalism and market institutions, the time is ripe to investigate sources of change in financial institutions and systems and correct the long-standing tendency to take the financial system as an invariant part of an explanation for other aspects of the domestic political economy. A small number of CPE scholars have placed emphasis on the agency of domestic actors in shaping national financial system change (Crouch 2005; Deeg 2007; Jackson and Deeg 2008). Busch (2009) and Deeg (2005) focus on the importance of governments in shaping financial systems through regulation and supervision. Parallel to this are studies by economists focused on the impact of regulation upon the behaviour of financial sector agents (see, for example, Hellmann, Murdock and Stiglitz 2000; Barth, Caprio and Levine 2006; Leaven and Levine 2009).

Government actions shaping national financial systems extend beyond regulation narrowly defined to 'industrial' or 'sectoral' policy that amounts to protecting certain financial business sectors from competition and/or encouraging development in new arenas. O'Sullivan (2007), for example, depicts the crucial role of the French state in directing financial market reform and driving the creation of the domestic bond market (see also Howarth, this volume). Similarly Posner (2005, 2009) outlines the role of the European Commission in pushing the creation of European stock markets. Other CPE scholarship aims to explain sources of change in national financial systems, emphasizing NFCs' funding strategies or bank–NFC interactions as the independent variable (Culpepper 2005; O'Sullivan 2007; Erturk and Solari 2007; Deeg 2010).

Generally, comparative political economists have not examined the role of bankers themselves as an autonomous and primary driver of change in national financial systems, as we do here. This is curious, given the importance of banks to most financial systems in providing a significant proportion of NFC external finance—even in the Anglo-American systems. The market-based banking model introduced here focuses on a particular set of business activities banks chose increasingly in many advanced industrial economies beginning in the late 1990s. The sources of dynamism in this volume are the choices of bankers about their business activities, and the aspects of the broader environment that shape those choices.

The chapters in this volume emphasize the role of banks as agents: making business decisions, engaging (or not engaging) in financial innovation, and responding to their own experience in the market (including their experience with global liquidity and previous banking crises) and not just as institutionally embedded actors (Crouch 2005; Hall and Thelen 2009). Nonetheless, the chapters that follow varyingly highlight one or more of six different institutional factors shaping bankers' business choices: banking regulation (including capital stringency), banking supervision, corporate governance rules, fiscal (including tax) policy, the structure of other financial institutions in place (notably equity and bond markets), and protectionism in the banking sector (both direct and indirect forms). There is overlap here: notably protectionism is often achieved through corporate governance rules and fiscal policies. In their depiction of these different considerations that may underpin bankers' choices about business activities, the chapters in this volume rub elbows with several other streams of research, such as the literature on the political economy of regulation and supervision (Pagano and Volpin 2001; Underhill, Blom and Mügge 2010; Quaglia 2011). Regulation and supervision can reflect the previous history of banking crises (Busch 2009; Royo, this volume; Kamikawa, this volume). Another related arena of inquiry addresses the impact of corporate governance structures on the behaviour of financial institutions (Barth et al. 2006). For example, Laeven and Levine (2009) point to riskier behaviour for banks where shareholders have more say.

National capital and regulatory regimes have shaped banking activities and have been widely perceived as the principal factors contributing to the impact of the financial crisis. However there are limits to the regulation, supervision, and corporate governance explanations for bankers' choices. The data produced by Barth et al. (2006) on capital stringency and bank regulation show the diversity of regulatory practice in our case countries and Table 1.3 juxtaposes these data with different levels of write-downs on financial assets and public funds drawn upon by banks in the financial crisis until 2010. Regulation is a moderately good predictor of the crisis with regard to Italy, Greece, and Spain, where market-based banking levels, especially with regards to assets, were comparatively low, in part because of capital stringency and regulation, and the direct impact of the financial crisis on banking systems limited. Clearly, however, as the relevant chapters make clear (Pagoulatos and Quaglia, this volume; Royo this volume), subsequent events have undermined even this moderately good prediction. However, regulation alone is anyway less useful in teasing out the differences with regard to other countries where scores are similar (as with the Netherlands, Germany, and France), but the forms of market-based banking and the impact of the financial crisis are considerably different. Such a superficial focus on regulation most obviously fails to predict the impact of the financial crisis on the US (see Hardie and Maxfield, this volume). One might criticize the values the authors assign to regulatory regimes, not the relevance of regulation *per se*. One might also recommend a more specific analysis focused upon national rules on the kinds of financial activities that contributed to the crisis: notably, off-balance sheet activities and securitization. However, it remains that several other factors contributed to the different levels and forms of market-based banking in national banking systems. Kamikawa's chapter on Japan is particularly noteworthy in this regard. He shows not only how low market-based banking limited the impact of the crisis on Japan's banks, but also how Japanese banks retreated from

Table 1.3. Capital and bank regulation, write-downs and public support (2007–10)

	Belgium	Canada	France	Germany	Greece	Italy	Japan	Netherlands	Spain	UK‡	US
Capital stringency*	NA	4	2	1	3	4	4	3	4	3	4
Restrict†	NA	7	6	5	9	10	13	6	7	5	12
Securities write-downs as a % total bank assets (2007)	0.44 (08–09 only)	0.84 (07–09 only)	0.38 (7/07 to 4/10 only)	2	0.012 (07–09 only)	0.086 (07–09 only)	0.22, (April 2009 est.)	1.8	0.17	0.52	2.6
Public funds drawn upon by banks (% 2007 GDP) by end 2009	6	0.5	1.1	4.9	0	0.3	0.2	2.5	1.1	6.5	4.8

*Capital stringency is an index of regulatory oversight of bank capital. This index is based on the following questions: is the minimum capital asset ratio requirement risk weighted in line with the Basel guidelines? Does the minimum ratio vary as a function of market risk? Are market values of loan losses not realized in accounting books deducted from capital? Are unrealized losses insecurities portfolios deducted? Are unrealized foreign exchange losses deducted? What fraction of revaluation gains is allowed as part of capital? Are the sources of funds to be used as capital verified by the regulatory or supervisory authorities? Can the initial disbursement or subsequent injections of capital be done with assets other than cash or government securities? Can initial disbursement of capital be done with borrowed funds? Thus, capital stringency does not measure statutory capital requirements. Instead, it measures the regulatory approach to assessing and verifying the degree of capital at risk in a bank (Laeven and Levine 2009: 263).

†Restrict is an index of regulatory restrictions on the activities of banks. 'This index measures regulatory impediments to banks engaging in securities market activities (e.g. underwriting, brokering, dealing, and all aspects of the mutual fund industry), insurance activities (e.g. insurance underwriting and selling), real estate activities (e.g. real estate investment, development, and management), and the ownership of nonfinancial firms' (Laeven and Levine 2009: 263).

‡Figures for the UK are not provided in the original study but are reproduced in Laeven and Levine 2008.

Sources: Barth et al., 2006 for the figures on capital stringency and banking restrictions. National Central Banks, 'Financial Stability Report' and IMF Global Financial Stability Report, April/October 2010 for figures on securities write-downs and public funds drawn.

market-based banking as a result of Japan's own crisis in the late 1980s and subsequent 'lost decade', and despite continued financial deregulation.

Table 1.3 also demonstrates the ambiguous correlation between the development of market-based banking, the impact of the financial crisis and traditional categorizations of varieties of (financial) capitalism. For example, in LMEs—notably the UK and US—market-based banking had developed further than most other national economies and the economies were hit particularly hard and early during the financial crisis. Similarly, the so-called MMEs of southern Europe—Greece, Italy, and Spain—developed less market-based banking and were far less affected during the early stages of the financial crisis, but have become a focus of attention later. There are also several cases where banking activities and the impact of the financial crisis do not conform to the VoC—thus several CMEs, including Belgium, Germany, and the Netherlands, were hit very hard by the financial crisis which has been otherwise associated with LMEs. Similarly, it can be added, LMEs including Australia and Canada suffered little (Porter 2010; Leblond 2011; Leblond, this volume). This lack of a clear correlation—demonstrated clearly by the eleven country cases analysed in this volume—suggests the need for a new way of analysing and distinguishing financial systems and one that provides an explanation of change.

Even in the cases where tight bank regulation corresponded initially to limited financial crisis, there remain significant differences in banks' engagement with the market. Market-based banking is multifaceted, and potentially involved both asset and liability sides of a bank's balance sheet. This influences both the nature and timing of the impact of the crisis. The Spanish central bank, for example, was widely praised for the regulation that limited banks' use of the off-balance sheet vehicles that caused bankruptcy at some German banks (see Royo this volume; Hardie and Howarth, this volume). However, Spanish banks were highly market based on the liability side of their balance sheets, especially in relatively high levels of securitized borrowing (that is, banks transforming loans into asset-backed securities (ABS)) which contributed to the property market bubble in that country. Thus, while the financial crisis did not have a devastating direct impact on most Spanish banks, the collapse in demand for ABS had a knock-on effect on Spanish bank lending, the bursting of the asset price bubble, and a seemingly rather more 'traditional' banking crisis.

An understanding of what shapes the extent to which bankers embrace different kinds of products or lines of business activity must take into consideration the broader range of variables outlined here. The chapters in this volume do not, however, test these variables formally. The focus is upon the activities of banks. However, most if not all of the variables are discussed in each of the chapters as relevant, to contribute to a more complete understanding of national financial, and specifically banking, systems. We argue that the level and form of market-based banking provide a better guide to the impact of the international financial crisis upon different countries than regulatory framework or political economy type. In the next chapter, we place national banking systems on a scatter plot graph and on a continuum, the position on which correlates more closely with the impact of the financial crisis.

The Impact of Market-Based Banking on the Domestic Political Economy

The chapters of this volume focus in detail on describing banking activity and the impact of the financial crisis, and secondarily on some of the factors that shape bankers' choices about the extent to which they engage in market-based banking. However, in addition to economics, our analysis of banking is also relevant to political economy and political science for its impact on social groups and governments. The starting point for our discussion of the ways market-based banking might impact upon the real economy, different stakeholders, and government, is how financial institutions make profits. The literature on varieties of capitalism implicitly suggests that financial institutions have two possible business models. In one model predominant in bank-based or credit market systems, financial institutions make loans at higher interest rates than they pay on deposits. The banks intermediate between household savers and entrepreneur borrowers and, usually, homeowners. Banks' 'funding base' in this system is household deposits, and banks are 'price setters' in the interest rates they pay to depositors and charge borrowers. In the second model which predominates in the capital market-based system, financial institutions underwrite initial stock or bond offerings and are fee-taking brokers buying and selling those stocks or bonds for retail or institutional customers and, usually, trading those stocks or bonds for 'the house' (the financial institution itself). In this system, financial institutions intermediate between saver–investors and entrepreneurs, with the financial institution as a price-taker earning a small fee for intermediation.

In the third model evident in the chapters included in this volume, financial institutions rely on the market to enable their lending in a variety of ways. To varying degrees in our different country cases, this business model exists alongside the more traditional business models. In this market-based banking, banks and other financial institutions themselves borrow to finance their own lending, often in complex 'production' chains of financial assets. As a result of that chain, a bank or financial institution intermediates between a saver and a household or entrepreneur borrower by making a loan, but the 'saver' is increasingly another financial institution investing through the market. In addition, another financial institution—most infamously AIG—may provide credit insurance (at a market-determined price), thereby assuming the credit risk inherent in the loan. This is a credit-driven model, but the loan originator, unlike the classic bank-based model, is less and less likely to be dependent on deposit-taking. In this model, commercial banks increasingly depend on borrowing and hedging from financial markets for their lending, and parallel banks, any financial institution that lends but does not take in deposits (and therefore does not ordinarily enjoy lender of last resort support from a central bank), have taken on a share of the loan origination business of commercial banks. These parallel banks are almost totally dependent on the market to finance their borrowing and determine the price of their lending.

The political economy of each system differs in simple but important ways. In the credit market-based system the major risk is borne by the banks in the unlikely case of a run by savers who withdraw deposits. In the capital market-based system as conceived in the existing VoC and VoFC literature, the financial institution pushes off risk of failure in the enterprise sector to the investing public. The main locus of risk in this system is the failing NFC enterprise (see Hardie and Maxfield, this volume).

In the third business model outlined in this volume, the financial institution transforms debt into investment by intermediating between debtors and investors who are predominantly other financial institutions. Pooling of underlying receivables in the creation of securitized assets appears to lower risk. Helping with this risk lowering are insurance companies. The entrepreneur from outside the financial sector is not a major focus in this business model. The main locus of risk is, as in the classic credit-based system, the financial institution. It faces the risk of a new type of bank run caused not by depositors but by other, much more skittish, financial institutions.

In this volume we label this third business model as market-based banking. This is closest to Aglietta and Breton (2001, 437), who recognize the change from a bank-based to a more market-based financial system, which they link to financial liberalization and financial innovation resulting from technological advance. They also recognize how banks add a 'new market portfolio' to their 'traditional credit portfolio' (Aglietta and Breton 2001, 441; see also Froud, Leaver, and Williams 2007). This market-based activity involves a range of activities: derivatives trading and investment in complex securities; raising funds on the wholesale markets (inter-bank borrowing, issue of securities, etc.). Securitization is an advanced form of market-based banking: the financial technique through which a financial institution converts assets (e.g. mortgages or other loans) into tradable instruments (such as ABS or asset-backed commercial paper) which financial institutions can sell off to raise financing. This permits these institutions to reduce the size of their assets and therefore reduce their solvency (leverage) ratio (assets/capital) and meet international and/or European guidelines. Securitization enables a financial institution to offer more lending or purchase other assets. Securitization also involves 'shadow banking'—that part of the financial system that is absolutely or partially off the balance sheet of banks only because of the availability of market funding (Pozsar, Adrian, Ashcraft, and Boesky 2010). The business model also includes, crucially, the market financing of banks' balance sheets; in other words, the 'traditional credit portfolio' has become less traditional, as it is financed by the market rather than deposits.

In economies where the third business model defined above increasingly dominated bank strategy and market-based banking spread, there was a rapid expansion of credit which fuelled significant growth in the financial sector compared with the non-financial sector and a dramatic increase in financial sector profits in both real and relative terms. The expansion of financial assets and more specifically bank assets since the 1980s has been dramatic and the expansion in the seven years from 2000 to 2007 quickened (see Table 1.2). The flip side was that where this business model increasingly dominated, governments faced increasing implicit liabilities associated with the threat of bank runs initiated not by depositors but other financial market actors, including other banks.

NFCs and households enjoyed more and lower cost options to borrow at arm's length from financial institutions thanks to supposedly risk-reducing loan pooling. As long as debt levels were sustainable and risk was genuinely dispersed in the financial sector, this system could permit consumption smoothing for households and investment smoothing for NFCs. This market-based consumption and investment smoothing was however a boon to governments only as long as it was sustainable. Incumbent elected politicians in several of our countries presumably benefited from the positive political pocket-book effect of consumers being able to use their houses as automatic teller machines but they took a drubbing when the boom went bust. While equity issuance may expose NFCs to greater short-term pressure than traditional relationship-based bank borrowing, the new market-based credit financing potentially exposed NFCs to greater volatility than equity-based financing. Kroszner, Laeven, and Klingebiel (2007) show how credit-dependent sectors grow faster in normal times and are hit harder in tough times.

Conclusion

This chapter started by pointing to the inability of economics and political economy to explain the differential impact of the financial crisis on older developed economies. We traced this inability back to the 'dichotomous framing' of financial systems dominant in economics which has underpinned the typologies with which many scholars have been working. This volume offers a complement to the traditional typology of financial systems by looking at the activities of banks. In particular we propose a market-based banking model as an analytical tool to explain change in national financial systems.

The importance for CPE of the focus of this volume on banking lies in three areas. First, banks are central to Hall and Soskice's (2001a) categorization of CMEs and LMEs, even though 'bank based' is not a term they use in their seminal chapter (2001b) and banks receive little attention. Second, our approach serves to highlight an underappreciated aspect of change within financial markets: the changing activities of the financial market actors themselves. While this has particular relevance within the CPE literature, where change at the level of market actors has focused on NFCs, it has more general relevance to the study of finance, incorporating the level of detail most commonly found in the financialization literature. Third, market-based banking provides CPE a vital tool not only to explain the differential impact of the financial crisis but also to examine critically the logic behind government policy responses.

Our application of market-based banking also challenges claims of convergence in contemporary capitalism by demonstrating the non-static nature of the 'Anglo-Saxon' model to which other varieties are seen as converging (if only in part). While we reject the notion of a teleological evolution toward a new hybrid-type system, we do see some common elements of market-based banking developing—more or less—in the eleven national financial systems examined in this volume. The bank-based/CME and the capital-market/LME categories provide no helpful indication of the relative presence of these elements. Overall these elements highlight a potentially profound shift that calls for reframing. Although it is not the focus of this volume, our analysis of market-based banking could be combined with the two other forms of market-based corporate financing—bonds and equities—to give an overall assessment of the extent to which NFC financing and the financial system depends on market influences, and therefore the degree to which each national financial system is market based.

Financial systems evolve and change: they do not necessarily conform to the stylized facts of any single type. The addition of market-based banking and the factors that it identifies helps us to depict financial institutions and analyse their evolution because they describe a way that financial intermediation can occur that has not been previously understood in political economy scholarship. Introducing a new model and considering it across a variety of cases can help scholars be more accurate in their depictions of finance and its implications for varieties of capitalism. An understanding and application of market-based banking can help scholars who want to understand the role of banks in national economies generally, as well as providing insight into the financial crisis that erupted in 2007. This is what we understand to be a major contribution of this volume to the literature on the political economy of finance.

References

Abdelal, R. (2007). *Capital Rules: The Construction of Global Finance*. Cambridge MA: Harvard University Press.

Aglietta, M. and Breton, R. (2001). 'Financial Systems, Corporate Control and Capital Accumulation.' *Economy and Society* 30 (4): 433–466.

Aguilera, R. V. and Jackson, G. (2003). 'The Cross-National Diversity of Corporate Governance: Dimensions and Determinants', *Academy of Management Review* 28 (3): 447–465.

Allen, F. and Gale, D. (2000). *Comparing Financial Systems*. Cambridge: The MIT Press.

Amable, B. (2003). *The Diversity of Modern Capitalism*. Oxford: Oxford University Press.

Andrews, D. M. (1994). 'Capital Mobility and State Autonomy: Toward a Structural Theory of International Monetary Relations.' *International Studies Quarterly* 38 (June): 193–218.

Bank of England. (2009a). *Financial Stability Review, December*. London: Bank of England.

Bank of England (2009b). *Credit Conditions Survey, Survey Results, 2008 Q4, January*. London: Bank of England.

Barth, J. R., G. Caprio Jr. and R. Levine. (2006.) *Rethinking Bank Regulation: Till Angels Govern*. Cambridge: Cambridge University Press.

Beyer, J., and M. Höpner. (2003). 'The Disintegration of Organized Capitalism: German Corporate Governance in the 1990s'. *West European Politics* 26: 179–198.

Busch, A. (2009). *Banking Regulation and Globalization*. Oxford: Oxford University Press.

Byrne, J. P. and E. Phillip Davis. (2003). *Financial Structure*. Cambridge: Cambridge University Press.

Clift, B. (2007). 'French Corporate Governance in the New Global Economy: Mechanisms of Change and Hybridisation within Models of Capitalism.' *Political Studies* 55 (3): 546–567.

Corrigan, E. G. (1982). 'Are Banks Special?' In *The Federal Reserve Bank of Minneapolis, Annual Report*, <http://www.minneapolisfed.org/pubs/ar/ar1982a.cfm>.

Crouch, C. (2005). *Capitalist Diversity and Change: Recombinant Governance and Institutional Entrepreneurs*. Oxford: Oxford University Press.

Culpepper, P. D. (2005). 'Institutional Change in Contemporary Capitalism: Coordinated Financial Systems since 1990.' *World Politics* 57 (2): 173–199.

Davis, E. P. (1996). 'The Role of Institutional Investors in the Evolution of Financial Structure and Behaviour', RBA Annual Conference Volume. In: *The Future of the Financial System Reserve Bank of Australia* (ed. M. Edey). Canberra: RBA.

Davis, E. P. and B. Steil. (2001). *Institutional Investors*. Cambridge, MA MIT Press.

Deeg, R. (1999). *Finance Capitalism Unveiled: Banks and the German Political Economy*. Ann Arbor, MI University of Michigan.

—— (2005). 'The Comeback of Modell Deutschland? The New German Political Economy in the EU.' *German Politics* 14 (3):1–22.

—— (2007). 'Complementarity and Institutional Change in Capitalist Systems.' *Journal of European Public Policy* 14 (4): 612–631.

—— (2010). 'Institutional Change in Financial Systems.' In: *The Oxford Handbook of Comparative Institutional Analysis* (eds M. Glenn, J. L., Campbell, C. Crouch, O. Kai Pedersen, and R. Whitley). Oxford: OUP, 312–351.

Erturk, I. and Solari, S. (2007). 'Banks as Continuous Reinvention.' *New Political Economy* 12 (3): 369–388.

Feeney, P. W. (1995). *Securitization: Refining the Bank*. New York: St. Martin's Press.

Froud, J., A. Leaver, and K. Williams. (2007). 'New Actors in a Financialised Economy and the Remaking of Capitalism.' *New Political Economy* 12 (3): 339–347.

Gourevitch, P. A. and J. Shinn. (2005). *Political Power and Corporate Control: The New Global Politics of Corporate Governance*. Princeton, NJ: Princeton University Press.

Guillén, M. F. (2001). *The Limits of Convergence: Globalization & Organizational Change in Argentina, South Korea, and Spain*. Princeton, NJ: Princeton University Press.

Hackethal, A. (2001). 'How Unique are US-Banks? The Role of Banks in Five Major Financial Systems.' *Journal of Economics and Statistics* 221: 592–619.

Hall, P. A. and D. Soskice, eds. (2001a). *Varieties of Capitalism: The Institutional Foundations of Comparative Advantage*. Oxford: Oxford University Press.

—— (2001b). 'An Introduction to Varieties of Capitalism.' In: *Varieties of Capitalism, The Institutional Foundations of Comparative Advantage* (eds P. A. Hall and D. Soskice). Oxford, Oxford University Press, 1–70.

Hall, P. A. and K. Thelen. (2009). 'Institutional change in varieties of capitalism.' *Socioeconomic Review* 7 (1): 7–34.

Hancké B. and M. Goyer. (2005). 'Degrees of freedom: Rethinking the institutional analysis for economic change.' In *Changing Capitalisms? Complementarities, Contradictions and Capability Development in an International Context* (eds G. Morgan, R. Whitley, and E. Moen). Oxford: Oxford University Press, 53–77.

Hancké, B., M. Rhodes, and M. Thatcher, eds. (2007). *Beyond Varieties of Capitalism: Conflict, Contradictions, and Complementarities in the European Economy*. Oxford: Oxford University Press.

Helleiner, E. (1996). *States and the Reemergence of Global Finance: From Bretton Woods to the 1990s*. Ithaca: Cornell University Press.

Hellmann, T., K. Murdock and J. Stiglitz (2000). 'Liberalization, Moral Hazard in Banking and Prudential Regulation: Are Capital Requirements enough?' *American Economic Review* 90 (1): 147–165.

Hicks, A. (1988). 'Social Democratic Corporatism and Economic Growth.' *The Journal of Politics* 50: 677–704.

Jackson, G. and R. Deeg. (2008). 'How Many Varieties of Capitalism? From Institutional Diversity to the Politics of Change.' *Review of International Political Economy* 15 (4): 679–708.

Katz, R. (1998). *Japan, The System That Soured: The Rise and Fall of the Japanese Economic Miracle*. New York: M.E. Sharpe.

Kaufman, H. (2009). *The Road to Financial Reformation*. Hoboken, NJ: John Wiley & Sons.

Krippner, G. R. (2005). 'Financialisation and the American Economy', *Socio-Economic Review* 3 (2): 173–208.

Kroszner, R. S., L. Laeven, and D. Klingebiel. (2007). 'Banking Crises, Financial Dependence, and Growth', *Journal of Financial Economics* 84: 187–228.

La Porta, R., F. Lopez-de-Silanes, A. Shleifer, and R. Vishny (1998). 'Law and Finance'. *Journal of Political Economy* 106 (6): 1113–1155.

Laeven, L. and R. Levine. (2009). 'Bank governance, regulation and risk taking', *Journal of Financial Economics* 93 (2): 259–275.

Lall, S. (2006). 'How to Characterize Financial Systems' IMF Global Issues Seminar Series, 25 October. Available at: <http://siteresources.worldbank.org/EXTABOUTUS/Resources/Lall-slides.ppt>, accessed 20 February 2012.

Leblond, P. (2011). 'A Canadian Perspective on the EU's Financial Architecture and the Crisis', In: *Europe, Canada and the Comprehensive Economic Partnership* (ed. K. Hübner). London: Routledge: 165–179.

Loriaux, M. (1991). *France After Hegemony: International Change and Financial Reform.* Ithaca, NY: Cornell University Press.

O'Sullivan, M. (2007). 'Acting Out Institutional Change: Understanding the Recent Transformation of the French Financial System.' *Socio-Economic Review* 5 (3, July): 389–436.

Pagano, M. and P. F. Volpin. (2001). 'The Political Economy of Finance.' *Oxford Review of Economic Policy* 17 (4): 502–519.

Pauly, L. (1988). *Opening Financial Markets: Banking Politics on the Pacific Rim.* Ithaca: Cornell.

—— (1995). 'Capital Autonomy, State Autonomy and Political Legitimacy.' *Journal of International Affairs* 48 (2): 369–388.

Porter, T. (2010). 'Canadian banks in the financial and economic crisis.' Paper prepared for presentation at the Policy Responses to Unfettered Finance Workshop North-South Institute Ottawa, Canada, June 8–9 2010.

Posner, E. (2005). 'Sources of Institutional Change: The Supranational Origins of Europe's New Stock Markets.' *World Politics* 58 (1): 1–40.

—— (2009). *The Origins of Europe's New Stock Markets.* Cambridge, MA: Harvard University Press.

Pozsar, Z., A. Tobias, A. Ashcraft, and H. Boesky. (2010). 'Shadow Banking', Federal Reserve Bank of New York Staff Report No. 458 (July).

Quaglia, L. (2011). 'The politics of insurance regulation and supervision reform in the European Union,' *Comparative European Politics* 9: 100–122.

Rajan, R. G. (1998). 'The Past and Future of Commercial Banking Viewed through an Incomplete Contract Lens,' *Journal of Money, Credit and Banking* 30 (3): 524–550.

Rajan, R. G and Zingales, L. (2003). 'Banks and Markets: the Changing Character of European Finance.' CEPR Discussion Papers 3865.

Schmidt, R. H., A. Hackethal and M. Tyrell (2001). 'The Convergence of Financial Systems.' Working Paper Series: Finance & Accounting, Johann Wolfgang Goethe-Universitat, Frankurt Am Main, no. 75, May. <http://www.finance.uni-frankfurt.de/wp/425.pdf>.

Schmidt V. A. (2002). *The Futures of European Capitalism.* Oxford: Oxford University Press.

Strange, S. (1988). *States and Markets*. London: Continuum.
—— (1996). *The Retreat of the State. The Diffusion of Power in the World Economy*. Cambridge: Cambridge University Press.
Streeck, W. (2004). 'Taking Uncertainty Seriously: Complementarity as a Moving Target.' *Workshop Proceedings of the Osterreichische Nationalbank*, 1: 101–115.
Underhill, G., J. Blom and D. Mügge, eds. (2010). *Global Financial Integration Thirty Years On: From Reform to Crisis*. Cambridge: Cambridge University Press.
Useem, M. (1996). *How Money Managers are Changing the Face of Corporate America*, New York: Basic Books.
Verdun, A. (2000). *European Responses to Globalization and Financial Market Integration: Perceptions of Economic and Monetary Union in Britain, France and Germany*. Houndmills: Palgrave Macmillan.
Vitols, S. (2004). *'Changes in Germany's Bank-Based Financial System: A Varieties of Capitalism Perspective'*. Berlin: Wissenschaftszentrum Berlin, Discussion Paper SP II 2004–2003.
Whitley, R. (1992). *Business Systems in East Asia: Firms, Markets, and Societies*. London: Sage.
—— (1999). *Divergent Capitalisms: The Social Structuring and Change of Business Systems*. Oxford: Oxford University Press.
Wood, G. and J. G. Frynas. (2006). 'The institutional basis of economic failure: anatomy of the segmented business system.' *Socio-Economic Review* 4 (2): 239–277.
Zysman, J. (1983). *Government, Markets and Growth: Financial Systems and the Politics of Industrial Change*. Ithaca: Cornell University Press.

2

Framing Market-Based Banking and the Financial Crisis

Iain Hardie and David Howarth

Introduction

In the immediate aftermath of the worst banking crisis in modern economic history, the question 'What were the banks doing?' is appropriate not only as a cry of exasperation, but as an area of academic inquiry. The crisis has revealed a lack of understanding, hampered often by a lack of information, of the implications of many bank activities across politicians, regulators, academics, and most bankers themselves. Increased disclosure by the banks since 2007 and increased attention by others is revealing the nature of bank activities. It is now clear that banking in developed world economies, to varying but significant degrees, underwent profound changes in the early years of this century. Amongst the casualties of this change is the distinction between 'bank-based' and 'capital market-based' capitalism. Banking, this volume argues, has, increasingly but to varying degrees across the countries studied, become 'market-based banking'. The change has had significant implications for the nature of credit provision in advanced capitalist economies, and therefore for how we consider national financial systems.

As the introductory chapter to this volume argues, we seek to show that typologies that distinguish between capital market-based and bank-based financial systems are now obsolete, and to highlight the role of financial market actors—particularly banks—in bringing about systemic change. We develop that argument here, based on three problems we perceive with the standard approach, when applied to modern financial markets. First, building on claims presented in the introduction, we show the approach does not fit the facts in the developed economies. The immediate pre-financial crisis period must be seen as a time of rapid expansion of financial, and especially credit, markets, as the result of market-based banking. Yet, across a number of countries, and notably a supposedly archetypical 'Anglo-Saxon', capital market-based financial system, the United Kingdom, there was dramatic growth in bank lending to non-financial companies (NFCs), both in absolute terms and relative to bond and equity market financing (Table 1.1 and Figure 1.1 in the introduction). The importance of banks was not diminishing, but increasing, highlighted also by dramatic increases in the size of banks relative to the size of their home national economies. The second problem is the lack of explanatory power of the standard analysis in terms of the impact of the crisis, whether in the fact that supposedly disintermediated banks faced massive, bankruptcy-threatening losses, or in the variable impact of the crisis across national systems, in terms of the timing of the impact, size, and nature of losses, required government support or the availability of credit to NFCs—the development of a 'credit crunch'.

These two problems stem, as the introductory chapter argues, from a third problem, which we seek to rectify here: the limited focus in the political economy literature on banking and banks. In this chapter, we seek to justify an increased focus on banks and banking by presenting a model of market-based banking and to show its explanatory power in our understanding of the impact of the worst financial crisis in over eighty years.

Market-Based Banking

The distinctive feature of traditional bank-based financial capitalism, epitomized by Germany, is patient capital. Banks have a close relationship with NFCs, bolstered by the banks holding shares in companies and bankers serving on those companies' boards. This results in banks being willing to be patient in their lending decisions, by being more long term in their initial loans, and/or being more willing to deal sympathetically with companies in difficulties. An underlying assumption of this conception of banking is a core, seemingly incontrovertible, idea: banks make their own decisions regarding whether to lend, and the amount, maturity, and interest rate of any loan: 'We will/will not lend your company €1 million for five years at an interest rate of 5 per cent because *the bank* thinks ... '. Outside influence on these decisions could come from national or regional government owners, such as in France as described by John Zysman (1983) and pre-1990s Italy or regional governments in Germany and Spain, but not from the market. It is this core idea of bank or bank owner (national or regional government but not private shareholder) decision making that we seek to challenge in our broader conception of market-based banking. The financial crisis has revealed that increasingly it is the market that determines both banks' capacity to lend and even the particular decision to lend. As argued in the introduction to this volume, central to patient capital is the view that banks have the 'financial power' to resist market pressures (Zysman 1983). This volume suggests that this financial power has increasingly disappeared. To lend to a company, a bank must have sufficient amounts of both capital—to be able to meet regulatory requirements—and liquidity—in simple terms, so as to have the cash to give the borrower. In a traditional bank, the profit/loss from lending decisions made by the bank adds to/detracts from capital, increasing/decreasing the capacity to lend. Customer deposits provide the cash to make loans, and banks maintain a prudential 'liquidity buffer' to meet withdrawals of customer deposits. Depositor runs on banks are rare (indeed, until Northern Rock in the United Kingdom, seemingly a thing of the past), and provided bankers do not make large numbers of bad lending decisions (never a thing of the past) banks are stable. The vast majority of bank assets are loans, and the vast majority of liabilities are customer deposits. As a result, neither assets nor liabilities are market based, as movements in financial markets do not have an impact on the profitability of assets or on the availability of financing. Banks have the 'financial power' to influence market prices and to protect NFCs from market pressures.

Such a conception is implicit in a largely 'black box' approach to banks within the political economy literature. Change can certainly come about at the level of banks, through privatization or increased numbers of foreign shareholders prioritizing short-term bank profitability, but changes in NFC financing are the main indicators of systemic change. An increase in financing through the bond and equity markets at the expense of bank borrowing means bank-based systems such as France and Germany are converging with capital market-based systems such as the United Kingdom. The focus, therefore, is on the disintermediation of banks (e.g. Hackethal 2001, 2004). Yet the reality is that in recent years this disintermediation has not been occurring.

We argue in this volume for a new typology of national financial systems that distinguishes systems not only by the use by NFCs of directly market-based sources of financing, but also by the extent to which bank lending is itself market based. We begin our analysis, therefore, by defining 'market-based banking'. This term is not new, but our use of it here is. Previously, market-based banking has been applied to the 'shadow banking system': those parts of the financial system that provide credit, but are not commercial banks, such as investment banks, money market funds, and some of the off-balance sheet vehicles made infamous by the crisis (see Adrian and Shin 2010). We broaden the definition to include all those parts of commercial banking that are also dependent on the market. This is particularly important for any cross-country comparison, which must include careful attention to banks' balance sheets. We also go beyond the concept of 'deal-based banking' (Deeg 2010), the focus on the changing sources of bank profits (Ertürk and Solari 2007), or the 'securitized banking' of the investment banks (Gorton and Metrick 2010) to include the financing and hedging of the assets on commercial banks' balance sheets.

Table 2.1 summarizes the contrast between traditional and market-based banking. 'Traditional' banking, in this context, is the conception of banks' business as making loans to customers, retained unhedged on their balance sheet and financed by customer deposits. Absent the unlikely event of a customer run on deposits, banks have a stable source of financing for their lending. Lending decisions are driven by the individual bank's view of a company's creditworthiness and the bank's relationship with the borrower. Once the loan has been made, the profitability of the bank's decision is determined by the borrower's payment of the interest and repayment of the loan, i.e. by the accuracy of the bank's initial lending decision. Banks, whether private, mutually or publicly owned, have the ability to play their coordination role within a coordinated market economy.

Market-based banking, in all its various forms, is very different. Put simply, the lending decision becomes: 'The financial institution engaged in banking will/will not lend you $5 million for five years at an interest rate of 5 per cent because *the market* thinks ...'. The terms of loans that are made with the intention of selling them into the market, directly or via securitization, are determined by the market price. If that market price suggests an interest rate of 4.9 per cent, rather than 5 per cent, 4.9 per cent is the interest rate

Table 2.1. Traditional versus market-based banking

	Institutions	Loans	Funding/ liabilities of loans retained	Credit risk of loans retained	Accounting of loans retained	*Official Support Pre-Crisis*
Traditional banking	Commercial banks/ savings banks*	Retained on balance sheet	Customer deposits	Not hedged	At cost	Central Bank Lender of Last Resort
Market-based banking	Commercial banks	Sold, in loan market, via securitization or to shadow banks (ABCP, etc.). 'Originate to distribute'	Wholesale market (inter-bank, bonds, etc.)	Hedged via CDS	Mark to market	Central Bank Lender of Last Resort
	Parallel banks (including investment banks)	Sold, in loan market, via securitization or to shadow banks (ABCP, etc.). 'Originate to Distribute'	Wholesale market (repos, bonds, etc.)	Hedged via CDS	Mark to market	None

*These institutions have different names in different countries, i.e. savings and loans, building societies, savings banks, mutual banks.

the borrower will pay.[1] Similarly, if the lender decides to retain the loan, but hedge (effectively, insure) the risk through a credit default swap (CDS), the price of hedging (insuring) the risk will be a key determinant of the terms of the loan.[2] In the case of market-based banking, the lender may not be what we would generally consider a bank: banking activities, including lending, are also carried out by 'parallel' banks (see SHADOW BANKING), usually outside the last resort support of the central bank.[3] While such parallel banks exist across the countries considered in this volume, they are only significant in the United States and are the key reason for the uniqueness of the US system (see Hardie and Maxfield, this volume).

Loans retained by a bank, rather than sold, have to be financed through bank borrowing. In traditional banking, this borrowing is by way of customer deposits, which, despite the recent experiences of Northern Rock and Washington Mutual, can be seen as 'sticky' (IMF 2008, 74), meaning it is not necessary to question the lender's ability to borrow the funds needed to complete a loan. In market-based banking, in contrast, the funds need to come not from depositors but from the market, i.e. from other banks or investors. The financial markets determine the availability and price of this financing, and thereby determine the ability of lenders to lend and the price at which they do so. As the financial crisis demonstrates, such funds are far from 'sticky' (see, for example, Basel Committee of Banking Supervision 2008, 2); they are in fact highly skittish, and if withdrawn, can force a contraction in lending: a credit crunch. As discussed later, however, the role of market prices is also procyclical.

There are three possible developments in the move to market-based banking. Non-market based liabilities (i.e. deposits) could finance market-based assets. In the countries studied here, deposits exceed customer loans in Belgium, Canada, Greece, and Japan: elsewhere only individual banks are in this situation.[4] Such a situation does not suggest the absence of market pressure on lending; firstly, because losses on market-based assets or on their financing will deplete the capital banks need to support lending and, secondly, because loans have themselves increasingly been traded, either directly or via securitization, and have therefore become market-based assets. Alternatively, where loans exceed deposits, market-based liabilities finance non-market-based

[1] We are, of course, simplifying here, and ignoring the many factors that are likely to determine the financial institution's required profit margin on the transaction.

[2] Data limitations preclude a comparison of CDS across countries, despite their widespread use (see, for example, Northern Rock 2007, 42). Nor is this confined to larger banks: Norddeutsche Landesbank offered 'the individual trading of borrower risks' to smaller savings banks (2007, 75).

[3] These are a close equivalent of the 'specialized lending institutions' Zysman (1983, 61) acknowledged in a seminal study of financial systems. Given their insignificance at the time Zysman was writing, he rightly largely ignores them.

[4] These banks include JP Morgan of the United States, which has recently (July 2012) reported a loss of at least US$5.8 billion in a part of the bank whose role includes investing excess deposits (Braithwaite and Scannell 2012).

assets. Increased lending is financed by wholesale funding in strong markets, but in weak markets banks face the risk of the equivalent of a bank run, but with wholesale lenders who are far more skittish than depositors. As in a classic bank run, banks hold long-term illiquid assets which they cannot sell or finance. This market-based financing of lending is crucial to any understanding of the nature of modern banking and, for all the focus on securitization in popular explanations of the crisis, in understanding the impact of the crisis, particularly in countries where the purchase of US subprime securitizations was insignificant (for example, Spain; Royo, this volume). An important third possibility also exists: market-based assets are financed by market-based liabilities, and this has also played a major role in the crisis. This resulted in 'an increased reliance on 'liquidity through marketability', based on the assumption that it was safe to hold long-term bonds funded by short-term liabilities because the assets could be sold quickly if necessary (Basel Committee on Banking Supervision 2009, 10). The fallacy of this assumption was central to the crisis. In this extreme version of market-based banking, 'the galvanising role of market prices reaches into every nook and cranny of the financial system' (Adrian and Shin 2010, 20). Of particular importance to the problem with the standard dichotomous understanding of financial systems, '[i]n a market-based financial system, banking and capital market developments are inseparable' (Adrian and Shin 2008, 1).

Of course, our distinction between traditional and market-based banking is stylized. Commercial banks usually carry out both activities simultaneously. In recent years, the activities of financial market actors have converged (see Hardie and Maxfield, this volume). Commercial banks have increased their activities in what have been seen as investment banking, in particular securities trading. Investment banks, meanwhile, have moved from primarily advising on and intermediating transactions to substantially increasing their balance sheets (Crotty 2008), including by making loans. Other financial market actors have also been active in certain areas of NFC lending (Ivashina and Sun 2010). There are three developments that are relevant to the contrast between banks and loans as largely synonymous and banks and loans as revealed by the financial crisis. The first is the extent to which lending is a reduced part of banks' business. In reality, banks have long done more than take deposits and make loans, and in many countries have always been universal banks. In 1983, only half of the assets of Deutsche Bank, the largest bank in the archetypal bank-based system, Germany, were customer loans.[5] However, central to our argument is the fact that commercial banks have become more market based. (The 2007 figure for Deutsche Bank loans is 10 per

[5] Authors' calculations from <http://www.bankgeschichte.de/en/docs/1983.pdf>, p.74, accessed 10 February 2010.

cent of total assets.[6]) The second development is the extent to which loans are not now retained on bank balance sheets and financed by stable deposits but instead are either sold to the market—directly or through securitization—or if retained on bank balance sheets are financed by banks themselves borrowing from financial markets and hedged through CDS. The third development, significant only in the United States and discussed therefore more fully in the chapter on the United States and United Kingdom, is the increasing involvement of parallel banks—themselves reliant on borrowing from the financial markets—in lending.

This first development is closest to that described by Aglietta and Breton (2001): the development of a 'new market portfolio' alongside a 'traditional credit portfolio'. These market assets are a multi-faceted development, but at its simplest are bank holding of debt securities, valued at market prices and financed in the market (see also Gorton and Metrick's (2010) 'securitized banking'). The second development, however, is best seen as the extent to which the 'traditional credit portfolio' is no longer traditional, but also market-dependent. The experiences of the countries considered in this volume with regards to these two developments have not been uniform. In Table 2.2, we show the first development as total customer loans/total assets, and the second as the funding gap (customer loans less customer deposits/ total assets), as of the end of 2007.

Table 2.2. Funding gap/assets and loans/assets, percentages, end 2007

	Customer funding gap/total assets	Loans (excluding to MFIs)/ total assets
Italy	25.3	58.9
Spain	16.8	67.3
Netherlands	13.5	45.9
UK	12.0	46.9
France	10.2	36.6
US	3.7	62.0
Germany	3.2	40.1
Greece	–2.8	65.2
Belgium	–5.7	42.2
Japan	–10.1	69.0
Canada	–10.6	52.8

Sources: ECB,[7] Cabinet Office 2008, Federal Reserve,[8] Office of the Superintendent of Financial Institutions of Canada.[9]

[6] Authors' calculations from <http://www.db.com/ir/en/download/Annual_Report_2007_entire.pdf>, p.104, accessed 10 February 2010.

[7] <http://www.ecb.int/stats/money/aggregates/bsheets/html/outstanding_amounts_nea_index.en.html> and <http://www.ecb.int/stats/money/aggregates/bsheets/html/outstanding_amounts_index.en.html>, accessed 12 November 2010.

[8] www.federalreserve.gov/releases/h8/current/default.htm, accessed 10 November 2010.

[9] www.osfi-bsif.gc.ca/osfi/index_e.aspx?ArticleID=554, accessed 12 July 2012.

Table 2.2 demonstrates how far modern banks in many of the countries discussed here have moved from the 'traditional' conception of banking. Low total loans/total assets show that lending is far from the only balance sheet activity in most banking systems. In systems as diverse, within the existing typology, as Belgium, France, the Netherlands, Germany, and the United Kingdom, loans are less than half of bank assets. Similarly, the customer funding gap shows that although loans are funded by deposits (or are very close to being so) in Belgium, Greece, Canada, Germany, the United States (commercial banks only), and Japan, they are, to varying degrees, financed by market borrowing in the other countries.

In terms of using these data to understand the crisis, a number of caveats must be addressed. First, the size of the banking system matters to the scale of the potential problem. Bank assets to gross domestic product (GDP) are shown in Table 2.3 and Figure 2.1 shows the absolute size of bank funding gaps (the extent to which loans must be financed in the financial market) and Figure 2.2 shows this relative to GDP from 2000. Note, however, that the countries with the largest banking systems are also those in which the banks are the most market based. 'Traditional' banks have not grown to such a significant size relative to their overall domestic economy.

The aggregate size of the funding gap is also of significance for those banks with a high need to borrow from financial markets. Although the country experiences clearly diverge considerably (and increasingly over the period), the overall trend is for the aggregate funding gap to increase markedly, from US$1.9 trillion in 2000 to 3.5 trillion in 2007 for these eleven countries. The funding gap is also only a part of the market borrowing requirement, given the need to also finance assets other than loans. By the end of 2007, the total market funding for all activities by commercial banks reached US$2.1 trillion in the United States (with the investment banks a further 3.7 trillion), US$12.4 trillion by the Euro area universal banks, US$4 trillion by United Kingdom banks and even US$1.4 trillion in Japan (IMF 2010, 67–8). This

Table 2.3. Commercial bank assets to gross domestic product (end 2007, percentages)

Belgium	502
France	335
Germany	196
Greece	160
Italy	178
Netherlands	302
Spain	203
UK	400
Japan	179
Canada	141
US	81

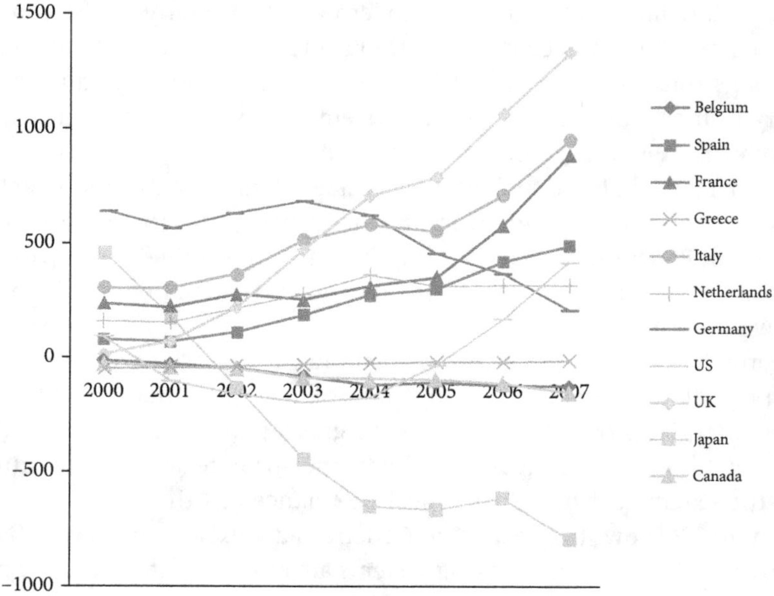

Figure 2.1. Bank funding gap (US$ billion), selected countries, 2000–7
Sources: ECB,[10] Cabinet Office 2008, Federal Reserve,[11] Office of the Superintendent of Financial Institutions of Canada[12]

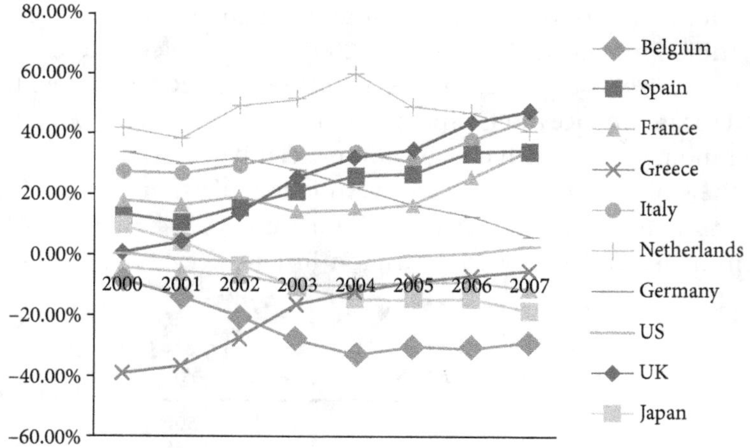

Figure 2.2. Customer funding gap (percentage of gross domestic product (GDP)), selected countries, 2000–7
Sources: As Figure 2.1; for GDP: World Bank

[10] www.ecb.int/stats/money/consolidated/html/index.en.html, accessed 12 November 2010.
[11] www.federalreserve.gov/releases/h8/current/default.htm, accessed 10 November 2010.
[12] www.osfi-bsif.gc.ca/osfi/index_e.aspx?ArticleID=554, accessed 1 August 2012.

overall dependence on wholesale funding is in itself a strong indicator of bank vulnerability during the crisis (Čihák and Poghosyan 2009; Huang and Ratnovski 2009; Poghosyan and Čihák 2009; Ratnovski and Huang 2009). However, it is also important to note that a large amount of this market financing is of assets, such as (some) government bonds, for which secured borrowing will be readily available in almost any market conditions.

A further caveat is that the studies cited immediately above look at individual banks. Given the heterogeneity of banks, aggregated data must be treated cautiously. This is particularly true in the United States. In addition, a large part of the crisis related, especially in the United States, to activities that were 'off-balance sheet', and therefore not visible to an analysis of bank balance sheets. We discuss this further in the section SHADOW BANKING. It is also important to note, even if obvious, that many banks faced crisis from 2007 stemming from 'traditional' activities. Bad property lending is central to any explanation of Spain's problems. However, this traditional lending was financed by borrowing from wholesale markets (see Royo, this volume). Further, in the context of the Euro area's sovereign debt crisis that erupted in 2009, it must be remembered that bank lending to governments is as old as banking and has long been predominantly through the buying of debt securities (a particular concern for Pagoulatos and Quaglia, this volume). Lastly, the details of the individual country experiences matter greatly. It is not only that banking is increasingly dependent on 'the market' that is central to understanding the financial crisis but, from a comparative perspective, that banking is dependent on a variety of markets with very different characteristics. We highlight some of those later, and the country chapters develop this further. One obvious distinction is the maturity of borrowing: borrowing short-term, such as from money market mutual funds or the US$ inter-bank market, gave a greater vulnerability to market pressures than borrowing long term. In addition, however, markets vary also in their fragility. For example, in the crisis, the 'covered bond' market[13] proved more stable than securitization. Banks borrowing more from the former (particularly German banks) suffered less impact than those, such as the United Kingdom's Northern Rock, with a heavy reliance on securitization. Similarly, market-based assets that are investments in relatively fragile markets (such as the now-infamous collateralized debt obligations (CDOs)) are likely to inflict greater losses, and more quickly, than investments in more stable markets, and longer maturity assets (increased maturity transformation by banks) are also likely to result in larger losses.

[13] A form of securitized borrowing, most heavily used in Germany (the *Pfandbriefe* market), in which assets remain on bank balance sheets (see IMF 2009a: 90). This market proved more stable during, though not unaffected by, the crisis.

Analysing Market-Based Banking

Having established our broad framework, the details of market-based banking are important to understanding both the extent that each banking system's lending depends on the market, and the nature of the crisis impact on that banking system. In this section, we outline comparative data across various aspects of market-based banking. Our focus is on differences in the nature of market-based assets and liabilities between the countries considered, to present a more nuanced picture than is possible from the data in Table 2.2 above. This involves considering in more detail the market-based assets and liabilities of the banks in the individual countries. To give one example: Italian banks had a wider customer funding gap than their Spanish counterparts, but Italian 'market-based' liabilities included a relatively high proportion of longer maturity bonds sold to the banks' own customers, a more stable source of market financing. Spanish banks, in contrast, borrowed relatively highly via securitization and from the US$ inter-bank market, one longer term but fragile, the other both short term and fragile. This overview chapter sets the overall framework for the volume and provides some examples of the varied nature of market-based assets and liabilities. Readers are directed to individual country chapters for greater detail.

Market-Based Assets

As discussed above, the maturity and fragility of assets are important to refining the impact of the market on banks, both in terms of the direct costs of the financial crisis, and the impact on bank lending. We first start this discussion by looking at the way in which market-based assets are valued by banks—marking-to-market—and its implications, before considering how banks invested in particularly fragile, longer maturity markets, especially securitizations, in a capital-efficient manner, through 'shadow banking', with disastrous consequences. We focus particularly on asset-backed commercial paper (ABCP) programmes.

'MARKING TO MARKET'

Financial markets reached their recent nadir in March 2009, before starting to recover. At that nadir, the Bank of England's estimate of worldwide losses across a broad range of assets, based on then-prevailing market prices, was equivalent to approximately 40 per cent of global GDP (Bank of England 2009, 6). A year later, the recovery in market prices was sufficient to reduce those losses by the equivalent of over 30 per cent of global GDP (Bank of England 2010, 38). Of equal importance, estimates on the losses on US subprime mortgage securities, based on prevailing market prices in 2008, were nearly 60 per cent greater than losses implied by a reasonable assumption of actual default-related losses, as a result of 'uncertainty ... and illiquidity' (Bank of England 2008, 16). For UK prime mortgage securities, losses were 85 per cent greater (Bank of England 2008; see also Hellwig 2008). Accounting matters. Bank assets that are not priced on the balance sheet according to market prices will remain at the price at which any transaction was originally completed, unless there is a clear reason for change (such as credit impairment on a loan). The value of those assets that are marked to market will move with the market, with implications for bank profitability and capital. The issue, however, is not one solely of losses, but of procyclicality, as market prices above credit fundamentals can also increase profitability and lending capacity (Hellwig 2008, 20).

A significant change occurs in the nature of lending decisions as a result. If a loan is to remain on a bank's balance sheet at its original value ('historical cost'), unless there is credit impairment, the profitability of that loan is determined by the bank's assessment of the creditworthiness of the borrowing company. With a loan that is marked to market, the profitability is determined by a successful assessment of the value the market will put on that asset. The extent to which banks mark their assets to market varies across countries, as shown in Table 2.4, although the data are incomplete.

Table 2.4. Mark-to-market accounting by country, 2007

	% of assets
France	46.5
BNP Paribas	65
Credit Agricole	44
Societe Generale	46
Germany	
Deutsche	75
Italy	19
Japan	27
Netherlands	28.4
Spain	17.2
United Kingdom	
Barclays	52
HSBC	40
Royal Bank of Scotland	45
United States*	26.9
Bank of America	27
Citigroup	39
Goldman Sachs	86
JP Morgan Chase	41
Lehman	42
Merrill Lynch	44
Morgan Stanley	44

*Commercial banks only.

Sources: Committee on the Global Financial System (2010), Fitch Ratings (2008) See also IMF (2008: 119).

The data make clear that the impact of market prices directly on the value of bank assets is low in Italy, Spain, and Japan, and relatively high in France, the United Kingdom, and, allowing for the investment banks, the United States. The Netherlands lies in between, and the data on Germany are too limited to make an assessment (although the one bank for which data are given, Deutsche Bank, is almost certainly an outlier). Although incomplete, the data demonstrate a close fit with Table 2.2, which shows loans as a percentage of assets, which we have used as a proxy for market-based assets. For those countries where a high proportion of bank assets were valued at market prices, the excessive weakness of market prices caused severe difficulties for banks, and for Hellwig (2008) explains why the subprime crisis became systemic. The controversial regulatory response was selectively to suspend the mark-to-market accounting rules: effectively it was decided that the market was wrong.

The market sensitivity and procyclicality of market-based assets are compounded when these assets are financed, as the vast majority are, by borrowing collateralized by the assets themselves, in the repurchase, or 'repo' market. This is particularly the case in parallel banking by the investment banks, which Gorton and Metrick (2010) refer to as 'securitized banking' (see also Gorton 2010). The importance of the repo market is highlighted by the analysis of the crisis in the United States as a 'run on repo' (Gorton and Metrick 2010; see also Acharya, Schnabl and Suarez 2010). The focus of these studies on the repo market serves to highlight that market-based assets are most commonly financed with market-based liabilities, and the difficulties of seeking to disentangle the two sides of bank balance sheets. However, the focus here on market-based liabilities as supporting lending is more appropriate for the situation outside the United States, and is therefore more useful to a comparative study.

'SHADOW BANKING'

The term 'shadow banking' has been used to describe banking activity outside the commercial banking system (e.g. Pozsar, Adrian, Ashcraft, and Boesky 2010; Tucker 2010). Pozsar et al. (2010, 66) differentiate between 'internal' and 'external' shadow banking and adopt a very specific definition of parallel banking related to the distinction between regulatory arbitrage and genuine competitive advantage. We follow here the distinction of Adrian and Shin (2010) between 'shadow'—banking activities undertaken by commercial and savings banks but either wholly or partially off the balance sheets of those banks—and 'parallel' banking—banking activities that take place outside the commercial and savings banks, and do not ordinarily benefit from lender of last resort support from a central bank. The former is addressed here, and the latter mainly in the chapter considering the United States (Chapter 3).

Single-purpose companies were established to allow banks to sell them assets. These purchases, often of securitizations, are financed by the single-purpose companies issuing securities. The most important of these companies, on which we focus, are ABCP programmes or conduits, which borrow short term, usually from US money market funds (for an overview, see Fitch Ratings 2007).[14] Banks sponsor the establishment of ABCP programmes, and provide them with credit support of various kinds. These programmes are therefore a capital-efficient and profitable way for banks to assume the risk of market-based assets.[15] In a strong market, the programmes make profit for their sponsoring bank from the difference between their interest income and cost of borrowing. ABCP programmes therefore, in good market conditions, increase the availability of credit in an economy, and also increase bank profitability. However, the banks' credit support leaves them committed to lending, secured on ABCP programme assets, if financing in the commercial paper market is unavailable. This resulted in the banks owning the underlying market-based assets of the ABCP entities to which they had provided credit support. In poor market conditions, therefore, ABCP causes an 'involuntary reintermediation', pressuring banks' capital and liquidity. Even where, as occurred with German banks LB Sachsen and IKB, the bank is not effectively bankrupted, further lending is constrained. In the United Kingdom, for example, banks had to borrow directly 7.7 per cent more as a result of the collapse of the ABCP market (Bank of England 2007, 33) at precisely the time such borrowing was becoming more difficult. This is therefore a further means by which lending in the economy becomes increasingly market based (and as a result procyclical).

Outstanding ABCP reached US$1.3 trillion in July 2007, larger than outstanding US government treasury bills, and a doubling since January 2004 (Acharya et al. 2010). However, the French bank BNP Paribas' decision to halt withdrawals from three funds on 9 August 2007 triggered a fall in outstandings to US$833 billion by December (Acharya et al. 2010.). Banks that had provided credit support were bitten by the shadow. Only 2.5 per cent of outstanding ABCP actually defaulted by December 2008, while commercial banks faced losses estimated at US$68–204 billion on assets they had involuntarily reintermediated (Acharya et al. 2010).[16]

The bank sponsoring an ABCP vehicle may well also provide the credit (or liquidity) support to that vehicle, but another bank may do so. Table 2.5 shows

[14] Another type of shadow bank, structured investment vehicles (SIVs), reached a total size of US$350 billion. Many of the comments here on ABCP apply also to SIVs, although the latter's borrowing was generally more medium term.

[15] See Acharya, Schnabl and Suarez (2010, 61) for estimates of 'missing capital'.

[16] This does not include Canadian ABCP (see Leblond, this volume), where the structure of the guarantees meant that ABCP investors assumed greater losses, meaning these programmes were closer to 'originate and distribute'.

Table 2.5. Liquidity support to asset-backed commercial paper vehicles by country

	Amount (US$bn)	% of GDP
Belgium	52.33	11.52
France	90.66	3.5
Germany	310.84	9.36
Italy	2.72	0.13
Netherlands	173.87	22.37
Spain	7.08	0.49
United Kingdom	214.25	7.75
United States	356.83	2.58

Source: Fitch Ratings (2007: 7–8).

the exposure of bank providers of liquidity support for ABCP programmes by country. It is, in effect, another way to present the variation in bank involvement in market-based banking. It shows the exposure of a country's banks to being forced to accept assets fully onto their balance sheets, with capital and liquidity implications, as a result of ABCP funding being unavailable.

Measured relative to GDP, the Netherlands has by far the biggest exposure (although the impact on the country was mitigated by the highly fortuitous sale of ABN-Amro to the Royal Bank of Scotland), followed by Belgium and Germany. The low figure for the United States is particularly noteworthy.[17] The nature of the assets included in ABCP programmes, including securitizations and CDOs which proved particularly fragile during the crisis, means that in those countries with high involvement in ABCP, the measure of market-based assets in Table 2.2 should be seen as an underestimation of the exposure of assets to market fluctuations. Acharya and Schnabl (2010) also show very low or zero figures for bank sponsorship of ABCP vehicles in Greece and Japan, a good proxy for liquidity support (see also Arteta, Carey, Correa and Kotter 2009).

Market-Based Liabilities

We move now to consider the market-based liabilities of banks, by which we mean the extent to which the capacity to lend is constrained by the availability of funding from the market. The liability side of the balance sheet has moved far from the traditional conception of bank lending funded by customer deposits. There is also significant variation across the countries

[17] Amounts sponsored relative to bank equity give a similar picture (Acharya and Schnabl 2010: 25). Figures on the amount of capital 'saved' as a result of the capital treatment of ABCP (Acharya et al. 2010: 62) and of liquidity support to ABCP entities relative to individual banks wholesale funding (Fitch Ratings 2007: 7–8), also show the high risks run by certain banks, especially in Germany.

analysed (see Raddatz 2010 for a similar approach). Although the funding gap does represent one measure of market-based liabilities (Table 2.2),[18] it is an incomplete picture of the market pressures on this side of bank balance sheets, because banks in different countries do not borrow from the financial markets in the same way.[19] There is substantial variation in the maturity of borrowing and in the fragility of the various financial markets of bank borrowing.

Table 2.6 demonstrates the different times that certain financial markets faced stress in the early stages of the financial crisis. This table is also important for the asset side of bank balance sheets, but, in terms of liabilities, the extent to which banks rely on wholesale funding increases the market-based nature of lending, as the lower difficulties in borrowing via deposits shows. Banks with greater access to deposits cut lending less over the crisis period (Ivashina and Scharfstein 2009). However, as Table 2.6 also shows, different wholesale markets experienced problems at different stages, and therefore the degree and timing of liquidity issues for banks and banking systems depended on the use of specific wholesale markets. The impact of problems in these markets on lending capacity was also influenced by the maturity profile of the financing in question: short-term financing resulted quickly in problems, whereas banks reliant on longer term sources of funding, such as bonds and covered bonds, did not face such immediate refinancing pressures.

Table 2.6. Financial markets during the crisis

	Pre-crisis	Aug 2007– Sept 2008	Lehman failure	After govt rescue plans
Short-term markets				
Inter-bank	○	•	•	•
Repurchase	○	•	•	◘
ABCP	○	•	•	•
CP	○	○	•	•
Deposits	○	○	c/◘	○
Long-term markets				
Bonds	○	◘	•	•/◘
Covered bonds	○	○	•	•
Securitization	○	•	•	•

Key: ○ Functioning Smoothly.
◘ Signs of Difficulties.
• Impaired.
Adapted from ECB (2009: 11).

[18] However, there is variation across countries even in the market-based nature of customer deposits. In the crisis, United Kingdom corporate deposits were withdrawn very quickly, while in France and Germany they proved stable. In addition, central banks, primarily in Asia and the Middle East, withdrew over US$250 billion from European banks during the crisis.

[19] The funding gap is an even less helpful measurement with regard to the United States, where market-based liabilities are primarily in the parallel banks. A large proportion of parallel banks' market-based liabilities were via the repurchase ('repo') market.

The different ways to measure the variation in the exposure to the market can be divided broadly into financing from other banks (with borrowing from international banks particularly vulnerable to withdrawal in the event of market weakness), and financing through the bond and money markets (with both the maturity of financing, and the fragility of certain bond markets concerns). It is generally the case that increased exposure to wholesale funding goes hand-in-hand with financing from less stable sources. For those countries where wholesale funding comes from relatively stable, longer-term markets, the funding gap (see Table 2.2) overstates the influence of financial market prices on lending. This is because the funding gap indicates solely the volume of wholesale financing of customer lending. Conversely, where wholesale borrowing is from short-term fragile markets, the impact of financial markets is likely to be understated by the funding gap.

The authors in this volume note a number of distinguishing issues regarding the composition of market-based liabilities that shaped their countries' experience of the financial crisis. For example, both the inter-bank and commercial paper markets were exceptionally short term immediately preceding the crisis. In July 2008, over 60 per cent of all commercial paper investment was one to four *days* in maturity; and this peaked at over 80 per cent during the crisis (Bank of England 2008, 23). European banks borrowed US$1 trillion in this market by mid-2007 (Baba, McCauley and Ramaswarmy 2009), with UK banks particularly active. British banks were also heavily exposed to inter-bank borrowing, especially international, much of which was overnight. This borrowing fell by US$812 billion in the second quarter of 2008 alone (Baba, Gadanecz and McGuire 2008, 25).

Overall, the market-based liabilities of the continental European banks most exposed to wholesale markets were comparatively more in markets that were a source of longer term funding, such as bonds in the case of France (Howarth, this volume) or covered bonds in Germany. Longer term funding lessened immediate pressures in the early stages of the financial crisis. There were, however, significant differences between European countries. Spanish banks also borrowed in the US$ inter-bank market to finance domestic lending, in contrast to other countries' banks, where such borrowing (or domestic borrowing) financed international activity (McGuire and von Peter 2009, 10).

The details of market-based assets and liabilities allow a more refined analysis of the market-based nature of bank balance sheets than the funding gap presented in Table 2.2. This involves considering banks' involvement, on both sides of the balance sheet, in short or long-term and/or fragile markets. There must, of necessity, be an element of subjectivity in this assessment, but it is based on the maturity and fragility of markets as set out in Table 2.6, and the available data regarding the nature of assets and liabilities in the national banking systems. We first set out our conclusions for each country, and then present this diagrammatically in Figure 2.3. In the cases of Canada, Greece, Japan, and the United States (in the case of commercial banks only), the available data suggest no under- or overstatement in the Table 2.2 figures.

United Kingdom

The customer funding gap in the United Kingdom is substantial, but this understates the market-based nature of liabilities, because of their short-term nature and high dependence on relatively fragile markets. The United Kingdom is most noteworthy in this regard for the banking system's high reliance on short-term markets such as the inter-bank (especially international) and commercial paper markets.[20] Similarly, on the assets side, ABCP sponsorship was high. Table 2.2 therefore understates the market-based nature of both assets and liabilities. The RBS takeover of ABN-Amro also increased the cost of the crisis for the UK government. The United Kingdom is our clearest example of highly market-based commercial banks, with the UK commercial banks demonstrating many of the vulnerabilities of the central actors in US parallel banking, the investment banks.

Belgium

In contrast to the Netherlands, Belgian banks do not rely on market-based sources of financing. However, Belgian banks were also heavily involved in supporting ABCP programmes. This suggests an understatement of market-based assets in Table 2.2, but to a lesser extent than in the case of the Netherlands.

Netherlands

On the assets side of the balance sheet, the Netherlands stands out in terms of the highest sponsorship of ABCP relative to GDP, twice the level of the next highest country, Belgium. This suggests that Table 2.2 understates market-based assets. It should be noted, however, in terms of the cost of bailout for the Dutch government, that ABN-Amro was the bank most involved in this market, and it was taken over by the Edinburgh-based Royal Bank of Scotland shortly before the crisis.

Germany

Overall conclusions regarding the German banking system must be cautious, because of its heterogeneity, and particularly because of the very large number

[20] At the end of 2006, a median of 44 per cent of major UK banks' wholesale funding matured within three months (Bank of England 2007: 34).

of small, traditional savings and cooperative banks. As Hardie and Howarth (this volume) make clear, the crisis in Germany was very much a problem of the larger banks. Nevertheless, even considering the liabilities of the larger banks, Table 2.2 overstates market-based liabilities because of the relatively high reliance in wholesale borrowing on the more stable and long-term covered bonds (and German *Pfandbriefe* were more stable than other covered bond markets), and bonds sold to retail customers or related savings banks. Inter-bank borrowing, especially internationally, was low. On the assets side, however, the high German involvement in ABCP suggests Table 2.2 understates market-based assets.

France

Relative to its very high market-based assets, French involvement in ABCP is low. This would suggest a slight overstatement of market-based assets in Table 2.2. Similarly, the relatively high borrowing via bonds, and a low reliance in the US$ inter-bank market (McGuire and von Peter 2009) suggests a small overstatement of market-based liabilities.

Spain

Spanish banks have a relatively high customer funding gap, meaning that market-based liabilities 'turbocharged' traditional lending (Royo, this volume). In this market borrowing, Spanish banks relied disproportionately on the US$ inter-bank market, a very short-term and fragile market, to finance domestic lending. It was the only country in a Bank of International Settlements study where this occurred (McGuire and von Peter 2009, 51). Bond issues were also of a shorter maturity than in Italy. This suggests that Table 2.2 understates the market-based nature of Spanish bank liabilities. The result is that 'Spanish deposit institutions have been affected by the international financial crisis because of the evaporation of the wholesale funding channel, which in the years prior to the summer of 2007 had contributed to funding a significant portion of growth in activity' (Bank of Spain 2009, 19).

Italy

Relative to total bank assets, Italy's customer funding gap is the largest of the countries considered and, as an absolute amount, it is second only to the United Kingdom. This suggests high levels of market-based liabilities. However, as Pagoulatos and Quaglia (this volume) make clear, Table 2.2 overstates the market-based nature of Italian bank liabilities. Italian banks borrow disproportionately via longer maturity bonds rather than from banks. These bonds are sold to their own retail customers, which are a more stable investor base than institutional investors. Inter-bank borrowing in Italy tends to come from other Italian banks rather than international banks, which is also more stable.

Figure 2.3 sets out our overall conclusions regarding the market-based nature of assets and liabilities on bank balance sheets in the national commercial banking systems of the countries in this volume. The positioning of countries stems from both their funding gap and our assessment of the extent to which assets and liabilities are exposed to market movements. The position of countries has been moved relative to the position implied by the data in Table 2.2, to reflect the particular assessments of national banking systems immediately above.

We divide our assessment of bank balance sheets into four sections, representing relatively high and low market-based assets and liabilities. The positioning of countries in these sections largely corresponds to the nature and timing of the crisis. We would expect the direct impact on banking systems and lending in the bottom left quadrant to be less and late (if at all). Ignoring the United States, in terms of direct impact, in Canada, Greece, and Japan, this is exactly what occurred. Greek banks have subsequently been victims of a sovereign debt crisis, rather than more central to that crisis. It seems highly likely, given the situation presented by Kamikawa (this volume), that Japanese banks would be very negatively affected by a sovereign debt crisis, as has been the case in Greece.[21] In the bottom right quadrant of the table are banking systems which we would expect to face few problems

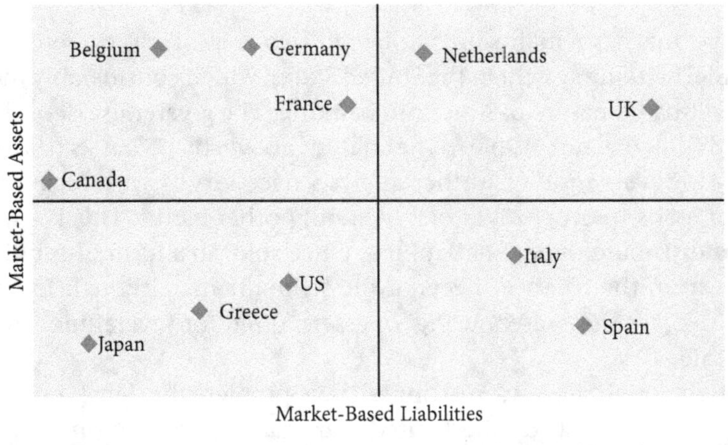

Figure 2.3. Market-based assets and liabilities on bank balance sheets, 2007

[21] Kamikawa also considers why Japan has not followed Greece's path despite its exceptional levels of government debt.

early in the crisis on the asset side of the balance sheet, but with the potential for subsequent difficulties, especially with market borrowing. Spain fits this description, although with the addition of severe problems with 'traditional' property lending.

The two quadrants at the top of the table both contain banking systems where market-based assets were important and where early problems from this source would be expected. Losses should be expected on assets other than loans (i.e. those that are predominantly market based), and difficulties with the financing of those assets early in the crisis. This was apparent across the countries in the top two quadrants and all the non-US bank casualties relatively early in the crisis—up to and including the immediate aftermath of the Lehman bankruptcy—come from these countries (although, as discussed by Howarth, this volume, France is a partial exception). The difference between the two quadrants relates to the nature of the financing of lending. Market borrowing to support lending was relatively low in Germany at the on-set of the crisis and non-existent (i.e. the funding gap was negative) in Belgium. The impact of losses on market-based assets can have a negative impact on lending, but direct difficulties in financing lending are less likely in the top left quadrant. In the top right quadrant, to varying degrees, there is a need to borrow from financial markets to finance lending. As before, it is the extent of this borrowing (the high absolute size of the UK funding gap, over US$1.3 trillion, up from zero in 2000, is particularly striking) that determines the degree of difficulties the individual banking systems faced.

'Originate and Distribute'

The above analysis remains incomplete in two areas. First, we must include the parallel banking system in the United States, which considerably increases the market-based nature of American banking. The greater use of off-balance sheet activities (i.e. not visible in the analysis above) by US banks has a similar impact. However, another further analysis necessary is with regards to the selling of loans to other investors, including other banks. This is the 'originate and distribute' model of banking. Once sold, this form of funding will not appear on the balance sheets of the selling bank, although the process usually involves the 'warehousing' of assets, often for several months, prior to their sale.

Although 'originate and distribute' is a problematic label for banking overall, especially outside the United States, and risks ignoring the extent to which distribution was to another bank, it is nevertheless an important component of modern banking and of any explanation of the crisis. Banks increasingly make loans not with the intention of keeping them on their own balance sheets, but of selling them to other financial market actors. The lending decision is therefore directly linked to the market via the ability to sell and the pricing of any sale. 'This is not the way that banks operated for hundreds of years' (Gorton 2010, 42). As a result, the distinction, central to the dichotomous understanding of financial systems, between loans that remain on bank balance sheets and market-based bonds and equities, has broken down. There are two broad ways in which such distribution can take place. The first is through direct sales of the loans themselves, the second is as a result of various forms of securitization. The securitized assets are then in turn sold directly to the market or to shadow banks.

Trading loans is a relatively new activity but has grown very rapidly in recent years. The trading volume of loans in the United States reached US$520 billion in 2007, a fivefold increase from 2000. The importance is such that US surveys of lending conditions do not ask about the availability of funding for the banks, but rather 'Decreased liquidity in the secondary market for these loans' (see Figure 1.1 in the introduction to this volume). Gorton (2010, 42) sees the ratio of secondary market loan sales to outstanding commercial and industrial loans by US banks peaking in 2007 at over 25 per cent. In contrast to the United States, in Japan there is no secondary loan market,[22] and the European market is 'relatively nascent' (Standard & Poor's 2010, 17), with volumes in 2007 of US$225 billion equivalent (Axa Investment Managers n.d.). No country breakdown is available. In this situation, the loan is made because it is expected to be sold, and the terms of the loan are determined by that sale. Much of these sales represent genuine distribution of risk outside the banking system: by 2007 non-bank institutional investors bought 62 per cent of leveraged loans[23] in the United States (Iveshina and Sun 2010); in Europe one estimate for 2006 exceeds 40 per cent (Morgan Stanley 2006, 12).[24] However, the slow process of distribution meant that when the market collapsed globally banks were caught with US$300 billion of loans they had planned to sell (Bank of England 2007, 36).

Loans are not only sold directly to the market, but are also sold by way of securitization: the repackaging of pools of loans into tradable bonds. Securitization has played a very significant part in the crisis, especially the securitization of subprime US residential mortgages, much of it bought by European banks. However, securitization of European assets has also been significant. Securitization, and the 'originate and distribute' model of banking, underpins increased bank lending in benign market conditions, but increases the severity of a credit crunch when markets fall. Deutsche Bank makes the

[22] Email communication with Loan Syndications and Trading Association, 16 September 2010.

[23] Loans to less creditworthy companies, including for the financing of takeovers of companies by private equity investors.

[24] These figures include sales via securitization (see Benmelech, Dlugosz and Ivashina 2008).

connection explicit in their (pre-crisis) 2006 annual report (2007, 110): 'A sudden drop in investor demand for asset-backed securities could cause us to restrict our lending thereafter for the types of loans we securitize'. The Bank of England (2009, 16) notes the growth of individual banks' mortgage lending and the percentage of mortgages securitized. The extreme example, Northern Rock, had securitized well over half its mortgage book by the end of 2007 (The Bank of England 2009, 17). The decisions by US, Euro area, and UK central banks to support the securitization markets are further proof of their importance (see Cheun, von Köppen-Mertes and Weller 2009). The IMF concludes: 'repairing securitization is critical to supporting the supply of credit'. This is particularly the case in the United States, where the extensive use of securitization is a significant contributor to our assessment of market-based banking being high even when the commercial banks themselves appear largely traditional. However, in the first quarter of 2009 securitization also accounted for 14 per cent of outstanding credit in the UK (half the US figure) and 6 per cent in the Euro area (IMF 2009a, 32). Within the Euro area there is significant variation in the importance of securitization to lending activity. Table 2.7 sets out the amount of collateral in securitizations, by country, as a percentage of GDP.

Clearly the United States stands far ahead of all other countries, including the United Kingdom, in the significance of securitization to lending. The substantial US figure includes the parallel banking market. Equally important for the analysis here, securitization was also an important influence on lending capacity in a number of continental European countries, including two, Spain and Italy, where bank purchases of such assets were very low. In some

Table 2.7 Securitization collateral by country (end 2007)

	Medium-term securitization collateral (% of GDP)	ABCP collateral (% of GDP)	Total
Belgium	2.3	1.5	3.8
Germany	1.6	1.2	2.8
France	2.9	0.8	3.7
Greece	4.4	0	4.4
Italy	7.8	0.8	8.6
Netherlands	24.1	6.8	30.9
Spain	16.9	0.4	17.3
UK	24.8	4.0	28.8
US	70.1	1.2	71.3
Japan	1.3	0	1.3

Source: Authors' calculations from European Securitisation Forum, Japan Securities Dealers Association.

Percentage of outstanding ABCP as of 28.2.08 versus total ABCP outstanding and GDP as of end 2007. Figures based on ABCP outstanding of €392 billion versus peak of €528.9 billion (Q2 2007). Figures also understated because do not include assets categorized as 'global' or 'Europe' (19 per cent of total).

countries where securitization activity was relatively low, however, growth was rapid. German securitization issuance, for example, was in 2006 over five times that in 2004 (IMF 2009b, 13). While much of the securitization market proved particularly fragile during the crisis, this is not uniformly the case. As in the United States, in Canada and the Netherlands there was extensive government support for mortgage securitization (Leblond, this volume; Chang and Jones, this volume). In December 2009, Dutch Mortgage Backed Securities had the lowest spreads in Europe, thanks to government guarantees (Netherlands Central Bank 2009, 20).

It is important to note, given our focus here on corporate financing, that this was not solely the securitization of residential mortgages. While residential mortgage-backed securities represented over 80 per cent of issuance in Belgium and the Netherlands, and 75 per cent in the United States, 68 in Spain and 62 in the United Kingdom, it was under half in Germany and Italy (as of Q1 2008). The importance of house prices, and therefore mortgage lending, to economic growth, and therefore corporate performance, in some countries highlights that residential mortgage securitization was indirectly important. However, of more direct importance to this volume is the fact that outstanding European securitized collateral other than residential mortgages totalled just under €600 billion at Q1 2008 (European Securitisation Forum 2008), with the United States at a further €1.5 trillion. Furthermore, although the Deutsche Bank statement above suggests effectively hypothecated securitization—with the securitization of assets prompting further lending in that specific type of asset—for other banks there also appears likely to be a more generalized 'freeing up' of the balance sheet to allow greater lending, for example as a result of the reduced capital required to support overall lending.

In terms of the financial crisis, the breakdown of the 'originate and distribute' banking model had two main effects. First, banks faced losses on those assets they held on the balance sheet only because they intended to sell them. As noted earlier, one estimate puts these assets at US$300 billion. In an extreme example such as Northern Rock in the United Kingdom, lending which has been intended for securitization continued, but was financed by increasingly short-term borrowing, ultimately threatening the bank's survival. Second, and of particular importance in the United States and to a lesser extent some European countries, was the impact not directly on the banks through their balance sheets, but on the availability of credit in the economy.

An Overall Assessment of Market-Based Banking

By combining the analysis summarized in Figure 2.3 with parallel banking, off-balance sheet activities and originate to distribute, we can reach a

Low										High
Japan	Greece	Canada	Italy	Spain	France	Germany	Belgium	Netherlands	UK	US

Figure 2.4. A continuum of market-based banking

conclusion as to the extent of market-based banking in each country, best displayed, as in Figure 2.4, along a continuum.

This figure represents the extent to which banking in the national economies is market based. As such, this already suggests a radical reshaping of the dominant bank-based/market-based dichotomy. There are profound implications for how we should understand some bank credit-based financial systems in the years preceding the financial crisis—notably Germany and Belgium. The eleven national banking systems examined in this volume can effectively be distinguished by the degree to which banking in each country has moved away from traditional banking (still seen in the countries on the left side of the figure) towards lending that depends on the market. In the United States we can see this as in part the rise of both the 'originate and distribute' banking model and parallel banks. In the United States it is no longer possible to see banks and loans as synonymous. This is also true in nearly all European countries, but to a lesser degree. The most important change in Europe is rather what has occurred on the balance sheets of the banks, with their increased holding of market-based assets and their increased financing from market sources.

The Impact of the Financial Crisis

We seek to show the explanatory utility of market-based banking in terms of the impact of the crisis, both its degree and timing. The fact that US subprime lending was the initial source of credit concerns does not explain the severity of the crisis for US financial institutions, or the early problems in various parts of the parallel banking system, most noteworthy of which was the US investment bank Bear Stearns. Outside the United States, the canaries in the national systems' coal mines were then the most market-based banks, particularly in the United Kingdom and Germany. The most market-based systems then faced further problems in the wake of the Lehman Brothers collapse, with those systems that were less market-based at this stage proving relatively immune, at least until more 'traditional' problems with lending and government debt emerged.

Government Intervention

While finding comparable data is challenging given different measurements by national bodies, we have enough data to demonstrate that public interventions to support banks—notably in terms of actual capital injections and loans—varied significantly across the different countries (see Figures 2.5 and 2.6).[25]

Of the financial systems that were worst hit by the financial crisis and therefore required the greatest government support, two were 'market based' (the United States and the United Kingdom) and two were 'bank based' by the traditional measure (the Netherlands and Belgium). Indeed, the size of the banking sector to GDP might be a more accurate indicator (the United Kingdom, Germany, the Netherlands, and Belgium suffered significantly). However, France's large banking sector was less badly affected, while a relatively small commercial banking sector did not protect the United States. Most noteworthy is that the greatest support was necessary at this relative early stage of the crisis in countries at the top of Figure 2.3. The crisis was initially one of losses on market-based assets and difficulties in the financing of those assets. Noteworthy also is the fact that Belgian, German, and UK support for their banks exceeded the US, measured relative to GDP.[26] We cannot simply conclude that the most market-based banking systems suffered the most in the crisis. Rather, it is necessary to consider the details of market-based banking. The explanation for the size of the impact and the timing of that

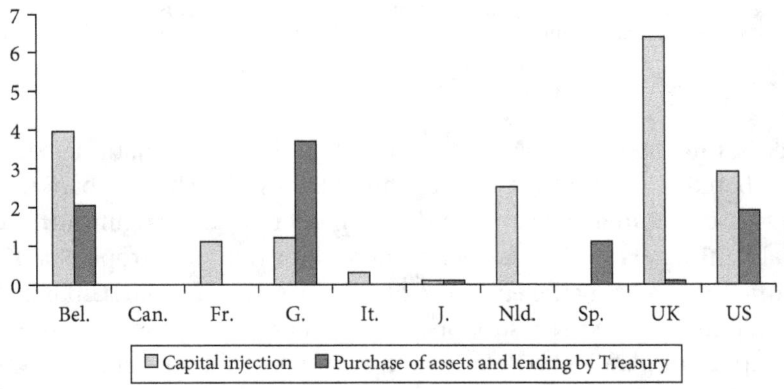

Figure 2.5. Public funds to banks (by end 2009 as a percentage of 2009 gross domestic product)

Sources: European Central Banks; National Central Banks; Spanish and Belgian figures for end of 2010. The large majority of the Belgian figures concern capital injections (etc.) in 2008. Banque Nationale de Belgique (2011) 'Rapport 2010 Evolution economique et financiere'

Note: The Canadian Mortgage Housing Corporation (owned by the federal government) provided liquidity support for mortgages worth C$69 billion to banks because of unavailable wholesale market funding

[25] The use of late 2009 figures for total government aid packages (as opposed to late 2008 figures) is more revealing because some of the initial credit guarantees and other elements of national rescue packages which were not drawn upon by banks were withdrawn prior to the end of 2009.

[26] The absence of the AIG bail-out from US figures should be noted.

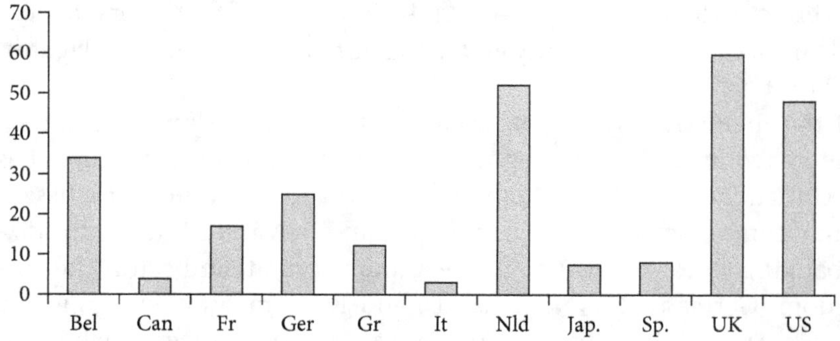

Figure 2.6. Public sector interventions* for the financial sector in selected countries to end October 2009 (as a percentage of 2007 gross domestic product (GDP))
*Includes capital injections, purchase of assets and lending by treasury and credit guarantees

Sources: From Miles (2009). Bank of England, HM Treasury, US Federal Reserve, US Treasury, FDIC, IMF World Economic Outlook (October 2009), BIS, ECB and Bank calculations; Bank of Japan, Banco de Espana, *Financial Stability Report*, 03/2010. (a) End of month data expressed as percentages of 2007 nominal GDP (b) Scale of interventions recorded as potential size of packages when announced, rather than as drawn. Total interventions include insurance, investments, and lending by central banks and governments to financial institutions under measures introduced after the crisis began. Investments are composed of capital injections to banks and SPVs, guarantees of first loss tranches and direct holdings of assets. Unlimited guarantees have not been included. (c) The US Guarantee Program for Money Market Funds expired on 18 September 2009 and the size of the UK Asset Protection Scheme was reduced on 3 November 2009. The estimates for the UK do not include purchases under the asset purchase facility

impact lies in the nature of market-based banking in the national systems. Parallel banking is very high in the United States, but shadow banking and market-based commercial banking is only moderate, and, significantly, commercial bank assets to GDP are very much lower than in Europe. So, despite the United States being the epicentre of the crisis, commercial banking in the United States required less support than in many European countries. The most important parallel bank failure, the investment bank Lehman, was not supported.

Tightened Lending Conditions from 2007

As discussed in the introduction to this volume, our engagement with the varieties of capitalism literature means we are ultimately interested in the impact of market-based banking on lending to NFCs and the wider economy. We are interested in the extent and timing of, and the reasons for, any tightening of credit conditions. We expect tightening to be greater and earlier in the more market-based systems, and to be, to a greater extent, the result of funding problems where market-based liabilities are high. We can explore these issues in a limited way through central bank surveys of bank loan officers. The overall question of tightening is problematic for our purposes, both because of the fact that these are changes in lending conditions, rather than an absolute measure, and because of the importance of overall economic conditions to bank lending conditions. The interaction between lending and the overall economy is a further complication.

While accepting these caveats, we present the survey data on tightening as a result of the 'cost and availability of funding' (although, as discussed, note the different wording of the question in the United States) and due to 'expectations about economic activities' from Q3 2007 until the end of 2011 (Figure 2.7). The greater impact of funding problems, both absolutely and relative to overall economic conditions, in the countries with more market-based banking, is clear.[27] In addition, it is the countries in the top right quadrant of Figure 2.3 (the United Kingdom and the Netherlands) where immediate funding problems are the most significant, as problems with market-based assets have a direct impact on lending. In Germany, despite problems with market-based assets, banks faced less pressure on the financing of loans. At this very early stage of the crisis, Italian and Spanish banks, thanks to their low involvement with market-based assets, did not yet face pressure on the ability to finance lending.

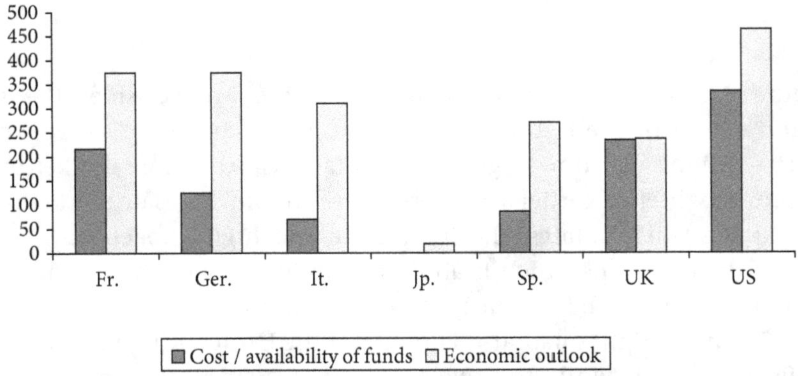

Figure 2.7. Tightening of banking lending due to 'cost and availability of funding' and 'expectations about economic activities' (net weighted percentage of responses; +tightening, –easing; total over six quarters, Q3 2007 to end Q4 2008; all firms)

Source: Bank lending surveys. No Japanese data are provided on tightening of banking lending due to 'cost and availability of funding'. Large companies only. France: 'capacité de la banque à accéder aux financements de marché'; UK 'changing cost/availability of funds'; Italy/Spain: 'banks' ability to access market financing (e.g. money or bond market financing)'; US: 'Decreased liquidity in the secondary market for these loans'

[27] Central banks in Belgium, Canada, Greece, and the Netherlands do not provide this breakdown, in large part because of confidentiality concerns in such concentrated banking systems.

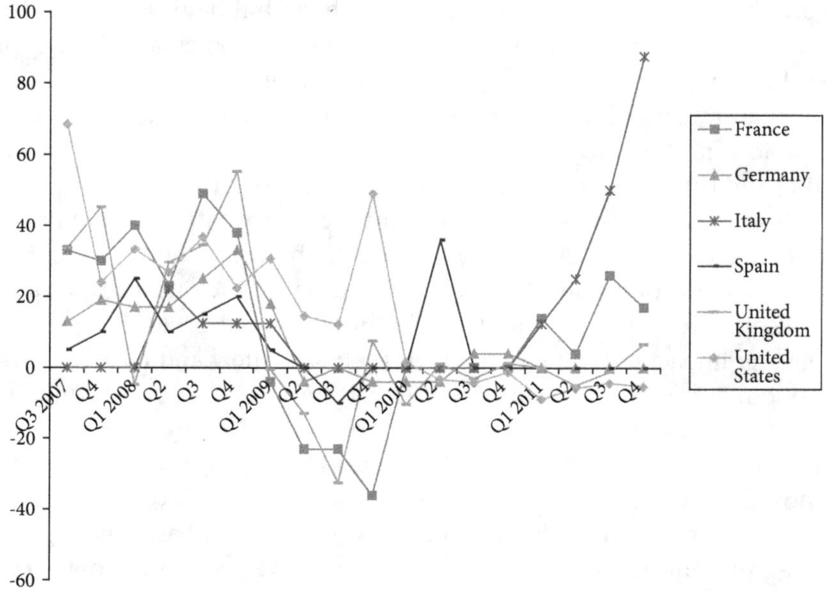

Figure 2.8. Tightening of banking lending due to 'cost and availability of funding'
Sources: National Central Banks: Bank lending surveys. France: 'capacité de la banque à accéder aux financements de marché'; UK 'changing cost/availability of funds'; Italy/Spain: 'banks' ability to access market financing (e.g. money or bond market financing)'; US 'Decreased liquidity in the secondary market for these loans'

Figure 2.8 takes this analysis slightly further, to consider the timing and extent of the tightening due to funding concerns. As we would expect—although acknowledging the limitations—the more market-based economies tightened earlier and more as a result of wholesale market problems. In the United States, the immediate and high impact may be the result of the question, which is about the ability to sell loans rather than financing them on the balance sheet. Two countries in or towards the Figure 2.3 upper-right quadrant, France and the United Kingdom, see early significant impact, while the two lower-right quadrant countries, Spain and Italy, at this stage see lower impact.

Conclusion

The most important source of change in most national financial systems studied in this volume has not been in the use of bond and equity financing by NFCs, but rather in changes in the nature of banks and banking. The one clear exception is Japan, while Spain is a partial exception given the strong rise in equity issued by NFCs in conjunction with the strong rise in bank lending (see Table 1.1 in the Introduction to this volume). The rise of market-based banking, we argue, has undermined the analytical usefulness of the bank-based/capital market-based dichotomy. We cannot understand change in national financial systems, or the onset and impact of the financial crisis, without understanding the actions of banks as agents of change. We have set out in this chapter the ways in which banks, to varying degrees, became increasingly market based, even in national systems where bank lending remained the dominant, and in some increasingly dominant, source of NFC external financing.

One important consequence of the approach taken here to market-based banking is to highlight the fact that the changes in the years immediately preceding the financial crisis were not entirely reversed in the years that followed. The SIV market did not survive, ABCP contracted, and investment banks disappeared or became commercial banks. Various aspects of the securitization markets seem unlikely to reappear. Overall, this represents a significant reduction in both shadow and parallel banking. However, the market-based nature of commercial banking across most countries remains high. Despite a very significant reduction in the funding gap in the United Kingdom, an extreme example before the crisis, the reliance on market-based sources of finance remains the most important continuing change in banking from the early 1980s. Indeed, much of the government and central bank intervention during the crisis—for example, extending government support to such entities as money market mutual funds or central banks buying securitizations—was in support of such market-based banking. Regulations were adopted with the aim of limiting the potential negative consequences of this exposure to the market, but appear unlikely to change the fact that bank lending, in nearly all the countries that are studied in this volume, remains dependent on financial markets. Mehrling (2011) argues that this dependence is significant enough in the United States to require changes in monetary policy that could include, *inter alia*, Federal Reserve support for the CDS market. As Kamikawa (this volume) shows, however, Japan moved from a significant funding gap to customer deposits exceeding loans by 2007. He explains this as the result of the long period of low Japanese growth, and the legacy of the bursting of Japan's own bubble economy. It remains to be seen whether European countries will follow this path. Regardless of whether or not this occurs in the near future, it is necessary, in order to both understand the financial crisis and follow subsequent developments, to replace the bank-based/market-based dichotomy with an analysis of market-based banking.

References

Acharya, V. V., and P. Schnabl (2010) 'Do Global Banks Spread Global Imbalances? Asset-Backed Commercial Paper during the Financial Crisis of 2007–09'. *IMF Economic Review* 58 (1): 37–73.

Acharya, V. V., P. Schnabl and G. Suarez (2010) 'Securitization Without Risk Transfer'. 15 June. Available at <http://pages.stern.nyu.edu/~sternfin/pschnabl/AcharyaSchnablSuarezJun10.pdf>, accessed 9 November 2010.

Adrian, T., and H. S. Shin (2008) 'Financial Intermediaries, Financial Stability and Monetary Policy', Paper Prepared for the Federal Reserve Bank of Kansas City Symposium at Jackson Hole, 21–23 August 2008.

—— (2010) 'The Changing Nature of Financial Intermediation and the Financial Crisis of 2007–09'. *Federal Reserve Bank of New York Staff Reports* No. 439 (April).

Aglietta, M., and R. Breton (2001) 'Financial Systems, Corporate Control and Capital Accumulation'. *Economy and Society* 30 (4): 433–466.

Arteta, C., M. Carey, R. Correa, and J. Kotter (2009) 'Revenge of the Streamroller: ABCP as a Window on Risk Choices'. Unpublished paper. Board of Governors of the Federal Reserve System, Division of International Finance (May).

Axa Investment Managers (n.d.) *Has the Dawn Risen on the European Loan Market?* Available at <http://www.axa-im-structuredfinance.com/index.cfm?pagepath=investment_expertise&CFNoCache=TRUE&servedoc=266DA5E7-1708-7D7E-1B46D0085C4C613A>, accessed 2 March 2011.

Baba, N., B. Gadanecz, and P. McGuire (2008) 'Highlights of International Banking and Financial Market Activity'. *BIS Quarterly Review* (December): 25–35.

Baba, N., R. N. McCauley, and S. Ramaswamy (2009) 'US Dollar Money Market Funds and non-US Banks'. *BIS Quarterly Review* (March): 65–81.

Bank of England (2007) *Financial Stability Review* (October). Available at <http://www.bankofengland.co.uk>, accessed 10 November 2010.

—— (2008) *Financial Stability Review* (October). Available at <http://www.bankofengland.co.uk>, accessed 10 November 2010.

—— (2009) *Financial Stability Review* (December). Available at <http://www.bankofengland.co.uk>, accessed 10 November 2010

—— (2010) *Financial Stability Review* (June). Available at <http://www.bankofengland.co.uk>, accessed 11 November 2010.

Bank of Spain (2009) *Financial Stability Review* (May). Available at <http://www.bde.es/webbde/Secciones/Publicaciones/InformesBoletinesRevistas/InformesEstabilidadFinancera/estfin16e.pdf>, accessed 14 June 2012.

Basel Committee of Banking Supervision. (2008) *Liquidity Risk: Management and Supervisory Challenges* (February). Available at <http://www.bis.org/publ/bcbs136.pdf>, accessed 12 November 2010.

—— (2009) *Report on Special Purpose Entities* (September). Available at <http://www.bis.org/publ/joint23.pdf>, accessed 11 November 2010.

Benmelech, E., J. Dlugosz, and V. Ivashina (2008) 'What lies beneath: An inside look at corporate CLOs collateral'. Available at <http://www2.lse.ac.uk/fmg/documents/events/seminars/lunchtime/1178_JenniferDlugosz.pdf>, accessed 8 November 2010.

Braithwaite, T., and K. Scannell (2012), 'JP Morgan roiled by the wake of the 'whale'', 13 July. Available at <http://www.ft.com>, accessed 18 July 2012.

Cabinet Office (2008) *Annual Report on the Japanese Economy and Public Finance 2008*. Available at <http://www5.cao.go.jp/j-j/wp/wp-je08/08.html>

Cheun, S., I. von Köppen-Mertes, and B. Weller (2009) 'The Collateral Frameworks of the Eurosystem, the Federal Reserve System and the Bank of England and the Financial Market Turmoil', European Central Bank, Occasional Paper Series, No. 107, December. <http://www.ecb.int/pub/pdf/scpops/ecbocp107.pdf>, accessed on 2 November 2010.

Čihák, M., and T. Poghosyan (2009) 'Distress in European Banks Before and During the Financial Crisis', Paolo Baffi Centre Research Paper Series No.2009–52. Available at <http://ssrn.com/abstract=1428806>, accessed 16 May 2012.

Committee on the Global Financial System (2010) The Role of Valuation and Leverage in Procyclicality. *CGFS Papers* No.34 (April).

Crotty, J. (2008) 'If Financial Market Competition is Intense, Why are Financial Firm Profits so High? Reflections on the Current "Golden Age" of Finance', *Competition & Change* 12 (2): 167–183.

Deeg, R. (2010) 'Institutional Change in Financial Systems' In *The Oxford Handbook of Comparative Institutional Analysis* (eds G. Morgan, J. L. Campbell, C. Crouch, O. K. Pedersen, and R. Whitley). Oxford: Oxford University Press, 312–351.

Deutsche Bank (2007) *Annual Report 2006*. Available at <http://www.db.com/ir/en/download/entire_Annual_Report_2006.pdf>, accessed 12 November 2010.

Ertürk, I. and S. Solari (2007) 'Banks as Continuous Revolution', in *New Political Economy* 12 (3): 369–388.

European Central Bank (2009) *EU Banks' Funding Structures and Policies*, May. Available at <http://www.ecb.int/pub/pdf/other/eubanksfundingstructurespolicies0905en.pdf>, accessed 11 November 2010.

European Securitisation Forum (2008) *Securitisation Data Report Q1: 2008*. Available at www.securitization.net/pdf/Publications/ESFData_2008Q1.pdf, accessed 8 November 2010.

Fitch Ratings (2007) 'Asset-Backed Commercial Paper & Global Banks Exposure—10 Key Questions'. Available at <http://www.fitchratings.com/dtp/pdf3-07/babp1209.pdf>, accessed 26 February 2010.

—— (2008) *Fair Value Disclosures. A Reality Check.* (26 June). Available at <http://www.fitchratings.com>, accessed 26 February 2010.

Gorton, G. (2010) *Slapped in the Face by the Invisible Hand.* Oxford and New York: Oxford University Press.

Gorton, G., and A. Metrick (2010) 'Securitized Banking and the Run on Repo'. Available at <http://ssrn.com/abstract=1440752>, accessed 3 March 2011.

Hackethal, A. (2001) 'How Unique are US-Banks? The Role of Banks in Five Major Financial Systems', *Journal of Economics and Statistics*, 221: 592–619.

—— (2004) 'German Banks and Banking Structure', In *The German Financial System*, 2nd edition (eds J. P. Krahnen and R. H. Schmidt). Oxford: Oxford University Press, 71–105.

Hellwig, M. (2008) *Systemic Risk in the Financial Sector: An Analysis of the Subprime-Mortgage Financial Crisis*. Max Planck Institute for Research on Collective Goods (November).

Huang, R. and L. Ratnovski (2009) 'The Dark Side of Bank Wholesale Funding'. Research Department, Federal Reserve Bank of Philadelphia Working Paper No. 09–3.

IMF (2008) *Global Financial Stability Report*, October. Available at <http://www.imf.org>, accessed 14 November 2010.

IMF (2009a). *Global Financial Stability Report*, October. Available at <http://www.imf.org>, accessed 14 November 2010.

—— (2009b) *Germany: 2008 Volume IV Consultation—Staff Report; Staff Supplement; Public Information Notice on the Executive Board Discussion; and Statement by the Executive Director for Germany*. IMF Country Report No.09/15. Available at <http://www.imf.org>, accessed 14 November 2010.

—— (2010) *Global Financial Stability Report*, October. Available at <http://www.imf.org>, accessed 2 March 2010.

Ivashina, V., and Z. Sun (2010) 'Institutional Demand Pressure and the Cost of Corporate Loans', available at <http://papers.ssrn.com/sol3/papers.cfm?abstract_id=1299300>, accessed 8 November 2010.

Ivashina, V. and D. Scharfstein (2009) 'Bank Lending During the Financial Crisis of 2008'. Available at <http://ssrn.com/abstract=1297337>, accessed 8 November 2010.

McGuire, P., and G. von Peter (2009) 'The US Dollar Shortage in Global Banking'. *BIS Quarterly Review* March: 47–60.

Mehrling, P. (2011) *The New Lombard Street*. Princeton and Oxford: Princeton University Press.

Miles, D. (2009) *The Future Financial Landscape*. Speech given at Bloomberg (16 December). Available at <http://www.bankofengland.co.uk/publications/speeches/2009/speech418.pdf>, accessed 12 November 2010.

Morgan Stanley (2006) *European & US Leveraged LCDS: Impact on the High Yield Market*, EHYA & LMA Panel Discussion (31 May). Available at <http://web.archive.org/web/20060818031932/http://www.ehya.com/docs/LLCDS_slides_distributed.pdf>. accessed 16 February 2011.

Netherlands Central Bank (2009) *Central Bank Statistical Bulletin*, December. Available at <http://www.dnb.nl/en/binaries/Statistisch%20Bulletin%20dec%202009_tcm47–228881.pdf>, accessed 12 June 2012.

Norddeutsche Landesbank (2007) *Annual Report 2006*. Available at <http://www.nordlb.de/fileadmin/Investor_Relations/Geschaeftsberichte/englisch/2006//www.nordlb.com/fileadmin/redaktion/branchen/investorrelations/geschaeftsberichte/2006/Annual_Report_2006.pdf>, accessed 12 October 2009.

Northern Rock (2007), *Annual Report and Accounts 2006*. Available at <http://nram.biz/~/media/Files/N/N-RAM/content/corporate-reports/res2006pr-annualreportandaccounts.pdf>, accessed 5 January 2010.

Poghosyan, T., and M. Čihák (2009) 'Distress in European Banks: An Analysis Based on a New Data Set', IMF Working Paper no. 09/9.

Pozsar, Z., T. Adrian, A. Ashcraft and H. Boesky (2010) *Shadow Banking*. Federal Reserve Bank of New York Staff Reports no. 458 (July).

Raddatz, C. (2010) 'When the Rivers Run Dry: Liquidity and the Use of Wholesale Funds in the Transmission of the U.S. Subprime Crisis', Policy Research Working Paper Series 5203, The World Bank. Available at: <http://ideas.repec.org/f/pra328.html>, accessed 3 March 2010.

Ratnovski, L., and R. Huang (2009) 'Why Are Canadian Banks More Resilient?' IMF Working Paper No. WP/09/152.

Standard & Poor's (2010) *A Guide to the European Loan Market*, January. Available at <http://www.lcdcomps.com/d/pdf/European_Loan_Primer.pdf>, accessed 15 February 2011.

Tucker, P. (2010) 'Shadow Banking, Financing Markets and Financial Stability'. Available at: <http://www.bankofengland.co.uk/publications/speeches/2010/speech420.pdf>, accessed 3 March 2011.

Zysman, J. (1983) *Governments, Markets, and Growth*, Oxford: Martin Robertson.

3

Market-Based Banking as the Worst of All Worlds: Illustrations from the United States and United Kingdom

Iain Hardie and Sylvia Maxfield

Introduction

In the wake of the 2008 global financial meltdown, French President Sarkozy reported that the world 'had turned the page on the Anglo-Saxon model'. But is there an Anglo-Saxon model?[1] Political economy scholarship largely takes it for granted. High stock market capitalization, dispersed shareholding, and a relatively high proportion of equity and bonds in corporate financing are all evidence of arm's-length interactions and impatient capital in a 'market-based' system. The literature on varieties of financial capitalism (VoFC), and the broader varieties of capitalism (VoC), represented most famously by Zysman (1983) and Hall and Soskice (2001), respectively, make much of the bank-based/market-based dichotomy. Neither work uses the term 'bank based', but the central role of banks is clear in the distinction between 'the impersonal arm's length dealings of capital markets' and 'the personal institutional ties of banks or lending institutions' (Zysman 1983, 63).[2] The United States and the United Kingdom have been, in this approach, the archetypal market-based financial systems.

Developments in these archetypal systems since 2000 and their experience of the 2007–8 financial crisis highlight the shortcomings of this market versus credit typology. Changes in the US financial system are in broad outline consistent with Zysman's typology, although they require some modification in

[1] We accept the problems with the term (Crouch 2005).

[2] The potential role of 'specialized lending institutions' is acknowledged (Zysman 1983, 61).

the details of the approach, most obviously in the stark distinction between loan and capital markets and the limited attention to money markets. The UK case, however, is more problematic. In the United Kingdom, bank assets have increased dramatically, far faster than equity or bond markets. In terms of NFC financing, bank loans have increased significantly, the proportion of long-term lending increased and bond markets remain small and have grown less quickly than bank loans. During the financial crisis, the three most prominent British casualties were commercial banks, albeit of different types: Northern Rock, Royal Bank of Scotland, and Halifax Bank of Scotland. In the United States, in contrast, a wide variety of institutions failed or needed epic bailouts: an insurance company, AIG, at least two investment banks, Bear Stearns and Lehman, a number of commercial banks, some heavily engaged in investment banking (Citibank), some not (Wachovia), and a savings and loan, Washington Mutual. Nevertheless, although a wide variety of different financial institutions were involved in the two cases, and the regulatory institutions were very differently structured, the early timing and severity of crisis in both countries were very similar. To understand developments in the US and UK financial systems and their experience of the financial crisis, we need to focus far more closely on the activities of financial institutions in general and banks in particular, and look to what can be learnt 'by following the money flows in the market economy and dissecting the institutions that structure that flow' (Zysman 1983, 11). As argued throughout this volume and true also of the United States and United Kingdom, the key change in the nature of financial systems in advanced economies in recent years is the rise of 'market-based banking' (MBB), and therefore of credit provision with availability and terms determined by market prices. The term is not new (see Adrian and Shin 2010), and in its so-far US-centric application it fits relatively well into the existing market versus credit typology of national financial systems. By contrast, the evolution of financial intermediation and the development of MBB in the other stereotypical example of a market-based system, the United Kingdom, highlight changes occurring in many supposedly bank-based European economies. Focusing on bank activities, as evident on both the asset (loans given and financial assets purchased) and liability (money borrowed and equity capital raised) sides of their balance sheets, the United States and United Kingdom represent the extreme version of MBB in the countries considered in this volume, but the two countries are also very different financial systems (see King and Wood 1999).

We do not see MBB as another manifestation of the existing conception of market-based systems, but rather as a financial system that shares negative characteristics of both bank- and market-based systems, with few of the positives and with additional sources of weakness. Following discussion of the limitations in the traditional typology highlighted by the US–UK comparison, the next section introduces second-order distinctions focused on the nature of exchange, information efficiencies, and risk distribution. The third section illustrates how these second-order distinctions comprise unique vulnerabilities for MBB as evident in the US and UK experiences of the financial crisis. This chapter is therefore both a discussion of two specific country case studies of highly MBB and a further consideration of the vulnerabilities of this model which has relevance to other countries considered in this volume.

Questioning the Traditional Typology of National Financial Systems

Recent work on the political economy of European finance illustrates the weakness of the traditional view of the United Kingdom as a market-based system (Howell 2007; Hardie and Howarth 2010). As discussed in the introduction to this volume, and Hardie and Howarth (this volume), we can distinguish financial systems within the existing typology either by the sources of financing for NFCs, or by consideration of the size of banks relative to equity and bond markets. By either measure, the United Kingdom would appear to have become more bank based in the period since 2000. In terms of market size, bank assets increased 49.2 per cent between 2000 and 2007, private bond markets increased by 19.2 per cent, while equity market capitalization fell by 26.5 per cent. Of the major economies, bank assets increased by more only in Spain, and UK bank assets to gross domestic product (GDP) are higher than nearly all the major European economies (see Hardie et al., this volume). This is not solely the result of increased foreign assets: since 1980, UK bank assets have increased approximately five times relative to the size of the UK economy, even excluding the banks' foreign currency assets (Miles 2009).

The problem of classification is immediately apparent. The US and UK's stock market capitalizations are the highest, as we would expect, although the difference from Spain, France, and Japan is not so large and the UK stock market includes many foreign firms with little or no connection to the domestic economy. Bond market size is not compelling in either case. US bank assets, the lowest of the countries listed, are as we would expect in a market-based economy, but the contrast with the United Kingdom is dramatic, even allowing for accounting difference. While bank assets in the United States are less than half the size of the private debt market, in the United Kingdom they are nearly four times larger. Given the importance to the existing typology of financial institutions' ability to dominate credit markets, the high concentration of the UK banking market is also noteworthy. The US banking system, as would be expected of a traditional market-based system, is highly fragmented.

In comparing the sources of NFC external financing for the United States and United Kingdom, the data further challenge the traditional typology. With bank lending growing more strongly than bond financing and equity being repurchased by listed companies, the United Kingdom became more bank based in this period (see Hardie et al., this volume). From 1999 until 2007, UK bank lending to NFCs grew at an annual rate of 10–20 per cent, even higher than growth in mortgage lending (Bank of England 2007, 35). As a result, at end 2008, loans to NFCs by UK banks peaked at 45.4 per cent of GDP, up from 27.2 per cent at year end 1999,[3] and the proportion of NFC external financing represented by loans rose from 18 to 37.8 per cent over the same period.[4] Furthermore, although UK banks continued to lend predominantly short term, the volume of long-term loans to UK NFCs increased by nearly three times in this period.[5] Far from an economy increasingly reliant on bond and equity financing, the Bank of England noted 'the potential benefits of lowering the economy's reliance on bank finance' (Bank of England 2009, 11) and the government announced a consultation paper exploring action steps to remedy this dependence. While the United Kingdom became increasingly bank based in its financing of NFCs, in the United States a range of institutions usurped the commercial banks' role. Of most relevance here, investment bank assets reached 30 per cent of those of commercial banks (Gorton and Metrick 2010, 11). Also, money market mutual fund assets were larger than US bank deposits on the eve of the crisis (Pozsar et al. 2010, 52), and, uniquely for developed economies, credit provision by 'other financial institutions' dwarfed that by deposit banks at the end of 2007 (Beck and Demirgüç-Kunt 2009). This last point is crucial to how we see the United States within the continuum developed in this volume. US commercial banks were more 'traditional' (see Hardie and Howarth, this volume) than their European counterparts, but 'parallel' banks (Hardie and Howarth, this volume) mean that credit provision in the United States is highly market based. By the primary empirical indicators used in the accepted comparative political economy (CPE) categorization of national financial systems, therefore, the United States and the United Kingdom exhibit important differences. The United Kingdom, in particular, does not fit the capital market-based category. However, we argue that both systems are centred on MBB.

Market-Based Banking and its Vulnerabilities: A Second-Order Comparison of Credit- and Market-Based Systems

The most critical distinguishing characteristic of MBB for the CPE of capitalism is that banks finance the assets on their balance sheets by borrowing

[3] Source: Bank of England, Office of National Statistics.
[4] Source: Eurostat.
[5] Authors' calculation from Eurostat.

from other financial institutions, because customer deposits do not suffice. By eclipsing the stabilizing role of deposits, this element of MBB eliminates an important basis for patient capital in the classic depiction of the credit-based model that underpins coordinated market economies (CME). Banks may be able to make long-term loans (as UK banks increasingly did pre-crisis), but only when market financing is available, rather than as the result of decision making that is independent from market pressures. In order to shed light on this and other implications of MBB for CPE, we extend the stylized comparison among the different types of national financial systems (see Hardie et al., this volume; Hardie and Howarth, this volume) to several second-order distinctions (Table 3.1). This evaluation points to systemic vulnerabilities of MBB in comparison with the two classic types of national financial systems. It is therefore relevant to systems which have been seen as CMEs in the prevailing analysis, as well as the liberal market economies (LMEs) of the United Kingdom and United States.

We focus on the quality of the financial institution–NFC interaction and information flows, liquidity characteristics, and on the locus and concentration of risk. We argue that in questioning the utility of the label 'bank based', we cannot simply see MBB as a market-based system as conceived

Table 3.1. Stylized second-order depiction of national financial system differentiation

		Capital market based	Bank based	Market-based banking
Second-order distinction	Nature of exchange	Arm's-length interaction (low basis for 'patience')	Relational exchange (basis for patience)	Arm's-length interaction
	Information	Requires transparency, markets gather information	Protects opacity, information is concentrated	Protects opacity, information is concentrated
	Liquidity	Can satisfy large financing needs, offers liquidity	Can't satisfy largest financing needs, relative illiquidity	Can satisfy large financing needs, offers liquidity
	Locus of risk	First-order risk is enterprise insolvency, risk dispersed	First-order risk is bank insolvency, risk concentrated	First-order risk is bank insolvency, risk concentrated
Overall assessment		Pros: transparency, financial resources easily mobilized, liquidity and risk held by capital recipients Cons: short-termism and potential harm to households	Pros: multiple bases for patience (household depositors, relational exchange) Cons: financing limited and risk concentrated on banks	Pros: large financing volume possible Cons: low transparency, risk concentrated within financial sector, little basis for patience ('banks finance banks' in arms-length transaction)

in the original VoFC and VoC literature. Instead, a system that shares the potential weaknesses of the bank-based system, none of its advantages, and with the additional vulnerability in the fragility of the market-based financial institutions upon which risk is concentrated has important implications for how we see recent developments in financial systems. A core argument of the VoC literature is that economic success can be achieved under either an LME or a CME system, even if the institutional and policy underpinnings of this success differ. In our comparative analysis of the stylized types of financial systems we highlight attributes suggesting the systemic vulnerabilities in a now-common form of market-based system, MBB.

In MBB, various forms of banking entities intermediate, and rely heavily on funding from other financial institutions, rather than on depositors (see Hardie et al., this volume; Hardie and Howarth, this volume). At the same time, the 'originate and distribute' model of banking undermines the relationship aspect of exchange between financial institutions and NFCs, reducing the incentives for information gathering and undermining a key perceived advantage of the traditional bank-based system (Hardie et al., this volume). The way the crisis unfolded in the US and UK highlights systems with high levels of MBB, where banks in particular, and financial market actors in general, intermediated between themselves—a system 'feeding on itself' (Trichet 2008)—in markets that involved negative aspects of the relationship exchange (i.e. information was kept private) traditionally associated with the bank-based, patient capital model, rather than the frictionless arm's-length exchange of the impatient capital markets-based system. Transactions typical of MBB activity also frequently involve not the one-off sale assumed in a market-based system but either an ongoing credit exposure to the counterparty, such as involved in credit default swaps (CDSs),[6] or the frequent repetition of transactions with the same relatively limited group of counterparties, as in the inter-bank and repurchase ('repo') markets. These transactions therefore have characteristics of relationship exchange, but do not involve the beneficial information qualities of relational exchange between banks and NFCs in the traditional bank-based system. Worse, they concentrate risk on the creditworthiness of a small number of large financial institutions, as occurs in a number of stereotypical bank-based systems, and despite the promises of risk dispersion in a market-based system. In the United Kingdom, this concentration was on the commercial banks, and in the United States, much of this centred on the investment banks that are uniquely important to the US system, and on AIG.

Information problems are compounded by the fact that many of the transactions that support this new bank intermediation activity, such as

[6] If credit risk is hedged (effectively insured) via a CDS, the buyer of the insurance pays a premium to the insurer, and in exchange the insurer commits to pay out in the event of a default.

those involved in inter-bank borrowing, repo agreements, derivatives, and derivative-based securities take place in markets very different from the public equity exchanges envisioned in the stereotypical capital market-based systems. Public exchanges require a relatively high level of disclosure, often enforced by regulation, that is not as important in the over-the-counter markets typical of the bilateral exchanges in MBB.

The Nature of Exchange

In arm's-length exchange, price aligns willingness-to-sell and willingness-to-pay. Markets determine price, parties to the transaction know about one another only what is required by law and accounting practice, and markets bring them into a one-time exchange. In a bank-based system, the parties to a transaction have previously exchanged information, and exchanges are repeated frequently over an extended period. Previous interactions and expectations of future transactions shape proclivities in any current transaction, and encourage patience. Parties transact directly, without an intermediary.

In several of the countries considered in this volume, and particularly in the United States and the United Kingdom, various aspects of the 'originate and distribute' business model, a key component of MBB, undermined relational exchange between banks and NFCs. In the outright sale of loans, incentives for banks to gather, and NFCs to share, information were reduced, as the availability, pricing, and profitability of lending was market determined. In the structuring of increasingly complex securities, these issues were compounded. Even though many of these transactions were not distributed, but retained on bank balance sheets, the banks relied not on information regarding individual borrowers, but on the apparent safety of diversified risk,[7] sanctioned by rating agencies and capital adequacy requirements. Meanwhile, the relational exchange typical of traditional bank-based systems, but without the information content and longer term time horizons expected of bank-based systems, came to dominate exchange between American and British financial institutions, both with each other and cross-border. The result is relational exchange without information or patience.

Many transactions in MBB take place on over-the-counter (OTC) markets and involve either exposure to a counterparty which must make ongoing payments similar to a borrower under a loan, as in CDS transactions, or repeated transactions with the same counterparty, either collateralized by securities, as in the repo market, or uncollateralized, as in the inter-bank market. The information challenge therefore involves not only identifying the fundamental value

[7] On the reduced incentives for information gathering in diversified portfolios, see Calvo and Mendoza 2000.

of the transaction, but also assessing the creditworthiness of the counterparty to the trade and the value of collateral (often derivatives-based bonds such as complex asset-backed securities, ABS). The ability of a counterparty to fulfil their promise, and in the case of collateral, deliver on unknown future promises, is an important calculation. The distribution of risk in this way is very different from the outright sale of a security. At best it is a more partial distribution of risk; at worst, risk is concentrated on the creditworthiness of the counterparty.

Information Flows in Market-Based Banking

The informational character of OTC markets is at the heart of the crisis. Information is elicited, synthesized, and distributed in different ways on these OTC markets than on public exchanges (Duffie, Garleanu and Heje 2005). Disclosure of information pertinent to valuing securities is critical for the public exchanges that are the main focus of VoFC analysis. Public exchanges require transparency to value securities, but such exchanges contribute to this transparency, and by mitigating counterparty risk, remove concerns regarding that risk.

OTC trading occurs through dealers who consummate deals through bilateral arrangements. Financial instruments involving securitization (mortgage-backed securities, collateralized debt obligations, CDS, etc.) are traded on OTC markets, as are instruments that dominate banks' wholesale funding markets such as asset-backed commercial paper (ABCP) and repo agreements. Prices in these trades are negotiated in opaque markets. Critical information in these exchanges includes counterparties' financial stability, which is not directly observable (Acharya and Bisin 2010). Counterparties must rely partly on reputation and signals, but repeated interactions should build trust (Lagos, Rocheteau and Weill 2009). Babus (2010) found banks in OTC markets forming core–periphery relationships in which repeated transactions created relationships, contrasting with a classic understanding of bank- and market-based systems in which the idea of securities trading involving relational exchange appears almost oxymoronic.

However, relationships in this system do not fully solve the information problem regarding the creditworthiness of a counterparty, and using collateral only increases market risk. The information problem regarding the component parts of many securities, especially those involving complex derivatives, remains, and valuation difficulties have a direct impact on the willingness to lend to a financial counterparty. Most ABS involve chopping up similar financial assets with different credit quality, such as mortgage loans, and recombining them into a new product with a credit rating assigned by a ratings agency, in an opaque process (BIS 2008, 132). When markets involve bilaterally negotiated exchanges of these hard-to-value securities, with no trade disclosure requirements, it is hard to use 'marking to market' valuation (SEC 2008). Relational exchanges in a modern market-based system are therefore different from relational exchanges in the classic bank-based system as well as from the non-relational exchanges of the archetypal market-based system. In relational exchanges in both traditional bank-based systems and systems with MBB, information is kept between the parties to the trade rather than being shared more widely, leading to informationally opaque systems. In classic bank-based systems, banks have sufficient information about the borrower from their relationship. In a system where the counterparties are financial institutions, all the evidence of the breakdown of lending between financial institutions, and of the unwillingness to take any form of credit risk during the crisis, points to repeated interactions and supposedly close relationships that did not yield sufficient information either about counterparty risk or underlying securities to have an impact on creditor behaviour.

Liquidity, Locus, and Concentration of Risk

In capital market-based systems, financial institutions make money from fees for services such as underwriting or trading and from short-term proprietary trading. In the existing understanding, bank-based systems are more vulnerable to liquidity crunches than capital market-based systems because the locus of risk lies with financial institutions, but risk is minimized by the stability of depositors and the lower liquidity. In contrast, the archetypical market-based system disperses risk among NFCs and offers more liquidity. The system operating in both the United States and the United Kingdom in the decade leading up to the financial crisis was a hybrid in which the presenting problem was typical of bank-based systems approaching crisis: a mismatch between short-term liabilities and longer term assets at large financial institutions, but the market-based nature of many short-term liabilities increased fragility.

Informational aspects of arm's-length versus relational exchange are related to liquidity characteristics. In archetypal bank-based systems, bank leverage normally remains fairly low, constrained by government regulations and savers' deposits. But liquidity is also relatively low, constrained by household deposits. Liquidity is higher in the capital market-based systems, constrained only by investors' appetite for stocks and bonds. 'Informationally efficient' capital markets also support liquidity by easily eliciting and centralizing information. The liquidity and informational characteristics of such a financial system are mutually reinforcing, and liquid markets facilitate price discovery (Levine 1997).

Another important difference between the traditional system types concerns the locus of risk. In traditional bank-based systems the first-order risk is bank solvency. Households trust their savings to banks in the form of deposits and banks are a primary source of financing for NFCs. Banks are the critical locus of risk. In capital market-based systems, in contrast, the primary locus of risk should be the NFCs in whom savers invest directly by purchasing bonds or stocks. In the traditional capital market-based model, therefore, risk is highly dispersed to NFCs that are of low systemic importance and heterogeneous. However, developments in both the United States and the United Kingdom in recent years have shifted the risk to default by commercial and investment banks or other very large financial institutions which facilitate MBB (such as AIG). The higher risk of financial institutions not lending to one another replaces the lower risk of customers withdrawing deposits. Risk is concentrated on the solvency of financial institutions that are increasingly large, thanks to the lack of constraint from retail deposits, and fragile, as a result of the same relative shortage of stable deposits (e.g. Basel Committee on Banking Supervision 2008; Adrian and Shin 2010).

Illustrating Market-Based Banking and its Vulnerabilities: American and British Experiences of the Crisis

MBB involves systemic vulnerabilities. These vulnerabilities are evident in the new types of bank activities associated with MBB that are at the heart of any story of the 2007–8 financial crisis. These are originate-to-distribute lending, shadow banking and wholesale funding by both commercial and parallel banks. Each of these activities comprises an important piece of the story of MBB in many countries in the first decade of the new millennium, and of the 2007–8 financial crisis. First banks and other financial institutions sold loans to one another in arm's-length (originate-to-distribute) transactions relying on information short cuts facilitated by the credit rating agencies. Second, banks also sold loans to new legal entities, but retained the risk if market financing was unavailable (shadow banking). This mechanism hid information, and while it facilitated increased lending, it also concentrated risk and the sources of liquidity, introducing potential instability. Thirdly, banks and shadow banks obtained money to make loans or purchase loans made by others, not from depositors, but by borrowing from one another (wholesale financing). This concentrated risk while shortening two legs of the traditional three-legged stool of financial intermediation involving banks, households, and NFCs.

Selling Loans

The 'originate and distribute' model of banking—making loans with the intension of selling them—was most enthusiastically practised in the United

States, in the US$500 billion loan trading market (no trading figures exist in the United Kingdom), and in a securitization market with outstandings (including through the parallel banks) equivalent to 67 per cent of GDP, far in excess of the United Kingdom, at 25 per cent.[8] Overall, securitization supported 28 per cent of outstanding credit in the United States, twice the UK figure (IMF 2010a, 320; see also Jiangli and Pisker 2008). The market determined the availability and pricing of these loans. This supports the blurring of Zysman's distinction between loans and securities (see Hardie et al., this volume), but it has further implications for the nature of MBB across all countries. Although where loans are sold, genuine risk distribution takes place, these loans are made through arm's-length transactions with reduced incentives to gather information for banks or the institutional investors buying the loans. Any reliance on rating agencies or use of CDS further reduces the incentives to gather information. In addition, in line with lending generally, the commitment to the borrower is made by the lending bank in advance of selling the loans. The likelihood is high that distribution will prove impossible in difficult market conditions, concentrating risk back on the original lending bank and increasing that bank's liquidity problems. This is what happened in the crisis, with 'involuntary' increases in bank balance sheets (Bank of England 2007, 14).

US banks were more reliant on selling loans to facilitate further lending than their UK counterparts. However, as is now clear, much of the distribution of risk, so central to a successful capital market-based system, was largely illusory. Rather than originate and distribute, this was 'originate, rate and relocate', even at times to another part of the same bank (Alexander et al. 2007). Banks retained the 'super senior'—the largest and most creditworthy—tranches of securitizations on their balance sheets, frequently with credit insurance from the insurance company AIG, which insured US$79 billion (Financial Crisis Inquiry Commission 2011, XIX), or a small number of specialist 'monoline' insurers, a further huge concentration of risk. One estimate is that of the US$240 billion super senior tranches of some of the most problematic securitizations,[9] two-thirds of the risk remained with arrangers with the remainder hedged with CDS. Importantly, in the United States, nine arrangers were each responsible for over US$10 billion of this risk, and one for over $50 billion (Alexander et al. 2007, 32). The overall result was 'the extreme concentration of risk in a highly leveraged financial sector' (Caballero and Krishnamurthy 2009,1). The concentration of risk was not confined to the largest institutions. Chains of transactions concentrated risk at the chain's

[8] Year-end 2007. Authors' calculations from European Securitization Forum. Available at www.europeansecuritisation.com/Communications/Archive/Current/2009Q2-ESFDataReport.pdf.
[9] Collateralized debt obligations based on ABS issued in 2006–7.

weakest link (Pozsar et al. 2010, 70). Those weakest links, for example AIG, the monoline insurers or one of the investment banks, like Bear Stearns or Lehman, gave rise to concerns regarding an institution being 'too connected to fail', even if it was not obviously 'too big to fail'. This is a risk that would not be expected in the archetypal capital market-based system. The locus of risk in MBB is large financial institutions, not relatively smaller NFCs. On the eve of the financial crisis in the United States these financial institutions were opaque, even to those counterparties with whom the frequency of transactions should give a relational characteristic to exchange, in large part because of the market-based nature of both their assets and liabilities.

Furthermore, despite their apparent different businesses, these financial institutions are not heterogeneous, as NFCs are, but rather face 'common market exposures' (BIS 2008, 133). The only variation was in ways which increased fragility, such as a lack of access to lender of last resort facilities in the United States. Indeed, in the years leading to the crisis, homogeneity had markedly increased, and not only as a result of commercial banks in both countries (as elsewhere) increasingly carrying out investment banking. In addition, investment banks made, and, particularly traded, loans, and an insurance company like AIG became active in CDS. Much of this activity involved the use of collateral, and homogeneity was readily apparent in the false comfort of market-based collateral.

Shadow Banking

Shadow banking, as defined in this volume, involves commercial bank lending that is wholly or partially removed from bank balance sheets as long as market financing is available. It is central to any conception of MBB (see Hardie et al., this volume, Hardie and Howarth, this volume). Despite frequent transactions between investors and the special purpose companies, exchange is arm's length, with the information difficulties inherent in such exchange, compounded by the complexity of the underlying assets held by these entities.

Shadow banking in the United States involved temporarily removing assets from the balance sheet. In the United Kingdom, assets generally remained on balance sheet, but enjoyed favourable capital treatment (Basel Committee on Banking Supervision 2008) and can therefore be seen as partially off balance sheet. Despite these differences, the outcomes in the crisis were very similar. The primary motivation for this activity, in both the United States and United Kingdom, was the reduction of the capital needed to support lending and increased profitability (Landsman, Peasnell and Shakespeare 2006). Shadow banking rested precariously on short-term funds from US money market mutual funds. This borrowing was exceptionally short term and therefore the liquidity risk was high: borrowing from money market mutual funds of one to four *days* in maturity reached 80 per cent of the total (Bank of England 2008, 23). The money market mutual funds were 'the lifeblood' of the shadow and parallel banking system (Pozsar et al. 2010, 50). The US money market mutual funds' need for short-term investment opportunities precipitated change in both the US and UK financial systems by offering a plentiful source of wholesale funding for all forms of banking. The liabilities of US shadow and parallel banks peaked in the summer of 2007 at close to US$20 trillion, at that point approaching twice the liabilities of traditional banks, before contraction that 'reduced the [US] financial system's lending capacity by several trillion dollars' (Acharya, Gale and Yorulmeyer 2010, 3). When commercial paper market funding contracted (as it did first in August 2007 but even more severely in October 2008), assets that had previously not appeared on the balance sheets had to be recognized as fully on balance sheet, increasing the need for funding and capital to meet regulatory requirements. In the United Kingdom, the increase in assets (allowing for their risk weighting) was estimated at £109.1 billion (Bank of England 2007). The lending was therefore again market based, and the risk, despite its apparent distribution, was once again with the large financial institutions. The problems were compounded by the fact that the banks had to value most of these assets at the prevailing market price using 'mark-to-market' accounting. 'Mark disputes', disagreements between counterparties as to the market price of a particular security, were common pre-crisis (SEC 2008), but during the crisis, the gap between market prices and any notion of fundamental value worsened (see Hardie and Howarth, this volume). Figures on marking to market in the two countries are incomplete, but suggest a contrast between 'traditional' US commercial banks, with 26.9 per cent of assets marked to market, and market-based US investment and UK universal banks. Although Goldman Sachs is an outlier with 86 per cent of assets marked to market at end 2007, Lehman, Merrill Lynch and Morgan Stanley, with 42–44 per cent, were no more market based on this measure than Barclays, HSBC, and RBS, at 40–52 per cent (Hardie and Howarth, this volume). This marking to market adds to the problems of information regarding the creditworthiness of financial counterparties, because of uncertainties regarding the value of market-based assets, particularly at a time when a largely homogeneous group of financial institutions are looking to sell those assets.

The largest component of shadow banking across all countries was ABCP (Hardie and Howarth, this volume). This is a type of short-term security issued by a special purpose company, secured by the assets the special purpose company holds, but with additional credit support from the sponsoring bank (see Hardie and Howarth, this volume). ABCP sponsorship by US entities (predominantly commercial banks) exceeded US$300 billion by the beginning of

2007, more than twice the UK figure (all by commercial banks[10]). However, UK banks were disproportionately active in programmes that an academic study has shown to be more risky (Arteta et al. 2008), and US bank activity relative to GDP (a key determinant of the fiscal impact of any support for the banks; see Hardie and Howarth, this volume) was lower. Shadow banking was important in both countries, both to lending before the crisis—US and UK assets were nearly half of the assets of ABCP programmes that totalled US$1.3 trillion—and to problems after. However, the UK banks were taking greater risks, relative to US banks, on the continued availability of market financing. This risk was highly concentrated: in both countries, three banks were responsible for approximately three-quarters of total sponsorship.[11] The ABCP market collapsed very early in the crisis. Information concerns regarding the special purpose companies' assets made mutual funds wary of purchasing. Support promised by banks was triggered, and banks also supported their ABCP companies for reputational reasons (Basel Committee on Banking Supervision 2009, 3). The risk concentration and liquidity risks involved in ABCP became apparent. Beyond the originate-to-distribute selling of loans, as practised in the US and the UK, shadow banking reflects dissolution of the relationship between banks, depositors and nonfinancial corporate borrowers at the centre of the classic bank-based financial system envisioned in the VoC literature.

Wholesale Funding of Bank Assets

Particularly important outside the US is market based, or wholesale, funding of assets that remain on commercial banks' balance sheets. In terms of a reliance on selling assets, either permanently or temporarily, US commercial bank lending would appear to be more market based than the UK. However, the more dramatic difference between the two countries' commercial banks lies in financing of the loans that were not sold. Increased reliance on wholesale funding has been a characteristic of banking systems across developed economies, but the US and UK did not follow the same path pre-crisis. UK bank dependence on wholesale funding—a funding gap (Hardie and Howarth, this volume) has, with the exception of HSBC, increased significantly as the rising volume of loans relative to deposits (loan to deposits ratio) facilitated significantly increased bank lending. In the United States, in contrast, the loan to deposits ratios of the commercial banks have remained

[10] UK banks' liquidity support to ABCP programmes reached the equivalent of 35 per cent of their lending to domestic non-financial companies (Bank of England 2007, 33).

[11] Citigroup, Bank of America, and JP Morgan Chase in the United States, HBOS, HSBC, and Barclays in the United Kingdom. Author's calculations from Acharya, Schnabl and Suarez 2010.

stable, indicating no relative increased dependence on market funding. In the United Kingdom, customer deposits have made up roughly 50 per cent of total commercial bank funding, compared with the United States where customer deposits have accounted for over 75 per cent (IMF 2010b, 67). In the United States, increased reliance on wholesale funding by commercial banks and other financial intermediaries was partially hidden in off-balance sheet activities, including ABCP discussed above,[12] and US bank selling of loans was far greater than in the United Kingdom. Nevertheless, in the financing of banks' loan assets on the balance sheet, the UK commercial banks are more market-based than their US counterparts.

The wholesale funding of banks mostly involved banks lending to each other through a variety of different OTC markets. Banks that were well known to each other interacted very frequently in short-term markets, thereby establishing what should be an information-rich relational exchange.[13] Yet this was not the case, and given the uncertainties regarding the financial market prices that are so central to the creditworthiness of market-based financial institutions, it is doubtful whether it was possible to acquire the necessary information. The result was very short-term, fickle funding that exacerbated liquidity risk while financing the increased size of the institutions upon whom the risk was increasingly concentrated. Markets involving frequent interaction between counterparties who were well known to each other collapsed in the crisis, necessitating the rescue in the United Kingdom of both RBS and HBOS as a result of inter-bank market problems, and Bear Stearns' takeover and Lehman's collapse as the repo market faced difficulties. Goldman Sachs increased margin calls on AIG and effectively started a 'margin run' on AIG (Gorton 2008). In the case of Lehman, the final collapse was arguably the result of increased collateral demands by JP Morgan, Lehman's 'clearing bank' and therefore the bank with which it had probably the most frequent interaction (Sorkin 2009, 281). None of the supposed benefits of relational exchange materialized. This fragile exchange between financial institutions then risks undermining the relational exchange between bank and NFC on which the VoFC and VoC literature has concentrated.

Figure 3.1 shows the total volume of wholesale funding by UK and US commercial banks and US investment banks in the period 2005–9. UK banks were far more exposed to the need to raise funds in the market, both relative

[12] For example, Citigroup brought US$ 25 billion of such assets back onto their balance sheet in 2008. Statement of John C. Dugan, Controller of the Currency, before the Financial Crisis Inquiry Commission 8 April 2010. <http://www.occ.treas.gov/newsissuances/congressional-testimony/2010/pub-test-2010–39-oral.pdf>.

[13] In addition, there is the friendship between the heads of Morgan Stanley and Lehman, that the head of Citibank had worked at Morgan Stanley and the head of Merrill Lynch at Goldman Sachs. See Sorkin 2009.

to their size, and in absolute terms, than their US counterparts. By 2007, UK commercial banks needed to borrow over US$4 trillion from the markets, nearly twice the volume required by the US commercial banks. The higher proportion of short-term (less than one year) funding by US banks (62.6 per cent of market funding at the peak against 51.7 per cent for the United Kingdom) does not make up for the difference between the two countries' commercial banks. Furthermore, in one area, UK banks were particularly exposed to market pressures: specifically the US$ inter-bank market (McGuire and von Peter 2009). Market borrowing of US dollars by non-US banks was a particular source of problems during the crisis, and UK banks cross-border borrowing from other banks approached the equivalent of half of UK GDP at end 2007, compared to less than 10 per cent for US banks.[14] Much of this was overnight borrowing and subject to 'home bias' during the crisis. The US investment banks, as Figure 3.1 shows, more than made up for the relatively low dependence of the US commercial banks on market financing. US investment banks' requirement for market funding reached US$3.7 trillion by 2007. Given the importance attached by some to the 2005 SEC decision to remove fixed leverage ratios for the investment banks (Blundell-Wignall, Atkinson and Lee 2008), it is important to note, however, that the US investment banks' market funding requirements were well below those of the UK commercial banks. Nevertheless, it is significant that this investment bank market borrowing was overwhelmingly short term (in 2007, 86 per cent). By 2007, commercial and investment banks in these two market-based economies were borrowing US$6.7 trillion (or 48 per cent of US GDP) which would have to be refinanced within a year.

Wholesale funding was increasingly short term, especially for parallel banks in the United States. US investment banks bought bad assets, but the key issue was their high dependence on market borrowing, and particularly short-term borrowing. Short term in this context means very short term, compounding liquidity risk: the investment banks had 'to roll over a large part of their funding on a daily basis' (Brunnermeier 2009, 80). US investment banks were heavily exposed to the overnight repo market: the proportion of assets financed by overnight repos doubled between 2000 and 2007 (Brunnermeier 2009, 5).

Repo agreements are like savings accounts for institutional investors, with excess cash deposited overnight or for a week or more with an investment bank like Bear Stearns, for interest. In addition to paying interest, Bear Stearns pledges collateral to back the cash deposit. Ideally the arrangement rolls over when the contract expires. If a repo borrower such as Bear Stearns faces

[14] Source for cross-border inter-bank borrowing: <http://www.bis.org/publ/qtrpdf/r_qa0806.pdf>, table 9C.

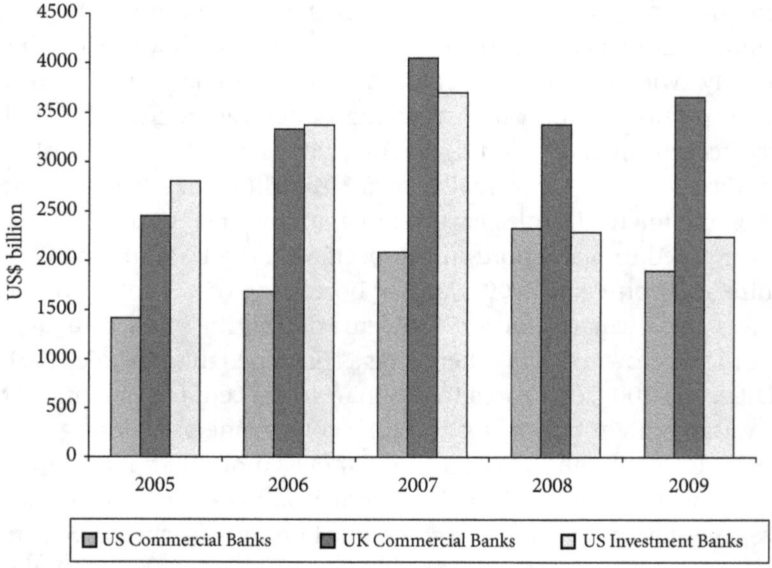

Figure 3.1. Wholesale funding in the United States and the United Kingdom

Source: IMF *Global Financial Stability Report* (October 2010) pp. 67–8. Largest US investment banks (Bear Stearns and Lehman excluded after 2007); 60 per cent of US investment bank assets are covered

difficulties, lenders are faced with the classic dynamics of a bank run in their incentive to seize and sell collateral first, in their lack of information regarding the bank's creditworthiness and in the way their self-interested actions, by pressuring financial market prices, have negative consequences for other actors (see Gorton and Metrick 2010). As prices fell and volatility increased during the crisis, repo financing terms (interest charged for depositing cash with the repo borrower) using *any* financial asset as collateral (including US government bonds) increased (Committee on the Global Financial System 2010, 2). Repo markets therefore faced many of the issues with information and liquidity discussed above.

Collateralized lending, a key element of the system of wholesale funding that became so short term in the lead-in to the crisis, is as old as lending itself and underpins modern banking. It hedges risk. Its underlying logic is simple: in the event of default, a lender seizes an asset. Lending that is protected by collateral is therefore lower-risk lending. In the case of retail mortgage lending, secured on housing, this is clearly the case, problems in subprime notwithstanding. The experience when collateral is financial assets has not, however, been as straightforward and can both exacerbate information problems and concentrate risk. Events in the repo market, the main source of short-term secured (collateralized) wholesale financing, illustrate this.

Because the collateral is a broad range of different credits, borrowers' funding risk is theoretically highly dispersed. If borrowers hold assets acceptable to repo lenders, funding should be available. Yet the 2007–8 crisis involved 'a run on repo' (Gorton and Metrick 2010). Globally, repo activity more than halved from June 2008 to December 2009 (Bank of England 2009, 40). Both the terms and availability of repo financing worsened dramatically, pressuring institutions dependent on this form of financing. This was particularly the US investment banks, which relied on this market for about half their funding. The nature of the assets—financial instruments—effectively homogenized the risk and concentrated it on those financial institutions reliant on repo borrowing. This risk is both that the borrower might fail, and, if that occurred, the collateral would not prove as valuable as expected, especially if others were simultaneously selling the same collateral. The borrowers, financial institutions, are not only themselves far more homogeneous than NFCs, but also are themselves exposed to the values in the same financial markets that value the assets they are pledging as collateral. Furthermore, activity in the repo market was heavily concentrated on a small group of financial institutions (Federal Reserve Bank of New York 2010, 14).US repo market problems were more severe than the United Kingdom or Euro area (Hördahl and King 2008, 38). Commercial banks, in the United States or United Kingdom, were not as heavy users of repos as investment banks (Gorton and Metrick 2010), but UK banks' foreign currency repos approached £300 billion equivalent by end 2007 (24 per cent of foreign currency liabilities),[15] and banks in both countries turned increasingly to this market as sources of unsecured borrowing dried up (Committee on the Global Financial System Markets Committee 2010, 5). Once repo financing became prohibitively expensive or unavailable for previously financeable assets, firms such as Bear Stearns and Lehman could not continue to operate, and central banks were forced to provide financing to others. Much of the popular discourse regarding the crisis has focused on losses on the purchase of 'dodgy assets. However, this is 'a comparatively small part of the story' (Borio 2008, 9). What is striking in both the United States and the United Kingdom is the impact of the market sources, and short-term nature, of liabilities, and therefore liquidity risk for a concentrated group of large financial institutions. Many (although by no means all) deposits can be withdrawn on demand, but short-term market financing is far more fickle. At end 2006, a median of 44 per cent of major UK banks' wholesale funding matured within three months (Bank of England 2007, 34), suggesting

[15] Source: Bank of England Monetary and Financial Statistics, April 2008, Table 1.21. Available at <http://webarchive.nationalarchives.gov.uk/20081231032945/http://www.bankofengland.co.uk/statistics/ms/2008/Apr/bankstats_full.pdf>, accessed 22 November 2010. January 2010 figures suggest around 10 per cent of this is probably within individual bank groups.

even the exposure to the market indicated in Figure 3.1 is understated. The inter-bank market was an important source of funds, especially for the UK banks. Despite the potentially relational nature of repeated transactions between familiar counterparties, the majority of unsecured inter-bank borrowing was for less than a week (IMF 2009, 75), and the market collapsed in the crisis. UK banks were also reliant on US money market funds. The ten largest money market mutual funds were directly lending UK banks US$80 billion during 2009 (Bank of England 2010, 37), only slightly less than their lending to US banks. Continental European banks (predominantly those in systems with higher MBB on the liability side of the balance sheet), similarly relied on the money market mutual funds, for about an eighth of their dollar borrowing requirements (Baba, McCauley and Ramaswamy 2009).

The financial crisis was primarily a liquidity crisis, but triggered by doubts regarding the value of market-based assets. Banks' increasing use of short-term borrowing left them particularly exposed to a collapse in funding liquidity. August 2007 saw sharp liquidity contraction in ABCP; in September 2008 the contraction was more widespread (Arteta et al. 2008). We can see the fragility and exposure to the market in the headline financial institution failures in the crisis. Differences between the two countries' financial institutions and bank activities had a number of implications for the two countries' experience. Both had high exposure to problems in the ABCP and securitization markets in August 2007. At this point, the heavily market-based Northern Rock, which relied on securitizations for over half its mortgage lending (Bank of England 2009, 17) but was not active in shadow banking, failed. While the proximate cause appeared to be a run on deposits, the initial problem was the high exposure to wholesale funding. At this early stage the ABCP and securitization markets—and write-downs on subprime lending—pressured commercial banks in both countries, but the main problems were amongst the parallel banking institutions in the United States, including the collapse of Bear Stearns. After the intensification of the crisis with the collapse of Lehman, it was largely the volume, rather than primarily the composition, of UK banks' wholesale funding that made them particularly exposed.

The liquidity explanation for the roots of the crisis is the focus of academic analysis looking at elements of the interaction between margin calls and market liquidity and the cyclicality of leverage (e.g. Adrian and Shin 2010; Brunnermeier 2009). The crisis demonstrates another aspect of the MBB system we outline here: liquidity was certainly high in the build-up to the crisis, motivating the originate-to-distribute model and financing the build-up of shadow and parallel banking and the increase in commercial banks' balance sheets. Our analysis of these three types of banking activities dominating MBB in the United States and the United Kingdom—selling loans, shadow banking, and wholesale financing—reveals some differentiation between the two countries. There was relatively more loan selling and shadow banking in the United States than the United Kingdom, but more wholesale financing in the United Kingdom than the United States. However, excess liquidity was a common denominator and proved equally transitory, with its disappearance the main reason that problems in a small asset class, subprime loans, became a global crisis. In the particular fragilities of MBB highlighted here—transactional exchange in informationally inefficient markets and risk concentrated on a relatively small number of increasingly-homogeneous financial institutions—we see similarities in the United States and the United Kingdom and other developed country financial systems. We also see the primary explanation of the crisis.

Conclusion

From the turn of the millennium both the United States and United Kingdom were increasingly market-based systems, but not as conceived in the existing VoC and VoFC literature. The US and UK systems had the disadvantages, without the advantages, of bank-based systems, compounded by the fragility of the financial institutions upon which risk was concentrated. The strengths of the traditional market-based system, particularly the diversification of risk across heterogeneous NFCs, did not materialize. The US and UK financial systems therefore represent, not the existing conception of either a market-based or a bank-based system, but rather a less stable hybrid of the two.

The systems we highlight contained financial institutions that intermediated between themselves in an increasingly concentrated sector, lacked the stabilizing connection to household savers through deposits, and were increasingly disconnected from corporate borrowers. At its best, the financial engineering-heavy market-based system facilitated bond issuance by NFCs because securitization and derivatives creation and trading allows for risk dispersion and risk insurance, both of which can minimize credit risk. When not at its best, however, the financial engineering laden system fuelled bank intermediated systems with markets characterized by opacity, liquidity vulnerability, and risk concentration. This poses an even greater danger to the non-financial sectors of the economy than the impatient capital associated with a traditional market-based system. From a VoC perspective, the classic capital market-based system should begin to appear desirable in comparison to MBB systems.

Our study also has implications for the principles of the ongoing regulatory response to the crisis. The two surviving large US investment banks emerged from crisis as commercial banks and insurance companies are unlikely to repeat AIG's involvement with derivatives markets, leaving a US system dominated by more tightly regulated universal banks, and therefore closer to the United Kingdom's system of banks engaged in high levels of MBB than the United States' pre-crisis institutional diversity. Meanwhile the Volcker Rules and the Vickers Report point in the direction of separating some (it remains unclear at time of writing exactly which) highly market-based activities from commercial banks.

This is to be welcomed, given the fragility we have discussed. Similarly, initiatives to move OTC derivatives onto centralized exchanges both decreases information problems and should also have some (possibly marginal) impact on the concentration of these businesses in a small number of market players. Ultimately, however, regulation needs to be targeted directly at risk concentration and high liquidity risk. Post-crisis initiatives have sought to target the latter to some extent, with higher capital requirements limiting leverage and higher requirements for the holding of genuinely liquid assets. The question of risk concentration, however, remains largely unresolved.

References

Acharya, V. V., and A. Bisin (2010) 'Centralized Versus Over-the-Counter Markets'. Available at: <http://papers.ssrn.com/sol3/papers.cfm?abstract_id=1573355>.

Acharya, V. V., D. M. Gale and T. Yorulmeyer (2010) 'Rollover Risk and Market Freezes'. Available at <http://papers.ssrn.com/sol3/papers.cfm?abstract_id=1325887>.

Acharya, V. V., P. Schnabl and G. Suarez (2010) *Securitization Without Risk Transfer* NBER Working Paper No.15730. Available at <http://www.nber.org/papers/w15730>, accessed 8 February 2011.

Adrian, T., and H. S. Shin (2010) 'The Changing Nature of Financial Intermediation and the Financial Crisis of 2007–09' Federal Reserve Bank of New York Staff Report no. 439.

Alexander, K., J. Eatwell, A. Persaud and R. Reoch (2007) *Financial Supervision and Crisis Management in the EU*, European Parliament Policy Department. Available at <http://www.europeansecuritisation.com/Market_Standard/Finance sector study.pdf>, accessed 10 November 2010.

Arteta, C., M. Carey, R. Correa, and J. Kotter (2008) 'Revenge of the Streamroller: ABCP as a Window on Risk Choices'. Unpublished paper, Board of Governors of the Federal Reserve System, Division of International Finance.

Baba, N., R. N. McCauley and S. Ramaswamy (2009), 'US Dollar Money Market Funds and non-US Banks', *BIS Quarterly Review* (March), 65–81.

Babus, A. (2010) 'Strategic Relationships in Over-the-Counter Markets' University of Cambridge. January. Available at: <http://ideas.repec.org/p/red/sed011/1405.html>.

Bank of England (2007) *Financial Stability Report.* October Available at <http://www.bankofengland.co.uk/publications/fsr/2007/fsrfull0710.pdf>, accessed 10 November 2010.

Bank of England (2008) *Financial Stability Report.* October. Available at <http://www.bankofengland.co.uk/publications/fsr/2008/fsrfull0810.pdf>, accessed 10 November 2010.

Bank of England (2009) *Financial Stability Report.* December. Available at <http://www.bankofengland.co.uk/publications/fsr/2009/fsrfull0912.pdf>, accessed 10 November 2010.

Bank of England (2010) *Financial Stability Report.* June. Available at <http://www.bankofengland.co.uk/publications/fsr/2010/fsrfull1006.pdf>, accessed 10 November 2010.

Basel Committee on Banking Supervision (2008) *Liquidity Risk: Management and Supervisory Challenges.* February. Available at <http://www.bis.org>, accessed 7 February 2011.

Basel Committee on Banking Supervision (2009) *Report on Special Purpose Entities.* Available at <http://www.bis.org>, accessed 7 February 2011.

Beck, T., and A. Demirgüç-Kunt (2009) 'Financial Institutions and Markets Across Countries and over Time: Data and Analysis'. World Bank Policy Research Working Paper No. 4943, May.

BIS (2008) *78th Annual Report.* Available at <http://www.bis.org>.

Blundell-Wignall, A., P. Atkinson and S. H. Lee (2008) 'The Current Financial Crisis: Causes and Policy Issues', *Financial Market Trends*, 95: 1–21.

Borio, C. (2008) 'The Financial Turmoil of 2007-?: a Preliminary Assessment and Some Policy Considerations'. BIS Working Papers No. 251. Available at <http://www.bis.org>.

Brunnermeier, M. K. (2009) 'Deciphering the Liquidity and Credit Crunch 2007–08' *Journal of Economic Perspectives* 23: 77–100.

Caballero, R. J., and A. Krishnamurthy (2009) 'Global Imbalances and Financial Fragility', *American Economic Review* 99: 584–588.

Calvo, G. A., and E. G. Mendoza (2000) 'Rational Contagion and the Globalization of Securities Markets', *Journal of International Economics* 51: 79–113.

Committee on the Global Financial System (2010) 'The Role of Margin Requirements and Haircuts in Procyclicality'. CGFS Paper No. 36. Available at <http://www.bis.org>.

Committee on the Global Financial System Markets Committee (2010) 'The Functioning and Resilience of Cross-Border Funding Markets' CGFS Paper No. 37. Available at <http://www.bis.org>.

Crouch, C. (2005) *Capitalist Diversity and Change, Recombinant Governance and Institutional Entrepreneurs.* Oxford: Oxford University Press.

Duffie, D., N. Garleanu, and L. Heje (2005) 'Over-the-Counter Markets', *Econometrica* 73: 1815–1847.

Federal Reserve Bank of New York (2010) *Task Force on Tri-Party Repo Infrastructure Report.* Available at <http://www.newyorkfed.org/prc/report_100517.pdf>.

Financial Crisis Inquiry Commission (2011) *The Financial Crisis Inquiry Report.* Available at <http://www.fcic.gov/report>.

Gorton, G. (2008) 'The Panic of 2007'. NBER and Yale University. Available at: <http://papers.ssrn.com/sol3/papers.cfm?abstract_id=1255362>.

Gorton, G., and A. Metrick (2010) 'Securitized Banking and the Run on Repo'. Available at <http://papers.ssrn.com/sol3/papers.cfm?abstract_id=1440752>.

Hall, P. A. and D. Soskice (2001), 'An Introduction to Varieties of Capitalism' In *Varieties of Capitalism* (eds P. A. Hall and D. Soskice). Oxford: Oxford University Press.

Hardie, I. and D. Howarth (2010) 'What Varieties of Financial Capitalism? The Financial Crisis and the Move to "Market-Based Banking" in the UK, Germany and France'. Paper presented at the ISA Conference, New Orleans.

Hördahl, P., and M. King (2008) 'Developments in Repo Markets During the Financial Turmoil', *Bank for International Settlements Quarterly Review*. December: 37–53.

Howell, C. (2007) 'The British Variety of Capitalism: Institutional Change, Industrial Relations and British Politics' *British Politics* 2: 239–264.

IMF (2009). *Global Financial Stability Report*. April. Available at <http://www.imf.org>.

IMF (2010a) *Global Financial Stability Report Market Update*. July. Available at imf.org.

IMF (2010b) *Global Financial Stability Report*. October. Available at imf.org.

Jiangli, W., and M. Pisker (2008) 'The Impacts of Securitization on US Bank Holding Companies'. Available at <http://ssrn.com/abstract=1102284>.

King, D., and S. Wood (1999) 'The Political Economy of Neoliberalism: Britain and the United States in the 1980s' In *Continuity and Change in Contemporary Capitalism* (eds H. Kitschelt, P. Lange, G. Marks, and J. Stephens). Cambridge: Cambridge University Press, 371–397.

Lagos, R., G. Rocheteau, and P. O. Weill (2009) 'Crashes and recoveries in illiquid markets'. NBER Working Paper, University of California at Los Angeles.

Landsman, W. R., K. V. Peasnell and C. Shakespeare (2006) 'Are Asset Securitizations Sales or Loans?' Available at <http://papers.ssrn.com/sol3/papers.cfm?abstract_id=924560>.

Levine, R. (1997) 'Financial Development and Economic Growth: Views and Agenda'. *Journal of Economic Literature* 35: 688–726.

McGuire, P., and G. von Peter (2009) 'The US Dollar Shortage in Global Banking'. *BIS Quarterly Review*. March, 47–60.

Miles, David (2009) 'The Future Financial Landscape'. Speech at Bloomberg, 16 December, 6. Available at <http://www.bankofengland.co.uk/publications/speeches/2009/speech418.pdf>.

Pozsar, Z., T. Adrian, A. Ashcraft and H. Boesky (2010) *Shadow Banking*. Federal Reserve Bank of New York Staff Reports no. 458. July.

SEC (Securities and Exchange Commission) (2008) *Report and Recommendations Pursuant to Section 133 of the Emergency Economic Stabilization Act of 2008: Study on Mark-To-Market Accounting*. Available at <http://www.sec.gov/news/studies/2008/marktomarket123008.pdf>.

Sorkin, A. R. (2009) *Too Big To Fail*. London: Allen Lane.

Trichet, J.-C. (2008) 'Remarks on the recent turbulences in global financial markets'. Keynote address at the Global Economic Policy Forum 2008, New York University, New York. 14 April. Available at <http://www.ecb.int/press/key/date/2008/html/sp080414_1.en.html>, accessed 18 November 2008.

Zysman, J. (1983) *Governments, Markets and Growth* Ithaca: Cornell University Press.

4

Belgium and the Netherlands: Impatient Capital

Michele Chang and Erik Jones[1]

Introduction

At the turn of the twenty-first century, the financial systems of Belgium and the Netherlands were among the most stable and dynamic in Europe. Finance comprised a significant portion of their respective economies and was an important engine of economic growth. Meanwhile the major banks of the two countries ventured increasingly into international markets and became deeply entrenched in the international financial system.

The banking systems of Belgium and the Netherlands were dominated by a small number of banks with relatively large capital buffers. In 2004, the International Monetary Fund (IMF) argued that the Dutch financial system was very stable: 'the stress testing indicated that the banking system could still absorb substantial shocks ... without significant problems, given banks' strong capital and asset quality, generally good profitability, diversification and good risk management processes' (IMF 2004, 5–6). Roughly two years later, the IMF declared that the Belgian 'financial system is generally sound, resilient to potential adverse shocks, and well supervised. Risks both on the international level and domestically appear well within the banks' capacity

[1] The authors would like to thank Jozefien Willemen and Jeroen Huiting for providing excellent research assistance. We would also like to thank Ivo Maes, Iain Hardie, David Howarth, and Amy Verdun for their useful comments, as well as the participants of the conferences 'The Financial Crisis, EMU and the Stability of Currencies and the Financial System' at the University of Victoria and the workshop 'Market Based Banking and the Financial Crisis' at the University of Edinburgh. The usual disclaimer applies.

to manage them and are well understood by the supervisor and overseer of the system' (IMF 2006a, 1), therefore 'near-term vulnerability appears low' (IMF 2006b, 6).

Despite such favourable evaluations, however, both the Belgian and Dutch financial systems were hit hard in the autumn of 2008 and required substantial government assistance. The explanation lies in the transformation of the banking systems of both countries during the preceding two decades. Belgium and the Netherlands were badly affected by the global financial crisis because major players in the markets including the IMF, ratings agencies, and national regulators failed to understand how their respective banking systems had become so vulnerable to changes in market conditions. Both financial systems were very international in orientation and dependent upon access to cross-border funding. The Belgian banks relied on inter-bank loans, Dutch banks relied on securitization, and both systems participated more heavily in shadow banking than any other country considered in this volume (Hardie and Howarth, this volume). Thus Belgium and the Netherlands suffered heavy losses when markets for asset-based securities and inter-bank lending dried up.

This vulnerability was not structurally predetermined and not all countries experienced similar developments. Even those countries with bank-based financial systems like those found in Belgium and the Netherlands at the end of the 1980s did not end up in the same place by the early 2000s. For example, George Pagoulatos and Lucia Quaglia in this volume outline how the bank-based systems of Greece and Italy weathered the early period of the global financial crisis relatively well—at least until the crisis spread to sovereign debt markets in 2009. In this sense, the classifications used in the varieties of financial capitalism literature fail to support straightforward predictions concerning the evolution of national banking systems over time (Hardie and Howarth 2009). Hence this volume argues that it is necessary to reassess the use of these labels and to focus more attention on comparisons over time within countries than on comparisons across countries at any given point in time.

This chapter has five sections. The first provides an overview of the origins of the Belgian and Dutch banking systems as they appeared in the late 1980s and places them within the context of the wider literature on the varieties of capitalism. The section then shows how the liberalization of banking regulations at home and capital markets abroad created new incentives for consolidation in both countries, moving them away from their ideal-typical origins. The second section examines how the new 'bancassurance' conglomerates that emerged from the 1990s were able to use excess savings to compete both within Europe and at the global level. The third explains what happened to these banks as a consequence of the global economic and financial crisis.

The fourth surveys the aftermath in Belgium and the Netherlands. The fifth section concludes with implications for our thinking about the characterization of national financial models.

Humble Origins

Belgium and the Netherlands are different in many respects—linguistically, socially, religiously, industrially, and geographically. But they are also similar. They share a common history as a buffer zone between Britain, France, and Germany. They have relied on similar consociational political formulas for managing deeply divided societies. And they have a legacy of financial integration that stretches back to the brief period in the early nineteenth century when the two countries were united within one Kingdom of the Netherlands and perhaps even further to the Golden Age when the Antwerp and Amsterdam markets were two of the most prosperous and active in Europe.

The challenge for analysis is to identify which of these characteristics, structures, or historical relationships are important as a means of predicting how the two countries will behave over time. The methodological assumption is that institutions matter and the question is if so, then how? The response offered by the varieties of capitalism literature is to focus on the nexus between industry and finance. The dichotomy is between the patient and forward-looking financial relationships that can develop between universal banks and their clients in industry, and the more dynamic and short-term relationships that operate between firms and their financial backers in merchant or commercial banks and on the stock exchange (Hall and Soskice 2001, 10). The longer-term or 'bank-based' relationships provide a more stable environment for the development of both physical and human capital; the shorter-term or 'market-based' relationship provides an environment more closely tied to the maximization of shareholder value.

The categories offered by the varieties of capitalism literature are useful for countries that fall close to one of the two ideal types—the classic example being Germany's approximation of the bank-based system and the United Kingdom's approximation of the market-based alternative. The categories are less useful, however, for countries that fall somewhere on the spectrum between the two extremes. Belgium and the Netherlands shared this attribute until the 1990s. If we focus on the late 1980s, for example, the two small northern European countries had relatively vibrant stock exchanges. According to data from the World Bank (2012a), the ratio of market capitalization to gross domestic product (GDP) in 1989 was 27 per cent for Germany, 46 per cent for Belgium, 66 per cent for the Netherlands, and 96 per cent for Great Britain. Moreover, the British case is probably an outlier; the United States is another 'market-based' economy and the US ratio of market capitalization to GDP was 64.5 per cent in 1989—just below the Netherlands and arguably more similar to Belgium than to the United Kingdom.

Another problem is that neither Belgium nor the Netherlands had banking systems similar to Germany. Instead they had a mix of savings banks, agricultural banks, postal banks, commercial banks, merchant banks, and insurance companies that more closely approximated the situation in Great Britain. World Bank (2012b) data suggest that the supply of domestic credit from the banking system to the private sector in the late 1980s was more comparable to Germany than to either Great Britain or the United States, but such data probably reveal the crowding out of domestic savings by government borrowing in the smaller countries more than the influence of relational banking as opposed to arm's-length banking transactions. Such crowding out was particularly acute in Belgium, where until the late 1980s the primary dealers in government obligations were paid a premium by the Belgian state to hold the public securities they purchased to term.

Neither Belgium nor the Netherlands is a liberal market economy in the standard varieties of capitalism categorization. The reason is the close coordination on display in so many other parts of the political economy in the two small countries and the willingness on the part of the Dutch government to accept a high degree of cartelization within Dutch industry. Both Belgium and the Netherlands contained the whole panoply of institutions for corporatist macroeconomic bargaining, and they continued to use those institutions to foster macroeconomic adjustment throughout the 1980s. Contemporary observers worried that centre-right coalitions elected in both countries at the start of the 1980s would abandon corporatist coordination strategies for a more extensive reliance on arms-length market mechanisms. By the end of the decade, it was clear that the Christian Democratic centre in both countries had opted for a corporatist revival instead (Jones 2008).

The illustrations from the late 1980s are important as a benchmark because the integration of European capital markets and the liberalization of the European financial space that started at the end of the 1980s and the start of the 1990s coincided with an important transformation in the financial structures of Belgium and the Netherlands. On the European side, some notable innovations include the liberalization of capital flows as part of the single market programme and the plans for a single currency by 1999. Meanwhile, the creation of an internal European banking market in 1993 contributed to the 'explosive' rise of bank claims abroad (CPB 2009, 17). The Second Banking Directive 1997 led to the provision of services in retail, wholesale and some investment bank activities in the EU under a system of mutual recognition, furthering cross-border transactions and the use of risk diversification to hedge against new financial instruments that were being developed.

On the domestic side, in 1990 the Dutch government ended the ban on banking and insurance mergers, paving the way for the creation of large bancassurance groups and contributing to cross-sector and cross-border growth (Prast and van Lelyveld 2005, 6). The Belgian government also undertook important reforms, including opening the public debt market to foreign firms and undoing the separation of deposit and portfolio investments in 1993 (Wyplosz 1999, 6). There, too, credit institutions became major stakeholders in insurance firms, or the reverse—hence, bancassurance—leading to further concentrated financial markets.

Other domestic policies had an indirect effect on the financial system by influencing the degree of leveraging of households and thus the funding structure of banks. For example, the Dutch government provided fiscal incentives for both homeowners and financial institutions to encourage housing purchases. The National Mortgage Guarantee System *Nationale Hypotheek Garantie* (NMGS) was introduced in the Netherlands in 1993, guaranteeing mortgages up to €350,000 and allowing buyers to purchase default insurance, thereby lowering the credit risk of banks supplying such loans. As a result, banks offered lower interest rates to homebuyers who took advantage of the NMGS, as their credit risk was also reduced as a result. Home owners also had the option of deferring loan redemption until maturity so as to take full advantage of the tax deductibility of mortgages (Vandeyvere and Zenthöfer 2012, 16). Financial institutions also enjoyed government guarantees for housing-related loans under the *Waarborgfonds Sociale Woningbouw* (Vandeyvere and Zenthöfer 2012, 16). Thus Dutch banks offered consumers a diverse range of credit instruments with long maturities (often 30 years) and flexible terms. The result was an increase in the leverage available to the housing market. Government guarantees also reduced the 'risk ... from the maturity and liquidity mismatches and different return profiles on either side of the balance sheets which can lead to a loss in net wealth and/or financial resources readily mobilized in times of financial stress' (Vandeyvere and Zenthöfer 2012, 11–12).

In the wake of these reforms, the financial institutions in both countries went through a period of consolidation to emerge as vertically integrated multinational conglomerates. Functionally, these entities were in many ways closer to the universal banks predominant in Germany than the fragmented, specialized, and domestically oriented banks and insurance companies that existed at the start. In terms of market concentration, however, Belgium and the Netherlands were in a different league altogether. According to data from the European Central Bank (ECB) (2012), the five largest Belgian credit institutions controlled 75 per cent of the assets in the domestic market in 1999; the share of domestic assets controlled by the five largest Dutch credit institutions that same year was 82 per cent. By contrast, the five largest

British institutions controlled only 28 per cent and the five largest German institutions just 19 per cent of total domestic banking assets.

Along the way, these emerging Belgian and Dutch financial conglomerates quickly outgrew any obvious relationship with the historical patterns for bank–firm relations or the established mechanisms for corporatist macroeconomic coordination and so became more focused on booking profits from their investments in both the European and global markets. In other words, isomorphism did not lead to iso-function and the more the financial institutions of Belgium and the Netherlands began to look like the large private banks in Germany, the less closely they approximated the behaviour anticipated by the bank-based ideal type in the literature on varieties of capitalism: patient capital was swapped for profit maximization. From an inter-temporal rather than cross-national perspective, this is hardly surprising. As Hardie and Howarth argue elsewhere in this volume, a similar evolution was at work in Germany itself.

The distinction made by the editors of this volume between traditional and market-based forms of banking is more appropriate than the categories used in the literature on varieties of capitalism for understanding the evolution of financial institutions in Belgium and the Netherlands during the 1990s. Even where banks continued to match lending and deposits within the domestic market, they became increasingly reliant on other forms of intermediation to generate profits abroad (Maes and Buyst 2009).

There was some variation within the general pattern. In Belgium, the appropriate contrast is between Fortis or Dexia, on the one hand, and KBC, on the other. Fortis was a Dutch insurance company that moved into the investment banking business in 1996 before acquiring both the largest Belgian bank Générale de Banque and the largest Belgian pension savings organization Caisse Générale d'Epargne et de Retraite by 1999. Dexia started out as the merger between local government lenders in France (Crédit Local de France) and Belgium (Crédit Communal de Belgique), which then went on to add Italian local government lender Crediop to the institutional portfolio. These were explicitly multinational organizations with a predominant position in the Belgian market. By contrast, KBC was much more locally oriented, having emerged from the fusion of the largest Flemish bank (Kredietbank) and two other Belgian institutions, the CERA bank and the ABB insurance company. As with Fortis and Dexia, the main consolidation of KBC was completed by 1999, but the scope was primarily domestic and the activities of the groups were more traditionally oriented.

In the Netherlands, the contrast is between ING or ABN-AMRO, and the Rabobank. ING evolved out of the merger between the Nationale-Nederlanden and the Dutch postal bank, but it grew rapidly beyond its domestic confines through a string of foreign acquisitions including the Belgian Banque

Bruxelles-Lambert. ABN-AMRO was created out of the 1991 merger of two historic Dutch merchant banks which then went on to make a string of acquisitions in the United States and elsewhere. ABN-AMRO did not break into the first tier of the Dutch financial system but it had a clear strategy for doing so through its activities on the world market—until it was ultimately acquired by a consortium of European banks including Fortis in 2007. Fortunately for the Dutch government, the Royal Bank of Scotland ended up with the riskier investment banking operations. By contrast, the Rabobank has been more conservative. Although it has extensive overseas operations, the Rabobank remained true to its origins as a network of cooperative agricultural lenders.

By the end of the 1990s, both the Belgian and Dutch banking systems were dominated by a small number of large financial institutions. Some of these banks were aggressive and others were more conservative. Some were more international than others as well. But they competed in the same domestic, European, and global markets and they sought to augment their profitability with a broader range of services that combined banking, insurance, and new forms of financial intermediation (Maes and Buyst 2009). Belgium and the Netherlands are different countries, but their financial industries at the start of the 2000s were closely integrated and in many ways similar (Figure 4.1).

Less traditional ←--→ More conservative

BE Fortis Dexia KBC

NL ABN -AMRO ING (NE) Rabobank (NE)

Figure 4.1. Continuum of major Belgian and Dutch banks, traditional to conservative

Increasing Risk

From a common starting point at the turn of the twenty-first century, the financial institutions of Belgium and the Netherlands had a common trajectory; the growth of the Belgian and Dutch banks in the early 2000s was dramatic. By 2007, bank assets as a percentage of GDP were higher in Belgium and the Netherlands 501 per cent and 302 per cent, respectively, than the Euro area 247 per cent, or even Germany 196 per cent, the traditional bank-based system (IMF 2008, 185). A 2008 IMF report indicated that the Belgian financial sector was behind only Ireland and Luxembourg as a percentage of GDP

(IMF 2008, 185). In the Netherlands, the assets and liabilities of financial institutions more than doubled as a percentage of GDP from 1990 to 2007 (CPB 2009, 16).

Both Belgian and Dutch banks took advantage of the globalization of international financial markets and the innovations that accompanied them. They had little choice but to do so: national and European-level deregulation had profoundly changed the investing environment, prompting larger and more international financial institutions, increased leveraging and the development of complicated risk management strategies. Growth had become an important strategic objective for most banks and was also considered to be a strategy against risk (Bellot, Coeme, et al. 2009, 108), undermining traditional notions of patient capital. Weak economic conditions and competition among lenders had put pressure on profits. A 2007 report by the Dutch central bank noted, 'The margins in traditional lending operations have been depressed for some time by strong competition and a flat yield curve' (DNB 2007, 16). Indeed, 'mortgage lending and expansion abroad became the key drivers of bank activity' (IMF 2006a, 16) as banks channelled the historically high savings rate in Belgium (IMF 2006b, 20) and consistent current account surpluses in Belgium and the Netherlands into international markets and the new financial instruments available under the shadow banking system (see below).

The banks thus moved away from traditional banking activities of deposits and loans into more market-based financial activities. This included greater reliance on wholesale funding and heavy involvement in the shadow banking system as well as a stronger international component to activities. The consolidated balance sheets of the major banks from 2002 until 2007 indicate the declining importance of loans to bank balance sheets and the rising importance of fees and commissions to banks' revenue for the 'origination and trading of sophisticated derivative products, trade finance, hedge fund platform, energy trading ... even credit insurance and guarantees for bonds, asset-back securities and structural finance' (Timmermans 2007, 490). The market for credit risk transfer rose by one third at the end of 2006 in the Netherlands, hitting \$34.5 trillion (DNB 2007, 8–9). By June 2006 outstanding credit default swaps in Belgium reached \$26 billion (Timmermans 2007, 47). All of the major banks in Belgium and the Netherlands participated in shadow banking markets that allowed them to issue more credit than would be allowed had they been forced to list them on balance sheets. They all also had exposure to what would prove to be risky assets. As noted in the introduction to this volume, the Netherlands and Belgium were the most exposed among the countries studied in this volume when measured as a percentage of GDP (Table 4.1).

Many, if not most, of these non-traditional assets were international. At least part of the explanation lies in the accommodating balance of payments

Table 4.1. Summary: rise of market-based assets

	Loan as % of assets	Monoline exposure	International
BE	Low	High	Very high
Fortis	36	verify	
Dexia	30	Via FSA	
KBC	41	Via MBIA	
NL	Low	High	Very high
ABN-Amro	39	Yes indirect	
ING	42	Yes	
Rabobank	65	Yes	

position. Both Belgium and the Netherlands ran substantial current account surpluses in the 1990s, making it not only possible but necessary for them to export capital as well. If anything, the export of capital lagged behind the growth of exports, putting upward pressure on the domestic currencies of both countries within the European Monetary System. Bank for International Settlement (BIS 2008, A8) figures indicate that when expressed as a percentage of GDP, banks in Ireland, Belgium, the United Kingdom and the Netherlands held a significantly higher percentage of assets abroad. The Dutch financial system had a lower degree of internationalization measured as a percentage of GDP than Belgium (180 per cent of GDP on the assets side) but considerably higher than other EU financial systems like France, Germany, and Spain (sources: BIS 2008, IMF 2008). Whereas in 1999 about half of the assets of Belgian banks were domestic, by 2006 the figure had fallen to 30 per cent (Timmermans 2007, 46).

This export of capital through the banking system carried significant and highly concentrated forms of geographic risk. The heaviest exposure of the Belgian financial sector was to France, the United States, the United Kingdom, and the Netherlands (IMF 2010b, 13). Belgium like the United Kingdom had particularly strong links to American markets, equalling 40 per cent of GDP. The American link was particularly significant in the context of the credit crunch, as these would have been the first assets affected by the subprime crisis in 2007. The large claims on non-residents via structured debt securities meant Belgian banks were significantly exposed to countries where housing bubbles were bursting (United States, United Kingdom, Spain, and Ireland) or being closely watched with concern (the Netherlands, France) or where foreign currency concerns exacerbated a shaky housing market due to risky mortgage loans (NBB 2008, 14). Belgian banks were also heavily exposed to eastern European countries: 25 per cent of GDP, compared to Dutch banks at the EU average of 8 per cent. The three major Belgian banks had invested heavily in the central and eastern European countries and Turkey: Fortis had subsidiaries in Poland and Turkey, KBC maintained links in the Czech Republic,

Slovakia, Hungary, Poland, and Russia, while Dexia had a Turkish subsidiary (NBB 2010, 52). Although problems in some of these markets caused concern, as with Greece and Italy (Pagoulatos and Quaglia, this volume), overall these were less problematic, more 'traditional' banking activities.

A related element is monolines that were needed to guarantee the non-traditional assets that were being issued by banks. Monoline insurers guarantee the status of underlying paper at an AAA level. Should a monoline come into trouble, the bonds that it had guaranteed would also run into problems. In Belgium, Dexia and KBC suffered heavily from monoline exposure. Dexia's monoline exposure grew from €935 million in 2005 to over €6 billion in 2008. KBC, an originator of structured collateralized debt obligations (CDOs), had purchased insurance from American monoline insurer MBIA (KBC 2008, 61). On the Dutch side, ABN-AMRO had an indirect exposure to monoline insurers through financial guarantees wraps that were purchased or embedded within different securities in the trading and available-for-sale portfolios (ABN-AMRO 2007, 26). ING's direct exposure was quite small, but it had insured €3.5 billion (0.3 per cent of assets) with several monoline insurers via wrapped bonds or through credit derivatives.

Table 4.2 summarizes the market-based elements on the asset side of Belgian and Dutch banks, emphasizing the declining importance of loans, monoline exposure and the internationalization of operations.

Table 4.2. 2007 inter-bank borrowing as percentage of liabilities

Bank	Percentage
BE	
Dexia	44
KBC	22
Fortis	22
NL	
ABN-AMRO	24
ING	9
Rabobank	24

Source: Annual reports of banks.

The funding side of bank expansion in Belgium and the Netherlands was equally problematic. Instead of relying solely on funds drawn from deposits, banks turned to the open market for financing (DNB 2007, 21). In 1995 the Dutch banking sector was dominated by more traditional funding sources (63 per cent); by 2006 this figure had shrunk to 42 per cent. The funding gap, which is the loan to deposit ratio, indicates the extent to which deposits are insufficient to fund lending. The funding gap in the Netherlands was among the highest of the countries studied in this volume, second only to the United Kingdom. Relative to banks elsewhere in the EU, the funding gap of Dutch banks €215.5 billion, or 40.53 per cent of GDP was higher than most except for the United Kingdom and Italy even though the Netherlands has a national savings surplus. Mortgage loans dominate the Dutch banking system, and as such savings deposits can only partly cover the extensive mortgage loan portfolios; the rest is made up by market funding (Vandeyvere and Zenthöfer 2012: 19). In contrast, the funding gap in Belgium was negative, indicating that Belgian bank lending was wholly funded by deposits.

The shadow banking system encouraged excessive lending in the run up to the crisis and, hence, there was strong growth in bank lending in the EU where securitization was widespread. In the Netherlands by early 2007 securitization reached almost €109 billion (DNB 2007, 16). In Europe, the United Kingdom (43 per cent), Spain (15 per cent), the Netherlands (11 per cent) and Italy (10 per cent) had the highest concentration of underlying collateral in CDOs at the end of 2007 (NBB 2008, 45). As seen in the contribution by Hardie and Howarth in this volume, the amount of collateral in securitization as a percentage of GDP revealed the Netherlands as an outlier at 30.9 per cent, higher than the United Kingdom's 28.8 per cent. The Dutch central bank estimates that the expansion of bank lending in the years prior to the outbreak of the crisis was a full percentage point higher than was reported in balance sheets in the Euro area, with Dutch bank lending likely to be closer to two percentage points higher (DNB 2007b, 17). Market-based liabilities—of a relatively stable nature—fuelled Dutch bank lending to a greater extent than in many parts of the EU, though clearly far less than in the United States (see Hardie and Howarth, this volume).

Although the various forms of securitization provide institutions with a more diverse set of funding sources, it can be difficult to regulate and makes banks more vulnerable to markets, both for income as well as balance-sheet and liquidity management. Such activities could also encourage riskier behaviour by banks under the presumption that the underlying risk can then be sold on in the markets, as with the American subprime mortgage loans (DNB 2007b, 18). Liquidity problems could emerge if long-term assets are financed through short-term instruments, as much of the securitization bought either directly by banks or via ABCP was before the outbreak of the crisis (Boot and Thakor 2009, 14).

Another source of wholesale funding is inter-bank borrowing. ECB data show that Belgium had the highest figure among the countries covered in this volume. Its banks had a history of making heavy use of inter-bank loans and deposits—in 2006 borrowing and lending from and to inter-bank markets constituting 29.2 and 19.2 per cent of the total balance sheet of Belgian banks, whereas the EU average stood at 16.9 and 13.1 per cent, making Belgium a net recipient of inter-bank loans. The importance of the inter-bank market in Belgium can be explained by the significantly lower levels of debt securities, as Belgium lacked a covered bond market; the low level of long-term interest rates also made uncovered bank bonds *bons de caisse* unattractive to investors (NBB 2008, 39). Bank-level data for inter-bank borrowing (Table 4.3) show that the major Dutch banks were less dependent on inter-bank lending than their Belgian counterparts. Nevertheless their activity was significant: a 2006 study noted that the Dutch inter-bank market in December 2002 held €193 billion in inter-bank assets and €364 billion in inter-bank liabilities, respectively 10 per cent and 20 per cent of total balance sheet value of the banks (van Lelyveld and Liedorp 2006, 106). Thus both Belgium and the Netherlands were particularly vulnerable to inter-bank lending being cut off.

Finally, the liabilities side of Belgian and Dutch banking also had a strong international component. In December 2007, the international liabilities of Belgium's financial system were roughly 210 per cent of its GDP. The Dutch financial system's international liabilities were lower though still high overall at approximately 150 per cent of GDP (BIS 2008; IMF World Economic Outlook database (www.imf.org/external/data.htm)). This recourse to international markets was never without risk. The problem is that while deposit runs are relatively uncommon, seizures in international wholesale markets may not be. Hence, while international wholesale markets provide access to new sources of funding, they also make banks vulnerable 'if financial submarkets evaporate' (DNB 2007, 21). Table 4.3 summarizes the situation in Belgium and the Netherlands regarding market-based liabilities

Table 4.3. Summary: rise of market-based liabilities

	Securitization	Inter-bank borrowing	International
BE	Low	Very high borrower	High
NL	Very high	High	High

Before the onset of the financial crisis, the risks involved in the rapid expansion of Belgian and Dutch financial institutions were poorly understood by the IMF, ratings agencies and regulators. Indeed the 2007 ratings from Moody's, Standard & Poor's (S&P), and Fitch of the major Belgian and Dutch banks gave the appearance of solid fundamentals. Regulatory authorities were similarly optimistic. At the start of the crisis, the Belgian central bank deemed 'Belgian banks ... in a good position to withstand financial shocks' (NBB 2007, 7). Similarly Dutch banks had not reported strong exposure to subprime-related paper, so the Dutch central bank was confident that 'in the Netherlands, there is no cause for concern that a US-style scenario may unfold,' (DNB 2007, 67) and although 'Dutch banks were impacted by the market turbulence their solvency buffers proved amply adequate' (DNB 2007, 65). However the problems faced by these banks during the autumn of 2008 did not correspond to these rosy outlooks due to their increasing dependence on market-based transactions.

The Reckoning

Inter-bank markets started tightening in the summer of 2007. As uncertainty regarding the nature and value of underlying assets of the credit risk transfer market increased, the financing of such instruments dried up. This led to speculation over the prospect of draw-downs of credit lines at the banks that sponsored them. Once the possibility of passing on credit risk for activities such as leveraged buyouts disappeared, banks' balance sheets came under further pressure. Structured credit products also took a hit, particularly the market for asset-backed commercial paper ABCP. For example, in mid-2007 the effect of the financial crisis on KBC's structured products totalled €6.5 billion, of which €5 billion had to be added back to the balance sheets (KBC 2008, 61).

In the Netherlands, securitized operations of banks and related special purpose vehicles rose precipitously towards the end of 2007. Banks took part in the in-house securitization of loans as opposed to making them for sale and offered them as collateral when seeking the central bank's credit facilities, which helped stabilize the situation and eased liquidity constraints in the short-term (DNB 2008a, 16). The Rabobank, for example, reported that it still had access to liquidity through securitization during this period (Rabobank Group 2008). By the middle of 2008, however, the figures for write-downs related to the credit crunch by Dutch banks had reached €15 billion (DNB 2008a, 16). ABN-AMRO, for example, reported a decrease in net trading income, with credit market write-downs against asset-backed securities equalling €1.6 billion and credit valuation adjustments against exposures to credit insurance counterparties amounting to €4.8 billion. These figures also incorporate losses from counterparty failures amounting to €1 billion, including losses from the Lehman Brothers bankruptcy and the Bernard L. Madoff fraud. Trading income suffered €500 million in losses because of changes in the valuation methodology of complex products that had to be adjusted to the same techniques as the RBS Group, one of ABN-AMRO's parent companies from 2007 (ABN-AMRO 2009, 34).

Developments in the monoline insurance market had a large impact on some banks. Dexia's high exposure to asset-backed securities can be traced to Financial Security Assurance (FSA), the American subsidiary of Dexia Crédit Local de France that was one the five leading monoline bond guarantors in the world. On 21 July 2007, Moody's considered downgrading FSA, leading Dexia to announce on 6 August that it would provide €300 million to recapitalize FSA (Dexia 2008). By 2009 the sharp decline in creditworthiness of

MBIA contributed to losses of over €4 billion for KBC in 2008 and €1.8 billion in 2009, eventually required a guarantee agreement with the Belgian government in May 2009 (KBC 2009, 40).

In 2008, ABN-AMRO reported a negative valuation adjustment on monoline insurers amounting to €606 million (ABN-AMRO 2008, 31), its net exposure to monoline insurers in 2008 being over €2 billion (ABN-AMRO 2008, 45). The downgrading of a monoline insurance led to a loss of €66 million on ING's profits by leaving €630 million of underlying assets unprotected (ING 2007). The Rabobank also suffered as a result of counterparty risk relating to monoline insurers, as value adjustments of €245 million were made in the first half of 2008 and an additional €148 million were recognized through profit and loss (Rabobank 2008, 57).

Problems continued to mount through the spring and summer of 2008 with the near collapse of Bear Stearns and the government bailout of US mortgage giants Fannie Mae and Freddie Mac. However, it was only the collapse of Lehman Brothers in the fall of 2008 that brought matters to a head. Inter-bank markets froze as only short-term maturity financing was accepted. Moreover non-prime collateral could no longer be used in secured financing transactions. The major banks in Belgium were hit simultaneously as their ability to obtain funding via unsecured financing from other financial institutions fell sharply in the last months of 2008 (NBB 2009, 14). The price of credit default swaps (CDSs) for Fortis and Dexia exceeded an annual premium of 500 basis points, significantly above the premium of a benchmark of European financial institutions. KBC's CDS premium also ran over this benchmark, though it was less extreme (NBB 2009, 29).

The first Belgian bank to require government assistance at this stage was Fortis, which could no longer refinance on the inter-bank and wholesale markets as professional counterparties withdrew their deposits (Fortis 2008,17). It also had the largest funding gap of the major Belgian banks. The amount of write-downs and the strong impact of the credit crunch were the result of a reliance on shadow banking as well as the unfortunate timing of the ABN-AMRO takeover. The €24 billion it had paid for its share of ABN-AMRO wiped out Fortis's capital, making it even more vulnerable to the sudden disappearance of market sources of liquidity. In early October, the Dutch government took over Fortis Nederland, followed by the Belgian government's purchase of the Belgian side a few days later on 9 October 2008. Dexia received a combined guarantee from the governments of Belgium, France, and Luxembourg for its liabilities (NBB 2009, 33–4). On 16 October 2008 the Belgian government constructed a temporary guarantee scheme to provide relief for credit institutions and financial holding companies seeking to obtain refinancing on inter-bank and other wholesale markets.

ING suffered from valuation losses and an overextended business model. ING's largest holdings were in Europe (Belgium, Germany, Poland), Canada, the

United States, and Asia. On 19 October 2008 it issued €10 billion of core Tier 1 securities to the Dutch state, thus improving its capital position. Continued market turmoil necessitated a second agreement with the Dutch government at the end of January 2009 on an Illiquid Assets Back-up Facility that covered 80 per cent of their €30 billion portfolio of residential mortgage-backed securities, giving the Dutch state 80 per cent of any profits or losses. Although it retained its privately owned and managed status, unlike ABN-AMRO or Fortis, ING's bailout came with conditions attached (CBFA 2008, 46; IMF 2010a, 35; ING 2009, 11).

On 14 November 2008 Dexia announced that monoline insurer Assured Guaranty would purchase its FSA subsidiary's holdings, except for the financial products executed by FSA Asset Management (FSAAM). So as to prevent the risks associated with FSAAM, Dexia constructed a put option that permitted the whole or partial sale of the portfolio to Dexia. The governments of Belgium and France then agreed to guarantee Dexia's commitment under the put option above and beyond the first \$3.1 billion in losses that exceeded its \$1.4 billion in reserves (NBB 2009, 33–4).

In 2008 the Dutch banking system recorded a loss of €27 billion, much of it due to write-downs on market-based assets that were valued at market value and then directly debited to the profit and loss account during the fourth quarter. Banks also needed to allow for the possibility of future write-downs as the crisis was expected to deepen (DNB 2009a, 20). The total was closer to €39 billion if one considers both the balance sheet and the profit and loss account (DNB 2008b, 81). The state injected €10.75 billion in capital in 2008 (DNB 2008b, 81). The IMF concluded that the Dutch problems resulted from 'foreign troubled assets and sizeable declines in asset prices' despite the stability of its mortgage and housing markets (IMF 2010a, 4). The difficulties in the Netherlands, in other words, were the result of high levels of market-based assets in relatively fragile markets.

The massive government intervention and prompt restructuring of Belgian banks towards domestic investment helped Belgium's recovery process greatly. By the third quarter of 2009 Belgian liquidity conditions had improved and banks were returning to pre-crisis levels of gross income. Banks were able to issue both covered and unsecured bonds in wholesale markets. However the impact of high loan losses due to deteriorating asset quality meant that KBC's net income in 2009 was inferior to that of 2008. Dexia did better. Having divested from its US monoline, FSA, it was able to post a better net income than in 2008 (IMF 2010b, 42). By 2009 credit conditions were slightly better than those found in other European countries (IMF 2010b, 49). Nevertheless real GDP fell in Belgium by 3 per cent in 2009 and unemployment continued to rise.

The initial effect of the crisis on the Netherlands was 'somewhat uneven' (IMF 2010a, 65). Its levels of financial stress remained on par or above that of the United States and above that of Germany, the United Kingdom, or Japan

(IMF 2010a, 8). Although the banking system suffered from reduced profitability, asset quality, and capital, loans to the private sector have been less affected and credit continued to be available. The fact that the financial sector made up 7.5 per cent of GDP in 2009 (higher than in most EU countries) meant that overall growth would be adversely affected. The financial cycle was estimated to have reduced GDP growth by up to 3 percentage points through the end of 2009 (IMF 2010a, 13–15), with GDP falling by 4.5 per cent in total in 2009. Exports dropped by 12 per cent during the year, as over 75 per cent of Dutch exports went to ailing European markets (IMF 2010a, 15).

The situation in Belgium was further complicated by the sovereign debt crisis. After Portugal, Ireland, Italy, Greece, and Spain—known collectively as the PIIGS—Belgium was one of the most closely watched due to uncertainty surrounding the future of its public finances. It had already entered the financial crisis with a relatively high level of public debt that was exacerbated by declining tax receipts and the massive outlay of public funds to save the financial system. Moreover, the political situation was tenuous, as the 2010 elections failed to yield a government, making the long-term solution to the Belgian debt problem uncertain. In February 2011, Belgium broke the record for the longest period without a government. By December, the spread between Belgian and German long-term sovereign debt yields soared to more than 3 percentage points. The government coalition negotiators met under intense pressure to avoid a full-blown sovereign debt crisis and agreed to form a government under the francophone socialist Elio Di Rupo. The pressure in the markets abated soon thereafter, and by mid-2012 Belgium emerged as a relative safe-haven for investors looking to purchase sovereign debt.

The Netherlands experienced none of this high drama. Although the public finances of the Netherlands also worsened as a result of the crisis—and the Dutch political environment experienced moments of volatility as well—the Netherlands' pre-crisis debt levels left it in a more sustainable condition and it is not considered to be a country vulnerable to sovereign default. If anything, the availability of Dutch sovereign debt markets as a safe haven has proven to be a boon for government finances, because the inflow of capital from distressed countries on the Euro area periphery has compressed debt servicing requirements.

The Aftermath

Whatever thin silver linings may be found, the impact of the crisis will continue to be felt in both Belgium and the Netherlands and on many levels—in terms of actual losses suffered, the size of government support that had to be pledged, and the extent of the credit crunch in the real economy as the financial systems of both countries deleveraged in order to improve their balance sheets.

The direct financial losses were enormous. In Belgium the damage in 2007 due to subprime-related ABS CDOs accounted for the €2.5 billion rise in impairment losses on financial assets that had been factored into 2006's profit and loss account (NBB 2008, 11). By 2008 this figure rose significantly, reversing the gains from 2008. Write-downs on CDOs had overall been 'moderate', but certain cases registered large losses (see Table 4.4). Despite the government support, 'Belgian banks lost more market capitalization than peer European banks' (IMF 2010b, 39). In the Netherlands, the four major Dutch banks had write-downs of €10 billion in 2007 as a result of losses related to the credit crunch, thus wiping out over half of their net annual profits (DNB 2008a, 16). Dutch income from banking activities dropped precipitously (see Table 4.5), and both Belgian and Dutch banks suffered significant losses and write-downs (see Table 4.6).

Table 4.4. Impact of valuation changes on financial assets held by Belgian credit institutions (billions of euros)

Impact via profit and loss account	2006	2007	2008
Realized or unrealized financial gains or losses on financial instruments	3.9	3.8	–3.8
Impairments	0.4	2.9	12.6

Source: NBB 2009, 13.

Table 4.5. Total Dutch income in banking in billions of euros 2004–8

	2004	2005	2006	2007	2008
Total income	50.1	54.9	61.7	57.4	20
Income from financial transactions	3.7	5.2	6	4.6	–27.9

Source: DNB Annual Report 2008, 81.

Table 4.6. Net losses and write-downs, 2008

Bank	Net losses 2008 in billions of euros	As percentage of assets	Write-downs in billions of USD August 2008
Fortis	20.6	1.25	7.4
Dexia	3.9	1.47	1.2
KBC	2.5	0.77	1.3*
ABN-Amro	3.6	0.5	
Royal Bank of Scotland RBS-acquired businesses	12.5	1.87	2.3
Dutch-state acquired business	0.47	0.7	
ING	0.729	0.05	5.8
Rabobank	1.1	0.23	1.7

*Year end, from 2008 annual report.

Sources: annual reports, <http://in.reuters.com/article/2009/04/08/financial-writedowns-idINN085275792009040> <http://www.bloomberg.com/apps/news?pid=newsarchive&sid=a8sW0n1Cs1tY>.

As expected given the variation across banks within countries, they were hit unevenly. Fortis by far suffered the most in absolute terms in 2008, with its total losses of €20.6 billion equal to 1.25 per cent of its assets (Fortis 2008, 17). Although Fortis had substantial investments in structured investment vehicles, much of its troubles were due to concerns over its acquisition of ABN-AMRO that depleted its capital base and therefore reduced its room for manoeuvre in the newly tight credit market. Roughly €12.5 billion of losses can be attributed to divesting from the Dutch side of the company FBNH (Fortis 2008, 17), including ABN-AMRO activities obtained in 2007 as well as the transactions undertaken in September and October 2008 that amounted to €9.7 billion as a result of the global financial crisis (Fortis 2008, 17). Fortis attributed almost half (€4.8 billion) to losses and depreciations due to the downgrading of its portfolio of structured credit instruments (Fortis 2008, 18). Another €1.3 billion was a result of its connections to failing banks likes those in Iceland as well as American firms like Lehman Brothers and Washington Mutual (Fortis 2008, 21). Almost another billion euros were lost on covered interest rate options and credit guarantees. The credit market collapse in non-domestic markets like the United Kingdom, Spain, and Poland also negatively impacted activities in commercial banking and real estate (Fortis 2008, 15).

On 27 and 28 September 2008 the Dutch, Belgian, and Luxembourg governments began the process of rescuing Fortis. On 3 October the Dutch state assumed Fortis' Dutch operations, including ABN-AMRO, for €16.9 billion (Fortis Nederland 2009, 17). On 6 October, the day the Dutch deal closed, the Belgian government purchased €4.7 billion in shares, giving it 99.93 per cent ownership and negotiated the sale of 75 per cent of its Belgian operations to French bank BNP Paribas in exchange for shares in BNP Paribas (Fortis 2008). Fortis received emergency liquidity assistance until 9 October, peaking at €51.3 billion on 3 October (NBB 2009, 30). In addition, in November 2008 the Belgian federal government guaranteed up to €150 million to Fortis for inter-bank transactions. The controversy surrounding the Fortis rescue contributed to the fall of the government of Yves Leterme in December 2008 over charges of political meddling with the judicial review of the bailout. In April 2009 the proposal passed, and the Belgian government also guaranteed the losses due to toxic assets up to €1.5 billion, provided that Fortis covered the first €3.5 billion of losses. Finally, the Belgian government committed to recapitalizing Fortis for up to 3 years and €2 billion.

Dexia lost €3.9 billion in 2008, 1.47 per cent of its total assets. Dexia's dependence on wholesale funding for financing its balance sheet which had significant maturity mismatches and its exposure to American asset-backed securities led to a loss of confidence that required emergency intervention (NBB 2009, 11). On 9 October, Dexia received a combined guarantee from the governments of Belgium, France, and Luxembourg amounting to a maximum of €150 billion, and covered its liabilities. Even this proved insufficient to the scale of the bank's foreign losses, however, and so in 2011 the Belgian and French governments had to negotiate a further guarantee package.

KBC fared much better in 2008 with a loss of €2.5 billion, less than 1 per cent of its total assets, due to the markdown of €4.5 billion in their CDO portfolio (KBC 2008). While KBC was not immediately affected by the credit crunch after Lehman Brothers' collapse, its CDS premium rose sharply in October, and subsequently it was downgraded by Moody's. The third quarter losses were posted at the same time various European governments embarked on plans to assist financial institutions to increase their capital buffers to protect against future losses. This combined with the tighter standards used to assess capital adequacy led the Belgian government to issue €3.5 billion of hybrid core capital securities. In January 2009 KBC received further assistance, this time from the Flemish government, for €2 billion in addition to a supplementary standby facility of €1.5 billion after Moody's revised its ratings for corporate synthetic CDOs at the end of 2008. In May 2009 KBC declared heavy losses on a portfolio of CDOs worth €14 billion that were guaranteed by monoline insurance company MBIA, contributing to a loss of €3.6 billion for the first quarter of the year. On 13 May 2009 the Belgian government gave KBC a guarantee on a structured credit instrument worth €22.5 billion and covering 90 per cent of the default risk above a first set loss (NBB 2009, 34).

In the Netherlands, the losses suffered by ABN-AMRO were assumed by Royal Bank of Scotland RBS at €12.5 billion, which was the equivalent of 1.87 per cent of its total assets. The bank itself posted a profit in 2008 of €3.6 billion. The Rabobank also remained profitable and managed to maintain its AAA rating. ING, on the other hand, suffered a loss of €729 million, its first, forcing it to turn to the Dutch government for guarantees and a capital infusion. In October 2008 the Dutch government granted ING €10 billion in the form of capital support. This was followed up in early 2009 with an Illiquid Assets Back-up Facility that goes towards 80 per cent of its portfolio of Alt-A close to subprime residential mortgage-backed securities (RMBS, see ING 2008, 14). When liquidity had dried up, market prices for these securities dropped, and the government intervention was seen as a measure for reducing uncertainty on any potential future losses of 80 per cent of the portfolio (ING 2008, 12).

The major weaknesses of the banks resulted from their heavy involvement in market-based banking activities. Banks with more traditional operations like the Rabobank in the Netherlands and heavier reliance on domestic markets like KBC in Belgium tended to do better. Overall, the crisis forced government reactions from Belgium and the Netherlands that were significantly higher when measured against GDP than for countries like Italy, Spain, and France, though lower than for the UK (see Figures 2.5 and 2.6 in Hardie and Howarth, Chapter 2, this volume). As in most of the other countries, save for Italy, the highest amount of funds went towards the provision of guarantees on bank borrowing in both Belgium and the Netherlands. The Belgian government provided equally important amounts of upfront financing and capital injection, while the Dutch government provided over the double the percentage of up front financing than capital injection (IMF 2010a, 33).

The combined impact of both the losses and the government bailouts was to focus the attention of the banks on the strength of their balance sheets. Much of the pressure to improve balance sheets came from inter-bank markets and corporate accounts. The systemically important banks in Belgium were hit directly by the drop in inter-bank liquidity, and professional investors withdrew their deposits in droves, further exacerbating the liquidity shortage (CBFA 2008, 36). Liquidity conditions in Belgium were tightest in October 2008 when inter-bank rates hit their heights (IMF 2010b, 24). This loss of support from the financial community left banks 'short of capital in view of the need to constitute provisions or to write off loans as counterparties defaulted and because the ratings of counterparties and/or securities held in portfolio had to be severely downgraded' (Dexia 2008, 12). Banks that had depended on inter-bank and bond financing were forced to raise capital, obtain state guarantees or undergo nationalization (Dexia 2008, 12). Total inter-bank deposits in Belgium fell from €409 billion at the end of 2007 to €319 billion at the end of 2008, though much of this was related to the deconsolidation of Fortis Bank Nederland (NBB 2009, 53–4). Rather than looking to book new assets, banks began to cut their leverage and pay down their debts. By the final quarter of 2008, deleveraging began with the separation of Fortis Bank Nederland, which resulted in a significant decline in the total assets of the Belgian banking system by €230 billion (NBB 2010, 35).

The major players in the markets also reacted to their own failure to estimate risks appropriately by demanding higher capital-adequacy ratios than before the crisis in order to continue lending. Hence even though the 'solvency position ... had been considered exceptionally strong until just before the crisis', they were no longer regarded as sufficient KBC 2008. Banks had to turn to governments for assistance in meeting these more stringent capital requirements as a result. They passed on this higher degree of risk aversion in their own lending practices as well. At the end of 2008, three-quarters of all Dutch banks indicated stricter residential mortgage and corporate lending standards (IMF 2010a, 13), the Dutch banking system was 'under historically high levels of distress' due to changes in stock prices and inter-bank lending rates at the height of the crisis (IMF 2010a, 65–6). In 2010 the IMF concluded that during the credit crunch from 2007–9, at its peak during the second quarter of 2008, credit demand exceeded supply by 6 per cent (IMF 2010a, 68–9).

Perhaps the largest change that occurred as the result of the financial crisis is that the need for the infusion of foreign capital to bail out the banking system left Belgium as a host country rather than a home country (High Level Committee 2009). In addition, the business models of the major banks have changed: Fortis was sold to BNP Paribas and has seen a shift back to separate banking and insurance bodies, as opposed to its pre-crisis integrated model. KBC and Dexia underwent major internal reforms requiring EU authorization, including a reduction of risk and the strengthening of its core and domestic retail franchises (IMF 2010b, 47).

The financial crisis also resulted in important changes in the Dutch financial system. First, it accelerated the national re-orientation of the banking system. The ABN-AMRO takeover led to the divestment of units in Italy, Brazil, and the United States. The nationalization of the Dutch branch of Fortis which had previously been a subsidiary of the Belgian group was another factor. Moreover, it drastically increased the proportion of state-owned banks, equalling over a third of the banking system (DNB 2009a, 20–1). The Dutch state completely owned the Fortis part of ABN-AMRO, Fortis Bank Nederland, Fortis Verzekeringen Nederland, and Fortis insurance (DNB 2008b, 17). The stock exchange ceased to include the biggest share of the Dutch banking system (DNB 2009a, 21). By the end of 2009 DNB had surmised, 'in the new situation the largest Dutch banks will be smaller in size than they were before the crisis, the number of large foreign players will increase, and the bancassurance model will definitely lose in importance' (DNB 2009a, 21).

The size and composition of the balance sheets of Dutch banks also changed as a result of the financial crisis. Formerly off-balance items once again became intermediated, and banks needed to deleverage in an effort to limit their exposure to risk though they remained highly leveraged, above the Euro area average. Moreover, banks increased their capital in order to compensate for stalled money markets as wholesale funding became harder to come by, making them increasingly dependent on central bank funding (DNB 2009a, 21). Like their Belgian counterparts, the crisis forced a change in business strategy. As Dutch banks slowly returned to profitability in 2009, banks reduced their risk profile and improved their level of capital, resulting in stronger solvency ratios. Banking became more directed towards national markets, and reoriented towards services to consumers and small and medium-sized enterprises rather than wholesale banking (DNB 2009b, 91–2). Market-based banking has clearly been reduced in the Netherlands, particularly on the asset side of the balance sheet.

Prior to the global financial crisis, Belgium and the Netherlands appeared to be in a strong and stable position. Finance was a major source of economic growth, and both of these small open economies fully participated in the expansion of credit that fuelled impressive returns for its major banks.

Banks in both countries relied less and less on traditional sources of funding, with the Netherlands becoming a major player in securitization to finance lending and Belgium in inter-bank borrowing to finance securities positions. Both banking systems participated heavily in shadow banking via support for ABCP programmes that was the highest in the countries in this volume as a percentage of GDP. Finally both banking systems were also highly international, thus offering much more growth than could be found from domestic markets but also making them vulnerable to outside shocks.

Implications

The large financial institutions that emerged in Belgium and the Netherlands during the 1990s and 2000s were greatly reduced in size in the aftermath of the financial crisis. Their international ambitions were sharply curtailed, their funding strategies became more conservative, and their asset portfolios showed a significant home bias. The range of services they offered remained broad and yet in political circles there was a renewed push to separate commercial and investment banking. Prudential oversight of individual institutions was reinforced, in the context of greater awareness of the potential vulnerability of the national financial systems as a whole. This retrenchment had little to do with bank-industry relations or with the bank-based, market-based dichotomy set out in the literature on varieties of capitalism. It had much to do with two middle-sized countries that found themselves in oversized financial trouble. Belgian and Dutch financial institutions staged a retreat from market based banking. But it is unlikely to be a permanent withdrawal.

The banks in Belgium and the Netherlands will have to compete with banks from other parts of the world as the integration of international financial markets recovers from the effects of the crisis. They will have to engage in market based banking activities and accept increasing levels of international exposure in order to do so. Like the other countries analysed in this volume, the Belgians and the Dutch cannot simply return to traditional banking practices. They will have to learn to live with market-based banking arrangements and with all of the consequences in terms of risk and volatility that such practices entail.

References

ABN-AMRO. Various years. *Annual Report*. Amsterdam: ABN-Amro.

Bank for International Settlements 2008 Quarterly Review. Available online at <http://www.bis.org/publ/qtrpdf/r_qa0806.pdf>.

Bellot, F., G. Coeme, H. De Croo, L. Van Der Auwera, and B. Collas 2009 'La Crise Financiere et Bancaire.' *Chambre de Représentants et Senat du Belgique*. Doc 52 1643/002 Chambre, 4–1100/1 Senat.

Boot, A. W. A., and A. V. Thakor 2009 'The Accelerating Integration of Banks and Markets and its Implications for Regulation' In *The Oxford Handbook of Banking* (eds A.Berger, P. Molyneux, and J. Wilson). Oxford: Oxford University Press. Available online at <http://www.accf.nl/uploads/boot-thakor-OUP-Handbookbanking-rev-jan30–2009%20_2_.pdf>.

CBFA Commission Bancaire, Financière et des Assurances. Various years. Annual Report. Brussels: CBFA. Available online at <http://www.cbfa.be>.

CPB Centraal Planbureau 2009 'The Credit Crisis and the Dutch Economy 2009–2010'. CPB Memorandum 221. Available online at <http://www.cpb.nl/node/9798>.

DNB De Nederlandsche Bank 2007 *Overview of Financial Stability in the Netherlands* September. Amsterdam: DNB.

DNB 2008a *Overview of Financial Stability in the Netherlands: September 2008*. Amsterdam: DNB.

DNB 2008b. *Annual Report*. Amsterdam: DNB.

DNB 2009a May. *Overview of Financial Stability in the Netherlands*. Amsterdam: DNB.

DNB 2009b *Annual Report*. Amsterdam: DNB.

Dexia. Various years. *Annual Report*. Brussels: Dexia Bank.

European Central Bank 2012 'Shares of the 5 Largest CIs in Total Assets.' Statistical Data Warehouse. <http://sdw.ecb.europa.eu/browseSelection.do?DATASET=0&sfl2=4&REF_AREA=65&REF_REA=262&REF_AREA=244&REF_AREA=160&sfl3=4&SSI_INDICATOR=S10&node=948387>.

Fortis. Various years. *Rapport Annuel*. Brussels: Fortis.

Hall, R. A. and D. Soskice 2001 'An Introduction to Varieties of Capitalism' In *Varieties of Capitalism: Institutional Foundations of Comparative Advantage* (eds R. A. Hall and D. Soskice). Oxford: Oxford University Press, 1–69.

Hardie, I., and D. Howarth 2009 'Die Krise but not La Crise? The Financial Crisis and the Transformation of German and French Banking Systems' *Journal of Common Market Studies* 47 November: 1017–1039.

High Level Committee for a New Financial Architecture 2009 Available online at <http://www.nbb.be/doc/ts/Other/Lamfalussy_final_report.pdf>.

IMF 2004 'Kingdom of the Netherlands-Netherlands Financial System Stability Assessment.' *IMF Country Report* No. 04/312 September.

IMF 2006a 'Belgium: 2005 Article IV Consultation' *IMF Country Report* No. 06/74.

IMF 2006b 'Belgium Financial Stability Assessment' *IMF Country Report* No. 06/75.

IMF 2008 'Financial Stress and Deleveraging: Macroeconomic Implications and Policy.' *Global Financial Stability Report* October.

IMF 2010a 'Kingdom of the Netherlands—Netherlands Staff Report for 2009 Article IV Consultation' *IMF Country Report* No. 10/34.

IMF 2010b 'Belgium' *IMF Country Report* No. 10/63. March.

Jones, E. 2008 *Economic Adjustment and Political Transformation in Small States* Oxford: Oxford University Press.

KBC. Various years. *Annual Report*. Brussels: KBC.

Maes, I. and E. Buyst 2009 'Financial Crisis and Regulation: An Overview of the Belgian Experience.' Paper prepared for the conference, 'Financial Market Regulation after Financial Crisis: The Historical Experience', Banca d'Italia, Rome. 16–17 April.

NBB National Bank of Belgium. Various years. *Financial Stability Review* Brussels: National Bank of Belgium.

Rabobank Group 2008 *Annual Report* Amsterdam: Rabobank.

Timmermans, T. 2007 'Structural Evolution and Prudential Surveillance of the Belgian Financial Market in the EU Environment.' Federale Overheidsdienst FINANCIEN—BELGIE, 67e jaargang, nr 2, 2e kwartaal.

Vandeyvere, W., and A. Zenthöfer 2012 'The Housing Market in the Netherlands' *European Economy Economic Papers* 457. June.

van Lelyveld, I., and F. Liedorp 2006 'Interbank Contagion in the Dutch Banking Sector' *International Journal of Central Banking* 2 2: 99–133.

World Bank 2012a 'Market Capitalization of Listed Companies % GDP.' <http://data.worldbank.org/indicator/CM.MKT.LCAP.GD.ZS?page=4>.

World Bank 2012b 'Domestic Credit Provided by Banking Sector % GDP.' <http://data.worldbank.org/indicator/FS.AST.DOMS.GD.ZS?page=4>.

Wyplosz, C. 1999 'Financial Restraints and Liberalization in Postwar Europe.' CEPR Discussion Paper 2253.

Zysman, J. 1983 *Governments, Markets and Growth* Ithaca: Cornell University Press.

5

A Peculiar Kind of Devastation: German Market-Based Banking

Iain Hardie and David Howarth

Introduction

During the international financial crisis that erupted in 2007, the German banking system was one of the worst hit in the world in terms of both total write-downs and write-downs to gross domestic product (GDP), yet German bank lending was only marginally affected by crisis and the core element of the German coordinated market economy (CME)—patient lending—barely undermined. Part of the explanation of this apparent paradox is obvious: hundreds of domestically focused smaller savings and cooperative banks which were not involved in market-based banking came to the rescue of the German economy. However, a full explanation rests on a nuanced understanding of market-based banking in Germany engaged in by both privately owned banks and publicly owned Landesbanks (LBs).[1]

The German economy was free from the asset price bubbles that afflicted several West European national economies during the 2000–7 period. There was no significant rise in public, private sector, or household debt, and house prices even fell slightly. Germany was also free from rampant growth in bank credit that hit a range of countries where market-based banking dominated. Most observers and senior policy makers thought that the German banking system overall would escape the difficulties hitting the British and Dutch systems. In the late summer of 2008, the German Finance Minister, Peer Steinbrück insisted upon the stability of the German system and its robustness

[1] Landesbanks are mainly owned by state (Land) governments and the savings banks of that state, for which they carry out investment banking and treasury-related functions.

compared to the American. On 26 September 2008, Steinbrück announced that the financial crisis was specifically an 'American problem', the product of an 'irresponsible rise of the laissez-faire principle' and the result of inept regulation.[2]

These claims appeared to ignore the obvious difficulties facing the German banking system. As early as August 2007, a small number of German banks faced collapse as a result of exposure to asset-backed commercial paper (ABCP) programmes (see Hardie and Howarth 2009, and the second chapter in this volume) and a range of banks had announced heavy losses by mid-2008. Less than a week after Mr Steinbrück's critical assessment of the American system, the finance minister announced the hitherto largest bank bail-out in German history—€35 billion to Hypo Real Estate (HRE). The perception that Germany would avoid the worst effects of the crisis failed to recognize the significant changes on the asset side of the balance sheets of the largest German banks in the years preceding the financial crisis. At the same time, this perception was correct in that, unlike elsewhere, banking troubles in Germany did not have an impact on the real economy by way of a domestic credit crunch. It is this apparent contradiction between high levels of market-based banking and limited impact that this chapter seeks to explain.

German banking was changing during the decade preceding the outbreak of the financial crisis, with commercial banks and Landesbanks moving away from the traditional model of banking to market-based banking, principally on the asset side of the balance sheet. By 2007, several held huge quantities of asset-backed securities (ABSs), either directly or through their activities in ABCP programmes. As a result, a range of German commercial and publicly owned banks were hit hard by the financial crisis. It is necessary to reassess the German banking system as 'market based' in that it became heavily dependent on the availability and pricing conditions of capital markets and exposed to market pricing through both balance sheet and off-balance sheet assets (see Hardie et al. and Hardie and Howarth, this volume; Adrian and Shin, 2010). Both the five largest commercial banks[3] and twelve LBs had long relied on wholesale market-based funding, but from more stable sources, such as longer term covered bonds and unsecured bonds sold to individual investors. However, they increasingly purchased, and indirectly took the risk on, securitized products. The LBs were particularly reckless in doing so, benefiting

[2] Bundestagsrede, September 2008, Plenarprotokoll 16/179, 25 September 2008. <http://www.google.co.uk/url?sa=t&rct=j&q=&esrc=s&source=web&cd=1&ved=0CCYQFjAA&url=http%3A%2F%2Fdipbt.bundestag.de%2Fdip21%2Fbtp%2F16%2F16179.pdf&ei=StN-UJCVFoua0QXj5oCQCQ&usg=AFQjCNEMl7wyeLFNbEkGu99Xr9DmZj3l-Q&sig2=iehuOePV830CPRhI7k_maw>, accessed 5 October 2012.

[3] During the decade prior to the financial crisis, the five largest commercial banks (by assets) were: Deutsche Bank, Commerzbank, Dresdner Bank, HypoVereinsbank (HVB) (subsequently part of UniCredit Bank) and Postbank.

from explicit government protection and a problem of moral hazard (Hardie and Howarth 2009, Fischer et al. 2011). The LBs and, to a lesser extent, the largest commercial banks (and one specialized lender, IKB) purchased securitized assets as the easiest way to expand in the context of low profitability and largely protected markets. Thus, even without domestic asset price bubbles and a boom in credit, the LBs and commercial banks faced high losses. Smaller German cooperative and savings banks were less affected during the crisis: many continued to make profits in 2008 and 2009 and expand their lending despite difficult economic conditions. Few of these banks were large enough to access global capital markets.

This chapter is structured as follows. The second section provides an overview of the impact of the financial crisis on the German banking system. The third section provides an overview of the banking system and its partial transformation from the 1990s. This is followed by two sections analysing the details of German market-based banking on the assets and liabilities sides of the balance sheet respectively. Prior to concluding, the sixth section briefly examines the impact of German market-based banking on non-financial companies (NFCs), the real economy, and the German CME.

A Peculiar Kind of Devastation

Even prior to the finance minister's assurance of stability in September 2008, German bank write-downs were massive. By August 2008, no less than twelve German banks had write-downs of more than $1 billion with a total of $55.9 billion for these banks (Bloomberg 2008). In July 2009, the International Monetary Fund (IMF) estimated that 9 per cent of total global write-downs were German versus 12 per cent for the United Kingdom and only 3 per cent for France (IMF 2009a). The IMF announced that German banks suffered around a quarter of Europe's write-downs (IMF, 2009b, 12). One credible estimate from April 2009 of write-downs directly linked to the crisis for larges international banks placed German losses at 33 per cent of Tier 1 capital, very close to British levels (37 per cent) and far higher than French levels (17 per cent) (Xiao 2009). Four German banks, including the country's third largest, effectively collapsed and only massive federal and regional government intervention—including the creation of a bad bank to soak up toxic assets and the purchase of shares—saved a number of banks. The publicly (or formerly) owned LBs—previously known largely for domestic retail and commercial lending—revealed major losses across a range of activities.

The five largest commercial banks and 12 LBs, representing 46 per cent of total German bank assets, enjoyed half of the profits of the German banking system between 2004 and 2007 but suffered the bulk of German bank losses

Table 5.1. Profits and losses of five largest commercial banks and Landesbanks (in € billion)

Type of bank (number)	Share of total German bank balance sheet	Cumulated profits 2004–7	Cumulated profits 2008–9
Largest commercial banks (5)	25.75	35.610	–24.524
Landesbanks (12)	20.67	10.304	–11.280

Source: Authors' calculations based on Deutsche Bundesbank. The five largest commercial banks change over time. During the 2004–07 period these were: Deutsche Bank, Commerzbank, Dresdner Bank, HypoVereinsbank (HVB) (now part of the Italian UniCredit Bank) and Postbank.

Table 5.2. Selected German bank write-downs on toxic assets and bad loans (2007–9) as of 31 December 2009

	Total write-downs at end of 2009 ($bn)	Write-downs/total assets (end 2007) (%)
IKB	14.4	22.68
LB Sachsen	2.5	3.69
Bayerische LB	18.8	4.52
Commerz	22.3 (including Dresdner Bank)	0.36 (2008); 2.01 (2009) including Dresdner Bank assets.
HSH Nordbank	4.1	2
Deutsche	21.4	1.89
DZ	7.6	1.76
HRE	7	1.74
WestLB	3.9	1.36
LBBW*	7.8	1.75

*LBBW took over LB Sachsen, and so there may be an element of double counting.

Source: Scotia Capital (2010, B15) and Reuters (2010). Reuters/annual reports/company filings. Estimates based on writedowns and losses from subprime securities, mortgages, CDOs, derivatives and SIVs, and losses on bad loans, or non-performing loans. The definition of a bad loan is complex and can vary between countries and often includes a provision for future loan losses.

in 2008–9. Kreditanstalt für Wiederaufbau (KfW)—a publicly owned development bank involved in the rescue of other banks—and smaller specialized banks—notably HRE, the mortgage lender, and IKB Deutsche Industriebank—accounted for the remainder. Table 5.2 sets out the losses for the worst hit German banks.[4] Amongst the most severely affected banks in Europe (losses to assets) were LB Sachsen, HRE, and IKB—which all effectively collapsed. (HRE figures appear low in Table 5.1 because the size of the balance sheet increased from 161.6 billion in 2006 to 400.2 billion in 2007 due to the lender having to return off-balance sheet assets to balance sheet.) It is the LB losses that challenge the standard view of conservative publicly owned banks, and further reinforce the claim of dramatic change. These losses had nothing to do with regionally based lending.

[4] From Bloomberg, 2008 and Reuters, 2010.

Despite this devastation and the severe economic recession of 2009, created largely by the considerable decline in exports, overall German bank lending was barely affected—as in France but unlike the United Kingdom (Figure 5.1). We disaggregate and explore these figures further in our examination below of the impact of market-based banking on the German CME (see Figure 5.5). While aggregate bank lending survey figures show some tightening of credit due to 'cost and availability of funding' from mid 2007, figures for France, the United Kingdom and the United States were far higher (see Hardie et al., this volume). Such tightening had eased entirely by mid-2009.

The Hidden Transformation of the German Banking System

The German banking system has for decades been one of the most fragmented in Europe, with over 3,000 monetary financial institutions still operating in the 2000s. On the eve of the financial crisis, the largest five banks held only 22 per cent of total assets (ECB, 2008). Only one German bank was found in the largest fifteen in Europe during the first half of the 2000s: Deutsche Bank.[5] Germany is traditionally described as having a three pillar decentralized universal bank-based financial system (Zysman, 1983; Deeg, 1999). The three pillars were (are) separated by financial structures, legal status, and

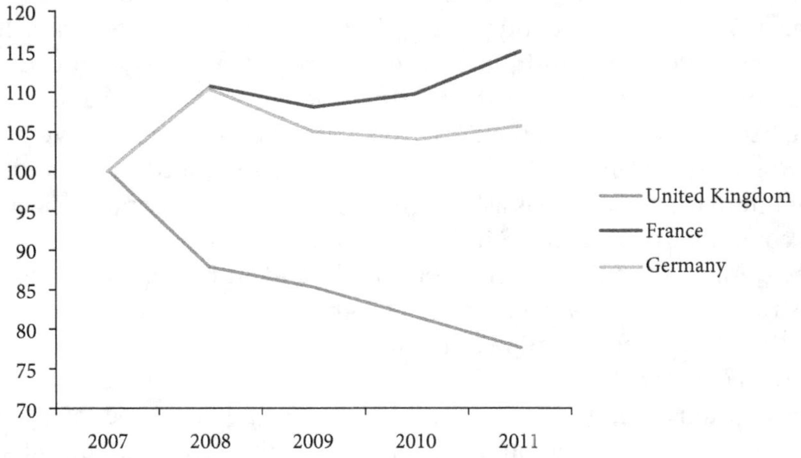

Figure 5.1. Monetary financial institution lending to non-financial companies only (national currencies); 2007 = 100

Source: ECB Statistical data warehouse. Domestic banking groups and stand alone banks only. All currencies combined. Figures for French and German banks include lending to the Euro area

[5] At the end of 2007, on the verge of the financial crisis, Commerzbank reached fifteenth place, but it was not in the 'trillion dollar club'.

governance systems. The first pillar consists of the private commercial banks (prior to 2008) and was relatively concentrated, with five 'big' banks, including the three largest, internationally present universal banks: Deutsche Bank, Commerzbank, and Dresdner Bank. The second pillar included the public sector banks: the twelve LBs and approximately 500 savings banks (Sparkassen), backed by state and local governments respectively and seen as 'not strictly profit-maximizing' (Hackethal 2004, 74). There is a long (though declining) tradition of Bundesland government interference in LB lending decisions and overall public sector ownership far exceeds that in comparable economies (IMF 2003). In the 1990s, four-fifths of retail and commercial banking activity in Germany was by publicly owned banks, which held approximately 50 per cent of retail banking assets in the early 2000s (Hackethal 2004). The publicly owned banks were seen as specializing in banking for the Mittelstand, Germany's small and medium-sized enterprises (SMEs) and the backbone of the German economy. Deeg (1999) and Krahnen and Schmidt (2004a) emphasize the continued domestic focus of the public sector banks and their close relationships as 'Hausbanks' with the Mittelstand. However, a fragmented domestic market restricted competition and profits, and this view of domestic focus only applies to the smaller savings banks, not the LBs. The banking system was one of the least profitable in Europe (Brunner et al. 2004), pushing both commercial banks and the LBs increasingly abroad to increase profitability. The German Finance Ministry itself encouraged financial innovation to strengthen both the LBs and German commercial banks but also to improve the performance of the German economy (Nawrath 2003, Asmussen 2006). The third pillar of the German banking system consisted of approximately 2000 cooperative banks, domestically focused and often specializing in specific economic sectors. However, the cooperative banks' functional equivalent of the LBs—DZ Bank—also engaged in some of the same international activities as the LBs, appearing, for example, as a significant counterparty of failed US insurance company AIG.

The German system was more protectionist and anti-competitive than the British and French in several ways. Until 2005, guarantees against bankruptcy from their Länder owners allowed LBs to borrow more cheaply than commercial rivals (Fischer et al. 2011). Furthermore, the LBs and Sparkassen did not compete against one another, retaining their own fiefdoms. German federal governments, the Association of German Banks, the European Commission, and the Bundesbank all supported the elimination of the three-pillar German system, but change was strongly resisted by Bundesland governments. Foreign penetration into the German banking market was amongst the lowest in the EU. In Germany, at the end of 2003, foreign bank branches held only 6.4 per cent of total bank assets (IMF 2006, 103), far below French (12 per cent) and British levels.

Unlike French, Italian, and Spanish bank retail-driven expansion abroad, the internationalization of the German commercial banks and LBs in the 1990s and 2000s was almost exclusively in corporate lending and investment banking. Investment banking in Germany was developed and expanded both by those commercial banks with (increasingly foreign) private shareholders and the LBs, following the pattern of the largest British and French banks. The LBs may not have been 'not strictly profit-maximising entities' (Hackethal 2004, 74), but this had no significant impact on their behaviour in this regard.

The nature of what can be broadly seen as 'investment' banking also changed over time. The initial impetus for the expansion into overseas investment banking may have been to acquire skills to assist in serving domestic clients (see Deeg 1999). The foreign firms purchased, largely in the United Kingdom, were largely advisory fee-earning, not proprietary trading, businesses, but over time, as will be discussed in greater detail later, proprietary trading and the purchase of securities increasingly dominated investment banking.

In the early 2000s, the German banking system lagged far behind a range of other European banking systems and the United States in the issuance of securitized debt (asset-backed securities and mortgage-backed securities). However, German governments pushed through several regulatory changes and promoted securitization actively (Nowak 2004). The October 2005 coalition agreement of the so-called 'Grand Coalition' between the centre-right CDU/CSU and the centre-left SPD included a statement on how to facilitate the growth of the German securitization market.[6] The aim of the government was to increase the use of securitization as a liabilities tool for the banks, as a means to distribute risk from bank balance sheets and increase domestic lending, i.e. to increase market-based liabilities. There was no desire or expectation that this (or even worse, American) risk would be concentrated in (market-based) bank assets.

Assets: Buying Toxic American

The asset structure of German commercial banks changed dramatically in the decade preceding the financial crisis, with loans to non-banks losing relative importance, as in other countries in this volume, to loans to banks (Figure 5.2). The asset structure of the LBs underwent change in the same direction but this was less pronounced, while change was marginal for savings and cooperative banks.

Positioning assets, especially securities, on bank trading books increased significantly by German commercial banks and LBs, as much as by their

[6] *Koalitionsvertrag* (2005). Available at <http://www.cducsu.de/upload/koavertrag0509.pdf>.

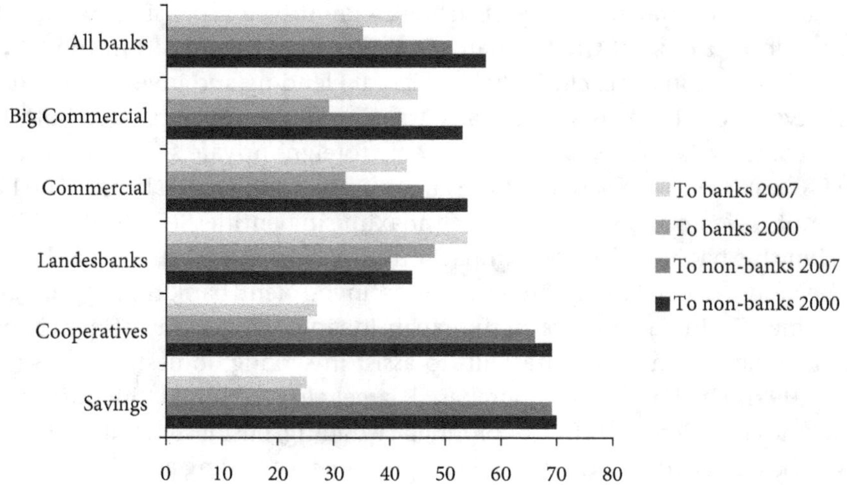

Figure 5.2. Monetary financial institution assets from 2000 to 2007 as a percentage of the total (end of year)
Source: Deutsche Bundesbank. Authors' own calculations

British and French competitors (Hardie and Howarth 2009, Table 5.1). This represented both an increase in genuine trading, but also a desire to take advantage of the lower capital requirements from having assets held as trading assets. Either way, however, the result was a significant increase in the exposure of bank profitability to movements in market prices (Hardie and Howarth, this volume). Derivatives trading far in excess of the amounts required for balance sheet and financing risk hedging also occurred (Hardie and Howarth 2009; Memmel and Schertler 2009).

The banks' reports do not give a single way to track increased positioning of assets as trading assets, but the data all point in the same direction. The available data include the percentage of total assets designated 'trading assets', or, more narrowly, the proportion of securities held that are said to be held for 'trading purposes'. Table 5.3 summarizes the available data for most of the largest German banks which suffered significant write-downs in the aftermath of the financial crisis.

For the German LBs, the figures, where available, show an increasing focus on trading, although this is by no means consistent across all banks. As would be expected, given their reputation as Germany's leaders in investment banking, the importance of trading for Deutsche and Dresdner was higher than other German banks. However, Commerzbank's trading assets figures were far lower than several LBs: as much an indication of changing LB activity as of Commerzbank's relative caution. In 2007, the average of trading assets for the three largest German commercial banks was higher than the average of

Table 5.3. Increased bank trading activity

Commerzbank	Trading assets as a percentage of total peaked at 24.0 in 2004.
Deutsche	Trading assets as a percentage of total peaked at 45.9 in 2006 (30.9 per cent in 2000).
Dresdner	Trading assets as a percentage of total peaked at 32.0 in 2007 (21.4 per cent in 2000).
HSH Nordbank	Trading assets as a percentage of total peaked at 13.4 in 2006. Proportion of securities held for trading purposes 55.7 per cent in 2006 (11.0 per cent in 2002).
LBBW	Proportion of securities held for trading purposes 30.9 per cent in 2006 (12.5 per cent in 2002).
LB Sachsen	Proportion of securities held for trading purposes 15.3 per cent in 2007, more than triple the 2003 figure.
WestLB	Trading assets as a percentage of total peaked at 32.5 in 2007. Proportion of securities held for trading purposes peaked in 2002 at 51.3 per cent (28.4 per cent in 2000 and 41.7 per cent in 2006).
DZ Bank	Trading assets as a percentage of total peaked at 30.1 in 2007. Proportion of securities held for trading purposes 58.0 per cent in 2007 (21.2 per cent in 2002).

Source: Bank registration documents, authors' calculations.

the three British banks with highest trading assets (42.4, 18.94, and 15.78 for RBS, HSBC, and Barclays, respectively).[7] This increased involvement in trading by Deutsche and Dresdner, however dramatic, did not represent any change from the general picture of the commercial banks, but the nature of investment banking, at least for Deutsche and Dresdner, had changed, as it had globally, to be focused far less on advisory and new issue businesses (as in the initial move into London-based investment banking) and more on proprietary trading and balance sheet expansion. The trading figures for the LBs also demonstrate an increased vulnerability to market movements, a central aspect of market-based banking (Hardie and Howarth, this volume). For a period, this appeared to be a successful strategy. Risk-adjusted trading results at the largest banks were seen as improving from 2005 until mid-2007. However, after that, the true nature of the market risk was revealed and heavy losses were made (Deutsche Bundesbank 2007a, 67). For the LBs there were additional incentives to increase their trading activities. The elimination of new government guarantees on their borrowing from July 2005, as the result of an EU ruling, encouraged LBs to borrow increased amounts at cheap levels before the guarantee lapsed.[8] This additional cheap borrowing led to an adjustment in their business models, resulting in higher lending to non-German banks (in the inter-bank market or by buying bank bonds), and buying of securitized bonds, including from the United States. This compensated for the decline in

[7] Figures are drawn from bank balance sheets and registration documents. Authors' own calculations.

[8] The guarantees lapsed only for additional borrowing after the 2005 cut-off, meaning outstanding debt continued to enjoy the guarantee.

domestic lending to both banks and non-banks.[9] LB loans to domestic banks and non-banks fell from over 80 per cent of assets as late as 2002 to less than 70 per cent in 2007. Loans to foreign banks almost doubled as a percentage of total assets (to approximately 20 per cent), as did the purchase of foreign securities (to approximately 10 per cent) (Sachverständigenrat 2008, 140). Although smaller as a proportion of the overall balance sheet, securities of foreign banks increased quite dramatically in relative terms. In the spring 2005, LBs held €2.2 billion in assets issued by foreign banks (principally equity and bonds); only two and a half years later, in the fall 2007, LB holdings had increased by almost 400 per cent to €8.5 billion (data from Deutsche Bundesbank). Most of this increase was based on the purchase of securitized products from foreign banks since they promised additional yield.

In the decade preceding the financial crisis, but in particular the four years, the off-balance sheet activities of a small number of commercial banks and LBs increased rapidly. The result was significant exposure to the contingent risks involved in ABCP conduits and special investment vehicles (SIVs) on the eve of the crisis (Table 5.4, see also Deutsche Bundesbank 2007b, 24).[10] The outstanding ABCP of the largest fourteen German banks reached US$74 billion (Deutsche Bundesbank 2010). It is not surprising that the banks with the highest figures relative to assets correspond to the banks which suffered the highest write-downs (relative to assets) as a result of the financial crisis.

High Market-Based Liabilities From Relatively Stable Markets

In Germany, the changes in market-based financing have been limited (Figure 5.3).

Table 5.4 Exposure of selected German banks to asset-backed commercial paper conduits and special investment vehicles, top five (2007)

Bank	Type	Per cent of capital	Per cent of assets
LB Sachsen	LB	1126	30.3
WestLB	LB	542	12.7
IKB	Com	494	20.5
Dresdner Bank	Large Com	364	9.9
Landesbank Berlin	LB	179	2.2

Source: Hüfner 2010, based on Fitch ratings 2007.

[9] See the section on Landesbanken in the Report by the German Council of Economic Advisors (Sachverständigenrat 2007, 137–41).

[10] Both ABCP and SIVs are off-balance sheet entities that buy assets like mortgage-backed securities, and finance the purchases through issuing debt, mainly short term. A bank's exposure comes from either holding the debt issued or through committing to provide financing if the debt cannot be sold.

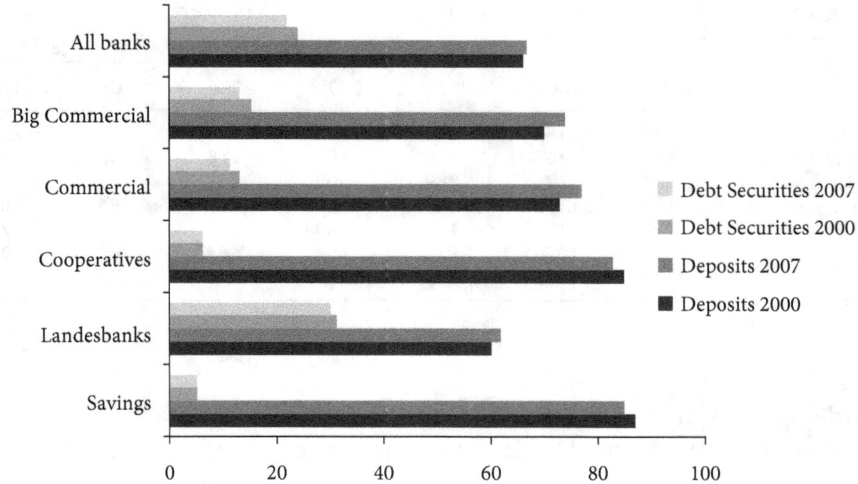

Figure 5.3. Monetary financial institution liabilities from 2000 to 2007 as a percentage of the total (end of year)
Source: Deutsche Bundesbank. Authors' own calculations.

While German bank assets internationalized rapidly in the early 2000s, bank liabilities remained stubbornly domestic. German banks therefore faced less of the exposure to international lenders than their counterparts in, for example, the United Kingdom and Spain (Hardie and Maxfield, this volume; Royo, this volume). Foreign exposure on the asset side of the balance sheet increased by 250 per cent between 2001 and 2007, whereas there was negligible change on the liability side.[11] As a result the net foreign asset position of German banks sky-rocketed from near zero in the late 1990s to over €1000 billion in 2007, reaching €1500 billion in 2008 before dropping—while the position of French banks only reached slightly in excess of €200 billion, the Italian position was close to balance, and Spanish banks' international liabilities exceeded international assets.[12]

Exposure to Wholesale Funding

Any bank lending more than it takes in deposits must finance this additional lending from wholesale markets and is therefore subject to the lending decisions of other market actors, including other banks (Hardie et al., this volume;

[11] Deutsche Bundesbank, Auslandsstatus, <http://www.bundesbank.de/Navigation/DE/Statistiken/Aussenwirtschaft/Auslandsstatus_der_Banken/auslandsstatus_der_banken.html#Start>, accessed on 24 October 2010.

[12] Achim Dübel, financial consultant, republished in the *Financial Times*, ft.com/alphaville, posted 18 March 2010. <http://ftalphaville.ft.com/blog/2010/03/18/177361/germanys-bank-asset-berg/>, accessed on 26 September 2012.

Table 5.5 The funding gap: non-financial company loans-to-deposits ratio (selected German banks, 2002–8)

	2002	2003	2004	2005	2006	2007	2008
Heleba	172	164	164	164	162	211	217
HSH Nordbank	159	165	169	188	218	207	224
LB Sachsen	168	174	189	200	228	276	N/A
NordLB	162	162	162	160	155	186	181
WestLB	139	121	112	160	142	346	378
HRE	1346	1090	873	757	668	786	1393
IKB	1229	1082	1225	1101	694	502	480

Source: Bank registration documents, authors' calculations.

Hardie and Howarth, this volume).[13] Thus, the 'bank funding gap' (NFCs loans to deposits ratio) is a useful indicator of exposure to wholesale, market-based funding. In the early 2000s, the German banking system's overall funding gap and gap to GDP was one of the highest in Europe and considerably higher than the British banking system (see Figures 2.1 and 2.2 in Chapter 2 in this volume).[14] Although this is a rather crude measure of exposure to wholesale funding, it supports the view that German banks have long been heavily exposed to market-based financing and that the German model of banking has long been to some degree 'market based'. However, in the years preceding the crisis, the funding gap dropped markedly for the German banking system as a whole, at a time when the gap for several other European banking systems rose considerably. The funding gap for the largest commercial banks and several LBs stagnated or dropped. Yet the gap for some German banks remained very high in comparative terms. Contrary to systemic trends, the funding gap for five LBs (WestLB, HSH Nordbank, Heleba, LB Sachsen, and NordLB) increased significantly during the decade prior to the crisis, while the gap for the mortgage lender HRE fluctuated at very high levels (Table 5.5). The funding gap for the specialist lender IKB dropped significantly but remained very high relative to most German and European banks. These two banks were hit particularly hard by funding difficulties early in the financial crisis.

[13] There are a number of issues with this measure. First, it can mask the most dramatic changes in bank balance sheets, as they move away from lending to holding financial assets which are subsequently sold. An extreme example is Deutsche Bank, where at the end of 2007 loans represented only 10.3 per cent of total assets. Second, not all deposits are equally stable. Obviously, as the bank run by individual depositors at Northern Rock demonstrated, no deposits are stable. Nevertheless, retail (individual) deposits are less likely to be withdrawn than deposits from companies and especially than deposits by other financial market actors. We will explore this further below. Third, size matters. The ratio, as a measure of the required wholesale financing, obscures the highly variable rates of growth in lending.

[14] Both Hackethal (2004) and the IMF (2009, 18) note the importance of wholesale funding for the LB, and the resultant vulnerabilities.

The IMF (2009b, 18) concludes: 'the financial crisis has revealed the serious risk—to their viability and, thereby, to systemic stability—associated with the [LB's] wholesale funding approach'. However, such an observation only partially holds true for the LBs' (and other German banks') more 'traditional' wholesale funding: that is, the sources of wholesale funding used widely before 2000, and continued thereafter. German banks have long financed themselves through the issuance of 'covered bonds', in Germany called *Pfandbriefe*, where the bonds are secured on a pool of assets ring-fenced for the purpose but remain on the issuing banks' balance sheet. The issuing bank remains fully liable for principal and interest payments. The assets are most commonly mortgages and public sector loans. By the end of 2008, covered mortgage bonds outstanding reached US$3 trillion, 40 per cent of European GDP (for an overview, see IMF 2009d, 90), with Germany by far the largest market. Furthermore, the German covered bond market has been established longer than those of other countries, and is generally seen as legally more safely underpinned (see Hardie and Howarth, this volume). German wholesale funding was overall of much longer maturity compared to most other European countries. At the end of 2007, only 3.8 per cent of German wholesale funding was less than a year compared to over a third for France and almost two-thirds for the United Kingdom.[15] Heavier reliance on longer-term debt also helps to explain the limited nature of Germany's credit crunch (Figure 5.1), at least early in the crisis.[16] The *Pfandbriefe* market did close down briefly in the autumn of 2008, and rating agency demands for increased asset cover constrained the amount of liquidity banks could raise (Hypo Real Estate 2009, 108), but the *Pfandbriefe* market was subsequently far more robust than the securitization market and also performed far better than other European covered bond markets.

In other areas of traditional wholesale funding, German banks also performed better than counterparts elsewhere, meaning that the impact of the crisis through the reliance on wholesale funding was limited relative to the overall level of market exposure (with the notable exception of HRE). The relatively heavy dependence on the inter-bank market was mitigated by the fact that borrowing by German banks was disproportionately from other German banks,[17] in marked contrast to the United Kingdom, where large amounts of bank borrowing were from abroad (with France and Germany

[15] ECB figures: <http://www.ecb.int/stats/money/aggregates/bsheets/html/outstanding_amounts_2007-12.en.html>, accessed 17 November 2010.

[16] The more recent flow of bank deposits from Euro area periphery countries to the core also benefited German banks, and reduced their need for market-based funding.

[17] All the LBs except Landesbank Sachsen give this figure. The percentage of bank deposits held by LBs coming from domestic banks ranges from 55 to 93 per cent at year end 2007. Of the other banks that give figures, only Deutsche (30 per cent) and Dresdner (29 per cent) are below 50 per cent (source: annual reports).

the two largest sources (IMF 2009c, 19)). In addition, for the LBs, bank deposits included deposits from affiliated savings banks (and for DZ Bank, from cooperative banks). A number of banks reported stability (Westdeutsche Landesbank 2009, 97) or increases (Bayerische Landesbank 2009, 33; HSH Nordbank 2009, 74; Landesbank Berlin 2009, 65; DZ Bank 2009, 110) in these deposits, despite the troubles of the recipient LBs, in marked contrast to the experience of a bank run in the United Kingdom and United States (Hardie and Maxfield, this volume). This is attractive 'rating-independent funding' (Landesbank Sachsen 2008, 15). Furthermore, savings banks continued to provide a means to distribute unsecured bond issues, a further 'traditional' source of funding. Westdeutsche Landesbank, despite its difficulties, increased long-term unsecured issuance by half in 2008, and sold three-quarters of the bonds to 'franchise clients such as savings banks' (2009, 97; also Bayerische Landesbank 2009, 33). In corporate deposits, another traditional source of wholesale funding, the contrast was similar. Whereas in the United Kingdom, corporate depositors were noteworthy for their speed of exit (interview, 24 February 2010), in Germany they were stable (Westdeutsche Landesbank 2009, 97; Bayerische Landesbank 2009, 70). Although it is certainly true that wholesale funding had long underpinned German bank lending, such 'traditional' wholesale funding continued to be generally available in the crisis. This is certainly not to argue that German banks did not face liquidity issues. They did and government and central bank actions were in part aimed at alleviating these issues. However, the situation in the United Kingdom and for the United States investment banks was far more severe, and the scale of intervention required far higher (Hardie and Maxfield, this volume).

Securitization

German bank borrowing through securitization was delayed but the rise was very rapid: issuance in 2006 was over five times the level in 2004.[18] The overall market-based liabilities of the German banking system via securitization were comparatively low. At the end of 2008, German outstandings reached €87 billion (4 per cent of GDP), which was far below UK levels (€579 billion, 32 per cent of GDP, and 40 per cent of the European total) yet considerably higher than French levels (€27 billion and 1 per cent of GDP) (European Securitisation Forum 2009; see also Hardie and Howarth, this volume; Hardie and Maxfield, this volume; Howarth, this volume). The securitization of NFC lending remained significant. Deutsche Bank (2009a) claimed effectively

[18] IMF 2009b, 13. Other figures on the issuance of securities show a rise of almost 1000 per cent from €4.28 billion in 2001 to €37.7 billion in 2006 (Association for Financial Markets in Europe, 'Monthly Securitisation Report', www.afme.eu, accessed 13 February 2010; authors' calculations).

hypothecated securitization—with the securitization of assets prompting further lending in that type of asset (see also Norddeutsche Landesbank below)—but for many other banks there appeared to be a more generalized 'freeing up' of the balance sheet to allow greater lending generally.[19] To be expected, given the sluggish domestic property market, residential mortgage-backed securities represented only 23 per cent of German collateral outstanding at the end of 2008, far less than in France (48 per cent) and the United Kingdom (78 per cent) (European Securitisation Forum 2009).

Details in bank annual reports on what was being securitized are scant. Deutsche Bank highlights both commercial real estate and loans to medium-sized German companies (Deutsche Bank 2009b, 45).[20] Norddeutsche Landesbank securitized 'loans to the East German housing industry'—noting that this allowed more lending to the same industry (Norddeutsche Landesbank 2007, 56)—and Landesbank Baden-Wurttemberg securitized receivables related to trade financing, leasing, commercial real estate, and lending to SMEs (Landesbank Baden-Wurttemberg 2009, 20). Despite the relatively low exposure to market-based liabilities through securitization, German exposure to ABCP conduits on the assets side of the balance sheet rightly received considerable public attention, thanks to the collapse of IKB and LB Sachsen early in the crisis, both as a direct result of exposure to ABCP. In addition, the problems in the commercial paper market were the main reason for the difficulties at the much larger HRE, although this was not directly the result of ABCP conduits. Overall, German banks provided only slightly less liquidity support to the conduits (Fitch 2007, 7; totals US$313 billion) than British ($322 billion), in marked contrast to the difference in securitization levels on the liabilities side.

'Synthetic securitization' was also widely used by banks as a means to reduce their risk-weighted assets and therefore potentially free up capital for further lending—as indicated in several German bank annual reports (HSH Nordbank 2009, 75; IKB Deutsche Industriebank 2009, 72; Hypo Real Estate 2009, 168).[21] This technique involves using credit default swaps (see Bomfim 2005) to transfer the risk from the bank's lending activities. This ability to 'trade corporate credit risk' could also be provided to the German savings banks (Sparkassen) by their regional LBs (Norddeutsche Landesbank 2007, 75). Although problems at AIG and Lehman Brothers subsequently demonstrated that the risk transfer was somewhat illusory, the activity nevertheless allowed increased lending.[22] However, the price at which the transfer of risk

[19] Telephone interview, former senior UK banker, 24 February 2010.

[20] Telephone interview, former senior UK banker, 24 February 2010.

[21] Basel II bans this activity.

[22] When the recipients of collateral postings for credit default swaps by AIG (using US government support) were revealed, named German banks received US$7.7 billion.

could take place was determined by the credit default swap market (see Hardie and Howarth, this volume).

Market-Based Banking and the German CME

The German banking system is widely seen as having been a key ingredient of the post-war German economic success story (Shonfield 1965). Banks contributed to the overall framework of a unique and highly consensual and cooperative 'German model' through the provision of 'patient capital' (Deeg 1999; Streeck 1997). The model involved a strong reliance of NFCs on bank loans and a limited role for equity capital; a strong institutional link between banks and NFCs through formal bank representation on the board of large firms; and a long-term relationship of trust between the Mittelstand (SMEs) and their 'Hausbank' as a lender with a special responsibility—so-called 'relational banking' (Deeg 2010; Hackethal 2004). Some elements of this central role played by banks in the German CME have been undermined since the early 1990s. For example, for the largest firms, the relationship with the 'Hausbank' declined in importance and banks divested themselves of the shares they held in large firms (Hall and Soskice 2001; Lütz 2000). However, most experts note continuity in most areas of German banking and the relationship of German banks with NFCs at least up to the mid-2000s (see, for example, Krahnen and Schmidt 2004b, 488).

Securitization was limited but its rapid growth from 2004–8 probably contributed to the overall growth in commercial and Landesbank lending to NFCs over this period and prevented a decline in the lending by the biggest commercial banks. Deutsche Bank makes the connection between securitization and lending explicit in their (pre-crisis) 2006 annual report (p. 110): 'A sudden drop in investor demand for asset-backed securities could cause us to restrict our lending thereafter for the types of loans we securitize'. However, the limited available data on securitized lending prior to 2009 prevent a clear comparative study: published Bundesbank figures start from after the start of the financial crisis. At the level of individual commercial banks and the LBs, the change in loans to NFCs and households between 2000 and 2007 varied from a fall of 54 per cent to a rise of 38 (bank registration documents, authors' calculations). (HRE was an outlier in this regard with an increase of 138 per cent.) By contrast, in the United Kingdom, where securitization contributed massively to lending, individual banks' loans to customers (NFCs and households) all increased by between 83 and 393 per cent during the same period. In Germany, the gentle decline in overall domestic bank lending between 2000 and 2005 reflects a moribund economy, while the rise from 2005 to 2008 likely reflects stronger economic growth more than the rapid rise in securitization (Figure 5.4).

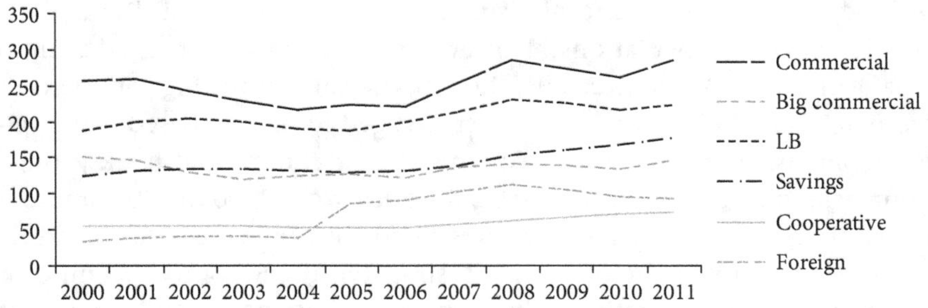

Figure 5.4. German and foreign bank lending to domestic non-financial companies (Q4 of every year, € billion, outstanding), 2000–11
Source: Deutsche Bundesbank.

Following the outbreak of the financial crisis, commercial bank lending dropped sharply (approximately 9 per cent to the end of 2010) and LB lending moderately (Figure 5.5). This reflected both a credit tightening due to 'availability and cost of funding' on short-term wholesale markets and temporarily on the *Pfandbriefe* market as well as the deep recession that the German economy entered due to the rapid drop in its exports. However, the lending by smaller savings and cooperative banks—less reliant on wholesale markets—rose steadily, which meant that overall bank lending to NFCs remained relatively steady following 2008. Thus the devastation wrought by market-based banking in Germany did not result in the kind of credit crunch experienced in the United Kingdom. Market-based banking appears to have had a limited impact upon the German CME due in large part to the diversity of the country's banking system.

Further, the impact of market-based banking upon the maturity of German bank lending is inconclusive. We show elsewhere in this volume that the rise of market-based banking, especially on the liabilities side of the balance sheet, can procyclically encourage longer-term lending (Hardie and Howarth; Hardie and Maxfield in this volume). While market-based banking fundamentally undermines 'patient capital' because lending becomes more directly linked to developments in the market, favourable market conditions (i.e. those that prevailed between 2000 and 2007) will result in increased longer maturity lending. This has been shown to have been the case in the Euro area generally, the United States, and the United Kingdom.[23] A superficial analysis indeed indicates that the average maturity of German bank lending rose significantly from the start of 2000 to the end of 2006, with the

[23] See ECB Euro Area Bank Lending Surveys April 2003–April 2012; Bank of England (Credit Conditions Survey) www.bankofengland.co.uk/publications/Pages/other/monetary/creditconditions.aspx, accessed 11 July 2012; and US Federal Reserve data on the maturity of loans <http://www.federalreserve.gov/boarddocs/snloansurvey/>, accessed 12 July 2012.

percentage of long-term lending rising from 60 to 73 per cent (Bundesbank statistics, authors' calculations). However, this percentage dropped again to 60 per cent by late 2008. Crucially, though, the data for the big commercials, commercials and LBs—the banks most engaged in market-based banking—are inconclusive in this regard. For the biggest commercial banks, longer maturity lending actually declined significantly from 2000 to 2008 (approximately 18 per cent), which contradicts trends in the United States and the United Kingdom. On the other hand, short-term lending rose significantly—despite strong fluctuations—by 76 per cent from its 2004 through to its mid-2008 peak and medium-term lending also rose. Evidence from the LBs is similarly inconclusive: although long-term lending rose, both medium-term and short-term lending rose more in relative terms. The most noteworthy development is the significant rise in maturity of savings and cooperative bank lending, two groups of smaller and largely domestically focused banks little engaged in market-based banking. Long-term lending by these banks, supported by covered bonds, continued to increase in both total and relative terms after the outbreak of the financial crisis in 2007, demonstrating the greater stability of this market at a time when the securitization market's closure was undermining the UK's Northern Rock but also the German IKB and HRE.

German NFCs became marginally less reliant on bank credit from the 1990s in relative if not real terms (Table 1.1, in the Introduction to this volume). The main change in German NFC financing took place in the first half of the 1990s with a significant shift from loan financing to equity financing and this was not linked directly to the activities of banks (see Deeg 2010; Krahnen, and Schmidt 2004a; Lütz 2000). However, in the decade prior to the financial crisis, lending by the large commercial banks to large German NFCs rose and, correspondingly, large German NFCs came to rely more on bank credit for their external funding. Bank credit accessed by large firms increased by about a fifth (18.9 per cent) between 1997 and 2004 and growth accelerated after 2004 due in large part to the securitization of bank lending.[24] In this, large German firms were more like NFCs in France (Howarth, this volume) and the United Kingdom (Hardie and Maxfield, this volume). At the same time, these developments did not reverse longer term trends and the equity stock of large companies grew by 53.8 per cent between 1997 and 2004 (rising to 62.9 per cent of external funding). Large German firms also experienced something of a credit crunch from 2007 as the large commercial banks became more reluctant to lend (IMF 2009b), pointing to the selective impact of market-based banking on NFC lending by the most market-based German banks. However,

[24] Deutsche Bundesbank, 'German enterprises' profitability and financing', Monthly Report, several years.

this decline was largely compensated for by increased lending year on year by both publicly owned savings banks and cooperatives.

The development in Mittelstand funding leads to different conclusions about the impact of market-based banking. Between 1997 and 2004, Mittelstand borrowing from banks dropped by almost a fifth in real terms (18.2 per cent) (Bundesbank 2006), while the equity stock of the Mittelstand grew by 149.6 per cent (from 6 to 15 per cent of the balance sheet total and to 25.7 per cent of external funding) (Bundesbank 2006). LB loans to the Mittelstand declined considerably right up to 2008 as a percentage of total LB assets, from 37.3 per cent at the start of 2000 to 25.6 per cent at the start of 2008 (Bundesbank 2006).[25] Prior to 2008, foreign banks stepped in to compensate. Thus, in the period leading to the crisis, for the Mittelstand backbone of the German economy, there was a significant decline in reliance on patient capital and relational banking—which nonetheless continued to dominate Mittelstand external funding. However, these developments must be put into perspective—bank lending remained of crucial importance to German SMEs' external funding. The development in bank lending since 2008, with a relative and real rise in Spaarkassen and Cooperative lending to NFCs, suggests that the 'patient capital' that is central to the German CME regained lost ground.

LB engagement in market-based banking contributed to the decline in lending to domestic NFC. The LBs sought higher returns through the purchase of securitized products and lending to banks. However, determining the precise relationship is impossible and other factors are relevant. Indeed, while the importance of domestic lending to LB assets declined during this period, LB lending to foreign NFCs increased significantly from 7.8 per cent of total LB assets in 2000 to 14.8 per cent in 2008. Thus, the LBs continued to lend. However, they did so increasingly abroad. Domestic lending patterns also reflect sluggish economic growth for part of this period and compartmentalized domestic markets, rather than low securitization levels per se. Interestingly, despite their huge write-downs at the height of the financial crisis in 2008 and 2009, official figures indicate that the LB also increased their lending markedly in both years—although this dropped from 2010. Heavily reliant on covered bonds for their funding and able to draw on support from their Bundesland owners, LBs also did not face the same pressures to raise funding or capital from markets. Thus the impact of losses on capital had less impact on LB lending than on lending by the commercial banks.

Much of our analysis on the asset side of German bank balance sheets might be interpreted as broadly supportive of the 'neoliberal convergence' thesis

[25] It should be noted that LB lending as a percentage of assets had been declining for over two decades from over 60 per cent of LB assets in the early 1980s.

(see, for example, Soederberg et al. 2005). Certainly, losses on assets played a significant part, via reduced bank capital, in the credit difficulties of German commercial banks. On the liability side of the balance sheet, however, we see continued and significant divergence. Change took place in Germany, but this was far less significant than what took place in the United Kingdom during the first years of the twenty-first century (Hardie and Maxfield, this volume). The fact that the UK banks became more market-based changed the determinants, even before the crisis, of their capacity to finance the UK economy. This was much less the case in Germany. Despite the early prominence of German banks in this crisis, thanks to market-based assets, relatively low market-based liabilities were central to Germany's NFCs facing less impact on their ability to borrow than NFCs in many other countries in this volume.

Conclusions

The German banking system was one of the worst hit in the very early stages of the international financial crisis both in terms of the absolute levels of write-downs and write-downs to GDP. At the same time, German bank lending was only marginally affected by the crisis and the core element of the German coordinated market economy—patient lending—was never fundamentally undermined. Part of the explanation of this paradox is obvious, and very much in line with the standard view of the German banking system: hundreds of domestically focused smaller savings and cooperative banks came to the rescue. However, the full explanation is that the big German commercial banks and public sector LBs were engaged in high levels of market-based banking on the asset side of the balance sheet but less so on the liabilities side—with some important exceptions. The nature of German bank assets, especially their involvement in ABCP programmes that threatened the survival of some banks, was not clear before the crisis, and is central to understanding the very serious difficulties in a country that had not seen house price appreciation and where the crisis was initially seen as an 'American problem'. The attitude was the same as the Japanese (Kamikawa, this volume), but the Germans were wrong. This activity had a material negative impact not only on the banks which actually or effectively failed but also on the capital positions of other banks. For those banks which rely on private markets to raise capital (i.e. the commercial banks), this appears to have had a direct impact on the ability to lend, compounded by the unusually high leverage of German banks. For the LB, with their state and savings bank support, it was the EU competition authorities which had the greater impact. In the case of Westdeutsche Landesbank, a serial offender in terms of problematic investment banking related activities, the EU requirements dissolved the bank.

German commercial banks and the LB appear to have long had a high dependence on borrowing from the market to finance their lending activities, suggesting they should have shared the experiences of, for example, UK (Hardie and Maxfield, this volume) and Spanish (Royo, this volume) banks in facing a 'credit crunch' as a result of difficulties for banks themselves to raise funding. In reality, however, the funding gap of German banks is not a good indicator of the likely impact of market pressures on lending in Germany. As in the Netherlands (Chang and Jones, this volume), market sources of funding were relatively more stable. Whereas UK and Spanish banks borrowed heavily from international banks, German banks borrowed from each other (on Italy, see Pagoulatos and Quaglia, this volume), including from connected smaller savings and cooperative banks which also purchased unsecured bond issues and sold them to their individual clients (as in Italy). Whereas UK and Spanish banks relied on securitization markets that closed early in the crisis, German banks were more dependent on the relatively less fragile covered bond market, and German covered bonds, *Pfandbriefe*, were seen by investors as more attractive than their equivalent elsewhere. Overall, market-based banking on the liabilities side of German bank balance sheets is relatively low, despite initial appearances. German banks therefore faced less difficulty in financing lending.

For all the sound and fury of the German experience of the financial crisis, and the important developments in the years preceding, it may be that the net result of this period will be a banking system that, at least in the immediate future, looks more, not less like the literature's standard perception of that system. Prior to the crisis, the market-based nature of German bank assets was increasing rapidly, and even smaller savings banks were being offered the opportunity to hedge the credit risks of lending using credit default swaps. The LBs were central to these developments. Despite being supposedly not strictly profit maximizing, they engaged in a range of activities that can only be explained as aimed at increasing profitability and, despite their lack of private shareholders, return on equity. LB Sachsen, which subsequently failed as a result of its ABCP activity, in 2003 set a target for return on equity higher than was then being achieved by Deutsche Bank (Kirchfeld and Simmons 2008). 'Never again' has been said often about some of the LB activities in the past, so any conclusions must be cautious, but there does appear to be a fundamental change occurring. It is certainly 'never again' for LB Sachsen and Westdeutsche LB. It appears highly likely that the LBs, a key driver of increased market-based banking in Germany, will not play this role again in the immediate future.

The other main drivers of market-based banking have been the large commercial banks. Just as in the United States, United Kingdom, and France, their investment banking activities have undergone profound change, from buying advisory-based British 'merchant' banks to the large balance sheet positioning of securities and derivatives. The future for these businesses is likely to mirror developments elsewhere, but initial moves in Germany are at least suggestive of a less market-based strategy: Deutsche Bank has taken over Postbank to bolster its German retail business, and Dresdner Bank has been taken over by the less market-based Commerzbank.[26] The large German commercial banks have faced serious problems during the crisis, with very clear parallels with the experience, for example, of the United Kingdom, but a significant difference has been the ability of smaller banks, so central to the distinctiveness of the German system, to fill any gap in lending that results.

The initial impact of the financial crisis on Germany was severe. German banks were amongst the first casualties, its third largest commercial bank was taken over with government assistance, and two of the LBs that regional politicians had previously seen as central to their local economies disappeared. These are significant developments, and came as a profound shock to initial German complacency that was more widespread than the focus on the quotation-worthy Peer Steinbrück might suggest. The stability of German banking was far more dependent on the market than was generally realized. However, this dependence was also far more concentrated on one side of the balance sheet than in the 'Anglo-Saxon' banking systems that also experienced early problems. This explains why Germany saw less impact on the real economy from the difficulties of German banking—although the collapse of exports caused an immediate and deep contraction. The future is, of course, uncertain, but initial developments point to a potential reduction in market-based banking in Germany as a result of the crisis.

References

Adrian, T. and H. S. Shin (2010). 'The Changing Nature of Financial Intermediation and the Financial Crisis of 2007–09'. Federal Reserve Bank of New Staff Reports No. 439 (April).

Asmussen, J. (2006). 'Verbriefungen aus Sicht des Bundesfinanzministeriums'. *Kreditwesen*, 19: 1016–1018.

Brunner, A. D., J. W. Decressin, D. C. Hardy, and B. Kudela (2004). 'Germany's Three-Pillar Banking System Cross Country Perspective in Europe.' *IMF Occasional Paper, No. 233.*

Bloomberg (2008). Available at <http://www.bloomberg.com/apps/news?pid=20601087&sid=a8sW0n1Cs1tY&refer=home>, accessed 17 June 2009.

Bayerische Landesbank (2009). *Annual Report 2008*. Available at <http://www.gb08.bayernlb.de/bayernlb/annual/2008/gb//English/pdf/report.pdf>.

[26] On Commerzbank pre crisis, see Hardie and Howarth 2009.

Bomfim, A. N. (2005). *Understanding Credit Derivatives and Related Instruments*, San Diego and London: Elsevier.

Deeg, R. (1999). *Finance Capitalism Unveiled: Banks and the German Political Economy*. Ann Arbor: University of Michigan Press.

—— (2010). 'Industry and Finance in Germany since Unification.' *German Politics and Society*. Issue 95 Vol. 28, No. 2: 116–129.

Deutsche Bundesbank (2006). 'The economic situation of small and medium-sized enterprises in Germany since 1997', Monthly Report, December

—— (2007a). *2007 Financial Stability Review*, November. Available at <http://www.bundesbank.de/download/volkswirtschaft/mba/2007/financialstabilityreiview2007.pdfm>, accessed 21 July 2009.

—— (2007b). *Annual Review 2006*. Available at <http://www.db.com/ir/en/download/entire_Annual_Report_2006.pdf>.

—— (2010). *Finanzstabilitätsbericht*. Frankfurt am Main: Deutsche Bundesbank.

Deutsche Bank (2009a). 'Basel II Pillar 3 Report 2008'. Available at <http://www.db.com/ir/en/download/Basel_II_Pillar_3_Report_2008_FINAL.pdf>, accessed on 4 January 2010.

—— (2009b). *Annual Review 2008*. Available at <http://www.db.com/ir/en/download/DB_Annual_Review_2008_entire.pdf>, accessed on 4 January 2010.

DZ Bank (2009). 2008 Annual Report. Available at <http://www.dzbank.com/components/getirdl.php?id=139>, accessed on 4 January 2010.

ECB (European Central Bank) (2008). *Annual Report*, Frankfurt.

European Securitisation Forum (2009). ESF Securitisation Data Report Q4: 2008. Available at <http://www.afme.eu/Documents/Statistics-and-reports.aspx>, accessed on 4 January 2010.

Fischer, M. J., C. Hainz, J. Rocholl, and S. Steffen (2011). 'Government Guarantees and Bank Risk Taking Incentives', AFA 2012 Chicago Meetings Paper. Available on-line; accessed on 12 September 2012.

FitchRatings (2007). Asset-Backed Commercial Paper & Global Banks Exposure—10 Key Questions. Available at www.fitchratings.com/dtp/pdf3-07/babp1209.pdf, accessed on 12 January 2010.

HSH Nordbank (2009). Annual Report 2008. Available at <http://www.hsh-nordbank.com/media/en/pdf/investorrelations/geschaeftsber/2008/gb2008/annualreport2008.pdf>, accessed on 4 January 2010.

Hackethal, A. (2004). 'German Banks and Banking Structure', In *The German Financial System*, 2nd edition (eds J. P. Krahnen and R. H. Schmidt). Oxford: OUP, 71–105.

Hall, P. and Soskice, D. (eds) (2001). *Varieties of Capitalism: The Institutional Foundations of Comparative Advantage*, Oxford, Oxford University Press.

Hardie, I. and D. Howarth (2009). 'Die Krise but not La Crise? The financial crisis and the transformation of German and French banking systems.' *Journal of Common Market Studies*, vol. 47, no. 5: 1017–1039.

—— (2011). 'Market-based banking and the financial crisis'. Working paper. Available at <http://www.pol.ed.ac.uk/staff_profiles/hardie_iain/?a=64561>.

Hüfner, F. (2010). 'The German Banking System: Lessons from the Financial Crisis'. *OECD Economics Department Working Papers*, No. 788.

Hypo Real Estate (2009). *Annual Report 2008*. Available at <http://www.hyporealestate.com/eng/pdf/AR2008_09_04_24_final_GL.pdf>, accessed on 4 January 2010.

IKB Deutsche Industriebank (2009) *Annual Report 2008/09*. Available at <http://www.ikb.de/content/en/ir/financial_reports/annual_report_2008_2009/Konzern_englisch_090821_sicher.pdf>, accessed on 4 January 2010.

IMF (2003). 'Germany: Financial System Stability Assessment', IMF Country Report No. 03/343, November, Washington: IMF, accessed on 14 February 2009.

—— (2006). Germany: 2005 Article IV Consultation—Staff Report; Staff Supplement; Public Information Notice on the Executive Board Discussion; and Statement by the Executive Director for Germany', January 2006, IMF Country Report No. 06/16, Available at <http://www.imf.org>, accessed on 4 February 2009.

—— (2009a). 'France: 2009 Article IV Consultation—Staff Report; Public Information Notice on the Executive Board Discussion; and Statement by the Executive Director for France, IMF Country Report No. 09/232, July. Available at <http://www.imf.org>, accessed on 10 August 2009.

—— (2009b). 'Germany: 2008 Article IV Consultation—Staff Report; Staff Supplement'; Public Information Notice on the Executive Board Discussion; and Statement by the Executive Director for Germany. IMF Country Report No. 09/15, 13 January. Available at <http://www.imf.org>, accessed on 10 August 2009.

—— (2009c). 'United Kingdom: Staff Report for the 2009 Article IV Consultation; Public Information Notice on the Executive Board Discussion; and Statement by the Executive Director for United Kingdom', Country Report No. 09/212. Available at www.imf.org, accessed on 10 August 2009.

—— (2009d). *Global Financial Stability Report*, October. Available at <http://www.imf.org>, accessed on 23 November 2009.

Kirchfeld, A. and Simmons, J. (2008). Lehman Toxic Debt Advice Led Leipzig Bank to Ruin Via Dublin. Bloomberg, 28 October. Available at <http://www.verantwortliche-kreditvergabe.net>, accessed 18 June 2009.

Krahnen, J. P. and Schmidt, R. H. (eds) (2004b). *The German Financial System*, 2nd Edition. Oxford: OUP.

—— (2004). 'Taking Stock and Looking Ahead: The German System at the Crossroads?' In *The German Financial System*, 2nd edition (eds J. P. Krahnen and R. H. Schmidt). Oxford: OUP, pp. 483–516.

Landesbank Baden-Wurttemburg (2009). 'Financial Stability Forum Report as of December 31, 2008'. Available at www.lbbw.de/imperia/md/content/lbbwde/ueberuns/geschaeftsbericht/2008/en/FSF_Report_en_2009.pdf, accessed on 4 January 2010.

Landesbank Berlin (2009). *Annual Report 2008*. Available at <http://www.landesbankberlin.corporate-reports.net/reports/landesbankberlin/annual/2009/gb/English/0.html>, accessed on 5 January 2010

Landesbank Sachsen (2008). *Annual Report 2007*.

Lütz, S. (2000). 'From Managed to Market Capitalism? German Finance in Transition.' *German Politics* 9(2): 149–171.

Memmel, C. and Schertler, A. (2009). 'The Dependency of the Banks' Assets and Liabilities: Evidence from Germany', available at <http://ssrn.com/abstract=1353927>.

Nawrath, A. (2003). 'Rahmenbedingungen für den Finanzplatz Deutschland: Ziele und Aufgaben der Politik, insbesondere des Bundesministeriums der Finanzen'. *Working Paper, Institute for Law and Finance, University of Frankfurt.*

Norddeutsche Landesbank (2007). *Annual Report 2006.* Available at www.nordlb.com/fileadmin/redaktion/branchen/investorrelations/geschaeftsberichte/2006/Annual_Report_2006.pdf, accessed on 4 January 2010

Nowak, Eric (2004). 'Investor Protection and Capital Market Regulation in Germany.' In *The German Financial System* (eds Jan P. Krahnen and Reinhard H. Schmidt). Oxford: Oxford University Press, 71–105.

Reuters (2010) 'FACTBOX-U.S., European bank writedowns, credit losses', 28 January, <http://www.reuters.com/article/idUSLDE60R0Z020100128>. Accessed 21 June 2011.

Sachverständigenrat (2007). *Gutachten 2007–2008: Das Erreichte nicht verspielen.* Sachverständigenrat zur Begutachtung der gesamtwirtschaftlichen Entwicklung, Wiesbaden.

Sachverständigenrat (2008). *Das deutsche Finanzsystem: Effizienz steigern—Stabilität erhöhen.* Sachverständigenrat zur Begutachtung der gesamtwirtschaftlichen Entwicklung, Wiesbaden.

Scotia Capital (2010) *Canadian Banks Annual Review*, February. Available on-line. Accessed 4 June 2012.

Shonfield, A. (1965). *Modern Capitalism. The Changing Balance of Public and Private Power.* Oxford: Oxford University Press.

Soederberg, S., G. Menz and P. Cerny (2005). *Internalizing Globalization: The Rise of Neo-Liberalism and the Decline of National Varieties of Capitalism*, Basingstoke: Palgrave.

Streeck, W. (1997). 'German Capitalism: Does it Exist? Can it Survive?' *New Political Economy* 2(2), 237–256.

Westdeutsche Landesbank (2009). *Financial Report 2008*, Available at <http://www.westlb.de/>, accessed on 4 January 2010.

Xiao, Y. (2009). 'French Banks Amid the Global Financial Crisis.' IMF working Paper, European Department, September, WP/09/201.

Zysman, J. (1983). *Governments, Markets, and Growth*, Oxford: Martin Robertson.

6

State Intervention and Market-Based Banking in France*

David Howarth

Introduction

French banks and their representative associations explain the comparative stability of the French banking system during the international financial crisis that erupted in 2007 in terms of a 'balanced business model' with both a strong retail base and a full range of investment banking activities (Lee 2010; Pauget 2009; Ministry of Finance officials 2010). This chapter explains this 'balanced business model' as the product of French state disengagement from the financial sector since the mid-1980s but also continued state intervention. The specificities of this intervention involved the creation of national banking champions, a highly consolidated, saturated, and competitive retail banking sector, cross-shareholding networks centred around banks, a closed banking system with only limited foreign presence due to both de facto protectionism (despite the encouragement of open equity markets) and a legislated bias towards retail for some of the mutual banks. The French state also deliberately—and very successfully—encouraged specific forms of financial innovation, notably derivatives. The unintended consequence of this action was that French banks downplayed securitization and the purchase of securitized products, thus limiting the impact of the financial crisis. The state was less successful in its repeated efforts to facilitate securitization. Banks themselves were agents of change, notably through their efforts to expand in the context of sluggish domestic economic growth and a saturated domestic retail market. French banks engaged increasingly in 'market-based banking' activities and

* 'This chapter borrows from David Howarth (forthcoming) 'France and the International Financial Crisis: The Legacy of State-Led Finance.' *Governance*.

expanded their retail operations abroad. The focus of this analysis parallels that of Mary O'Sullivan (2007), which emphasizes the French state's role in directing financial market reform but also highlights the post-liberalization role of economic actors in shaping the financial system. However, the focus here is on how the intended and less deliberate effects of state action shaped the features of French banking that can be described as systemic.

John Zysman's (1983) analysis of France as the best example of a state-led credit-based financial system provides little guidance as to the French variety of financial capitalism today. However, the footprint of the state, through a directed and incomplete liberalization, has created a specific kind of financial system, the intended and unintended features of which have been revealed in the impact of the international financial crisis on the system since 2008. The argument of this chapter thus builds upon the comparative political economy literature that stresses the transformation of French capitalism away from a state-led model yet struggles to categorize France in the liberal market economy (LME)/coordinated market economy (CME), dichotomy of the varieties of capitalism (VoC) literature (Hall and Soskice 2001; Culpepper 2008), or depicts it as a unique hybrid form (Boyer 1997; Hancké 2001).[1] The argument here about the development of the French banking system also aligns with the conclusions reached by Vivien Schmidt (2003, 2009), who describes France as a state-enhanced/state-influenced form of capitalism. However, the claim of an important legacy of state intervention does not suggest, let alone prove, continued state intervention, even of a more modest kind.

Similarly, France's financial system cannot be easily categorized. It contains features of the liberalized, deregulated, and more capital market-based British system but also features of the more protected, regulated, and bank credit-based financial systems of southern Europe and Germany. In Zysman's (1983) depiction of the French financial system as 'state-led credit-based', the French state directed finance through state owned banks in the *Circuit du Trésor* system (see also Loriaux 1991). Despite liberalization and the privatization of most of the large French banks from the mid-1980s, studies from the mid-1990s continued to assign a central importance to the state in the context of a 'financial network economy' (Story and Walter 1997; Underhill 1997). This description was already being challenged (Morin 1998, 2000) and had become less valid by the early 2000s. Yet France remained difficult to situate in terms of the credit-based/capital-based dichotomy, with Andreas Hackethal (2000, 13) describing the French financial system as a 'special case which seems hard to classify'.

Indeed, snapshots of the French financial system tell us very different stories if we look at non-financial company (NFC) external funding or total

[1] France has also been described as a Mixed Market Economy (MME) along with southern European forms of capitalism, but this is a broad category containing considerable institutional variety (Hancké, Rhodes, and Thatcher 2007).

Table 6.1. Non-financial company finance 1970s to 2000 (percentage of total)

	Bank lending	Debt securities	Equity (listed and unlisted)
1978–84 average*	67.4	3.5	29.1
2000**	16.1	3.4	79

*The NFCs do not include state-owned companies and public utilities. The total figure covers only lending, bonds and equity, excluding trade credits and other sources of external finance.
**The remaining 1.4 per cent consists of monetary market instruments.

Source: 1978–84 figures from Cobham and Serre 2000, 49; 2000 figures from Byrne and Davis 2002, 89.

financial system assets—two typical measures used to categorize financial systems. French NFC external finance moved from heavy reliance on bank lending prior to the 1990s to heavy reliance on equity finance by 2000 (Table 6.1). The French financial system had, by this important measure, become more 'Anglo-Saxon' than the United Kingdom by the late 1990s (80 versus 70 per cent equity in 2000).

However, if we look at total financial assets (which is standard for categorizing financial systems; see Allen and Gale 2000) banks continued to dominate the French financial system. Bank assets increased significantly rising to 334.8 per cent of gross domestic product (GDP) in 2007 (up from 140 per cent in 1993). The French banking system was one of Europe's largest, and broadly similar in size to Germany's despite the smaller French economy. In terms of bank assets to GDP, France's banking system was only somewhat smaller than the United Kingdom's (399.7 in 2007) and considerably bigger than Germany's (195.5 per cent).[2] Equity market capitalization also increased significantly in real terms reaching a peak of 105.5 per cent of GDP in 2007 (up from 36 per cent in 1993).[3] However, the importance of bank assets increased as a percentage of total French financial assets, which paralleled the trend in most developed economies (see Figure 1.2 in the Introduction to this volume).

France thus might be best described as having an 'equity-dependent but still largely bank-based financial system' an apparent contradiction explained largely in terms of the limited position of domestic lending in total bank assets (see Table 6.4). Yet in the 2000s, bank lending rose in real and relative importance as a source of finance for NFCs in relation to equity issuance and securities (Table 6.2), paralleling developments in several advanced

[2] The French financial system remains considerably smaller than the British owing to the comparatively limited development of other financial market actors (including hedge funds).

[3] As a percentage of total financial assets, equity rose from 3.7 per cent in 1980 (a third of UK levels) to 21 per cent in 2000 (just short of British levels at 24.1 per cent). Equity market capitalization as a percentage of GDP can fluctuate significantly. The figures used (from 2000 and 2007) represent peaks: the relative size of bank assets was larger between these years.

Table 6.2. Finance raised by French non-financial companies since 1990 (outstanding, € billion)

Funds by source/ date (end of year)	Bank loans from domestic credit institutions only	Securities (in all currencies combined)	Equities (listed only)
1990	440.6	101.1	206.2
1995	441.5	134.1	308.4
2000	507.3	233.1	1235.3
2005	579.6	279.3	1119
2006	630.5	280.1	1379.2
2007	713.3	275	1501.1
2008	781.6	295.9	891.7
2009	769.3	345.9	1080.2

Source: 'Loans: Banque de France, Credit Institution Credits to NFCs.' Available online at <http://www.banque-france.fr/fr/statistiques/base/statmon/telnomot/mh.m.ec.credit.3.r.1b.to.t.m.x.b.x.csv>. Securities and equity, ECB Statistical Data Warehouse.

industrialized economies, including the United States and United Kingdom (Hardie and Maxfield in this volume). Contradicting previous trends and expectations, this largely reflected the end of big privatization programmes, bear equity markets and low real interest rates. As will be shown below, 'market-based banking' also contributed to the real and relative rise in bank lending.

The Significant but Comparatively Limited Impact of the Financial Crisis on France

Total French bank losses have been lower than those in the United States, United Kingdom, and Germany, and losses to bank assets and GDP have been far lower than a range of additional European countries, including the Netherlands, Belgium, and Switzerland (see Table 1.3 in the Introduction to this volume).[4] Moreover, French banks needed far less government support to cope with the crisis than the banks in these other countries. At the same time, France was far worse hit than the financial systems of southern Europe, at least in initial stages of the crisis. French bank losses have been on an unprecedented scale: total write-downs for the 2007–10 period for the five largest banks reached US$72.4 billion (Reuters 2011). Table 6.3 sets out French bank losses from 2007 to 2010 and the announced areas of those losses, sourced from the banks' reports and accounts. The data are possibly partial because they show what the banks have deemed material enough to highlight.

[4] One international comparison (Xiao 2009; IMF 2009, 15) on the direct cost of the crisis for large international banks shows that the direct cost for French banks (to April 2009) was about 18 per cent of Tier 1 capital, lower than that of Germany (about 33 per cent), the United Kingdom (about 37 per cent), the United States (about 86 per cent), and Switzerland (about 87 per cent).

Table 6.3. French bank losses

	Total Write-downs 2007–10 ($US bn)	Write-downs 2007–10/total Assets (at end 2007) per cent	CDO/ MBS	LBO	Mono-line*	ABCP/ SIV	Other Trading	Iceland/ LLehman/ Washington Mutual
BNP-Paribas	28.3	1.67	X	X	X		X	X
Société Générale	18.6	1.74	X		X			
Crédit Agricole	18.6	1.32	X		X		X	
Crédit Mutuel	N/A	N/A	X				X	X
Caisse d'Epargne	Share of Natixis 6.9	N/A	X		X	X	X	X
Banques Populaires	Share of Natixis 6.9	N/A	X		X	X	X	X

*Exposure to insurance companies that provided guarantees for various types of securities.

Source: 'FACTBOX-U.S., European bank writedowns, credit losses', Reuters, 24 February 2011. Available online at <http://www.reuters.com/article/2011/02/24/banks-writedowns-losses-idUSLDE71N1J720110224>. Reuters/ annual reports/company filings/registration documents. Author's own calculations. Estimates based on write-downs and losses from sub-prime securities, mortgages, CDOs, derivatives and SIVs, and losses on bad loans, or non-performing loans.

The information about bank losses points to important features of French bank liberalization and investment banking activities which will be linked back to state intervention in the analysis later in this chapter. Notably, the crisis affected both commercial and mutual banks alike. Mutual banks are majority owned by their depositors and, at least in principle, operated for their benefit, rather than, as with the listed commercial banks, for the benefit of private shareholders. Given their more limited exposure to commercial pressures, many observers were taken by surprise by their losses (Hardie and Howarth 2009). Two mutual banks, Banques Populaires and the Caisse d'Epargne, were badly affected through the difficulties faced by their common investment banking arm, Natixis, and merged in 2010 to form BPCE. Crédit Agricole, the part mutual bank, suffered significant losses, notably through its investment banking arm, Calyon (renamed Crédit Agricole CIB in 2010), which was badly exposed to US subprime. These losses demonstrate the shift in mutual bank operations that took place in the decade prior to the financial crisis.

However, the figures also show that individual French banks were in good shape comparatively. In terms of total write-downs, the biggest French loser, BNP-Paribas, was (at the end of 2010) in sixteenth place globally and in distant seventh place in Europe (Reuters 2011). The two largest French commercial banks—BNP-Paribas and Société Générale—and Crédit Agricole reported profits in both 2008 and 2009, with each suffering only one quarter loss during the two-year period despite rising write-downs in 2009. The persistently high French bank leverage ratios (assets/shareholder equity) suggest a weak capital position (an average of 46 in 2010, well above the European average of 35) (Crédit Suisse 2010) and a high potential exposure to the financial crisis. However, these concerns over the leverage of French banks were mitigated by their comparatively strong Tier 1 capital ratio (Crédit Suisse 2010; *Financial Times*, 23 July 2010). French banks were exposed to the secondary effects of the financial crisis but less to domestic write-downs caused by slow domestic economic growth and more through their portfolio of international loans and government sovereign debt. French banks were heavily exposed to several Euro area countries more at risk of default—notably the southern European countries—and thus the impact of a traditional banking crisis. Much of the exposure in Italy and Greece owes to the expansion of retail banking activities in those two countries, an important feature of French bank internationalization.[5]

How Gallic 'Market-Based Banking' Limited the Impact of the Financial Crisis upon France

French banks and government officials claim that the large retail banking businesses and diversified operations of the French banks—that is, their 'balanced business model'—lessened the overall impact of the crisis. Retail banking continued to dominate domestic banking activities with over three-quarters of total domestically held bank financial assets throughout the 2000s (Table 6.4). Retail bank lending (both domestic and international) declined significantly as a percentage of the total bank financial assets between 2000 and 2007. Retail lending nonetheless increased significantly in total terms at both the domestic and international levels (Table 6.4). The internationalization of French banking contained an important retail element (see also Table 6.5). In comparison, the internationalization of German and British banking was almost exclusively in corporate lending and investment banking (on the United Kingdom see Hardie and Maxfield in this volume; on Germany see Hardie and Howarth in this volume and Hackethal 2004, 77). The internationalization of French bank assets and liabilities increased significantly in the decade prior to the crisis. However, this internationalization remained moderate compared to other large banking systems at just over 30 per cent of the total for both assets and liabilities and 100 per cent of GDP (2007 figures).[6]

Despite the comparative importance of retail banking and the comparatively limited internationalization of assets and liabilities, French banks were still heavily engaged in market-based banking. Indeed, by two measures—reliance

[5] Total French bank exposure to the so-called PIGS (Portugal, Ireland, Greece, and Spain) reached €334.8 billion in 2010 (BIS, December 2010). French banks were the most heavily exposed to Greece (€67.8) and the second most exposed to Spain. French banks were also the most exposed to Italy at €336.3 billion (end September 2010 figures, BIS).

[6] The internationalization of British assets and liabilities was far higher at well over 60 per cent of the total for both and 250 per cent of GDP. German internationalized assets were at 55 per cent of the total and at a similar level of GDP (ECB Statistical Data Warehouse).

Table 6.4. French financial institutions, financial assets 1980–2007 (billion euros)

	Total held in France (excl. Banque de France)	Total domestic lending (incl. MFIs and public sector)	Total lending to private sector	Total Euro area (lending, debt, shares and financial products)	Total rest of world (lending, debt, shares and financial products)	Total international lending (incl. MFIs and public sector)	Total lending/ total assets (%)	Total not linked to geographic zone (incl. financial assets held for trading/ derivatives)	Total
1980	601	558	305	25	61	N/A	N/A	65	752
1990	1610	1433	820	101	256	N/A	N/A	223	2190
1995	1984	1664	838	133	359	326.6	90.9	297.3	2763.3
2000	2561	2003	1046	314	468	341.6	62.7	395	3737
2004	3203	2416	1264	555	609	378	60.5	417	4784
2007	4129	3211	1732	1012	1004	732.3	55.3	976	7120

Source: Banque de France. 'Statistiques monétaires mensuelles: France, Bilan des Institutions Financières et Monétaires hors Banque de France (encours)'. Available online at <http://www.banque-france.fr/fr/statistiques/base/statmon/html/tmf_mens_france_fr_bilifmhbdfe.htm>, and 'Statistiques monétaire trimestrielles, Créances et engagements des Institutions Financières et Monétaires.' Available online at <http://www.banque-france.fr/fr/statistiques/base/statmon/html/idx_tmf_trim_ifm_fr_fr.htm>.

Table 6.5. French Bank internationalization (lending exposure)

BNP-Paribas	Lending outside France rose from 61 per cent in 2001 to 65 per cent in 2007. Lending business to the rest of the European Economic Area rose from 18 per cent of total in 2001 to 30 per cent in 2007.
Société Générale	Lending outside France rose from 35 per cent in 2003 to 50 per cent in 2007. Exposure outside Europe rose from 10 per cent in 2003 to 19 per cent of total in 2007.
Crédit Agricole	Lending outside France rose from 18.4 per cent 2001 to 56.3 per cent in 2007. Lending business in the rest of the EU increased from 4.9 per cent to 33.9 per cent. Lending to the rest of the world increased from 14.5 per cent in 2001 to 22.4 per cent.

Source: Bank registration documents. Authors' own calculations.

on loans and deposits as a percentage of, respectively, total assets and liabilities, the French banking system was one of the most market based on the planet and had moved furthest from the 'traditional' model of banking of deposit taking and lending out of all the banking systems examined in this volume. At the end of 2007, French bank deposits were only 20.3 per cent of total liabilities, with the United Kingdom the next lowest at 26.2 per cent. French bank loans were only 36.6 per cent of total assets, with Germany the next lowest at 40.1 per cent. It is necessary to examine the patterns of French market-based banking in order to understand the limited impact of the financial crisis on French banks.

Assets

The trading activity of French banks and, in particular, the use of derivatives in trading activities increased rapidly in the decade leading to the crisis

(Table 6.6). Taking the banking system at large, financial assets held for trading *exceeded* both German and UK levels in 2008 (38 per cent of total assets versus 34.5 and 36.7 per cent) (ECB Statistical Data Warehouse). French banks specialized in equity, interest, and exchange rate derivatives. Over the two decades prior to the crisis, French banks consistently engaged in approximately a quarter of global equity derivatives trading (Fédération Bancaire de France, 2007). For several years (2003–7) Société Générale was one of the world's leading traders of equity derivatives and for five years running (2003–7) reported more profits from equity derivative trading than any other bank globally. Earnings growth from these business lines mitigated the impulse to extend into credit derivatives (securitization) to the same extent as UK, US, or, even, German banks. Thus French banks were comparatively less exposed to the immediate effects of the financial crisis which hit hard trading in asset-backed securities (ABS), asset-backed commercial paper (ABCP), collateralized debt obligations (CDOs), and credit default swaps (CDS).

Yet some French banks were also heavily involved in the forms of market-based banking that were most linked to the financial crisis. Crédit Agricole, through its investment bank Calyon, was the world's sixth largest trader of CDOs (Barnett-Hart 2009, 19; with figures from credit rating agencies), more than any European bank apart from UBS and more than several of the largest US investment banks combined.[7] Two French banks

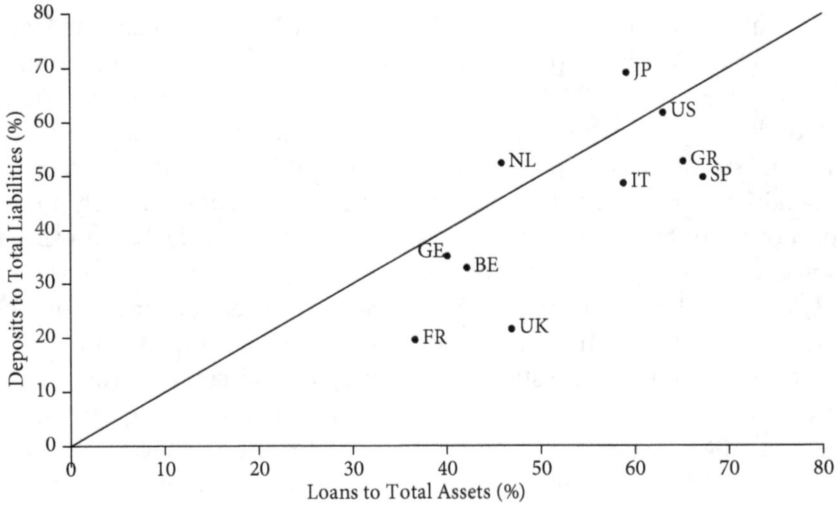

Figure 6.1. Loans to assets and deposits to liabilities, selected countries, end 2007

Sources: ECB (www.ecb.int/stats/money/consolidated/html/index.en.html); Cabinet Office 2008; Federal Reserve (www.federalreserve.gov/releases/h8/current/default.htm); IMF 2010, 16.

[7] Calyon issued more CDOs than Goldman, Lehman, Bear Stearns, Morgan Stanley, or JP Morgan.

Table 6.6. Increased bank trading activity (trading assets as a percentage of total assets, peak year)

BNP-Paribas	51.8 (2007) (14.2 in 2002).
Société Générale	31.9 (2006) (more than double 2002). Fall to 28.6 in 2007.
Crédit Agricole	30.2 (2007).
Caisse d'Epargne	10.5 (2007).
Crédit Mutuel	13.8 (2008) (2007 not available).

Source: Bank registration documents; author's own calculations.

were heavy traders in CDS. When the recipients of collateral postings for CDS by the American insurance giant, AIG (using US government support) were revealed, Société Générale headed the list, receiving US$11 billion, 22 per cent of the total. Calyon, the Crédit Agricole subsidiary, received a further US$2.3 billion. Named UK and German banks received less than their French counterparts, respectively, US$12.7 billion and US$7.7 billion. Luck therefore helped to diminish the impact of the financial crisis on French banks. The decision by the US Federal Government to bail out AIG meant that French bank losses were considerably lower than they could have been.

Liabilities

On the funding side, French banks relied *more* on wholesale markets than banks in most other European countries: 59.4 per cent of total liabilities in 2007 (Bank of France statistics). On the eve of the financial crisis, the French bank customer funding gap (loans minus deposits) was one the highest in the EU (see Figures 2.1 and 2.2, in Hardie and Howarth). The high level of French bank trading activities explains this heavy dependence on wholesale funds.

As with the assets side of the balance sheet, it is necessary to enter into the details on French bank liabilities to explain the comparatively limited impact of the financial crisis on French bank funding. French banks were less exposed to funding through off-balance sheet special investment vehicles (SIVs) and ABCP vehicles than banks in several other countries (Financial Intermediation Research Society 2008).[8] Banks were forced to bring these vehicles onto their balance sheet at the time of the financial crisis and find liquid funds to cover them. Globally, French banks were the fifth largest issuers of ABCPs. However, liquidity support to ABCP vehicles[9] in France reached only US$90.66 billion in 2007 or 3.5 per cent of GDP, far lower than in those European countries most affected by the crisis (Table 2.5 in Hardie

[8] See Hardie and Howarth (Chapter 2 in this volume) for a further discussion of off-balance sheet activities with regard to banks.

[9] Liquidity support to ABCP vehicles shows the exposure of a country's banks to being forced to accept assets fully onto their balance sheets, with capital and liquidity implications, as a result of ABCP funding being unavailable.

and Howarth). Twelve of the fourteen largest French banks did not sponsor ABCP vehicles at all.[10] Further, the limited securitization of bank lending in France diminished the effects of the financial crisis on the supply of credit. Outstanding collateral in securitizations at the end of 2008 was only 1.4 per cent of GDP in France—one of the lowest levels in western Europe—compared with 3.5 in Germany, over 10 per cent in Italy, over 20 per cent in Spain, and over 30 per cent in the United Kingdom.[11] The figure for ABCP collateral is 0.8 per cent of French GDP versus 4 per cent for the United Kingdom. Unlike in the United Kingdom, the Netherlands and even Spain, securitization was not crucial to the rise of French bank lending in the 2000s.

The sources of French bank funding help to explain the banks' relative stability in the context of the financial crisis. French banks financed themselves through debt securities more than the banks in more exposed European countries (€984 billion outstanding versus the United Kingdom's €553 billion) (although much less than Germany's €1638 billion) (ECB Statistical Data Warehouse). French bank debt was of a much lower maturity by Euro area standards, with 36.6 per cent up to a year in 2007 compared to German figures of 3.8 per cent.[12] French banks were thus potentially exposed to the difficulties of refinancing given the market conditions following the collapse of Lehman Brothers. However, refinancing was made easier because 'French banks' net foreign position (foreign claims minus foreign liabilities) was almost entirely denominated in euros, which could be financed directly by domestic sources.... UK, Swiss, German and Dutch banks built up large net foreign positions denominated in US dollars' (BIS CGFS 2010, 1).[13] This was largely a reflection of the comparatively limited exposure of French banks to the dollar-denominated securities of US banks, which is explained below. French bank funding relied considerably less on short term inter-bank lending and considerably less on inter-bank lending from beyond the Euro area and, specifically, from US banks—which froze up during the financial crisis—than funding in several other European countries. Only about a quarter (25.6 per cent in 2007) of French inter-bank lending came from beyond the Euro area, compared to over half (51.7 per cent) for the Netherlands (BIS data).

[10] Société Générale and Natixis were exposed to a total of US$0.72 billion and US$2.82 billion of ABCP respectively and only Natixis suffered major losses in ABCP. In contrast more British and German large banks sponsored ABCP vehicles (5 out of 11 and 14 out of 25, respectively) (Arteta, Carey, Correa, and Kotter 2010).

[11] Author's calculations from SIFMA (2008) 'ESF Securitisation Data Report. Q4: 2008', 30 December, available at www.afme.eu/Documents/Statistics-and-Reports.aspx

[12] ECB figures: <http://www.ecb.int/stats/money/aggregates/bsheets/html/outstanding_amounts_2007-12.en.html>

[13] The euro denominated net foreign position owed to limited French bank exposure to US assets (including securities) and the Euro area focus of French bank internationalization.

How Declining State Intervention Shaped French Market-Based Banking

French banks were engaged in many of the same market-based banking activities as British and German banks. However, French banks were far smaller investors in the assets that became toxic (notably financial products based on American subprime mortgages), less involved in setting up off-balance sheet vehicles, relative to their size, less engaged in the securitization of lending, and less reliant on short-term inter-bank lending. These features of French banking can in part be explained in terms of bank strategy—some aspects of which are specific to individual banks. However, most of these features are broadly similar to all or most of the largest French banks (both the mutual and commercial banks) and should be described as systemic. They can ultimately be traced back to government policy: deliberate state efforts to build the French financial system in the 1980s and 1990s, strategy on national champions and explicit and implicit forms of protectionism.

The liberalization of the French financial system from the mid-1980s was substantial. All French banks were subject to the same broad legal framework, adopted in 1984, which allowed them to become universal banks. Prior to 1987, all the largest French banks were state owned. With the privatizations of 1987–2002, four of the largest French banks—Société Générale, Banque Nationale de Paris (BNP), the now defunct Crédit Lyonnais, and Crédit Commercial de France—became fully commercial operations, listed on the French stock exchange, the CAC-40. BNP's takeover of Paribas, an investment bank, in 1999, further expanded its trading activities. However, the comparative strength of all these banks remained in retail. Several others, most importantly Crédit Agricole, opted to become non-listed mutual banks, owned by smaller regional cooperative banks.[14] Three of the six largest French banks were mutuals (and one part-mutual in the case of Crédit Agricole) and engaged principally in retail banking. The late arrival of the mutuals to investment banking (starting in 1999) may explain the difficulties faced by their investment banking arms—and Calyon's heavy exposure to CDOs—given the push to expand rapidly. However, the retail focus of Natixis' and Calyon's parent mutual banks limited the overall damage. German Landesbanken (LBs), the publicly owned regional banks, did not have this retail focus which explains why their expansion owed more to investment banking activities to which they similarly came late (Hardie and Howarth 2009). Further, the two French commercial banks and Crédit Agricole were also big and listed (and thus could issue equity to fund foreign acquisitions) an option unavailable to the German LB and banks in some smaller European countries.

[14] Crédit Agricole was later part-listed on the CAC-40 stock exchange.

The 'balanced model' of French banking—and the relative importance of retail—can in part be explained by regulatory constraints. By the 2000s, French regulation was far less restrictive of investment banking than in some European countries, notably Spain or Italy, where regulation made it prohibitively expensive for banks to create off-balance sheet vehicles (Royo 2008, this volume; and Pagoulatos and Quaglia, this volume). All French banks were encouraged by French governments to engage in a full range of investment banking activities, including off-balance sheet securitization. Further, French banks were able to avoid building capital reserves in line with assumed risks. Neither the Basle II capital adequacy requirements and the EU capital requirement directive nor domestic legislation addressed this issue (Bank of France officials 29 January 2008; Banking Commission officials 9 December 2009). By the mid-2000s, World Bank indicators gave France comparatively low scores in measures of 'capital stringency' and of 'restrictions' imposed on banks' activities (see Table 1.3 in the Introduction to this volume) (Laeven and Levine 2008; data from Barth, Caprio, and Levine 2006).

However, the history of French regulation on securitization and off-balance sheet activities helps to explain comparatively limited usage. The French state actively encouraged banks to engage in securitization, starting with the creation of a legislative framework in 1988 which was intended to boost confidence in the financial technique by creating clear legal, accounting and tax rules, unlike the United Kingdom which opted for a laissez-faire approach (Baum 1994). The official aim of the French Treasury at the time was to help French banks cope with new BIS solvency ratio guidelines and EC rules (Directive no. 89/647, Solvency I) set to come into force at the start of 1993. The French state also wanted to support the international competitiveness of French banks and was concerned that British banks and American banks based in London would dominate securitization in Europe (Baum 1994; International Securitisation Report 1993). Securitization would give French banks access to the same funding options available to American and British competitors, in order to replace traditional funding sources, such as retail deposits and commercial paper, the costs of which were rising in the 1980s. Further, French governments saw in securitization a mechanism to increase lending to NFCs, especially medium-sized companies. Securitization, however, took off only slowly due in part to the intentional and unintentional technical, legal and financial obstacles in the 1988 legislation (Baum 1994), which limited the types of assets that could be securitized and created disincentives through rigid bankruptcy provisions that stemmed from existing French law. These obstacles were only gradually and partially eliminated over the next decade—the result being more limited securitization than in most other West European countries (relative to banking activities) into the 2000s. A significant part of the problem was the application to securitization of existing French investor protection rules—notably lengthy procedures and safeguards in the creation of SIVs—and accounting rules which discouraged off-balance sheet securitization into the 2000s. French governments pushed through a series of legislative changes starting in 1993 to facilitate securitization (Touraine and Grillo 2004; Ministry of Finance Officials 2010) with significant changes in 2003 (Doat and Nugue 2005) and as recently as 2008 (Burnat 2009).

Limited French government success in encouraging banks to increase their engagement in securitization owes in large part to the success of state action encouraging other forms of financial innovation. In particular, the French state encouraged the trading of equity, interest rate and exchange rate derivatives, on which French investment banking became more heavily reliant than banking in other European countries. In February 1986, the socialist government established the French futures market, the MATIF, and appointed a senior Treasury official and financial inspector, Gérard de la Martinière, to run it. The MATIF served several purposes (Mamou 1988; Story and Walter 1997). It provided market-enabling institutional investors to hedge against the risk of volatile interest or exchange rates. It represented France's response to the creation of the London-based LIFFE in 1982. It brought the Paris market into the world web of futures markets. Above all, the MATIF was a central element in modernizing issuance of state paper. All its major derivative products originated with the Treasury. The French state floated a long-term ECU contract in October 1990 with the specific aim of developing Paris as the centre for trade in ECUs, the euro's predecessor. Paris rapidly became the second market for futures in Europe and by the early 1990s, the MATIF was engaged in trading levels that were only marginally lower than the LIFFE. In 1987, Société Générale started derivatives trading within two months of being the first state-owned bank privatized. The rapid expansion of bank trading activities in the decade leading up to the crisis (Table 6.6) both reflects the saturation of domestic markets and the relative strength of French investment banking.

Other forms of state intervention help explain the retail focus of the French banking system and bank internationalization. Government legislation strongly affected the composition and allocation of a large part of financial savings through numerous schemes to mobilize and direct savings and credit towards programmes judged to be in the public interest. These schemes encompassed certain controls on interest rates and fees, the design by the government of various savings products (notably the *Livret A*), the centralization of about a quarter of bank deposits in a fund managed by the state-owned *Caisse des Dépôts et Consignations* (CDC), restrictions on the use of funds collected through some savings products, and significant differences in tax treatment between financial products. In 2003, about 80 per cent of bank deposits (including cheque accounts) were subject to significant product and/or price prescriptions, and differences in tax treatment have steered household savings towards life insurance products and saving for house purchases (IMF 2004). Amongst other effects, these policies distorted competition in the banking sector by restricting the distribution of certain products with only certain institutions, notably the public sector or mutual banks, allowed to offer specific tax-exempt or high rate savings products, thus placing commercial banks, both domestic and foreign, at a competitive disadvantage (Candida 2000). For example, the Post Office and two mutual banks, Crédit Mutuel and Caisse d'Epargne, were alone allowed to maintain the tax-exempt *Livret A*—until the start of 2009 from when all banks could offer this savings vehicle.[15] Fiscal policy thus unintentionally contributed to the retail-focus of the French mutual banks, a highly saturated domestic retail market, into which few foreign banks entered,[16] and a strong retail component to French bank internationalization—the saturated domestic market forced French banks to expand internationally. The kind of protectionism that persisted in Germany was markedly different. German Lander governments continued to provide guarantees to credit issued by the LBs until 2005, and the LB and Sparkassen continued to operate in what were in effect fiefdoms closed to other public sector banks. The comparison of French and German protectionism is revealing. French protectionism encouraged domestic retail activities, resulted in the saturation of the domestic market and retail expansion abroad. German protectionism created a moral hazard for German public banks to invest actively in ABS created by American banks.

In the 1980s and 1990s, French conservative governments encouraged the emergence of a limited number of large, vertically integrated banking groups controlled by French corporate shareholders—in a complex network of cross-shareholding with national firms, both to improve the stability of the system and to foster national champions—and a reflection of long-standing industrial strategy (Cohen 1995; Hayward 1995; Schmidt 1996). In response to increasing international and domestic competitive pressures, economic recession and sluggish growth from 1993, there was considerable concentration in the French banking sector, with eight of the largest banks created (or transformed) as the result of mergers (often steered by the French state)

[15] A significant part of the *Livret A* financed social housing (and was placed on the balance sheet of the CDC) and thus did not constitute a resource for other banking activities. Nonetheless, the *Livret A* effectively distorted competition in retail banking.

[16] In 2008, France was in fourth place in the EU for the number of branches per capita (ECB 2008). French owned credit institutions held 85 per cent of bank-held assets throughout the 2000s (IMF 2004, 103; IMF 2009, 44). This was lower than some parochial continental European banking systems—domestic banks controlled 92.8 per cent of bank assets in Spain (December 2005) (IMF 2006b)—but far below the foreign presence in the British banking sector, reaching up to 55.2 per cent in 2005 (ECB 2010).

from 1995 to 2004 (Fédération bancaire française 2009).[17] The French banking system became one of the most concentrated in the EU. Figures from 2007 show that the five largest French banks held 51.8 per cent of total assets, compared to 22 per cent in Germany, 33 per cent in Italy, 41 per cent in the United Kingdom, and 41 per cent in Spain (ECB 2008). By the late 1990s, four French banks were in the top 15 European banks by asset size.

Morin (2000, 37) describes the France of the 1980s and 1990s as a 'financial network economy'. The French government aimed to emulate the long-standing German practice of cross-shareholding networks, centring these around the then three largest commercial banks (BNP, Société Générale, and the now defunct Crédit Lyonnais) and the insurance giant AXA—a central feature of the national champion strategy—with the state retaining, indirectly, part ownership through the CDC, the para-statal financial institution that manages state pensions, and NFCs part-owned by the state. The 'hard core' concept reserved 25 per cent of privatized firms' capital to major bank or corporate shareholders, selected by the state. The expectation was that the state would be able to manipulate this 'hard core' to influence strategic management decisions and block takeovers by foreign banks. Most of the largest banks were directed by former ministry of finance officials, advisers to the finance minister and, in several cases, members of the financial inspectorate, the elite network, *grand corps*, of financial sector administrators (Schmidt 1996; Maclean, Harvey and Press 2001). 'Security and market transparency' legislation adopted in 1989 strengthened the *Commission des Operations du Bourse* to protect companies against hostile takeovers by other companies by forcing owners of over 33 per cent of a listed company's shares to make a bid for at least 66 per cent of shares. Despite increased competition among French banks, the government also encouraged the practice of 'interbancarité', with cooperation amongst the biggest banks through an electronic banking card system (Story and Walter 1997). The minitel information system, developed by the state-owned telecommunication monopoly, France Telecom, enabled French banks to access households directly, over fifteen years prior to the advent of internet banking in other countries (*Le Monde*, 22 October 1992). Thus while no explicit law blocked foreign take-overs of banks, throughout the 1990s it was widely believed that no French government would sell a privatized bank to foreigners and that the state would also step in to block foreign firms from taking too large a shareholding of the listed banks. The decision by the socialist-led Jospin government to allow the London-based HSBC to take over the regional branches of France's seventh largest bank Crédit Commercial de France (CCF) in 2000 could be seen as a sign of changing government attitudes (see *Le Monde*,

[17] The number of French credit institutions declined from 1556 in 1984 to only 959 by 2003 and 450 by 2008.

4 April 2000). However, no other French bank has since been taken over by a foreign bank and in 2008 Banques Populaires bought these branches back from HSBC.

There is a caveat to this picture of a protectionist French banking system. Within a few years of privatization, the cross-shareholding networks began to unravel and foreign control of the largest national banks increased (Culpepper 2005; Clift 2007; Maclean, Harvey, and Press 2001). Although French banks dominated the domestic banking system, the actual equity ownership of the two large commercial banks became increasingly foreign owned in the 1990s and 2000s. In 2002, foreigners owned 67 per cent of BNP-Paribas' equity capital and 50.8 per cent of Société Générale's. The two large French commercial banks were similar to other EU commercial banks in this regard with rapidly rising foreign ownership over the past two decades.[18] Despite the decline in cross-shareholding portfolios, important features of the 'financial network economy' remain (Dudouet and Grémont 2010; Clift 2011b), including shareholding pacts as between BNP Paribas and AXA. French mutual banks mostly did not open their capital, but Crédit Agricole—one of the largest retail banks in Europe—was partially opened to private shareholding in 2001. The actual impact of rising foreign ownership on bank operations is hard to isolate. Nevertheless, this opening and partial breakdown of cross-shareholding in French banks—and thus the decline of an important form of patient capital (Culpepper 2005)—is a likely influence on the pursuit of increased profits through more aggressive strategies including investment banking. Sluggish economic growth in France over much of the decade prior to the financial crisis encouraged expansion abroad. The relationship of French banks with NFCs—never as close as in Germany—became more distant (Bertero, 1994; O'Sullivan, 2007) as elements of the 'financial network' economy deteriorated (Morin, 1998, 2000). The importance of bank finance for French companies—especially the largest CAC-40 listed companies—declined dramatically in the 1980s and 1990s, and large French banks compensated by expanding retail operations abroad and by developing investment banking activities (Bank of France officials 29 January 2008).

To conclude, French banks operated as profit-maximizers and pursued domestic and international expansion. However, the manner in which they did this was dictated by conditions in the French banking system established to a large extent by deliberate state intervention. State efforts in actively prodding recently privatized banks to engage in derivatives trading and securitization also point to the relevance of work by scholars who emphasize

[18] For example, Deutsche bank, the largest German bank, was foreign-owned at 55 per cent in 2007, while the second largest Spanish commercial bank, BBVA, was foreign-owned at 45 per cent in 2008. See Deutsche Bank (2010). 'Shareholder Structure.' Available at <http://www.deutsche-bank.de/ir/en/content/shareholder_structure.htm>.

continued but more limited forms of state intervention to cope with contemporary challenges in global capitalism—in additional to Schmidt (2003, 2009), see Levy (2006), and Ben Clift's (2011a,b) elaboration on *post-dirigisme*. French government efforts to facilitate financial innovation fit well with Chris Howell's (2009) 'paradox of French state intervention' which suggests that the French state is engaged in new kinds of state activism—but that the upshot of this activism is a retreat from interventionism in the economy, and the increasing exposure of the institutions of the French economy to international market forces.

Conclusion

This chapter has sought to explain the limited but significant impact of the international financial crisis on the French banking system. The rise of market-based banking significantly changed the country's financial system over the past two decades, notably through the substantial rise in derivatives trading in the 2000–7 period. However, retail banking remained important both at home and in international operations. The strong retail component to French bank internationalization is in marked contrast to the internationalization of German and British banks which had, on average, far greater exposure to securitized assets and liabilities. For Italian and Spanish banks, meanwhile, internationalization was largely about the expansion of international retail banking activities (IMF 2006a,b; Quaglia 2009; Royo 2009), even though their engagement in securitization was, on average, at a higher level than French banks.

The crisis did not bring substantial changes to the French banking system and even encouraged certain trends. The scaling down of some trading activities amidst the rhetoric of governments and many banks themselves for a necessary 'return' to traditional banking activities represents a time-honoured, and most likely time-limited, response to business problems (*Financial Times*, 10 September 2008). A retreat to the more cautious nationally-oriented banking of the past was highly unlikely in all but the very short term: the opportunities in domestic markets were limited and the lure of profits in risk-taking connected to derivatives trading remained. French banks—commercial and mutual—sought to expand their foreign retail and trading operations in order to increase profitability after the lean years of the mid-1990s. The result was record levels of profits for all six of the largest banks in the 2003–7 period.

Soft forms of protectionism and limited foreign penetration remained features. The upswing in state intervention as a result of the crisis was temporary. The state emerged as a substantial shareholder, in the case of BNP-Paribas the largest, but without voting rights. These shares were bought back by the banks in 2009 and 2010. The state-led merger of Caisse d'Epargne and Banques Populaires appears something of a throw-back to state interventionism. However, despite government rhetoric to the contrary, there was no state involvement in the micromanagement of the new bank. Rather the merger should be seen as an opportunistic move to further concentrate the banking system—by 2008 only 415 banks (715 credit institutions) continued to operate in the country down from 481 (975) in 2002 (Fédération Bancaire de France 2009; IMF 2009).

There was no significant overhaul of French regulatory and supervisory regimes that by 2008 provided full support to market-based banking, encouraging off-balance sheet activities and other financial innovations made difficult in the banking systems of southern Europe. The domestic regulatory response to the worst financial crisis affecting French banks since the Second World War was negligible (Hardie and Howarth 2009). The Bank of France and the government repeatedly challenged the assumptions behind 'Too big to fail' concerns (Noyer 2010; *Financial Times*, 16 November 2009). BNP-Paribas—actively supported by the French government in its take-over of Dexia and Fortis' Belgian and Luxembourg operations (Hardie and Howarth 2009)—became the largest bank in the world by assets in 2010, recording an increase of 34 per cent in three years. While the financial crisis resulted in a retreat in the international activities of British and German banking activities, the internationalization of French banking, principally in retail operations, proceeded apace.[19] From 2009, French banks were far more affected by the sovereign debt crisis afflicting the Euro area, suffering a significant downgrading by the three main credit rating agencies and major losses due to the internationally agreed 'haircut' on Greek sovereign debt holdings.

Over the twenty years prior to the international financial crisis that erupted in 2007, French governments repeatedly sought to facilitate securitization. However, the French state was more successful in encouraging banks to develop other operations—which resulted in the downplaying of securitization and the construction of a 'balanced business model' which sheltered French banks from the impact of the international financial crisis. The French state deliberately—and very successfully—encouraged derivatives trading through the creation of the MATIF and through Treasury issues. Ironically, it was the failure of repeated state efforts to facilitate securitization—in part due to well-rooted regulation that effectively hindered

[19] The non-French financial assets (loans, securities, shares and other financial products combined) held by French monetary financial institutions rose from 36.4 per cent of total financial assets at the end of 2007 to 38.1 per cent at the end of 2010. See Banque de France. 'Statistiques monétaires mensuelles: France, Bilan des Institutions Financières et Monétaires hors Banque de France (encours)'. Available at <http://www.banque-france.fr/fr/statistiques/base/statmon/html/tmf_mens_france_fr_bilifmhbdfe.htm>.

this form of financial innovation—that helped to shelter France from the financial crisis. Deliberate state efforts—reflecting a long-standing 'national champions' strategy—resulted in the construction of a small number of large French banks with a strong retail base and international retail presence—the unintentional consequence of which was to create a buffer for French banks facing significant losses due to the financial crisis. This construction of large retail-focused national champions was helped by a lingering protectionism that contributed to a highly saturated and foreign-bank unfriendly domestic retail market. Clearly, a crucial transformation in French political economy remains the move to a 'financial market' form of capitalism, as large and many medium-sized NFCs turned increasingly to the equity markets (often foreign) for finance and French banks looked abroad and to other activities to compensate (Morin, 1998, 2000). The drive of French banks to expand, with foreign equity issues and forms of market-based banking, contributed to the unravelling of the cross-shareholding groups created in the 1980s and 1990s and centred around the largest commercial banks. This chapter does not deny the importance of bank or NFC agency in reshaping the French financial system (Culpepper 2005; O'Sullivan 2007). However, state action played a crucial and largely deliberate role in shaping the French bank business model, internationalization and the peculiarities of French market-based banking.

References

Allen, F. and Gale, D. (2000). *Comparing Financial Systems*. Cambridge: The MIT Press.

Arteta, C., M. Carey, R. Correa and J. Kotter (2010). 'Revenge of the Steamroller: ABCP as a window on risk choices', 27 July. Available on-line at <http://apps.olin.wustl.edu/FIRS/PDF/2009/787.pdf>.

Bank of France officials (2008). *Interviews with the author*. Paris, 29 January.

Banking Commission officials (2009). *Interviews with the author*. Paris, Banking Commission, 9 December.

Barnett-Hart, A. K. (2009). 'The Story of the CDO Market Meltdown: An Empirical Analysis', BA Economics thesis, Harvard College, Cambridge, 19 March. Available on-line at <http://www.hks.harvard.edu/m-rcbg/students/dunlop/2009-CDOmeltdown.pdf>.

Barth, J. R., G. Caprio, and R. Levine (2006). *Rethinking Bank Regulation: Till Angels Govern*. New York: Cambridge University Press.

Baum, Th. (1994). 'Asset Securitization in Europe'. Working paper, 02/94 Frankfurt: Goethe University.

Bertero, E. (1994). 'The Banking System, Financial Markets, and Capital Structure: Some New Evidence from France.' *Oxford Review of Economic Policy* 10, 4, 68–78.

BIS CGFS. Committee on the Global Financial System (2010). 'The functioning and resilience of cross-border funding markets.' Paper no. 37, March.

Boyer, R. (1997). 'French Statism at the Cross-roads.' *Political Economy of Modern Capitalism*, eds. Crouch, Colin and Streeck, Wolfgang. London: Sage, 71–101.

Burnat, F. (2009). 'The Revival of French Securitisation: A Study of the 2008 Reform.' *Law and Financial Markets Review*, 3, 3, May: 227–231.

Byrne, J. P. and Davis, E. P. (2002). 'A Comparison of Balance Sheet Structures in Major EU Countries.' *National Institute Economic Review* 180: 83.

Candida, D. (2000). *The Future of European Retail Banking*. Reuters Business Insight. Available online at <http://reutersbusinessinsight.com/allreports.asp?pa=FS&page_no=8>.

Clift, B. (2007). 'French Corporate Governance in the New Global Economy: Mechanisms of Change and Hybridisation within Models of Capitalism.' *Political Studies*, 55: 3, 546–567.

— (2011a). 'French responses to the global economic crisis: the political economy of "post-dirigisme" and new state activism.' In *Aftershock: The Global Financial Crisis and its Aftermath*, eds. Wyn Grant and Graham Wilson. Oxford: Oxford University Press, forthcoming.

— (2011b). 'Comparative Capitalisms, Ideational Political Economy and French Post-Dirigiste Responses to the Global Financial Crisis.' *New Political Economy*, forthcoming.

Cobham, D. and J.-M. Serre. (2000). 'A Characterization of the French Financial System.' *The Manchester School*, 68, January: 44–67.

Cohen, E. (1995). 'France: National Champions in Search of a Mission.' In *Industrial Enterprise and European Integration* (ed. J. Hayward). Oxford: Oxford University Press, 23–47.

Crédit Suisse (2010). 'French banks: Stress testing the French banks.' Equity Research, 2 July. Available online at <http://www.scribd.com/doc/33859604/CreditSuisse-French-Banks-20100702>.

Culpepper, P. (2005). 'Institutional Change in Contemporary Capitalism: Coordinated Financial Systems since 1990.' *World Politics*, 57:2, January, 173–199.

Culpepper, P. (2008). 'Capitalism, Coordination, and Economic Change: the French Political Economy since 1985.' In *Changing France: The Politics that Markets Make*, eds. Culpepper, Pepper, Hall, Peter, Palier, Bruno, Palgrave: Basingstoke, 29–49.

Deutsche Bank. 2010. 'Shareholder Structure'. Available online at <http://www.deutsche-bank.de/ir/en/content/shareholder_structure.htm>.

Doat, P. and Nugue, Ph. (2005). 'Whole Business Securitisations in Civil Law Jurisdictions: The French Example.' In *Securitisation of derivatives and alternative asset classes: yearbook 2005*, eds. Jan Job de Vries Robbé, Paul A. U. Ali. The Hague: Kluwer Law International, 381–386.

Dudouet, F.-X. and Grémont, E. (2010). *Les grands patrons en France: du capitalisme d'état* à *la financiarisation* Paris: Editions lignes de repères.

ECB (2008). *EU Banking Structures*. October, Frankfurt: ECB.

ECB (2010). *EU Banking Structures*. September, Frankfurt: ECB.

Fédération Bancaire de France (French Banking Federation) (2007). *Rapport d'Activité*. Paris: FBF.

Fédération Bancaire de France (2009). *Rapport d'Activité 2008*. Paris: FBF.

Financial Intermediation Research Society (The) (2008). 'Revenge of the Steamroller: ABCP as a Window on Risk Choices.' October 24. Washington University in St. Louis. Available online at <http://apps.olin.wustl.edu/FIRS/PDF/2009/787.pdf>.

Hackethal, A. (2000). 'How Unique Are US Banks? The Role of Banks in Five Major Financial Systems.' Johan Wolfgang Goethe-Universität Frankfurt Am Main Fachbereich Wirtschaftswissenschaften, Working Paper Series: Finance and Accounting, 60 December.

— (2004). 'German Banks and Banking Structure.' *The German Financial System*, 2nd edition, eds. Jan P. Krahnen and Richard H. Schmidt. Oxford: Oxford University Press, 71–105.

Hall, P. A. and Soskice, D. (2001). 'An Introduction to Varieties of Capitalism.' In *Varieties of capitalism: the institutional foundations of comparative advantage*, eds. Hall, Peter A., and Soskice, David. Oxford: Oxford University Press, 1–68.

Hancké, B. (2001). 'Revisiting the French model: coordination and restructuring in French industry.' In *Varieties of capitalism: the institutional foundations of comparative advantage*, eds. Hall, Peter A., and Soskice, David. Oxford: Oxford University Press, 307–337.

Hancké, B., M. Rhodes and C. Thatcher (2007). *Beyond varieties of capitalism: conflict, contradictions, and complementarities in the European economy*, Oxford University Press, Oxford, UK.

Hardie, I. and Howarth, D. (2009). 'Die Krise but not La Crise', *Journal of Common Market Studies* 47, 5, November, 1019–1039.

Hayward, J. (1995). 'Introduction.' In *Industrial Enterprise and European Integration* (ed. J. Hayward). Oxford: Oxford University Press, 1–21.

Howell, Chris (2009). 'The Transformation of French Industrial Relations: Labor Representation and the State in a Post-Dirigiste Era.' *Politics and Society* 37, 2, June, 229–256.

IMF (2004). 'France: Financial System Stability Assessment.' *IMF Country Report* 04/344, November. Washington: IMF.

— (2006a). 'Italy: Financial System Stability Assessment.' *IMF Country Report* 06/112, March. Washington: IMF

— (2006b). 'Spain: Financial System Stability Assessment.' *IMF Country Report* 06/212, June. Washington: IMF.

— (2009). 'France: 2009 Article IV Consultation—Staff Report; Public Information Notice on the Executive Board Discussion; and Statement by the Executive Director for France.' *IMF Country Report* 09/232, July. Washington: IMF.

— (2010). *Global Financial Stability Report*, October. Available at <http://www.imf.org/External/Pubs/FT/GFSR/2010/02/index.htm>.

International Securitisation Report. 1993. 'Country Report and Database: France', in: International Securitisation Report, March.

Laeven, L. and R. Levine (2008). 'Bank Governance, Regulation, and Risk Taking.' NBER Working Papers, 14113. Available online at <http://papers.ssrn.com/sol3/papers.cfm?abstract_id=1142967>.

Lee, P. (2010). 'BNP-Paribas: The model that worked.' *Euromoney* January. Available online at <http://www.euromoney.com/Article/2376062/BNP-Paribas-The-model-that-worked.html>.

Levy, J. (2006). 'The State Also Rises.' In *The State After Statism: New State Activities in the Age of Liberalization* (ed. J. Levy). Cambridge: Harvard University Press.

Loriaux, M. (1991). *After Hegemony: International Change and Financial Reform*. Cornell: Cornell University Press, 1991.

Maclean, M., C. Harvey and J. Press (2001). 'Elites, ownership and the internationalization of French business.' *Modern & Contemporary France* 9(3), 313–325.

Mamou, Y. (1988). *Une Machine De Pouvoir: La Direction du Trésor*. Paris: La Découverte.

Ministry of Finance Officials (2010). *Interviews with the author*. Bercy, Paris, 20 October.

Morin, F. (1998). *Le Modele Francais de Detention et Gestion du Capital*. Paris: Les Editions de Bercy.

— (2000). 'A Transformation in the French Model of Shareholding and Management.' *Economy and Society* 29, 1, 36–53.

Noyer, C. (2010). 'Financial Stability in Europe and in the World: a French perspective.' Speech at the Open podium debate on 'The Euro in the Financial Crisis—lessons and perspectives.' Copenhagen, 22 March. Available online at <http://www.banque-france.fr/gb/instit/telechar/discours/2010/discours-Copenhague-Gouverneur-Noyer-22–03–2010.pdf>.

O'Sullivan, M. (2007). 'Acting out institutional change: understanding the recent transformation of the French financial system.' *Socio-Economic Review*, 5, 3, 389–436.

Pauget, G. (2009). 'The future of French banking.' *The Banker* 2 February. Available online at <http://www.thebanker.com/World/Western-Europe/France/The-future-of-French-banking>.

Quaglia, L. (2009). 'The Response to the Global Financial Turmoil in Italy: "A Financial System that Does Not Speak English".' *South European Society and Politics* 14, 1, March 2009, 7–18.

Reuters (2011). "FACTBOX-U.S., European bank write-downs, credit losses." February 24. www.reuters.com/article/2011/02/24/banks-writedownslosses-idUSLDE71N1J720110224(March 5, 2011).

Royo, S. (2009). 'After the Fiesta: The Spanish Economy Meets the Global Financial Crisis.' *South European Society and Politics* 14, 1, 19–34.

Schmidt, V. (1996). *From State to Market? The Transformation of French Business and Government*. New York and Cambridge: Cambridge University Press.

— (2003). 'French capitalism transformed, yet still a third variety of capitalism.' *Economy and Society* 32, 4: 526–554.

— (2009). 'Putting the Political Back into Political Economy by Bringing the State Back in Yet Again.' *World Politics* 61, no. 3 (July 2009), 516–546.

Story, J. and I. Walter. (1997). *Political Economy of Financial Integration in Europe: The Battle of the System*. Cambridge: The MIT Press.

Touraine, H. and Grillo, F. (2004). 'Overview of the French securitisation market recent innovations and market trends.' Paris: Freshfields Bruckhaus Deringer. Available online at <http://www.freshfields.com/publications/pdfs/places/DB04_France.pdf>.

Underhill, G. (1997). 'The making of the European financial area: global market integration and the EU single market for financial service.' In *The New World Order in International Finance (*ed. G. Underhill). London: Macmillan: 101–123.

Xiao, Y. (2009). 'French Banks Amid the Global Financial Crisis.' IMF working Paper, European Department, September, WP/09/201.

Zysman, J. (1983). *Governments, Markets and Growth.* Cornell: Cornell University Press.

7

A 'Ship in Trouble': The Spanish Banking System and the International Financial Crisis[1]

Sebastián Royo

Introduction

It is rare that central bankers refer to shipwrecks when talking about the institutions they oversee. However Miguel Angel Fernández Ordoñez (MAFO), governor of the Bank of Spain, described his job dealing with the financial crisis as 'doing a double job on *a ship in trouble*, at the same time as ordering the evacuation of the passengers it was necessary to repair the lifeboats'.[2] This description sums up the situation. In the run up to the global financial crisis, the Spanish financial system earned itself a nice reputation. A culture of invasive supervision from the regulators, coupled with a conservative policy and regulatory frameworks that required higher provisioning, meant that most Spanish banks were prepared with plump cushions to absorb the losses caused by the outset of the global financial crisis. However, this proved short lived. When the crisis intensified, it exposed the weakness in the policy and regulatory frameworks and an over-reliance on wholesale funding, specifically for mortgages and construction; the financial system was unable to escape its dramatic effects.

In this volume, we develop the concept of 'market-based' banking (MBB), which considers the extent to which the banks' ability to supply credit to the economy is driven by market pressures on both the asset and liability sides of their balance sheets (see Introduction). This chapter aims to examine changes in Spain's national financial system and the extent to which

[1] This chapter borrows from S. Royo (2013) *Lessons from the Economic Crisis in Spain*. NY. Palgrave, Chapter 6; and S. Royo (forthcoming) "How Did the Spanish Financial System Survive the First Stage of the Global Crisis?" *Governance*.

[2] As quoted in 'Spain bank chief faces reform battle,' in *Financial Times*, 16 April 2012.

it has been affected by the international financial crisis of the late 2000s. It addresses the following question: what factors explain the way in which the Spanish financial system has been affected by the crisis and has reacted to it? This chapter argues that a key feature of MBB, namely the degree of 'financialization' of national financial systems, defined in this volume as the trading of risk, is instrumental in understanding the impact of the financial crisis. Financialization is operationalized by looking at Spanish banks' assets (i.e. the size of the trading book and the presence of toxic assets), and liabilities (i.e. the funding base of banks, their reliance on wholesale market rather than retail deposits for funding, the securitization of lending, and the use of structured investment vehicles (SIVs)).

In Spain, banking exposure to wholesale markets has increased significantly over the last decade and, therefore, has become MBB, with significant implications for the nature of credit provision and the nature of the Spanish national financial system. The lower reliance on bank lending proved to be beneficial at the beginning of the crisis. While most market-based systems faced further problems in the wake of the Lehman Brothers collapse, Spanish banks performed relatively well. However, the crisis eventually had a major impact, once more 'traditional' problems with government debt and lending emerged. This chapter analyses this reversal and explains its causes.

Spanish regulators placed emphasis upon pre-existing regulatory and supervisory frameworks, which initially shielded the Spanish financial system from the direct effects of the global financial crisis. This contributed to their initial positive performance compared with their European counterparts. However, as in Ireland, the collapse of the real estate markets eventually led to a traditional banking crisis fuelled by turbo-charged lending by MBB on the liability side of the Spanish bank's balance sheets.[3] In order to explain the Spanish version of MBB, this chapter focuses on the following factors: first, the regulatory framework; second, the institutional features of the banking system, including the role of the Bank of Spain; and third, the impact of macro-economic developments, notably the real estate bubble.

In this volume, some chapters examine MBB as the dependent variable. In the case of Spain, it is explained as a dependent variable, but it is also examined as an independent variable that can be wielded to help explain Spain's supposedly 'traditional' bank crisis as well as the country's devastating sovereign debt crisis. This chapter shows that MBB allows us to better understand what happened during these crises. MBB explains the dramatic increase in lending, which was also crucial to explain the Spanish crisis. In addition,

[3] The global financial crisis and the subsequent credit crunch had a simultaneous effect: on the one hand, it reduced banks' ability to borrow and therefore to continue lending, thus leading to the property collapse; on the other, the property collapse contributed to reduce banks' ability to borrow.

MBB also explains the ongoing credit crunch in Spain: when the crisis hit, international and wholesale funding dried up, affecting bank lending.

However, this chapter also argues that the outcome is historical and contingent: there have been other causal independent variables of Spanish political and economic life that can be wielded to explain the crises. For instance, in Spain current account deficits (which reached close to 10 per cent of gross domestic product (GDP) just before the crisis) explain why MBB grew (that is, why Spanish banks became so dependent on wholesale banking and international lending). Finally, one of the interesting aspects about the Spanish crisis is that MBB was having its impact prior to much awareness regarding the crisis.[4]

Finally, Spain is unique among the countries in this volume in the fact that the largest banks did not face problems (and indeed, as described below, they were buying foreign banks early in the crisis). The real problem was largely at the next level down, with the *cajas* (or unlisted savings and loans). In this regard Spain is different from Germany, where both the large private banks and the *Landesbanks* were badly impacted by the global financial crisis (see Hardie and Howarth, this volume).

The chapter proceeds as follows. Section one examines the initial impact of the crisis and shows the partial success of Spanish banks. Section two explains the reasons for that resilience, focusing on the regulatory framework and the institutional characteristics of the Spanish financial system. Finally, section three analyses the deteriorating performance of Spanish institutions in the latest stages of the global financial crisis and explains this reversal. It focuses on the following variables: deteriorating economic conditions; the implosion of the real estate market; the dependence on wholesale funding; weaknesses in the regulatory framework; and the role of the Bank of Spain.

The Spanish Financial System

Prior to the liberalization of the late 1980s and 1990s, the Spanish financial system (like those of Greece and Italy) was a typical credit-based Mediterranean system, characterized by extensive interventionism, state control over the banking system, and underdeveloped capital markets (Pérez and Westrup 2010). The role of financial institutions was to provide funding to contribute to the process of economic development and industrialization (Pérez 1997;

[4] Lending figures from the Bank of Spain suggest a tightening due to cost and availability of funding since mid-2009, and they have mostly have remained tight since them. The more gradual but constant tightening from late 2007 to mid-2009 was clearly more significant—which shows that despite all the talk at the time about the limited problems in Spain, beneath this there was a tightening that was hitting mortgage/construction lending hard and contributed to the bursting of the bubble.

Lukauskas 1997), and bank deposits were turned into low-interest credit for industrial enterprises and the government (Deeg and Pérez 2000). The oligopolistic nature of the sector generated significant costs for Spanish firms outside the finance sector (Pérez 1997).

The liberalization of the sector started in the second half of the 1980s, driven by the country's accession to the European Community and the subsequent European single market programme. In Spain's case, the process of financial liberalization was also part of the Bank of Spain's effort to achieve effective disinflation (Pérez and Westrup 2010). The European integration process, and particularly the Single Market Programme and the European Monetary Union, was a driving factor in subsequent developments. While financial regulations remained the responsibility of the national governments, in reality over the last two decades there was a harmonization process throughout all the member states. This process led to the liberalization, modernization, consolidation, and opening up of the system.

Yet, the degree of financialization of the sector was relatively low prior to the crisis. Indeed, the majority of banks' *assets* were loans to customers, and a significant part of banks' assets involved Spanish government securities, which were considered among the safest possible asset investments. It is on the liabilities side of the balance sheet where MBB was most present in the Spanish banking system and, as we will see contributed significantly to the crisis as it unfolded in Spain. As in Italy and Greece, on the *liabilities* side Spanish banks had a broad and stable funding base. However, while funding from retail customers constituted a large share of their total liabilities, Spanish banks still had a significant dependence on wholesale inter-bank funding. The regulatory framework, as we see below, imposed important restrictions on the extent to which there could be securitization on the liabilities side; and banks sponsored by asset-backed commercial paper (ABCP) were close to zero.

At the outset of the crisis, the governor of the Bank of Spain characterized Spanish banks' assets and liabilities the following way:

> On the liabilities side ... they have focused on the longer maturities. This has given them greater peace of mind with regard to the structure of their liabilities ... Spanish banks' recourse to wholesale markets has taken the form of various instruments, including asset-backed securities. However, Spanish securitization bears little resemblance to that which is currently proving highly problematic. First, because of the high quality of the securitized portfolios. And second, because securitization was not conceived of as a business in itself to transfer risk ... It should not be forgotten that Spanish banks have traditionally maintained a solid deposit base. This is largely explained by the particular banking model followed in Spain. Activity is focused on retail business....
>
> On the assets side, Spanish banks have not invested in the complex and opaque products that have turned out to be highly problematic or, as people usually now

say, 'toxic'. Spanish banks' assets, even taking into account the rise in doubtful assets, are largely of good quality (Fernández Ordóñez 2008).

Indeed, Spanish banks have 'traditional' assets and liabilities. However, the funding gap was high, thus MBB was largely concentrated on the liabilities side of the balance sheet, with a significant element of bank lending prior to the crisis funded on wholesale markets (Figure 7.1). In this speech, Governor Ordonez underestimated the vulnerabilities of MBB liabilities; he downplayed the risks associated with Spanish banks' inter-bank borrowing (McGuire and von Peter 2009). He will come to regret it. In this regard, Spain is similar to Ireland, where Northern Rock's mortgage assets were similarly seen as high quality (and, it appears, unlike in Spain, will have low default rates) and securitizations were long term. However, by September 2007, Northern Rock needed liquidity support from the Bank of England because the securitization market dried up (see Hardie and Maxfield, this volume).

Once the crisis started, this became a major source of vulnerability because banks were no longer able to access funding on wholesale markets (see Hardie and Howarth, this volume). Governor Fernández Ordóñez recognized as much later on when he stated that 'the high dependence of the Spanish economy on external financing, as a result of many years of spending reliant on foreign savings, made it particularly sensitive to any turbulence that might undermine confidence and obstruct the access of banks to international financial markets.'[5] This is exactly what happened when the wholesale financial markets on which Spanish banks depended for liquidity drip up starting in particular in May 2010 after the bailout of Greece. In addition, stage one and two of the crisis (global banking crisis, credit crunch, and the

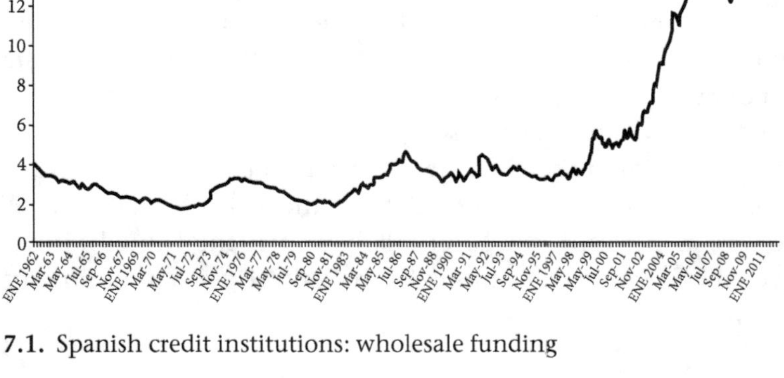

Figure 7.1. Spanish credit institutions: wholesale funding

[5] 'Dublin bail-out spooks investors in Spain,' in *Financial Times*, 27–28 November, 2010.

recessionary impact on the real economy) led to the bursting of the real estate market bubble, which led to significant problems on the assets side of bank balance sheets because of the property loan.

The relatively low degree of financialization of Spanish banks (as with Italian and Greek banks) can be explained by the slow evolution of the national financial system and Spanish banks' reluctance to change a business model that had been consistently successful for decades. At the same time, as we will see below, conservative regulatory framework and supervisory practices have played a crucial role in limiting the risk exposure and excessive leverage of the Spanish financial system.

Yet, as we describe below, the lending was largely concentrated in the construction/real estate sector, thus creating a very traditional bubble. The relatively high customer funding gap meant that market-based liabilities 'turbocharged' traditional lending. Further difficulties were created because Spanish banks' market-based liabilities were also disproportionately sourced in more fragile markets, especially securitization and the inter-bank market.

Spain had very high levels of securitized lending (that is, banks transforming mortgages into asset-based securities (ABSs)), which contributed to the property market bubble. Moreover, while Spanish banks were relatively unexposed to market-based assets because gains in the domestic real estate market and through retail expansion abroad were profitable enough; market based assets were still relevant and Spanish banks had write-down linked to securitized assets. Indeed, Santander and BBVA were already making substantial losses in 2007 and 2008 before the real estate collapsed.[6] While these write-downs were well below the levels of the United Kingdom or the United States, they were still significant.

Indeed, between 2000 and the summer of 2007 both the securitization market and the covered bond market expanded significantly in Spain. The outstanding amount of ABSs and covered bonds issued by Spanish institutions rose from €18 billion and €12 billion in 2000 to €298 billion and €168 billion in the second quarter of 2007. Furthermore, the outstanding amount of other fixed-income securities issued by financial institutions also expanded rapidly, albeit to a lesser extent. The growth of these markets in Spain was much faster than in other European countries; between 2004 and the second quarter of 2007, the weight of the Spanish market for ABSs in Europe was 14 per cent, the second largest after the United Kingdom. In the covered bond market, Spain had a share of 21 per cent during the same

[6] According to Reuters Factbox Santander: €4.8 billion in 2007 and €8.3 billion in 2008. BBVA had €2.7 billion in 2007 and €4.2 billion in 2008.

period, again the second largest in Europe, although in this case the leading market was Germany. In terms of outstanding amounts, as of June 2007 Spain had a share of around 13 per cent and was ranked second (after the United Kingdom) in Europe in the securitization market and third (after Germany and Denmark) in the covered bond market. Yet, it is important to highlight that in Spain the originators of ABSs did not issue these securities as a means to transfer the credit risk of their loan portfolios to other investors, as it happened in other countries. On the contrary, these securities were issued for funding purposes. Between 2000 and 2007, the net flow of loans was persistently above the flow of deposits, and Spanish financial institutions relied on the bond markets as a way of funding this gap. Financial institutions relied not only on the securitization market, but also on other fixed-income markets for the same purpose, including notably the covered bond market (Blanco 2011, 17–18).

One of the consequences of the global financial crisis has been the evaporation of market liquidity and its impact has been particularly severe for ABSs because market liquidity is a very important characteristic of those assets. Shortening the maturity of these products is not possible with ABSs because the maturity of these bonds is the same as the maturity of the underlying assets. At the same time, another consequence of the financial crisis has been a deterioration of the credit quality of financial institutions' portfolios. The impact of this factor was stronger in the case of ABSs owing to the lower level of protection in comparison with covered bonds (i.e. covered bonds have dual protection against losses, the issuer, and the underlying portfolio, but ABSs do not) (Blanco 2011, 19).

The Initial Impact of the Global Financial Crisis

Contrary to their counterparts all over the world, during the first two years of the global financial crisis, most Spanish banks appeared to have escaped the worst direct effects of the crisis (Royo 2012). The timing of the problems (the effect of the crisis was less intense in its early stages) and the nature of the problem (Spanish securitization levels were moderately high by EU levels, and this was largely undertaken by the *cajas*). Indeed, when looking at the performance of the Spanish financial system, it is very important to distinguish between the large banks and the *cajas*; the large banks performed relatively well while the *cajas* suffered from a somewhat traditional financial crisis. Much of what the *cajas* were doing was lending to non-financial companies (NFCs) in construction, rather than just mortgage lending. Yet, a key element that separates this crisis from a traditional one, particularly on the *cajas'* side, is the role of MBB liabilities (Carballo Cruz 2011). This distinction is unique in comparative terms; in no other country were small banks uniquely hit and large banks left largely unscathed.[7]

Initially, the crisis had positive as well as negative impacts on Spanish banks (Barrón 2009). On the positive side, Spain still had two of the most creditworthy banks in the world, Banco Santander and BBVA, and the crisis had not yet affected their solid foundations in terms of exposure to MBB (although they have been severely affected by the wider economic crisis in Spain). On the contrary, they continued to generate profits in the aftermath of the international financial crisis. Of the top five banks in the world in terms of 2008 pre-tax profits, two—Santander and BBVA—were Spanish (the other three, Chinese), with BBVA making €2.8 billion and Santander €4.5 billion of net profit. Moreover, while their main competitors in other countries were severely affected, and in many cases had to be rescued by their governments, in Spain, Santander and BBVA were in need of neither state assistance nor liquidity injections. In contrast, Spanish banks emerged as rescuers in foreign markets; Santander has expanded in the United States, United Kingdom, and Germany, while BBVA and Banco Sabadell (another private bank) in the United States. They also successfully raised funds from the flotation of their subsidiaries (i.e. Santander did it with its Brazilian subsidiary in one of the world's largest public offerings in 2009) (Mallet 2009, 3). By November 2009, only one financial institution had collapsed due to solvency problems after overextending itself in loans to local projects and had to be taken over by the Bank of Spain, Caja Castilla la Mancha. But this only represented 1 per cent of total assets.

The weak underbelly was principally the *cajas*—unlisted in the stock market, regionally based, and often politicized savings banks—accounting for half of the financial sector's assets. During the boom years, they successfully captured market shares from the banks, investing heavily in real estate (lending both to consumers and companies). They are now exposed to the collapse of that sector and the payment difficulties of mortgage holders. *Cajas*, highly dependent on international wholesale financing, were also forced to turn to the government and the European Central Bank (ECB) for liquidity when wholesale markets froze, thus confirming the vulnerability associated with MBB liabilities.

The crisis also affected bank profitability, particularly in the Spanish market where their profits decreased 10 per cent in 2009. Fortunately for the largest Spanish banks, their geographical diversification helped them to counterbalance their domestic losses. Indeed, the largest Spanish banks were active

[7] In France, the investment banks connected to the mutuals were also hit very badly (notably Natixis but also Calyon). In the United Kingdom, Northern Rock (a building society) was also devastated and a few other building societies were affected badly. Even in Germany a mortgage lender, HRE, was severely hit, and IKB was the first one to go under in 2007.

with foreign acquisitions during the past two decades in the United States, Mexico, Brazil, and the United Kingdom, among other countries. For instance, about a fifth of Santander's profits come from Brazil and another fifth from the United Kingdom. This limited their exposure to the weak economy of the home country and allowed Spain's largest banks to fund themselves locally in countries where they had substantive investments, particularly throughout Latin America and the United Kingdom.

Nevertheless, the loan delinquency rate continued to rise, reaching 5.35 per cent in August 2010 and, for the first time during the crisis, the delinquent rate was higher for the banks (5.35 per cent) than for the *cajas* (5.31 per cent).[8] At the same time, the problems of the sector were reflected in the difficulties that they experienced raising funds in international markets. The ECB played a crucial role to compensate for this situation; the debt of Spanish financial institutions with the ECB reached €81.88 billion in March 2010. This unprecedented level of borrowing from the ECB was a consequence of the struggle that Spanish financial institutions had in raising funds from the international capital markets and provided further evidence of the acute tensions in the Spanish banking system.

The results of the *cajas* continued to deteriorate during the first quarter of 2010; Caja Madrid announced a fall of almost 80 per cent in revenues and La Caixa, 11.4 per cent. The larger banks, however, continued growing, albeit many with lower profits. By May 2010, thirty-four of the forty-five *cajas* were involved in merger and restructuring discussions; it was expected that that would lead to the creation of eleven new *cajas*. It also became apparent that simply merging or combining weaker institutions would not fully address the sector's woes. The Bank of Spain also pushed for significant restructuring that would deliver efficiency savings and cost cuts.

Concerns over the strength and solvency of the financial sector led Spanish authorities to push for the publication of the 'stress tests' that the main European banks underwent in 2010. When the results of these tests were made public on Saturday, 23 July 2010, only five of the 17 *cajas* failed: Banca Cívica, Banca Espiga, Caja Catalunya's group, Unimm, and CajaSur. It is important to note, however, that although five of the seven institutions that failed the tests were Spanish savings banks, it was partly because all Spanish lenders were subjected to the tests. Indeed, contrary to other European countries, Spain subjected 95 per cent of its banking system to these stress tests (the average in the EU was 50 per cent). The overall good result for the Spanish financial system confirmed the benefits of the counter-cyclical capital regime, which proved to be the best rescue plan for the Spanish banks because it allowed

[8] These data have been questioned, as many doubted whether the *cajas* were still recognizing the reality of their loan problems.

many of these institutions to pass the stress tests. The twenty-seven banks and *cajas* that were included in the tests still held €19,796 billion in these kinds of provisions, available in case of a further crisis. The initial response of the markets to these results was very positive and helped to push down the country's risk premium. Given what we know now, these assumptions proved overoptimistic.[9]

In sum, despite all the challenges facing the Spanish financial sector, it was one of the least affected during the first phase of the crisis. Of the forty financial institutions that requested direct assistance from Brussels prior to mid-2010, none were from Spain (whereas a dozen were from Germany, five from the United Kingdom, six from the Benelux, and four from Ireland). The support provided to Spanish institutions (loans at a 7.7 per cent interest rate) only reached €30 billion by mid-2010 (0.9 per cent of the EU total). In December 2010, Moody's ranked the Spanish banking system as the third strongest of the eurozone, only behind Finland and France, above the Netherlands and Germany, and well ahead of Portugal, Ireland, and Greece. Finally, Santander and BBVA showed new strength with profits of €4.4 billion and €2.8 billion, respectively, during the first half of 2010.

This relative success, however, proved to be short-lived. Indeed, while Spanish banks faced fewer problems in the wake of the Lehman Brothers collapse than those countries with banking systems that were more market based, eventually the crisis caught up with them when more traditional problems with lending and government debt emerged after 2008.

What Made the Spanish Banking System Different?[10]

The structure of the banking sector sheltered Spanish banks from the crisis. Spanish banks had vibrant and efficient branch networks that helped them to develop strong relationships with their customers. Indeed, three Spanish banks were ranked by Arthur D. Little in 2010 among the world's top ten based on their cost to income ratio (Banco Popular was number 1, BBVA 7, Caja Madrid 10, and Banco Santander 20). An additional factor explaining the strong performance of the sector was the existence of a well-coordinated regulatory framework, in which the Bank of Spain plays a crucial supervisory role, working closely with the consumer protection agency and the finance ministry. The Bank of Spain discouraged lenders from adopting risky 'off-balance sheet' accounting methods and from acquiring billions of Euros of repackaged US subprime mortgages and other toxic assets. At

[9] Subsequent events seemed to show that they were not facing up to the reality of the situation, the assumed fall in property prices proved to be overoptimistic.

[10] From Royo 2012.

the same time, the Bank's onsite supervisors, who were posted in the head offices of commercial banks and *cajas*, were diligently overseeing risk decisions (clearly this was not enough, based on later discoveries). Moreover, the Bank of Spain was instrumental in forcing banks to focus on quality of capital, limiting their leverage, and the debt to equity ratio. For the Bank of Spain, enforcement was key, and they focused on principles (such as the need for conservative risk management, or for higher provisioning), not merely the legalistic approach that is more typical of the Anglo-Saxon countries. Finally, the reports from the Bank of Spain were instrumental in pushing for the necessary implementation of the Bank of Spain's requests. In sum, bank supervision under the management of the Bank of Spain contributed to the stability of the domestic banking system in the years leading up to the crisis.

The regulatory framework was also crucial. In Spain, the regulation and supervision of the financial system seek two main objectives: to guarantee the correct functioning of its markets and to protect the consumers of financial services. Regulation, defined as the development of the norms that rule the activities of financial markets and institutions, must be distinguished from supervision (the guardianship of the fulfilment of the norms). The regulatory organs of the Spanish Financial System (SFS) are all the institutions with competences to dictate legal norms (i.e. the government, Congress, and the Ministry of Economy), while the supervisory organs are the Bank of Spain and the National Stock Market Commission (Comisión Nacional del Mercado de Valores, CNMV). The CNMV, created by the 24/1988 Law, is the entity in charge of supervision and inspection of stock markets and the activities of legal and physical people involved in these markets.

The distinction between banks and *cajas* is crucial for our analysis. As indicated, their performance has been very different. A crucial reason for this divergence was the difference in their regulatory framework. *Cajas* are very peculiar credit institutions because they used to dedicate a significant portion of their provisions (usually over 20 per cent) to social causes, and, prior to the crisis, they had strong links with the regions in which they operate. They were regulated by both the national government (in charge of basic norms) and by the autonomous communities governments (in charge of application and development of the rules established by the central government). Political institutions (parties and unions) participate in their governing bodies. This proved to be a gaping hole in the regulatory framework, and had devastating consequences.

The Bank of Spain was so influenced by previous crises that it prevented the banks from indulging into reckless leverage and off-balance sheet accounting. In this regard, the single most important factor to account for the performance of the Spanish financial system during the initial stages of the crisis was the implementation prior to the crisis of a 'dynamic provisioning system', which established a counter-cyclical capital regime for banks:

a. Starting in 2000, the Bank of Spain forced banks to make provisions for latent portfolio losses, defined as those likely to occur, but which may be undetected by conventional accounting. This method allowed for the creation of a buffer in the form of a reserve deducted from capital in good times and released in times of downturn.
b. At the same time, the central bank also prevented the provision of dividend increases at times of growth that might undermine banks' solvency in the long term.
c. Finally, the central bank, through its directives, prevented banks from developing off-balance sheet activities, which sunk banks elsewhere, and forced Spanish banks to stay away from such toxic assets (Plender 2009).

This mandate provided Spanish banks with a countercyclical mechanism that was essential to overcome the first phase of the current crisis. Indeed, obstacles to off-balance sheet activities relate to dynamic provisioning requirements because these obstacles effectively contributed to a sound capital position. For instance, Banco Santander built more than €6 billion of generic loan loss provisions. While these provisions helped the banks during the initial stages of the crisis, they proved to be insufficient, as will be shown in the next section.

Government regulation was also deeply informed by the historical experience and previous financial crisis. Indeed, Spanish central bankers learned from the crises of the 1970s, 1980s, and early 1990s and adopted measures to prevent any repetition. The idea of an anti-cyclical fund was an old one and had been a source of constant confrontations with the banks. Between the banking crises of the 1970s until the bankruptcy of Banesto in 1993, the Bank of Spain witnessed the disappearance of 40 financial institutions. This experience convinced the leaders of the Bank of Spain of the need to establish special anti-crisis preventive measures. The collapse of Banesto in 1993 led Luis Angel Rojo, Governor of the bank at that time, to establish such provisions in an internal document (a 'circular'), which his successor, Jaime Caruana (2000–6), started to implement in 2000. As often happens with regulations, later events seemed to suggest that the Bank of Spain had learned from the previous experiences, but was not yet prepared to deal with what happened in this particular crisis.

The comparatively strong performance of Spanish banks in the early stages of the international financial crisis can also be explained by their focus on retail and commercial banking. Following the Bank of Spain's guidelines, they largely ignored the risky attractions of opaque investment banking operations. An additional important strategic factor, particularly for the larger banks, was their strategy to diversify internationally, primarily into Latin America, which has allowed them to compensate for the poor performance in the Spanish market. For instance, Latin American operations – including units in Brazil, Mexico and Chile – represented 50 per cent of the bank's profit in the first nine months of 2012 and it is estimated that within eight to ten years, it may reach 75 per cent. In 2011, Santander received nearly 70 per cent of its profits from economies outside the Euro area.

Finally, at this early stage, intra-Euro area flows were not as badly affected as international ones; in 2010, Spanish banks stood out for their limited funding from outside the EU (i.e. non-Euro). Indeed, only 19.4 per cent of their wholesale funding is external to the EU, which stands in contrast with other countries like Germany (60.4 per cent) or Ireland (56.9 per cent). Their market-based funding was actually relatively low compared to other countries' banks. Spanish banks' international inter-bank borrowing stood at only 26.7 per cent of GDP, in contrast to countries such as Ireland with 108.8 per cent. Even where market-based funding was relatively high (as with securitization), it had longer maturity than inter-bank borrowing (much of which less than a week), so the Spanish banks were not caught in the early waves of panic in the inter-bank market.

The Canary in the Coal Mine: How More 'Traditional' Problems Led to a Greater Crisis?

In the run up to the crisis, the Bank of Spain and the regulators earned themselves a fine reputation. The regulatory framework described above and the strong culture of invasive supervision meant that most Spanish banks had significant cushions to absorb the initial losses caused by the global financial crisis. Miguel Angel Fernández Ordoñez stated in October 2008, after the collapse of the banking system in many other countries, that 'the sector is in a strong starting position, and the Bank of Spain has the capacity and the tradition to know how to resolve the most complex situations without trauma for the depositors, or the overall economy'. He added: 'I am convinced that our entities, which knew how to manage the expansive cycle, will also know how to adopt the management decisions and implement the adequate strategies that will allow them to confront the difficulties with success.'[11] They did not, and the socialist government did not either. Spanish banks would come to regret such complacency.

[11] He also warned of the need to clean up the bad loans, in 'Tres años, cuatro reformas y varios cadáveres por el camino,' in *El País*, 11 May 2012.

Indeed, the relative success in dealing with the crisis has proved short-lived. When the economic crisis deepened, it led to a traditional banking crisis caused by the collapse of the real estate market, unemployment records, increasing government debt, and difficulties accessing credit in wholesale markets. The real estate boom–bust cycle, which materialized in particular in the *cajas* sector, exposed weaknesses in the policy and regulatory frameworks, as well as the sector's over reliance on wholesale funding. In the end the financial system was unable to decouple itself from the economic cycle and the huge macroeconomic crisis that has besieged the country. This section seeks to account for this reversal.

The deteriorating situation is illustrated by the interest margin of the Spanish banking system—the difference between what banks earn on loans and the cost of funding—which fell about 20 per cent since July 2007 to 0.86 percentage points at the end of 2011, the lowest since 1970 when the Bank of Spain started to compile the data. For the first time since 1985, return on equity was negative at the end of 2011, as a result of the economic crisis and increasing provisions against losses on real estate debt.

While there has been significant progress in trying to address the consequences of the crisis (i.e. €112 billion in extra provisions for bad property loans since 2007, which are expected to increase to €147 billion by the end of 2012, or 14 per cent of GDP; higher capital ratios; a 12 per cent fall in bank branches and a 10 per cent cut in staff; and the absorption through mergers of 30 weaker institutions, all but two of them *cajas*),[12] Spanish banks have continued to suffer from a range of problems:

1. *Adverse operating conditions*: a second recession in two years, the ongoing real estate crisis, and persistently high levels of unemployment.
2. *Reduced creditworthiness of the Spanish sovereign*, which impacts banks' standalone profiles and affects the capacity of the government to support banks.
3. *Rapid asset quality deterioration*: non-performing loans to real estate companies are increasing rapidly and mortgages are expected to deteriorate.
4. *Restricted market funding access in wholesale markets* intensified the ongoing Euro area debt crisis, and growing investor concerns about Spanish banks.

By May 2012, the government had been forced to intervene and/or nationalize eight banking institutions. On Wednesday, 9 May 2012, the government was pressed to nationalize Bankia, the country's largest real estate lender (and

[12] 'Spain bank chief faces reform battle,' in *Financial Times*, 16 April 2012.

the result of the merge of several *cajas*), which again validated the concerns about insufficient regulatory oversight, and the perception that banks and the Bank of Spain had played down the risk posed by real estate loans. This was the largest bank nationalization in the country's history. Bankia's non-performing loan rate was running at 8 per cent at the time of the nationalization. The cost of the nationalization was expected to reach €23 billion. This nationalization shows that some of the *caja* mergers that the Bank of Spain and the previous government pushed for were dysfunctional. Billed as the 'leader of the new banks' and as evidence of the success of the socialist government's crusading banking reforms, Bankia proved to be a monumental fiasco and it shows the refusal to acknowledge the true extent of the country's real estate problem. Concerns about Spanish banks' undercapitalization led to the announcement of an EU banking bailout for Spain in June 2012.

However, it is important to highlight, yet again, that as late as May 2012, analysts and markets were still drawing a distinction between strong and weak banks; and recognizing the management and lending standards of the so-called 'Big Three'—Banco Santander, BBVA, and La Caixa—as opposed to those of many *cajas*, which were often run by politicians with little (if any) financial and banking experience. While the *cajas* were struggling under the weight of bad mortgages and loans to construction companies, the 'Big Three's' exposure to toxic assets associated with the Spanish real estate sector was a relatively small problem for them; BBVA and Santander diversified internationally giving them access to greater resources, funding and capital, which allowed them to liquidate the toxic property assets at a lower price than their rivals, and with limited damage to their earnings. Net profits for the first quarter of 2012 at Santander (€1.6 billion and €1 billion respectively) were more than ten times greater than their nearest rival, La Caixa, which lacked the international diversification of the other two and depended largely on a powerful branch network that was located in a market mired in recession.[13] How do we account for the deteriorating performance of Spanish banks?

The Impact of Economic Conditions

Between 1996 and 2008, Spain witnessed one of its most spectacular periods of economic growth. During this period, Spain grew at a fast pace; 3.8 per cent annually (whereas the EU15 average was 2.5 per cent) and it created eight million jobs in ten years, almost 30 per cent of the jobs created in the EU. Unemployment decreased from 22 per cent in 1996 to 7.4 per cent in 2007. The flip side was the low productivity growth (it grew a meagre 0.5 per cent between 1997 and 2006 versus the 1.3 per cent average in the EU); the loss

[13] 'Two tiers, one crisis for Spanish Banks,' in *Financial Times*. Friday, 18 May 2012.

of competitiveness marked by record high trade deficits (over 10 per cent of GDP); and the dependency in the construction sector.

The global financial crisis that started in 2007 exposed these weaknesses and brought an abrupt end to the unprecedented era of economic growth. By the summer of 2008, the effects of the global crisis were evident in Spain; and since then, the country has suffered one of the worst recessions in history. In 2010, Spain's GDP fell 3.6 per cent, the worst performance since data have been compiled; the public deficit reached over 11 per cent; public debt increased from 36 per cent to 50 per cent; and housing construction fell 20 per cent. In 2012, the deficit was expected to reach 5.3 per cent; unemployment stood at over 24 per cent with more than 5.6 million people unemployed; and the debt was expected to reach 79 per cent of GDP.

The deteriorating economic conditions are having a severe impact on the banks' balance sheets. Indeed, the second recession in three years and the record-high unemployment, close to 25 per cent in mid-2012 (and 50 per cent for those twenty-five years old and younger), is triggering new loan losses in the Spanish mortgage market and increasing the percentage of non-performance loans (see later).

This collapse was not fully unexpected. Yet, it is important to emphasize that in Spain the crisis did not originate with wildly mismanaged public finances; Spain had a budget surplus between 2005 and 2007, and public debt stood at 36 per cent of GDP before the crisis. On the contrary, it has largely been a problem of ever-growing private sector debt, compounded by reckless bank investments and loans, particularly from the *cajas* (to developers and construction companies rather than to homebuyers), as well as aggravated by competitiveness and current account imbalances.

Indeed, while Spain has a relatively low ratio of public debt (70 per cent in 2011, compared with 165 per cent for Greece or 120 per cent for Italy), the non-financial private sector debt is 134 per cent of GDP, higher than any major economy in the world with the exception of Ireland (and in the case of Ireland, figures are skewed because of the outsized presence of foreign multinationals). Yet, it is worth emphasizing that the debt of financial institutions is lower than the eurozone average (102 per cent versus 128 per cent). Their main problem is not the level of debt, but where it is invested: principally in real estate assets.

Finally, the austerity policies implemented since May 2010 are aggravating the fiscal position of the country. The ratio of Spain's debt to its economy was 36 per cent before the crisis and is expected to reach 79 per cent in 2012, and 84 per cent by 2013 (and this is even based on optimistic growth assumptions). The shrinking economy will continue raising the debt, as well as reducing government revenue. The premium Spain pays to borrow over Germany reached a Euro-era record of 485 basis points in June 2012, and yields on government bonds have increased to over 7 per cent.

In sum, Spain seems to have fallen into the doom loop that has already afflicted Greece or Portugal and led to their bailouts. The sustainability of the Spanish government debt may come back to haunt Spanish banks (including BBVA and Santander) because they have been some of the biggest buyers of government debt in the wake of the ECB long-term refinancing operation liquidity infusions (the percentage of government bond owned by domestic banks reached 30 per cent in mid-2012, while the percentage of bonds held by foreign investors declined from a high of over 56 per cent in 2011 to less than 39 per cent in mid-2012).

The Collapse of the Real Estate Sector

Land prices increased 500 per cent in Spain between 1997 and 2007, the largest increase among the countries examined in this volume. The country's credit boom peaked in 2008, when the supply of cheap, and largely external, finance began to dry up. The real estate sector fit like a glove with a financial sector that was seeking rapid growth. At the end of 2010, the International Monetary Fund (IMF) reported that Spain had the largest real estate bubble in the developed world. But the global financial crisis burst it. Indeed, by the end of 2011, land prices, adjusted for inflation, had fallen about 30 per cent from the 2007 peak, and home prices were off about 22 per cent. House prices fell by 11.2 per cent in 2011 alone, while in Madrid, prices were down by 29.5 per cent. Many analysts estimate that house price adjustment is still less than halfway complete, and expect that real estate prices will fall to the levels of the mid-1990s.

The implosion of the real estate market has exposed the vulnerability of the banking sector to that market, which constituted 60 per cent of the banking loans (i.e. loans to families, enterprises in the real estate sector or direct real estate assets). Consequently, Spain has been suffering a property-linked banking crisis exacerbated by obstacles to financing created by the international crisis.

Four years after the crisis started, the quality of Spanish banks' assets continues to plummet. The estimated losses for banks are in the range of €130–300 billion. The banking sector will need between €100 and 250 billion in recapitalization in 2012 to maintain the 9 per cent minimum required by the European Banking Authority. Spanish banks still hold €308 billion in total real estate assets. As property prices continued to fall and bad loan ratios to increase, the Bank of Spain classified €180 billion as troubled assets at the end of 2011, and in 2011 alone they added €45 billion to their problematic assets. In addition, banks are sitting on €656 billion of mortgages and 2.8 per cent are classified as non-performing. The *cajas* are the ones experiencing the most difficulties because they financed much of the real estate boom.

Spanish financial institutions at the end of 2011 accumulated €405 billion in loans associated with the real estate sector given to developers and companies, and, of those, €188 billion were considered toxic and at risk of default. The *cajas* had to write down €50 billion in their property portfolios in 2011. As of December 2011, banks had already made provisions for 30 per cent of the €170 billion of property assets concerned, but some land holdings could not be priced or sold. The Bank of Spain announced that bad loans on the books of the country's commercial banks, mostly in the real state sector, had reached 7.4 per cent of total lending. In May 2012, the Bank of Spain disclosed that the value of bad loans held by Spanish banks increased by a third over the previous year to €148 billion, and loans in arrears accounted for 8.4 per cent of the sector's loan portfolio in March 2012. Barclays estimated that non-performing mortgages could reach up to 5 per cent with €16 billion in losses. In other words, the provisioning does not seem to be keeping pace with the crisis, and no one seems to know where the bottom is (Table 7.1).[14]

The problem has been compounded by the increase in bad loans, which reached almost 8 per cent in 2012, the highest level in 18 years as a percentage of total lending, forcing them to offload real estate assets from their balance sheets, and hindering their ability to lend to the real economy.

As of July 2012, despite raising billions of Euros since the collapse of the real estate market, the banking sector was still perceived as woefully undercapitalized and there were still serious questions about the full extent of the sector's real estate problem. The continuing recession led to further decline in property prices and put in question the value of previously performing loans. This concern extends even to the largest banks, with the potential impact on earnings and capital reserves.[15]

Wholesale Funding

According to the ECB, Spanish banks, on average, funded 46 per cent of total assets with deposits at year-end 2011, a relatively high level compared to other countries' banks examined in this volume. Yet, they still rely, to

Table 7.1. The financial sector and the exposure to real estate risk

	Consolidated assets (billion euros)	Exposed to credit to developers (million euros)	% of credit	Total at risk (million euros)	% of credit	Total covered by provisions (billion euros)	% Covered
Total Cajas	1 255	151 648	19.3%	128 601	16.4%	42 373	33%
Total Banks	2 187	69 774	11.4%	59 375	9.7%	18 420	31%
Total	3 442	221 423	15.8%	187 976	13.4%	60 793	31%

Source: *El País*, Wednesday, 9 May 2012: 24.

[14] 'España, duda permanente,' in *El País*. Sunday, 20 May 2012.
[15] Non-performing rates were running at 4 per cent at Santander and BBVA.

varying degrees, on market funds, which make them vulnerable to growing market tensions over the Greek crisis, and the sovereign and financial crisis in Spain. In addition, Spanish banks also funded themselves in the US dollar inter-bank market to finance their domestic lending (McGuire and von Peter 2009, 51). This was a market that was particularly fragile during the crisis.

Significant levels of market-based liabilities were taken on by both the big Spanish banks and the *cajas*, but in particular by the *cajas* in the context of their efforts to expand and strengthen their national presence, as illustrated most visibly by a rapid growth in the number of employees and branches (Figure 7.2). Their market share measured in terms of total assets, increased from around 20 per cent in the 1980s to 40 per cent in 2010. This aggressive expansion went hand in hand with increased lending to construction companies, real estate developers, and to households for mortgages, which was increasingly financed by the wholesale market. As a result, the *cajas'* share of total assets funded by domestic deposits (public and private sector, excluding credit institutions) trended downward from over 80 per cent in the early 1980s to 64 per cent in 2010 (IMF 2012, 9).

Indeed, another significant weakness has been the dependence of Spanish banks on wholesale funding for liquidity since the crisis started, and, in particular, their dependence on international wholesale financing, as 40 per cent of their balance depended on funding from international markets in 2012. Spanish banks have increased their ECB borrowings by more than six times since June 2011, to the highest level in absolute terms among Euro area banking systems by April 2012. Funding from the ECB has mitigated short-term

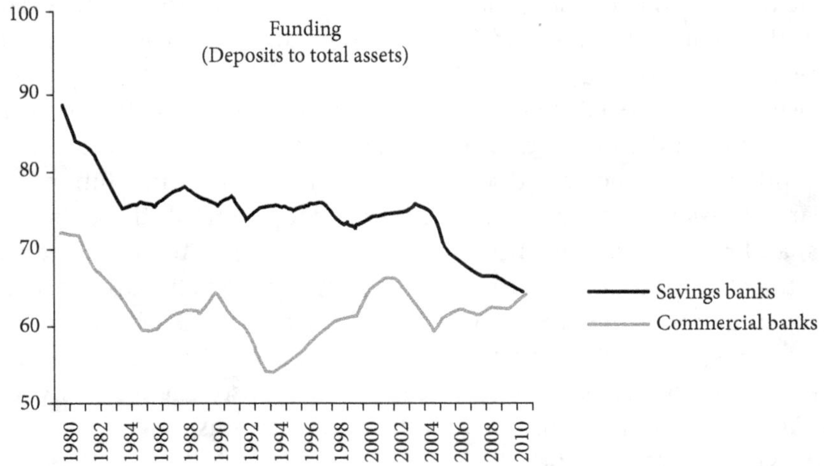

Figure 7.2. Spain: savings versus commercial banks, 1980–2010
Source: IMF 2012.

funding needs; in March 2012, Spanish banks borrowed a record €316 billion from the ECB, 28 per cent of the eurozone total. However, their reliance on the ECB raises concerns over their ability to reduce their dependence on ECB funding over time, which makes them very vulnerable and open to attacks from the markets.

Finally, on the liabilities side, funding was complicated by the difficulties of accessing international wholesale markets, because the securitization markets, and others, such as the inter-bank or senior debt markets, were still not completely open to small and medium-sized institutions. The Bank of Spain acknowledged as much: 'Spanish deposit institutions have been affected by the international financial crisis because of the evaporation of the wholesale funding channel, which, in the years prior to the summer of 2007, had contributed to funding a significant portion of growth in activity' (Bank of Spain Financial Stability Review, March 2010, 19). And the banks themselves: 'on the liabilities side, funding was complicated by the difficulties of accessing international wholesale markets through securities issues, asset securitization or borrowing on the interbank market' (*Caja Madrid Annual Report* 2007, 22).

Weaknesses in the Policy and Regulatory Framework

As seen in the previous section, at the beginning of the crisis, the financial regulatory framework was widely praised. Yet, it has been unable to cope with the crisis, which exposed the weaknesses of the system. The most evident sign of failure has been the fact that the country adopted four financial reforms in three years, as well as implemented two rounds of bank mergers (and was starting a third in the summer of 2012).[16] These efforts have all proven inadequate thus far in addressing the crisis. They have been largely perceived as 'too little and too late', and they failed to rebuild investors' confidence in the Spanish financial sector.

Indeed, the approved 'low-cost' reforms have not solved the problems. Both socialist and conservative governments have been reluctant to admit the depth of the liquidity and solvency problems of many institutions (particularly the *cajas*, where politics has continued to play a role throughout the crisis) and the reforms have been insufficient to address them. At the same time, the attempt to force restructuring through mergers has also backfired, as proven by the Bankia fiasco. The governments have also failed to recognize that merging weak banks does not create a strong one. The €100 billion assigned so far to deal with the crisis seem woefully insufficient and investors seem to be waiting for additional funding (and reforms) once the external auditors complete their work (Table 7.2).

[16] From 'Tres años, cuatro reformas y varios cadáveres por el camino,' in *El País*, 11 May 2012.

Table 7.2. Restructuring of the financial sector with Fondo de Restructuración Ordenada Bancaria assistance (as of 8 May 2012)

Bank	Process	Guaranteed Assistance (bn Euros)	Type of Assistance
Catalunya Caixa	Integration	1,250	Preferential Stock
	Recapitalization	1.718	Ordinary Stock
NovacaixaGalicia	Integration	1,162	Preferential Stock
	Recapitalization	2,465	Ordinary Stock
Caja Espanha-Duero	Integration	525	Preferential Stock
Bankia	Integration	4,465	Preferential Stock
Mare Nostrum	Integration	915	Preferential Stock
Cívica	Integration	977	Preferential Stock
CajaSur	Restructuring	392	Protection of risky assets
B.CAM	Restructuring	5,249	Ordinary stock Protection of assets Liquidity support
Unnim	Restructuring	953	Ordinary stock Liquidity support
B. Valencia	Restructuring		

Source: Fondo de Restructuración Ordenada Bancaria.

The loss of confidence from foreign investors is reflected by the fact that they withdrew €31 billion in just one month (March 2012). There is growing consensus that the banking and securities regulators' independence needs to be strengthened. The Bank of Spain needs further authority to address pre-emptively that build-up of risk in the system; the sanctioning regime in banking and securities supervision needs to be strengthened (IMF 2012).

The Role of the Bank of Spain[17]

At the beginning of the crisis, the Bank of Spain's policies, its experienced and respected professional staff, and its thorough supervisory processes were all praised and modelled by other countries. Time, however, has tempered that praise and the Bank of Spain is now criticized for its actions and decisions (or lack thereof) during the crisis.

The Bank of Spain anticipated the potential pitfall from the real estate bubble as early as 2003, when it alerted in one of its Economic Bulletins that the magnitude of the bubble could be as high as 20 per cent. This caused a conflict with the conservative government and Rodrigo Rato, the minister of finance at the time, questioned the report. This was the first instance of a battle that marked the course of action in subsequent years and this, despite the Autonomy Law, which protected the Bank of Spain against political interference. Indeed, the conflicts between the government and the Bank of Spain,

[17] This section borrows from 'El día que el Banco de España se doblegó,' in *El País*, 13 March 2011 and 'Un gobernador entre dos fuegos,' in *El País*. 13 May 2012.

between the political and the financial powers, are crucial to understanding what has happened as well as why the Bank of Spain failed to act to burst the real estate bubble and to address the recapitalization of the *cajas* until it was too late. Naturally, any action to burst the bubble was opposed by the governments (both the Partido Popular, PP; and Partido Socialist Obrero Español, PSOE) because of the negative impact that it would have had on economic growth.

When Jaime Caruana became governor in 2000, he knew that the economy had been overheating since 1995; he was also fully aware that the banks and *cajas* were assuming large risk in the real estate sector. In his first speech to the *cajas* on 18 April 2001, he asked for four things: not to abuse industrial investments because they could be 'foreign to their and traditional nature and objectives'; to reduce the emission of preferential stock, which had become a major source of unlimited liquidity; to control the expansion of credit; and to professionalize their administrative counsels and reduce the political weight in the sector. These recommendations proved to be prescient. Some of these recommendations had to do with the MBB framework discussed throughout the chapter (as in the need to control the expansion of credit), while others dealt with other problems, but had they been heeded, the *cajas* would not be facing the crisis that later materialized. Ten years later, the *cajas* continued to face most of these problems, which, in many cases, led to their collapse. Unfortunately, the leaders of the *cajas* disagreed with these suggestions, which in effect led to a confrontation that was only ended in April 2010 in with the selection of Isidro Fainé as president of the CECA (the Spanish Confederation of Cajas de Ahorros). Having worked in banks since 1964, he had the appropriate and extensive financial background to push for the necessary reforms.

Despite Caruana's warning, mortgages continued growing at a fast pace: a 20 per cent annual rate. On 21 June 2003, he warned, yet again, that 'the increase in the real cost of housing may have surpassed coherent levels', and asked 'for a progressive reconciliation and moderation of the credit to families and companies involved in the real state sector'.[18] He concluded that unless action was taken, there would be 'more abrupt adjustments'. Unfortunately, banks and *cajas* continued to ignore his recommendations. Pushed by intensifying competition for growth and market share, BBVA increased its mortgages by 17 per cent; La Caixa by 23.4 per cent; Caja Madrid by 24.9 per cent; and Banco Santander by 14.9 per cent. The herd logic, once again, triumphed.

Compounding the problem was the lack of political will to change a model that had resulted in unprecedented levels of growth. The Socialist Party, at the

[18] 'El día que el Banco de España se doblegó,' in *El País*, 13 March 2011 and 'Un gobernador entre dos fuegos,' in *El País*. 13 May 2012.

time in opposition, often criticized the conservative government. Rodriguez Zapatero, leader of the opposition, blamed the conservative government for the bubble several times in parliament and promised a shift in the growth model when his party won the elections. Yet, when he won the election in 2004, he did little to change the growth model and reduce the dependency on the construction sector (and this, despite a commitment, included in the Socialist Party's election manifesto).

Indeed, the government was too slow in reacting and acknowledging the depth of the crisis, something that has been established as a pattern throughout the crisis (Royo 2019. As late as May 2007, when the crisis was already brewing in the United States and the stock market was penalizing construction companies' stock in anticipation of the crisis, the socialist minister of finance, Pedro Solbes, provided a quote for the history books: 'I do not see the construction sector affected at all, it is just a small deceleration which will allow it to adjust to a new reality that will logically result in lower demand', and added 'of course this is an issue that has to be monitored, but I would not give it too much importance'. Clearly the forthcoming election (which took place in March of the following year) was on his mind. At the same time, the regional governments and municipalities, which were very dependent on construction for tax revenues, continued resisting reining in the *cajas*.

Governor Miguel Angel Fernández Ordoñez has also been severely criticized. A Socialist Party militant who served in government in different capacities since the 1980s, he had scant financial experience when he became governor of the Bank of Spain (this shortcoming has been used by many observers to explain the deficiencies in the design and implementation of the financial reforms). Prior to assuming the governor's position, Governor Ordoñez played a very prominent and public role in the Spanish media, criticizing the country's growth model and its dependence in the construction sector. However, he failed to heed his own advice when he became governor.

The Bank of Spain inspection services had already alerted his predecessor, Jaime Caruana, about the dangerous emergence of a real estate bubble. While he sought to address it, he found obstacles that he was unable (or unwilling) to overcome, principally the opposition from politicians and regional governments who controlled the *cajas* and were very reluctant to relinquish their power. Governor Ordoñez was unable (or did not dare) to confront them. This was a key factor in explaining the delays in the Bank of Spain' intervention, which often waited too long and/or acted when it was too late, resulting in the problems getting out of hand (as had happened with the *cajas* from the Valencia region, the Galician ones, or even with Caja Madrid).

The Bank of Spain also approved mergers that proved to be economically absurd (i.e. Bankia). The Bank of Spain, under his leadership, focused too much on economic reforms (the Popular Party accused him of acting like a minister of finance rather than as a governor of the Bank of Spain) and did not push enough for the necessary financial reforms, which were often delayed and largely insufficient. For instance, the decision to intervene in Caja Castilla la Mancha was interpreted more as a signal and as an example (it was controlled by the Socialist Party, then in power at both the regional and national level) rather than as a decisive step to address the problems (if that was the case there were other *cajas* that should have been intervened even earlier: Cajasur, CAM, Bancaja, or others that were absorbed through mergers). The official line from the Bank of Spain was that it 'could not intervene until there were solvency problems', claiming 'banks do fulfil the coefficient requirements, and interventions are the most traumatic and expensive options, therefore the bank sought other alternatives'.[19] This approach helps explain what happened with Caja Castilla la Mancha and Cajasur. The positive result of the stress test may have also influenced the actions of the Bank of Spain and contributed to the decision to delay the interventions.

The arguments often mentioned by the Bank of Spain—that it lacked control of monetary policy (in the hands of the ECB), that it would have been counterproductive to burst the bubble because it was already declining, and that it did not have the tools to burst the bubble—seem disingenuous at best.[20] The government also had options; it could have eliminated housing tax breaks and/or established higher stamp duty on property sales, or raised capital gains tax on second properties. It is true that the establishment of the counter cyclical regime was costly for the Bank of Spain and led to significant confrontations with the banks that complained bitterly arguing it placed them at a disadvantage with their international competitors because it reduced their profit margins. There was also a sense of complacency that the regime would provide a sufficient cushion if the real estate sector fell down. Yet, it was the Bank of Spain itself that approved the high concentration of risk in the real estate sector. Moreover, there were other actions that the Bank of Spain could have taken to reduce the risk from and dependence on the construction sector, such as increasing the required provisions together with the ECB, or strengthening the regulatory framework. Political considerations (both Caruana and Fernández Ordoñez wanted to avoid a confrontation with

[19] 'Un gobernador entre dos fuegos,' in *El País*. 13 May 2012.

[20] The Bank of Spain defended itself with seven arguments: it lacked the appropriate instruments to address the crisis until 2009; the economic deterioration was far longer and intense than anticipated; the government had decided to reject the creation of a 'bad bank'; international banks were unable and unwilling to participate in the merge and acquisition process that was taking place in Spain because of the crisis; they could not use the traditional tool to liquidate banks, namely forcing bondholders to take loses because of the potential contagion effect to other banks and *cajas*; that the corporate governance system of *cajas* was very deficient and politicized; and finally, the autonomous governments refused to approve the mergers during the restructuring process. See 'El Banco de España se defiende de su lentitud con siete argumentos,' in *El País*, 11 June 2012.

the PP and the PSOE) and concerns over potential litigation drove the agenda and precluded more decisive action to address the problem.

In the end, the Bank of Spain chose the path of least resistance: alerting as to the risks but failing to act decisively, even though some people within the bank had been very critical of such inaction and lack of leadership. The Inspectors Association of the Bank of Spain published in May 2006 a letter to the minister of finance, Pedro Solbes, criticizing Governor Caruana's passivity in the face of the accumulated and growing risk associated with the real state sector. They attributed the extraordinary growth of real estate prices to the 'excessive growth of bank lending', fuelled by MBB liabilities, and accused the governor of lacking determination in demanding 'rigour' from financial institutions 'when assuming risks'.[21]

This experience shows that, in the absence of appropriate leadership supported with the necessary regulatory and financial controls, the actions of the Bank of Spain were influenced by political considerations that ended up undermining its role. If anything, it shows the increasing concentration of power away from the Bank of Spain, in the hands of the government, and the banks.

Conclusion

Contrary to Greece or Italy, the financial crisis in Spain originated from private sector over-indebtedness (as in Ireland). Yet, Spanish financial institutions (unlike those of the Anglo-Saxon countries) were originally sound and well capitalized. The relatively low degree of financialization sheltered the Spanish economy from the initial stage of the crisis, which was particularly severe in countries (like the United States or the United Kingdom) that were heavily exposed to 'toxic' financial products.

Indeed, the Spanish financial system in the first stages of the crisis was one of the strongest and better regulated financial systems in the world. Initially, Spanish financial institutions were less 'financialized', had a stronger retail focus and relatively low leverage, and were soundly capitalized. However, the implosion of the real estate bubble, their dependence on MBB liabilities, and the depth of the economic crisis weakened them and made them far more vulnerable.

There is consensus that the stern regulations of the Bank of Spain played a key role in the performance of Spanish banks—and these clearly contained the development of Spanish MBB, explaining notably the absence of off-balance sheet securitization. However, regulation was not enough, particularly for the *cajas*. As the international crisis dragged on, the banking sector could not

[21] 'El día que el Banco de España se doblegó,' in *El País*, 13 March 2011 and 'Un gobernador entre dos fuegos,' in *El País*. 13 May 2012.

escape its dramatic effects. Deteriorating economic conditions, the implosion of the real estate market, the dependence on wholesale funding, weaknesses in the regulatory framework, and the role of the Bank of Spain all help to explain this reversal.

In the end, Spain could not escape the ensuing effects of the crisis: the liquidity and credit crunch as well as the collapse of the real estate sector. Initially, the strong fiscal position of the country (particularly in comparison to Italy or Greece), combined with the some of the features that characterize the Spanish 'model of capitalism' (namely, a relatively strong public sector, the informal economy, and the role of the family) (see Royo 2008) contributed to shelter the country from the effects of the crisis.

As we have seen, the funding gap was high and MBB was largely concentrated on the liabilities side of the balance sheet, with a significant element of bank lending prior to the crisis funded on wholesale markets. While the financial crisis did not have a devastating direct impact on most Spanish banks during the first phase of the crisis, the difficulties accessing wholesale funding eventually had a knock-out effect on Spanish bank lending, thus leading to the bursting of the asset price bubble and a seemingly rather more 'traditional' banking crisis.

This volume examines the experience of Japan. Is Japan the future of Spain? While there are some similarities on the assets and liabilities side, there are also key differences; in Spain, the purchase of sovereign bonds depends to a significant degree on international markets (this is not so much the case in Japan, where domestic savings are a major source of funding). In Japan (unlike Spain), during the lost-decade citizens still invest in banks despite the bubble, and there was limited capital flight in Japan. Finally, Spain has a much larger funding gap, hence a larger dependence on wholesale markets.

Fortunately, the bubble was smaller in Spain; property prices rose about three times in the mid-1990s, compared with 4.5 times in Ireland, and real estate loans peaked at 77 per cent of the Irish economy, compared with 29 per cent in Spain. Moreover, the crisis as of June 2012 has largely affected the second tier of Spanish banks. Santander and BBVA, far more diversified and with major international operations, were affected to a lesser degree. At the same time, Spain unlike Ireland, has established a recapitalization instrument and process based on the Fondo de Restructuración Ordenada Bancaria. The problem, of course, is that it lacked enough funds, which led to a financial bailout in June 2012. However, she Spanish bailout is also 9 per cent of its economy, compared with €63 billion, or 43 per cent, in Ireland.

The Spanish government (as well as the Bank of Spain and the ECB) failed to cope with the asset bubble and its imbalances. Hence, the Spanish experience shows that financial stability cannot be divorced from economic policy; while regulation matters, macroeconomic factors do too. The banks are still dealing with their toxic assets and should heed the lesson from other countries; they must be cleaned up, not just merged into a bigger problem. Bankia is a perfect example of that failure. In the end, Spain did not heed the lessons from previous crisis: do not lend excessively to property developers; burst the bubble before it is too late; recognize that retail banking is not a low-risk activity; avoid over-concentration in property loans; and remember what happened before.

From a theoretical standpoint, the Spanish financial sector's response to the global financial crisis shows that cross-national differences persist. While financial capitalist states have converged as a result of the combined processes of globalization and European integration rendered the 'Mediterranean' financial model far less distinct from other models than before, in the case of Spain, the crisis has led to extensive regulatory intervention that has served to reinforce the pre-existing model; changes in the years immediately preceding the financial crisis have not been reversed.

Furthermore, this chapter shows the importance of focusing on the concept of MBB and the need to examine the activities undertaken by financial institutions on the assets and liabilities sides of their balance sheets. On the assets side, the deterioration in the quality of loans caused by the collapse of the real estate market has led to the repeated downgrade of Spanish financial institutions and a financial bailout, turning a banking crisis into a sovereign debt crisis. At the same time, the financial crisis has intensified the credit crunch and worsened the recession. On the liabilities side, initially Spanish financial institutions were sheltered by their reliance on domestic deposits, and their limited exposure to 'toxic' assets. Yet, they were very vulnerable to wholesale funding and ABSs, which they issued for funding purposes to close the gap between the net flow of loans and the flow of deposits. This dependence, contributing to the real estate bubble, led to the downgrading (and collapse) of several *cajas*, as well as to the financial bailout.

Additionally, the degree of financialization, key to MBB, is also an important element to account for the way in which the crisis played out in Spain, specifically the response of the Spanish authorities. The collapse of the real estate markets eventually led to a traditional banking crisis fuelled by turbo-charged lending by MBB on the liability side of the Spanish bank's balance sheets. MBB explains the dramatic increase in lending, and the ongoing credit crunch in Spain; when the crisis hit, international and wholesale funding dried up and it affected bank lending. In this regard, the main 'toxic' assets held by Spanish banks are domestic bad loans and mortgages.

Finally, one of the interesting aspects about the Spanish crisis is that MBB was having its impact prior to keen awareness regarding the crisis and it was largely overlooked as a source of the bursting bubble. In this sense, although the Spanish banking crisis has been labelled as a traditional bank crisis, it was more than that.

References

Bank of Spain (2010) *Financial Stability Review*. Madrid: Bank of Spain March.

Barrón, I. (2009) 'Lehman no ha hecho daño hasta ahora ... ' [Lehman did not hurt up to now ... ']. *El País* (September 13).

Blanco, R. (2011) 'The Securization market in Spain: Past, Present and Future', In *Working Party on Financial Statistics: Proceedings of the Workshop on Securitisation* (ed. M. Chavoix-Mannato), *OECD Statistics Working Papers* (2011/03), OECD Publishing.

Caja Madrid (2007) *Caja Madrid Annual Report 2007*. Madrid: Caja Madrid.

Carballo Cruz, F. (2011) 'Causes and Consequences of the Spanish Economic Crisis: Why the Recovery is Taken so Long?' *Panoeconomicus*, 3: 309–328.

Deeg, R. and S. A. Perez (2000) 'International Capital Mobility and Domestic Institutions: Corporate Finance and Governance in Four European Cases', *Governance*, 13(2): 119–53.

Fernández Ordóñez, M. (2008) 'The challenges to the Spanish banking system in the face of the global crisis'. Lecture at the 50th anniversary of ESADE. Barcelona, (October 30). Fondo de Restructuración Ordenada Bancaria (FROB): <http://www.frob.es/index_en.html>.

International Monetary Fund (IMF) (2012) *Spain: The Reform of Spanish Savings Banks Technical Notes*. IMF Country Report No. 12/141.

Lukauskas, A. (2007) *Regulating Finance* Ann Arbor: Michigan University Press.

Mallet, V. (2009) 'Prudence pays off for big banks'. *Financial Times. Special Report: Investing In Spain*. (October 2): 3.

McGuire, P., and G. von Peter (2009) 'The US dollar shortage in global banking'. *BIS Quarterly Review* (March).

Pérez, S. A. (1997) *Banking on Privilege*. New York: Cornell University Press.

Pérez, S A. and J. Westrup (2010) "Finance and the Macroeconomy: The Politics of Regulatory Reform in Europe." *Journal of European Public Policy*, 17 (8): 1171–1192.

Plender, J. (2009) 'Respinning the Web', *Financial Times*. (June 22): 5.

Royo, S. (2008) *Varieties of Capitalism in Spain* NY: Palgrave.

Royo, S. (2009) 'After the Fiesta'. *South European Society & Politics* 14, (March): 19–34.

Royo, S. (2012) How Did the Spanish Financial System Survive the First Stage of the Global Crisis?" *Governance*. (Forthcoming). [Article first published online: November 6, 2012. DOI:10.1111/gove.12000].

Royo, S. (2013) *Lessons from the Economic Crisis in Spain* NY. Palgrave.

8

Turning the Crisis on its Head: Sovereign Debt Crisis as Banking Crisis in Italy and Greece

George Pagoulatos and Lucia Quaglia

Introduction

The economic and financial crisis that broke out with full force in the autumn of 2008, though sharing some common features worldwide, affected various countries in different ways. Whereas some countries, such as the United Kingdom (see Hardie and Maxfield, this volume) and Ireland, were badly hit by banking crises in the early part of the crisis, and by subsequent credit crunch and recession, others, such as Italy and Greece, were moderately affected at this stage by the banking crisis and the credit crunch, but were severely affected by subsequent difficulties in financing sovereign debt.

What explains similarities and differences in the way in which national financial systems have been affected by the crisis and have reacted to it? This chapter sets out to address this question by carrying out a structured comparison of two southern European countries: Greece and Italy. These two have been chosen because they share important similarities: their national financial systems have evolved as bank-based systems; they were latecomers in liberalization, subject to regionalization rather than globalization in their banking systems; and, as the analysis of the bank balance sheets reveals, relied to a limited extent on market-based banking, compared with the more advanced financial systems in the European Union (EU).

As noted in the introductory chapter of this volume, the literature on national financial systems has classified them either as 'bank based', such as those in most continental European countries, or as 'market based', first and foremost in the Anglo-Saxon countries (see Allen and Gale 2000). We aim to move beyond this traditional distinction, developing the concept of 'market-based' banking, which considers the extent to which the banks' ability to supply credit to the economy is driven by market pressures on both the asset and liability sides of their balance sheets (see the Introduction to this volume). As for liabilities, we look at the funding base of banks, in particular their reliance on retail deposits or on wholesale markets for funding, including inter-bank borrowing from abroad, which increased the banks' dependence on international funding. As for assets, we look at the trading of securities (i.e. the size of the trading book), the presence of toxic assets and the use of structured investment vehicles (SIVs). As part of the banks' business model we also examine the expansion of their activities abroad, in particular the banks' expansion into retail banking in other countries, or into international investment banking, including the investment in securities, many of which subsequently proved toxic.

Empirically, the chapter proceeds as follows. The second section outlines the evolution of the national financial systems under scrutiny and of their regulatory environment. This is followed by an analysis of market-based banking in Italy and Greece (third section). The fourth section examines how Italy and Greece have been affected by the financial (banking) crisis, and the fifth section analyses the unfolding of the sovereign debt crisis. The sixth section explains how the sovereign debt crisis turned into a banking crisis in Greece and belatedly in Italy. Finally, the chapter draws some insights concerning the limited extent and specific features of market-based banking in these two countries.

The Evolution of the Italian and Greek Financial Systems

Until their liberalization in the late 1980s and 1990s, the southern financial systems of Italy and Greece (like those of France and Spain) were typical credit-based Mediterranean systems, characterized by extensive state control over the banking system, underdeveloped capital markets, and pervasive financial interventionism (Perez and Westrup 2010).

Under the post-war developmentalist economic orthodoxy, financial interventionism was deemed necessary to accelerate the process of economic development, which in the 1950s and 1960s was considered as almost synonymous with industrialization; the 'later' the industrialization (Italy was a 'late', Greece a 'late-late' industrializer) the more active the state in engineering financial interventionism. Financial interventionism over the post-war period became a prerequisite both for autarkic development strategies based on import substitution industrialization (where heavy protectionism, capital controls, and subsidized credit to industry were the main instruments) and for open trade strategies of export-led growth (employing favourable financial regulations for manufacturing and exports) (Loriaux 1997; Pagoulatos 2003a; Perez 1997; Woo-Cumings 1999; Zysman 1983).

In all such cases, financial interventionism served as the institutional apparatus that directed national savings exclusively into the national banking system and subsequently transformed bank deposits (trapped into national banking systems sheltered through capital controls and market protection) into low-interest credit for 'productive' sectors, industrial enterprises, and, most notably, the government itself (Deeg and Perez 2000). Indeed, in southern countries characterized by public deficits and balance of payments deficits, largely resulting from weak tax bases, financial interventionism taxed the domestic banking system and depositors in order to secure cheap government finance, penalize consumption and other 'non-productive' activities and bolster export-oriented sectors.

Then, from the second half of the 1980s, southern financial systems were liberalized, in a process that was crucially driven by the European single market programme (Story and Walter 1997). Financial liberalization was, to a significant extent, a necessary prerequisite for the central banks' programmatic effort to achieve effective disinflation (Perez and Westrup 2010). For the south, at a subsequent stage, a stabilization strategy based on monetary austerity entailed the significant political advantage of allowing governments to eschew a more radical pace of fiscal adjustment (Pagoulatos 2003b). As a result, fiscal consolidation in the European south during the 1990s, especially Greece and far less so Italy, was mainly revenue based rather than structural, and was relaxed following European monetary union (EMU) accession (Blavoukos and Pagoulatos 2008). Italy ran uninterrupted primary surplus from 1992 to 2009, and between 1997 and 2002 these surplus were as high as 5 per cent of gross domestic product (GDP). Moreover, in the run up to EMU, the country reformed its income policy, pension system, and parts of the public administration. This is an important observation, because it helps understand the background of the 2010 sovereign debt crisis. But before we come to that, let us take a look at the two countries' financial systems.

Until the 1990s, the Italian financial system was mainly 'bank oriented', in that it was characterized by an extensive activity of financial intermediation performed by banks (Allen and Gale 2000).With the reform of banking, finance and corporate legislation in Italy in the 1990s, the financial system was liberalized, and new life was breathed into an anaemic stock market (Deeg 2005). However, this did not imply the reduction of the role of the banks, which engaged extensively in securities trading and, as in Germany and Japan, held shares in non-financial companies (Ciocca 2005). In the same decade, segmentation in the banking sector came to an end: the formal change took place with the transposition in 1992 of the Second Banking

Directive, which introduced the all-purpose universal bank in Italy. At the same time, the banking system was privatized, modernized, and consolidated (Panetta 2004; Giordano 2007). The pace of consolidation accelerated following the establishment of EMU in 1999 and the Financial Services Action Plan issued by the European Commission and endorsed by the member states in 2000. Yet by 2007, the five biggest banks in Italy held only 33 per cent of total assets, one of the lowest figures in the EU (ECB 2007a). Foreign operations represent about a third of total assets for the top five banking groups (OECD 2010). Other banking groups operate mostly in the domestic markets, where a large number of small banks, including cooperative banks specialized in local financing, are also active. Unlike the *cajas* in Spain, which got into trouble during the financial crisis (see Royo this volume), the small local banks in Italy were not subject to political interference.

Until the early 2000s there was a relatively limited penetration of foreign banks and financial institutions in Italy for a variety of reasons, most notably the lukewarm attitude towards foreign ownership of Italian banks by the Bank of Italy under the governorship of Antonio Fazio (1993–2005) (Quaglia 2008a). Increasingly into the 2000s, pressure from other EU member states, the European Commission, and financial markets, coupled with sharp domestic criticisms from part of the business community led the Italian banking system to open up, following the resignation of Governor Fazio (Quaglia 2008b). By the mid-2000s, there was significant foreign penetration into the Italian banking system approaching 19 per cent in 2006, compared with an average 10.5 per cent market share of foreign banks in Germany, France, and Spain (Saccomanni 2008). Foreign banks acquired major Italian banks, including the Banca Nazionale del Lavoro by BNP Paribas, and Antonveneta by the Dutch ABN-AMRO, although it was subsequently sold to the Italian bank Monte dei Paschi in 2008.[1] In 2007, there was the merger of the Borsa Italiana (Italian Stock Exchange) and London Stock Exchange, which contributed to the internationalization of securities trading in Italy. At the same time, Italian banks began expanding abroad, mainly through subsidiaries.

Similar was the course of Greece. In Greece, financial liberalization over the 1990s changed the structure of a traditionally state-controlled, heavily regulated, and bank-based financial system. Deregulation, followed by EU-driven re-regulation (such as the implementation of the capital adequacy and other EC directives from the early 1990s onwards) subjected the financial and banking system to a common, less interventionist European regulatory framework. The state retreated from the ownership of banks, either completely privatizing banks in a market that was soon to be dominated by private credit institutions

[1] This was the result of Royal Bank of Scotland's problems after it took over ABN-Amro, rather than being indicative of any Italian hostility to foreign banks.

or limiting itself to control in some banks through minority equity ownership. The financial system was transformed towards a more market-based structure, as viewed by the existing varieties of financial capitalism typology, but one in which new financial market instruments and institutions were colonized by existing banks and their subsidiaries (Pagoulatos 2003a).

Over the 1990s the Greek financial system was transformed momentously. Annual credit expansion led economic growth from the late 1990s through the 2000s. Following the trajectory of other emerging markets of the 1990s, the Athens capital market boomed after 1998. In addition, from the 1990s and especially into the 2000s, the Greek banking market opened up to foreign institutions. The market share of foreign branches and subsidiaries over total Greek banking system assets was 37 per cent in 2006 (European Central Bank 2010).

Market-Based Banking in Italy and Greece

Despite the privatization, modernization, consolidation, and opening up of the Italian and Greek banking systems, the degree of market-based banking in both countries was relatively low prior to the crisis. In the run up to the crisis, in both countries the majority of banks' *assets* were loans to customers, with only a small component of derivatives, approximately 3 per cent of banks' assets (Table 8.1). The European Central Bank (ECB) figures reported in Table 8.2 give a breakdown of the assets of the Italian, Spanish, and Greek banks.[2] A greater percentage of the assets of Italian and to a lesser extent Greek banks were national government securities—than were Spanish banks (Royo this volume).[3] Hence, Italian and Greek banks had more exposure to their government (assuming Euro area government lending was overwhelmingly to the banks' home government) than Spanish banks. Italian banks did not fuel a property bubble: they lent to households far less than either Spanish or Greek banks. Lending to non-financial companies (NFCs) was higher in Spain than in Italy and Greece, though not really dramatic. However, in Spain NFC lending included a very large proportion of property developers, which was much less the case in Italy. Data from the Bank of Italy (see Table 8.3) suggest that Italian banks were predominantly lending to NFCs, and that amongst NFCs, the bulk of the loans went to services and industry, not building. Obviously, a property bubble can come also from residential mortgage lending, but there was no significant rise in consumer lending in the years preceding the crisis.

[2] With the Euro area as a whole, rather than by individual countries, as a limitation.

[3] At that time Spain had a much lower public debt than Italy and Greece. In the pre-2008 world, euro-denominated government securities were considered among the safest possible asset categories.

Table 8.1. Assets of Italian and Greek banks

Assets	Italy	Greece
Loans/assets (%)	59	65
Securities/assets (%)	16	15
Derivatives/assets (%)	3.5	3.2
Internationalization of assets (%)	30.5	40

Sources: AFME-ESF (2008), BIS (2008a) (2008b), ECB (2007b), Individual banks' 2007/08 annual reports, five major banks in Italy and Greece, World Bank (2007).

Table 8.2. Breakdown of the assets of the Italian, Spanish, and Greek banks (with the Euro area as a whole, rather than by individual countries, a limitation), end 2007

	EA Banks	EA Govts	EA NFC	EA Households	EA Other	External To EA	Other
Italy	21.6	11.9	24.2	13.6	7.1	3.1	18.5
Spain	13.7	4.6	30.2	28.1	5.9	6.6	10.9
Greece	11.4	8.2	22.1	24.0	6.4	16.4	11.5

Source: (<http://www.ecb.int/stats/money/aggregates/bsheets/html/outstanding_amounts_2007-12.en.html>).

Table 8.3. Italian banks' loans distribution by: customer segment of economic activity

	September 2007	October 2008
Total loans (million of euros)	1,453,323	1,500,679
Segment of economic activity		
General government	56,985	58,357
Financial companies	161,470	168,448
Non-financial companies	775,447	809,079
Of which: Industry	*259,068*	*274,649*
Building	*108,621*	*110,943*
Services	*393,365*	*408,285*
Producer households	88,665	89,645
Consumer households	370,809	375,151

Bank of Italy (2008). *Summary Report of the Statistical Bulletin 2007–2008*, Data on credit, securities business and interest rates, quarter 4, p. 3.
Figures in italics represent subcategories of non-financial companies.

The internationalization of Italian and Greek bank assets was 30 per cent and 40 per cent respectively (Table 8.1), largely because of retail bank expansion in central and eastern Europe. For Italian banks such exposure topped €148 billion in December 2008, 5 per cent of the Italian banking system's total assets (OECD 2010). In absolute terms, Italian banks were mostly exposed to Poland, Croatia, Hungary, and Russia. Total assets of foreign subsidiaries and branches of Greek banking groups in 2008 amounted to €118 billion, an equivalent 28 per cent of total banking system assets and 49 per cent of Greek GDP; of that, the banking system assets in the emerging eastern European economies amounted to €51 billion. Turkey, Bulgaria, and Romania represented the lion's share of Greek banking group foreign assets in emerging eastern Europe, followed by Poland, Serbia, Albania, the former Yugoslav Republic of Macedonia, and Ukraine.

Some of the countries in which Greek and Italian banks were active experienced difficulties during the crisis, resulting in some pressure on the banks (Pagoulatos and Triantopoulos 2009). Overall this regionalization resulted in far less concern than the market-based globalization in some northern European countries (Chang and Jones, this volume; Hardie and Howarth this volume; Hardie and Maxfield this volume) or even the regional expansion of French banks (Howarth this volume).

As far as *liabilities* are concerned, Italian and Greek banks had a broad and stable funding base.[4] Funding from retail customers, more stable than wholesale funding, constituted a large share of the total liabilities in both countries, though this is less the case for Italian banks. The relatively high dependence of Italian banks on wholesale inter-bank funding (Table 8.4)—which underscores the importance of market-based banking in the country—suggests high exposure to the tightened credit conditions from 2007. However, several factors sheltered the Italian banking system from the worst of the credit crunch. First, Italian banks tended to lend mostly to each other. The average home bias for Italy was the highest in the Euro area's national banking systems (Manna 2011). At the height of the crisis, banks cut their lending to banks in other countries far more than their lending to banks in their own country, so the fact that Italian banks lent to each other suggests that inter-bank borrowing was more stable than in those systems (like Spain) where inter-bank funding was largely from abroad.

Second, although Italian banks have high levels of wholesale funding, this is relatively longer term (see Hardie and Howarth, this volume).[5] Ninety-three per cent of debt securities issued by Italian banks are over two years in maturity and none is under one year. For Spanish banks, the figures are 73 and 22 per cent, respectively. Although Italian banks relied on wholesale market funding far more than Greece and Spain—they were less like France (Howarth this volume) (and pre-2008 UK), which relied more on short-term funding. Italian debt maturity was more like that of Germany (Hardie and Howarth, this volume), comparatively long. From early 2011, the difficulties of Italian banks in providing credit due to the cost and availability of funding owed to the spike in bond yields fed principally by market concerns over Italian sovereign debt and the relatively high dependence of banks on bond sales to fund lending.

[4] Bank of Italy (2010, 36). 'Italian banks are distinguished internationally by a high proportion of retail funding, which provided funding stability during the crisis'.

[5] See<http://www.ecb.int/stats/money/aggregates/bsheets/html/outstanding_amounts_2007–12.en.html>

Third, several of the debt securities issued by Italian banks were sold to their customers, which made this sort of funding less subject to the vagaries of the financial markets. Italian banks have greater access to retail investors for their bond issues than elsewhere in Europe (Bank of Italy 2011). According to the Bank of Italy figures, fundraising 'least sensitive to market movements' (retail bonds and deposits combined) constitutes 54.1 per cent of the total. The figure is far higher for smaller banks. Moreover, a high proportion of wholesale funding is from domestic sources.

In a comparison between Italy and Spain (Royo this volume), although banks in both countries were borrowers through securitization, as a percentage of GDP, Italian assets in securitizations were half that of Spain, as a percentage of GDP (Hardie and Howarth this volume). So lending in Italy depended less heavily than in Spain on this relatively fragile market. Moreover, under half of Italian securitization was of residential mortgages, the most fragile securitization, while in Spain it was two-thirds. Inter-bank borrowing from abroad in Italy and Greece was about 10–13 per cent of GDP (Table 8.4). Spanish banks borrowed in the US inter-bank market to finance their domestic lending (Hardie and Howarth this volume; Royo this volume).

Greek banks have had a strong tradition, dating back to the times of financial 'repression', of financing their loans largely through deposits. Thus, in Greece dependence on the inter-bank market, and the associated liquidity shocks during the financial crisis, was limited. As in Italy, bank sponsorship of assed-based commercial paper (ABCP) was close to zero (Acharya and Schnabl 2010). At the end of 2007, the exposure of Italian banks to structured products amounted to €4.9 billion, only about 2 per cent of supervisory capital, thanks to the rule and practices of the national supervisory authorities. Consequently, write-downs due to losses on these products were limited for top banking groups, totalling €4.5 billion by the end of 2008 (OECD 2010).

Table 8.4 Liabilities of Italian and Greek banks

Liabilities	Italy	Greece
Deposits/total liabilities (%)	41	63
Wholesale funding/total liabilities (%)	42	13
Other liabilities/total liabilities (%)	19	27
Funding gap: Weighted average of individual banks' loans/deposits	168	117
Funding gap: loans/deposits (MFI's aggregate data)	129	93
Deposits/total Liabilities	41	63
Use of securitization, per cent securitization issuance/GDP	1.25	1.7
Amounts owed to credit institutions	15.6	16
Inter-bank borrowing from abroad/GDP (%)	13.5	10

Sources: AFME-ESF (2008), BIS (2008a,b), ECB (2007b), Individual banks' 2007/08 annual reports, five major banks in Italy and Greece, World Bank (2007).

The Impact of the Banking Crisis in Italy and Greece

The peak of stage one of the global crisis (as banking crisis) was reached on 15 September 2008, when the investment bank Lehman Brothers filed for bankruptcy in the United States and was not rescued by the US authorities. Amongst the various European countries, neither Italy nor Greece was hard hit by the first stage of the financial crisis. The average ratio of losses to loans at the end of 2008 for the five main Italian and Greek banks averaged approximately 1 per cent.[6]

Because of the low degree of market-based banking, Greek and to a lesser extent Italian banks were relatively sheltered from the most intense forces of global financial contagion. The expansion abroad of Italian and Greek banks was mostly in retail business, with ownership of retail subsidiaries and participation in banking groups in central and eastern Europe, for Italian banks, and south-eastern Europe, for Greek banks. As opposed to German banks (Hardie and Howarth, this volume) Italian and Greek banks did not invest in 'fancy' financial products that later proved to be 'toxic'. When the financial crisis spread to central and eastern Europe, Italian and Greek bank balance sheets were affected through the deterioration of local economies, even though risks remained relatively moderate. Greek banks channelled part of the government finance they received to stabilize them in late 2008 to bolster their Balkan subsidiaries. This move created repeated tensions with the Bank of Greece, paralleling difficulties between Austrian banks and their national supervisor.

The Sovereign Debt Crisis as Experienced in Greece and Italy

As explained earlier, financial liberalization after the 1990s radically altered the features of traditional Mediterranean, interventionist, bank-based financial systems. But some of the structural underpinnings that had led to financial interventionism in the first place persisted. Government deficits remained a problem, as witnessed by the large public debt levels; and from the moment finance was liberalized, the current account deficits shot up. This was especially so in countries with weak exports, such as Greece and Spain, but not Italy, whose economic growth has been export led to a significant degree. For every single year since its accession to the euro, Greece exhibited higher than Euro area average inflation, which was also attributed to the demand boom created by credit liberalization and low interest rates. As a cumulative result, over the 2000s, Greece suffered an estimated real exchange rate appreciation

[6] Authors' own calculation on the basis of individual banks' annual reports.

of 25–30 per cent, leading to declining competitiveness and a 14 per cent current account deficit in 2008. The pattern behind Spain's current account deficit was similar (Marzinotto, Pisani-Ferry and Sapir 2010). Overall Italy suffered a loss of competitiveness as labour costs rose relative to the core countries, but the export sector was able to remain competitive, meaning the current account did not move into nearly as substantial a deficit.

In 2008, both Italy and Greece had similar public debt levels close to 110 per cent of GDP. In both countries the large public debt levels were not a matter of huge private debt (as in Spain or Ireland) turning into public debt, but public debt to begin with. Both the Italian and the Greek private sectors remained significantly underleveraged compared with the Euro area average, despite the higher annual growth rates of private debt in the 2000s. Relatively lower private debt levels reduced the risks of transferring private debt to public debt, as happened in Spain, Portugal, and Ireland as the financial crisis proceeded. In 2009, Italian private debt reached only 224 per cent of GDP and Greece's 219 per cent of GDP, compared with a Euro area average 249 per cent, and significantly higher figures for Spain, Ireland, and Portugal (268, 273, and 314 per cent, respectively).

However, the external debt of both countries did converge to eurozone and EU15 average levels. Lower interest rates underpinned the consumption boom that followed EMU accession, as opposed to the much higher rates prior to 1998. Interest rates had been previous low during the era of 'financial repression' (1960s to 1980s) but there was no one else apart from the government sector and subsidized production sectors to take advantage of them as consumption and mortgage credit were heavily restricted (Perez and Westrup 2010).

However, the low interest rates of the 2000s followed the higher rates of the 1990s, during which the debt servicing burden for high public debt countries had risen. Between 2001 and the beginning of 2008, the Greek government bond spread from the German Bund usually ranged in the low 20 to 40 basis points area, or even lower. To take a random example, on 1 April 2004, the German bond yield was 3.95 per cent and the Greek one was 4.12 per cent, just 17 basis points higher. Combined with the boundless opportunities for public debt management (and window-dressing) created by securitization and financial accounting innovation, Greece benefited from a soft budget constraint that postponed hard fiscal consolidation decisions (Blavoukos and Pagoulatos 2008). Unlike Italy, Greek government budget primary surpluses (i.e. excluding interest payments on the debt) were short-lived, generated only in the end 1990s and sustained for just half of the 2000s.

The Greek economy expanded from the late 1990s through the 2000s with an average annual real GDP growth rate above 3.5 per cent. Economic growth was driven by domestic demand, consumption, and construction, financed by an annual credit growth rate that was among the highest in the eurozone. Despite the higher credit growth rates, the Greek household leverage ratio (household debt as percentage of gross disposable household income) remained consistently below the eurozone average (rising from 35 to 70 per cent in 2003–9, compared with the 80–90 per cent for the eurozone) (Bank of Greece, 2010).

In contrast, the Italian economy exhibited a low average annual GDP growth rate in the 2000s (0.54 per cent annual average real GDP growth between 2000 and 2010 versus 1.37 per cent for the eurozone), but posted a primary budget surplus from 1995 to 2008. Far more export led than all other southerners, Italy also had a very low current account deficit, 3.2 per cent in 2009, which paled in comparison to Greece's staggering 11.2 per cent in the same year. Thus Italy entered the 2008 crisis with far healthier macroeconomic fundamentals than Greece.

Italy's membership of the eurozone helped stabilize the situation during the financial turmoil because it effectively eliminated the risk of currency crisis, that is a run on the lira and inability of the Italian government to pay short-term foreign debts for lack of access to 'hard currency'. This was even more so the case for Greece, another notoriously weak-currency country prior to its euro accession. However, some risk of a solvency crisis remained, not so much for Italian banks, as pointed out earlier, but for the Italian state, given the high levels of public debt and deficit. Gross public debt was around 106 per cent of GDP in 2008 and it reached over 115 per cent of GDP in 2010, with an annual deficit of 5.3 per cent of GDP. For the first time since 1992, Italy ran a primary deficit in 2009 and 2010, which was mainly due to a falling growth rate. About one sixth of existing public debt has to be refinanced every year and around half of Italian government debt is held abroad (OECD 2010), unlike Italian banks that mostly fund themselves on the domestic market.

Signs of declining fiscal creditworthiness in Italy as well as in other eurozone member states were evidenced by the fact that the spreads between the ten-year treasury yields of Italy and those of Germany rose from thirty-five basis points in 2007 to 140–150 basis points in late 2009—the highest since the launch of the single currency in 1999 (Dinmore 2008). However, Italy, unlike Greece, did not suffer a fully fledged sovereign debt crisis as early as Greece and did not have to turn to the EU and International Monetary Fund (IMF) for financial assistance in 2010.

That the Italian public debt was not perceived at an imminent threat of default risk is evinced in the credit default swap (CDS) rates. Sovereign (five-year) CDS rates for Greece went from 120 basis points in September 2009 to 900 basis points in September 2010, while for Italy they ranged from 67 in September 2009 to 190 one year later, lower than Spain, Portugal, and Ireland (335, the second highest after Greece). As a result of its good fundamentals,

Italy in autumn of 2010 was estimated at the lowest risk of debt restructuring among all peripheral countries (Greece, Ireland, Portugal, and Spain), as was demonstrated in the CDS rates. Thus, at the time when the financial crisis was evolving into a Greek sovereign debt crisis, the Italian authorities were not forced to take special measures, like those adopted in Greece. For these reasons Italy, despite its large public debt to GDP ratio, eschewed the sovereign debt crisis faced by Greece in 2010, though it was subsequently affected by it.

The main reason for Greece becoming the first eurozone country to be bailed out, and the largest bailout in history, was a nasty combination of an unsustainable level of public debt (115 per cent in 2009), 80 per cent of which was external, combined with a staggering public deficit of 12.7 per cent of GDP revealed after the October 2009 elections,[7] against a 6 per cent level officially estimated by the previous conservative government. The revelation of the actual public deficit levels by the new socialist government prompted an unprecedented market speculation against Greek sovereign debt, with the spreads and CDSs reaching record levels. Borrowing spreads on ten-year Bunds jumped to 300 basis points in early 2009 (the highest in the Euro area) then receded temporarily before shooting up to prohibitive levels later in

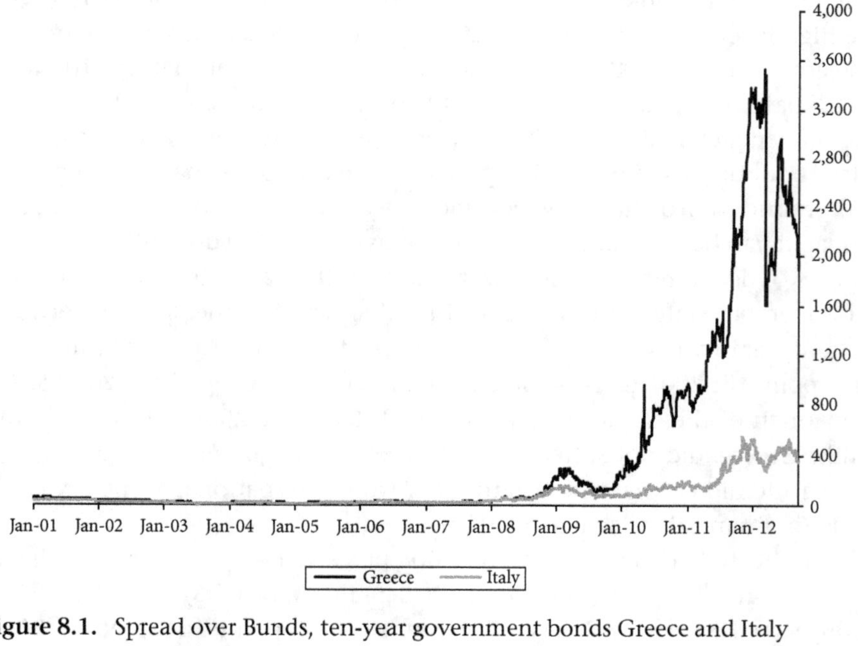

Figure 8.1. Spread over Bunds, ten-year government bonds Greece and Italy
Source: Datastream.

[7] Finally, in November 2010, Eurostat revised the 2009 deficit to 15.4 per cent GDP.

the year (Figure 8.1). Greece was downgraded by Standard & Poor's to two notches from minimum ECB collateral standards in early 2009 subsequently—the ECB changed its rules on collateral rating—and finally downgraded to junk bond status by two credit rating agencies in spring 2010, after which the bond spread settled in the 700 basis points area or above.

In the first months of 2010, an overwhelming majority of market analysts forecasted a Greek default. As market prices became prohibitive, the Greek government was forced, in late April 2010, to resort to an EU/ECB/IMF €110 billion Emergency Financing Mechanism, followed by a rigorous three-year conditionality programme. The Greek crisis and bailout was only the first chapter in the domino effect of eurozone sovereign debt crises, which subsequently spread to the rest of the eurozone periphery. The EU/IMF €750 billion European Financial Stability Facility (EFSF),[8] set up in May 2010 to avert speculation against other weak peripheral economies, did not succeed in this aim; Ireland was the second victim of the eurozone debt crisis, and resorted to an European Financial Stability Facility bailout in November 2010.

Thus, the 2008–9 financial crisis found Italy in a relatively sound and Greece in an extremely precarious fiscal position. The preconditions were there for the financial crisis to develop into a sovereign debt crisis for Greece but not yet for Italy, despite their almost similar public debt to GDP levels. The explanation for why Italy eschewed a debt crisis as early as Greece has emerged from their comparison: though at equal levels of public debt, Italy depended on the markets for refinancing only one-sixth of its debt, as compared with Greece having to refinance more than one-fifth; Italy had a far lower public deficit in the sensitive year 2009, and a consistent track record of fiscal discipline and credibility over the 2000s, and, more importantly, only 50 per cent of Italian public debt was held abroad, as opposed to 80 per cent for Greece.

In the past, for example through the 1980s and much of the 1990s, excessive public deficit and debt levels in Greece were prevented from turning into a sovereign debt crisis by the fact that the vast majority of that debt was domestic, held by the Greek banking system, most of which was also state controlled.[9] This was no longer the case in the 2000s. Public debt management was modernized, making use of advanced financial instruments such as extensive securitization, SIVs, and financial accounting innovation techniques, which allowed easy access to global money markets during the halcyon days of the global savings glut.

[8] This consisted of €440 billion eurozone funds, €60 billion EC budget funds, and €250 billion IMF funds.

[9] The domestic control of the public debt also explains why countries like Japan, whose public debt well exceeds 200 per cent of its GDP, are not under threat of a sovereign debt financial crisis.

For example, Greece resorted to advanced financial technology instruments, like a 2002 \$15 billion bond sale and currency swap organized by Goldman Sachs, through which Greece raised \$1 billion of off-balance sheet funding.[10] The public debt conversion from domestic to foreign was accelerated into the 2000s. Hence, Greece pushed its debt servicing burden to the future while becoming highly exposed to global debt market fluctuations. However, this global financial market exposure accumulated risks which materialized as soon as global liquidity dried out and markets became jittery about sovereign debt following the Dubai public debt crisis in late 2009. When the Greek GDP growth rate turned negative and bond yields shot up, the country's public debt outlook became unsustainable, prompting the devastating sovereign debt crisis from which Greece could only be rescued by an organized bail out.

Unlike Greece, Italy seemed to have been only marginally affected at the beginning of the sovereign debt crisis in 2010. However, Italy began to face serious problem in the bond market in the summer of 2011: the spread between Italian ten-year bonds and their German counterparts widened; Italian sovereign debt yields moved above those charged to Spain; and rating agencies downgraded the creditworthiness of the Italian government. Consequently, Italian banks faced an increase in their borrowing costs. In the countries most severely hit by debt market tensions, namely Italy and Spain, stock index levels fell close to the lows reached in March 2009, a few months after the collapse of Lehman Brothers. Stock prices also fell in the banking sector, both in the Euro area countries experiencing problems in the sovereign debt market as well as in other Euro area countries, because of the concerns about their banks' exposure to sovereign risk (*Wall Street Journal* 12 July 2011).The ECB intensified its purchase of Italian bonds in the secondary markets in an attempt to reduce borrowing costs. The deterioration of the fiscal situation and the inability of the centre-right government of Silvio Berlusconi to put together a convincing adjustment package, led to the government resignation and the nomination of the 'technocratic' government headed by Mario Monti in November 2011 (Jones 2012).

In December 2011, the ECB launched a programme of long-term refinancing operations (LTROs), issuing loans at the interest rate 1 per cent for a period of three years to European banks, accepting government bonds, mortgage securities, and other commercial papers in the portfolio of the banks as collaterals. At the same time, the ECB changed its rules on collaterals, accepting lower quality collaterals in return for its loans. Under this programme, the

[10] The swap was still legal under Eurostat rules in 2002, but the 2008 Greek government chose to withhold it from the Commission authorities, with the consequence of aggravating the credibility crisis in 2010 when the swap was revealed.

ECB loaned €489 billion to 523 banks,[11] mainly in Greece, Ireland, Italy, and Spain. Indeed, Italian, and Spanish banks took about 60 per cent of all the net new loans from the ECB, with Spain's overstretched banks taking marginally more than Italy's.[12] The banks used these funds to buy government bonds, effectively easing the debt crisis.

In February 2012, the ECB held a second three-year auction of €529 billion to 800 European banks. Although the ECB programme did not target specifically Italy, the country benefited through a temporary reduction of its borrowing costs. The ECB lent to Euro area banks, which in turn lend to Euro area governments, and then used the government debt they bought as collateral for yet more loans from the ECB. Arguably, the dependence of some Euro area banks on loans from the ECB can be seen as evidence that these banks have already failed, and so have the government of those countries, though how to define a sovereign debt crisis is a matter of controversy in the literature.

Sovereign Debt Crises as Banking Crises

We have seen so far that the banking systems of both Italy and Greece withstood the initial effects of the 2008 global financial crisis as a result of their limited market-based banking. However, these southern European banking systems carried a heavy toll as a result of the sovereign debt crisis, being critically affected by their respective country risk. Thus the Greek sovereign debt crisis also turned into a Greek banking system crisis; and in the summer of 2012 Italy was at risk of following a similar fate.

A strong starting position for capitalization (at 11.2 per cent regulatory capital to risk weighted assets in 2007, well above the 8 per cent regulatory minimum) provided the Greek banking system considerable resilience in the face of the crisis. The strong capital standing of Greek banks if compared with many advanced European banking systems was demonstrated in the relatively low leverage ratios. The leverage ratio of Greek banking groups (total assets/shareholder equity) was 13 in 2007, 17 in 2008 and down to 14 in 2009, following a significant increase of own funds. These leverage ratios were far lower than the ratios for large eurozone banking groups (at an average of 28 in December 2009), reflecting the strong capitalization of Greek banking groups (Bank of Greece 2010). Indicatively, in 2008, Crédit Agricole had an estimated leverage ratio of 40, Deutsche Bank around 50 (liabilities

[11] <http://www.economist.com/blogs/freeexchange/2012/02/europes-central-bank-and-euro-crisis>

[12] <http://www.bbc.co.uk/news/business-18058270>

exceeding 80 per cent of Germany's GDP), and Fortis 33 (liabilities several times Belgium's GDP) (Gros and Micossi 2008, see also Carmassi, Gros, and Micossi 2009). Gros and Micossi (2008) attribute the large gap between leverage ratios and official regulatory ratios mainly to the massive in-house investment banking operations performed by large European banking groups that were not subject to any regulatory capital requirements. Greek banks, as well as Italian banks engaged to a more limited extent—as compared to banks in other countries—in market-based banking, and thus created relatively lower systemic risks of a 'too big to fail and too big to be saved' type.

Very soon after the financial crisis erupted in the advanced financial systems on both sides of the Atlantic, contagion spread to the eurozone including the south. Bank funding costs rose, and asset quality in Greece and south-eastern Europe declined. Greek bank profitability decreased rapidly in 2009 and 2010, and share prices fell steeply. By 2010 Greek bank equity prices had collapsed to 20–30 per cent of their 2007 levels. Though operating income remained stable at elevated levels, the need for larger provisions against non-performing loans drove the Greek banking system as a whole in 2010 into a loss after including provisioning and taxes. Since 2009, the Greek banks have been supported by purchasing Greek government bonds and depositing them as collateral for lower-interest rate ECB finance, benefiting from the spread. However, the depreciation of their government securities portfolio in 2010 developed into a major burden for the Greek banking sector, affecting particularly the banks with the largest government debt holdings. From spring 2010, Greek banks followed the government in successive downgradings by credit rating agencies. Thus Greek banks became victims of the public debt crisis, the related economic slowdown and the country risk associated with their highly indebted sovereign.

The effects of the crisis became visible in the liability structure of the Greek commercial banking system. Bank bond issues declined from 10 per cent in 2005 to 6 per cent in 2009. In such a serious crisis, even deposits declined, and eurosystem financing increased from 1 per cent to 11 per cent (Bank of Greece 2010). Far better was the standing of Italian banks, corresponding to the lower perceived sovereign risk. In 2009–10, the funding structure of Italian banks was deemed among the best in Europe, facing very low refinancing risk (Credit Suisse 2010). Contrary to Greek banks, which relied extensively on the ECB, Italian banks in 2010 made little use of ECB funding.[13]

[13] Total ECB funding to Greek banks was estimated at an equivalent of 35 per cent of Greece's GDP, as opposed to 2 per cent GDP for Italian banks—Ireland received the equivalent of 45 per cent of its GDP in ECB funding, and Portugal 13 per cent (April 2010) (Credit Suisse, 'Equity Research', Europe/Italy, June 2010—source: ECB, national CBs).

During the first semester of 2010 an estimated €20 billion worth of deposits (representing around 9 per cent of total banking system deposits) left the Greek banking system. Though much of that was due to tax reasons, the threat of a run on the banks and consequent bank collapse was a crucial factor. Even more crucial was the overhanging threat of redenomination of deposits in a devalued currency in the event that Greece was forced to leave the euro. The deposit flight was forestalled only when the EU/IMF emergency financing mechanism was set up, providing explicit additional guarantees for the banking system and establishing, in the summer 2010, a Financial Stability Fund for bank recapitalizations.

Sovereign risk was taking a heavy toll on Greek banks, which in the second half of 2010 faced the same CDS rate levels as the Greek government. Greek banks were able to deposit Greek government bonds as collateral for receiving ECB finance after the eurosystem decided to accept as collateral government bonds from all eurozone member states regardless of credit rating. While Greek sovereign paper remained eligible with the ECB, its rating as non-investment grade meant that it was subject to a 5 per cent higher haircut,[14] which put renewed pressure on the banks' liquidity positions (IMF 2010).

In the summer of 2011, Italian banks were also hit by the sovereign debt crisis in Italy. Shares of Intesa Sanpaolo SpA, Italy's largest bank by assets, fell 7.7 per cent, and UniCredit SpA, the second-largest lender, lost 6.3 per cent. Other bank shares posted similar declines. Italy's two largest banks lost nearly 30 per cent of their market value between April and June 2011. Intesa and UniCredit held a total of €228 billion ($325 billion) of government debt as of the end of April (*Wall Street Journal* 12 July 2012). Moreover, as the conditions of the Italian economy deteriorated, Italian banks were hit by high levels of nonperforming loans because a number of their customers struggled to repay their debt.

Italian banks remain however well capitalized, as revealed by the stress tests carried out by the European Banking Authority and the national supervisory authorities in EU member states, in close cooperation with the European Systemic Risk Board, the European Central Bank, and the European Commission. Five Italian banking groups participated in the European stress test: Unicredit, Intesa Sanpaolo, Monte dei Paschi di Siena, Banco Popolare, and UBI Banca. After applying the stress test severe hypothetical conditions, for each one of the five groups—at the end of 2012—the Core Tier 1 ratio—referred to capital of higher quality—would be much above the 5 per cent threshold established by the competent authorities as a reference value to

[14] A haircut, in this context, determines the over-collateralization of secured borrowing. So a 10 per cent haircut would mean a bank could borrow €90 for every €100 of bonds posted as collateral.

assess the need for recapitalization measures. The banks involved in this exercise represent more than 62 per cent of the total assets of the Italian banking system.[15]

In Greece, the sovereign debt crisis was transformed into a banking crisis, despite the sound starting position and low market-based nature of Greek banks. Greek banks were affected by the country risk and collapsed sovereign creditworthiness, leading to the inability to raise funds from the inter-bank market, the almost complete dependence on the ECB, the depreciation of large asset portfolios of Greek government bonds, and the collapse of bank equity prices that rendered them vulnerable to a hostile takeover. Deposit flight was only contained by the 'imported' safety guarantees under the EU/IMF financing mechanism. Italy, being on a sounder fiscal footing, was belatedly hit by the sovereign debt crisis and the ensuing banking system crisis; the same forces that generated the Greek crisis played out in the case of Italy as well, but their intensity and timing was different.

Conclusion

Contrary to the financial systems of the Anglo-American variety or other eurozone countries (such as Ireland or Spain), the financial crisis in Italy and Greece did not originate from private sector over-indebtedness or the domestic financial systems, which were sound and well capitalized. On the contrary, in Greece, the global financial crisis was mainly internalized as a sovereign debt crisis, which thereafter turned into a banking crisis. In mid-2011, Italy seemed to be following a similar route. The state of the two countries public finances at the time of the crisis, and especially the structure of their public debt, was a crucial factor that defined the timing and intensity of the crisis.

The relatively low degree of market-based banking (although somewhat higher on the liabilities side in the Italian case) sheltered the two economies from the first stage of the crisis (global banking crisis) which affected mainly globalized banking institutions exposed to 'toxic' financial products. However, one way through which Italian and Greek banks were hit during the first stage was their operations abroad. In the second stage of the global crisis (credit crunch and recessionary impact on the real economy) both countries were hit by the recession that coincided with the credit crunch. However, the crucial features of the 'Mediterranean' model of capitalism (extensive public sector, relatively closed economy—more for Greece than for Italy—extensive small and medium-sized and family-owned enterprise sector, flexible in

[15] <http://www.bancaditalia.it/stress_test-2011;internal&action=_setlanguage.action?LANGUAGE=en>

adjusting to external economic shocks, widespread informal economy and tax evasion suggesting a cushioning of the effects of the crisis on real income) collaborated in somehow cushioning the intensity of the crisis. Italy, a more open and export-led economy was hit earlier than Greece.

The 'southern' or 'Mediterranean' Italian and Greek banking systems—less market based, regionalized rather than globalized, relatively 'traditional', retail oriented, low-leveraged, able to rely on wide domestic deposits (the result of a long tradition of underdevelopment of alternative investment channels), and soundly capitalized—withstood the effects of the crisis. The relatively low leverage of the private sector in both countries prevented private debt from turning into public debt. Thus, the features of a 'southern' financial model cushioned the initial effects of the global financial crisis.

However, as the global financial crisis deepened, high public debt levels became the crucial destabilizing factor (stage three of the crisis). Italy eschewed a true sovereign debt crisis until mid-2011 thanks to its moderate deficit levels and relatively favourable public debt structure. Lacking these mitigating circumstances, Greece took the full blow of a sovereign debt crisis, which subsequently affected its otherwise healthy banking sector. The fact that the Greek public debt over the 2000s was mostly sold abroad was a crucial factor that rendered Greece extremely susceptible to global market pressures, turning the financial crisis—as soon as debt-servicing ability was seriously questioned—into a public debt crisis. Creative Greek public debt management encouraged policy complacency that helped Greek governments over the 2000s eschew the necessary fiscal consolidation. When the surrounding circumstances changed, the GDP growth rate turned negative and bond yields shot up, the public debt that Greece had failed to curb in good times became unsustainable, under those same forces of internationalization and 'euroization' that had until then allowed easy and cheap government borrowing.

With reference to the overall theme of this volume, the Greek and Italian cases suggest that the concept of 'market-based' banking provides a crucial contribution to understanding national financial (banking) systems in the twenty-first century, beyond the traditional division between bank-based systems and credit market-based systems. In other words, it is important to pay attention to the activities undertaken by banks on the assets and liabilities side of their balance sheet. On the assets side, we saw that the large share of (erstwhile considered as risk-free) depreciating government securities and loans to government in the portfolios of Greek banks led to the downgrading of Greek credit institutions, thus turning a public debt crisis into a banking crisis. This consequently aggravated the credit crunch and recession, as banks, being under stress, cut down their lending even to healthy borrowers.

On the liabilities side, Greek and Italian banks were sheltered by extensive reliance on deposits and comparatively limited exposure to wholesale funding. Italian banks relied on inter-bank funding. However, comparatively little of this funding came from non-Italian banks. A strong liabilities structure mitigated the impact of the crisis throughout its evolving stages. The concept of market-based banking is less successful in explaining differences between Greece and Italy, which is mainly a matter of fiscal management and current account deficit. The main value of the concept is in the comparison between Italy and Spain, which helps us to understand why, in the stage three government debt crisis, Spain, which has lower levels of government debt than Italy, is the focus of the market's attention.

Compared to other EU countries examined in this volume, Italian and Greek banks retained a relatively low degree of market-based banking of assets and liabilities prior to the crisis, as explained in 'Market-based Banking in Italy and Greece'. Greek and Italian expansion abroad took place mainly in the retail sector in their respective neighbouring regions, incorporating mostly emerging market risk. This proved to be far less contagious than the strategies of other European banking systems, taking the form of international investment banking or toxic securities investments. At the end of the day, the principal 'toxic' asset contained in the portfolios of Greek, and to a lesser extent Italian, banks were domestic bad loans and government paper.

References

Acharya, V. V. and P. Schnabl (2010) 'Do Global Banks Spread Global Imbalances? The Case of Asset-Backed Commercial Paper During the Financial Crisis of 2007–2009', *IMF Economic Review*, 58 (1): 37–73.

Allen, F., and D. Gale (2000) *Comparing Financial Systems*. Cambridge, MA: MIT Press.

Association for Financial Markets in Europe-European Securities Forum (AFME-ESF) (2008). *Securitization Data Report*, www.afme.eu/Documents/Statistics-and-reports.aspx (accessed 18 Aug 2012).

Bank of Greece (2010) *Annual Report*. Athens.

Bank of Italy (2008) *Summary Report of the Statistical Bulletin 2007–2008*, Data On Credit, Securities, Business and Interest Rates, Quarter 4. Rome.

Bank of Italy (2010).*Financial Stability Report*. Rome: December.

Bank of Italy (2011) *Financial Stability Report*. Rome: November.

Bank for International Settlements (BIS) (2008a) *Quarterly Review*. Basel: June.

BIS (2008b) *Quarterly Review Statistical Annex*. Basel.

Blavoukos, S., and G. Pagoulatos (2008) 'The Limits of EMU Conditionality: Fiscal Adjustment in Southern Europe', *Journal of Public Policy*, 28 (2): 229–253.

Carmassi, J., D. Gros, and S. Micossi (2009) 'The Global Financial Crisis: Causes and Cures', *Journal of Common Market Studies*, 47 (5): 977–996.

Ciocca, P. (2005) *The Italian Financial System Remodelled*. Basingstoke: Palgrave Macmillan.

Credit Suisse (2010) *Equity Research*. Europe/Italy: June.

Deeg, R. (2005) 'Change from Within: German and Italian Finance in the 1990s', In *Beyond Continuity: Institutional Change in Advanced Political Economies* (eds W. Streeck and K. Thelen). Oxford: Oxford University Press, 169–202.

Deeg, R., and S. A. Perez (2000) 'International Capital Mobility and Domestic Institutions: Corporate Finance and Governance in Four European Cases', *Governance*, 13(2): 119–53.

Dinmore, G. (2008) 'Rome Promises Banks as Much as They Need', *Financial Times*, 14 October.

European Central Bank (ECB) (2007a) *Aggregated Balance Sheet of Euro Area Monetary Financial Institutions, Excluding the Eurosystem*, <http://www.ecb.int/stats/money/aggregates/bsheets/html/outstanding_amounts_2007–12.en.html> (accessed December 2011).

ECB (2007b) *Consolidated Banking Data* , <http://www.ecb.int/stats/money/consolidated/html/index.en.html> (accessed December 2011).

ECB (2010) *Structural Indicators for the EU Banking Sector*. Frankfurt.

Financial Times, 11 February.

Giordano, F. (2007) *Storia del Sistema Bancario Italiano*. Roma: Donzelli.

Gros, D. and S. Micossi (20 September2008). 'The Beginning of the End Game ...', VOX [online], <http://www.voxeu.org/index.php?q=node/1669> (accessed December 2011).

International Monetary Fund (IMF) (2010) *Country Report: Greece. Stand-By Arrangement. Review Under the Emergency Financing Mechanism*, 10/217. Washington DC: July.

Jones, E. (2012). 'Italy's Sovereign Debt Crisis survival: Global Politics and Strategy'. *Survival*, 54 (1): 83–110.

Loriaux M. (1997) 'Capital, the State and Uneven Growth in the International Political Economy' In *Capital Ungoverned* (eds M. Loriaux, M. Woo-Cummings, K. Calder, S. Maxfield, and S.A. Perez). Ithaca, NY: Cornell University Press, 208–229.

Manna, M. (2011) 'Home Bias in Inter-Bank Lending and Banks' Resolution Regimes', *Bank of Italy*, Working Papers No. 816, <http://www.bancaditalia.it/pubblicazioni/econo/temidi/td11/td816_11;internal&action=_setlanguage.action?LANGUAGE=en>, (accessed June 2012).

Marzinotto, B., J. Pisani-Ferry, and A. Sapir (March 2010) 'Two Crises Two Responses', *Bruegel Policy Brief*, <http://www.bruegel.org/publications/show/publication/two-crises-two-responses.html> (accessed December 2011).

Organisation for Economic Co-operation and Development (OECD) (2010) *Economic Survey of Italy 2009: The impact of the crisis and the potential for fiscal stimulus*. Paris.

Pagoulatos, G. (2003a) *Greece's New Political Economy: State, Finance and Growth from Postwar to EMU*. Basingstoke: Palgrave Macmillan.

Pagoulatos, G. (2003b) 'Financial Interventionism and Liberalization in Southern Europe: State, Bankers, and the Politics of Disinflation', *Journal of Public Policy*, 23(2): 171–199.

Pagoulatos, G., and C. Triantopoulos (2009) 'The Return of the Greek Patient: Greece and the 2008 Global Financial Crisis', *South European Society and Politics*, 14(1): 35–54.

Panetta, F. (ed.) (2004). *Il Sistema Bancario Italiano negli Anni Novanta*. Bologna: Il Mulino.

Pérez, S. A (1997) *Banking on Privilege, The Politics of Spanish Financial Reform*. Ithaca, NY: Cornell University Press.

Perez, S. A., and J. Westrup (2010) 'Finance and the Macroeconomy: The Politics of Regulatory Reform in Europe' *Journal of European Public Policy*, 17 (8): 1171–1192.

Quaglia, L. (2008a) *Central Banking Governance in the European Union: A Comparative Analysis* London: Routledge.

Quaglia, L. (2008b) 'Explaining the Reform of Banking Supervision in Europe: An Integrative Approach', *Governance*, 21 (3): 439–463.

Saccomanni, F. (2008) 'Il Processo di Internazionalizzazione del Sistema Bancario: La Presenza delle Banche Estere in Italia', *Bank Of Italy*, <http://www.bancaditalia.it/interventi/intaltri_mdir/saccomanni190208/Saccomanni_190208.pdf> (accessed December 2011).

Story, J. and I. Walter (1997) *Political Economy of Financial Integration in Europe: The Battle of the System*. Manchester: Manchester University Press.

Woo-Cumings, M. (ed.) (1999) *The Developmental State*. Ithaca, NY: Cornell University Press.

World Bank (2007) *Data Bank: Italy and Greece*, <http://data.worldbank.org/> (accessed December 2011).

Zysman, J. (1983) *Governments, Markets and Growth*. Ithaca, NY: Cornell University Press.

9

Cool Canada: A Case of Low Market-Based Banking in the Anglo-Saxon World

Patrick Leblond

Introduction

When the global financial crisis reached its apex in the fall of 2008 and governments in Europe and the United States were busy putting together bailout packages for their failing banks, Canadian banks were continuing to generate positive (though somewhat lower) returns on equity, unlike their American and European peers (Bank of Canada 2011, 6). In other words, although the Canadian financial skies were grey with heavy rain (coming from the south), things were otherwise pretty calm. There was no panic, just concern and vigilance. Canada kept its cool.

It is now well known that Canada did not experience a banking crisis like Europe and the United States in 2007–9. Because its economy is closely linked with those two regions, it nevertheless suffered a recession and its financial system recorded billions of dollars in losses. For example, according to regulatory filings with the Office of the Superintendent of Financial Institutions (OSFI), Canadian banks recorded impairment charges of C$7.1 billion and C$13.8 billion in 2008 and 2009, respectively. However, when compared to their North Atlantic counterparts, Canadian banks suffered much less; for instance, in 2008 total bank write-downs in Canada were around 0.8 per cent of gross domestic product (GDP) while those in Europe and the United States stood at around 3 per cent of GDP (IMF 2009, 4). Given its superior performance, it is reasonable to ask why Canada's financial system remained relatively stable during the global financial crisis. According to the market-based banking framework developed in this volume, the reason should be that Canada's banking system was not very reliant on positive financial markets for its financing and profitability. This chapter shows that this is indeed the case and that the Canadian case does in fact support the main argument advanced in this volume.

Although Zysman (1983) did not include Canada in his seminal study, Canada has generally been placed in the 'Anglo-Saxon' category alongside the United Kingdom and the United States in terms of the importance of capital markets for corporate financing (e.g. Davis 2001, 6; Schmidt and Tyrell 1997, 334). According to the Bank of Canada (2008a, 10), loans by Canadian financial institutions to non-financial corporations represented only 15 per cent of all corporate financing in Canada in 2007; for their part, equities accounted for 73 per cent of Canadian corporate finance. Therefore, it is surprising to observe that its banking system is less market based than those found in the United Kingdom and the United States (see Hardie and Maxfield, this volume) and closer to the Japanese one (see Kamikawa, this volume). So why does Canada have a banking system that is less market based than one might expect given its liberal market economy (Hall and Soskice 2001)? According to Bordo et al. (2011), it is because of a grand bargain between the government and the banks, whereby the banking sector is protected from competition in exchange for tight regulation that ensures the system's stability (see also Brean et al. 2011).

The present chapter is structured as follows. First, it describes the Canadian banking system and, following Hardie and Howarth in this volume, assesses how important capital markets was for Canadian banks' operations. Second, the chapter examines the main reasons why the Canadian banking system was less market based than in most of the countries studied in this volume. Finally, the chapter concludes on the implications of the Canadian case for the argument advanced by this volume.

The Canadian Banking System

At the start of the financial crisis, at the end of 2007, Canadian banks held just over a half of total financial system assets (see Figure 1.2 in the Introduction to this volume). More than 90 per cent of bank assets were concentrated among the so-called 'Big Six',[1] which were (are) financial groups that provide the full range of financial services, from traditional retail banking activities to investment banking and wealth management. The concentration of the Canadian banking sector is long-standing. According to Bordo et al. (2011), the Canadian banking system was already 'oligopolistic' in the early 1900s.[2]

[1] The big six banks are Bank of Montreal (BMO), Bank of Nova Scotia (ScotiaBank), Canadian Imperial Bank of Commerce (CIBC), National Bank of Canada, Royal Bank of Canada (RBC), and TD Canada Trust.

[2] By 1920, five banks dominated the system (Bordo et al. 2011, 33).

Following a series of legislative changes aimed at increasing competition in the Canadian financial services industry, banks gradually moved to the universal banking model in the late 1980s and early 1990s (Bordo et al. 2011; Brean et al. 2011; Freedman 1998). As such, they acquired existing brokerage firms (or built their own as the Toronto Dominion Bank did) and expanded into the mutual fund and wealth management business. Nevertheless, these additional financial services did not overtake traditional banking activities focused on lending and deposit taking (see later).

The big six banks are also active internationally, with overseas operations located primarily in the United States, Latin America, and the Caribbean. These operations are focused primarily on traditional banking activities resulting from the creation (often through acquisitions) of retail branch networks. Like their French counterparts (Howarth, this volume), Canadian banks aim to export the model that has made them successful in their domestic market. Their internationalization also shares the same 'traditional' characteristics as those pursued by large Spanish and Italian banks (Royo, this volume; Pagoulatos and Quaglia, this volume). International activities contribute close to half of Canadian banks' income (Financial Stability Board 2012, 8) and one-third of the banks' total assets (author's calculation based on Bank of Canada banking and financial statistics).[3]

The profitability of the major Canadian banks is generally high, with annual return on equity being around 20 per cent in the years before the global financial crisis. Even during the crisis, the big six banks managed to generate returns on equity above 10 per cent.[4] In terms of return on assets, the banks' profitability has also been very good in general, averaging 0.75 per cent over the last years,[5] which puts them in the top quartile among G10 banks (IMF 2008, 14).[6]

According to Calmès and Liu (2009), the Canadian banking system has become increasingly market based since the 1990s. For instance, they show that the contribution of interest income to overall bank profits has been decreasing since 1980; net interest income represented 79, 69, and 44 per cent of net operating revenue in 1980, 1990, and 2000, respectively (Calmès and Liu 2009, 131). According to the authors, the difference has been taken up by income generated from non-traditional banking activities, most especially

[3] For a detailed analysis of Canadian banks' international activities, see Létourneau and Heidrich (2010).

[4] Data are from Canadian Bankers Association (2012, 9) and Bank of Canada (2008b, 22).

[5] Calculation based on data from Canadian Bankers Association (2012, 9) and International Monetary Fund (2008a, 14).

[6] The Australian banking system enjoys many similarities with the Canadian one, which is why it also weathered the global financial crisis very well, with its banks maintaining relatively high returns on equity throughout the crisis. For details on the Australian banking system and comparisons with Canada, see Allen et al. (2011) and Bologna (2010).

market-based ones. Interestingly, they show that this diversification in terms of income sources has neither brought 'extra' profitability (beyond what interest income could have generated) for the banks nor reduced the volatility of their earnings. In fact, Calmès and Liu find that income volatility has increased along with Canadian banks' greater involvement in market-based activities, which is probably explained by the latter's procyclical nature (Hardie and Howarth, this volume). According to the authors, these results are in line with those found for US banks (see also Hardie and Maxfield, this volume).

How Do Canadian Banks Make Their Money? The Debit Side of the Balance Sheet

In terms of the evolution of the banks' balance sheets, this suggests that loans and deposits have slowly played a decreasing role over time in favour of non-traditional, more market-oriented banking activities such as investment banking and wealth management; however, traditional activities related to deposit-taking and lending remain dominant at Canadian banks (Figure 9.1). There are two types of non-interest income-generating activities: fees for services rendered (e.g. underwriting securities, providing advice on mergers and acquisitions, or simply service charges for bank accounts) and gains on the buying and selling of securities (also known as trading).[7] With respect to fee-generating activities, the benefit is that banks do not need to hold assets since they mostly involve people being at work rather than assets. In principle, this means that this fee-income should boost both return on assets and return on equity (by increasing profits without increasing assets and equity). In 2006, the year before the crisis began, Canadian banks generated 17 per cent of their total income from fees (Figure 9.1). Of this percentage, 60 per cent came from non-traditional banking services such as investment management, custodial services, brokerage commissions, securities underwriting, etc. The remaining 40 per cent of fee income corresponded to more traditional banking activities such as services charges of deposit accounts, fees for credit cards, loans, and mortgages as well as letters of credit. Canadian banks' fee income situation was pretty much the same in 2000. In 1997, however, fee income from non-traditional banking activities represented a smaller share to total income: 8 per cent. Thus, in line with Calmès and Liu (2009), fees generated from non-traditional activities have grown in importance over time,

[7] When establishing the level of non-interest income generated by a bank in order to determine the extent to which its revenues depend on market-based activities, it is important to make a distinction between fees that are generated from traditional banking activities (e.g. fees related to bank account transactions) and those that are generated from actual market-based banking activities (e.g. underwriting securities). Otherwise, if a bank's non-interest income is assumed to be all derived from market-based activities, the latter's relative importance will be overstated.

although they represented a small proportion of total gross income generated by banks in Canada before the global financial crisis.

Non-interest income arising from trading securities, for its part, most often requires adding assets to the balance sheet and financing these assets with either liabilities or equity.[8] The benefit here is that the expected returns on equity enjoyed through trading activities tend to be greater than on traditional lending activities; however, this is because the risk of substantial losses is also greater.[9] In 2006, income from trading activities generated 5 per cent of Canadian banks' total gross income (Figure 9.1). In 2000 and 1997, the share of trading income was 4 and 2 per cent of total income, respectively, which represents a small increase and a low figure relative to other countries considered in this volume.

In sum, non-traditional, market-based activities accounted for only 15 per cent of Canadian banks' total gross income in 2006, the year when such activities should have been at their zenith. Interest income from lending, however, has continued to represent more than half of the banks' total income (Figure 9.1). So, although market-based activities have played a greater role over time at Canadian banks, their relative significance has remained limited when compared to traditional banking activities such as

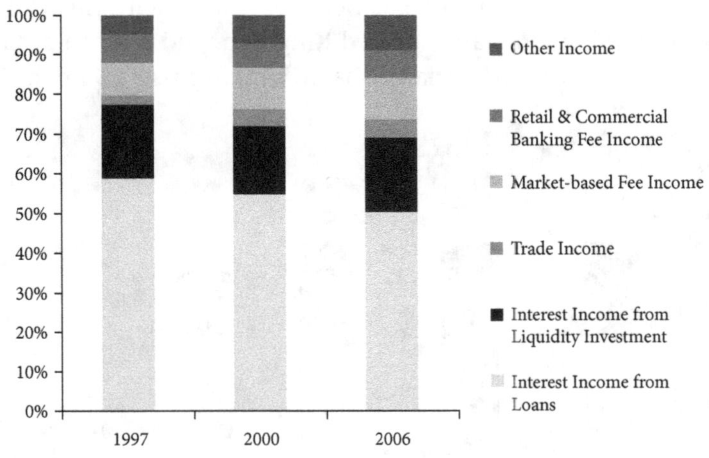

Figure 9.1. Distribution of gross income of all banks in Canada
Source: Office of the Superintendent of Financial Institutions of Canada.

[8] If no amount of regulatory capital needs to be set aside for these kinds of assets, then banks will most likely rely on debt financing rather than equity financing. This increase in leverage will boost return on equity but not return on asset (see Haldane 2011).

[9] This explains in good part why, in practice, market-based activities tend to be no more profitable than traditional banking ones: market-based non-interest income is much more volatile (risky) than interest income arising from the difference between interest collected on loans and interest paid on deposits (see Calmès and Liu 2009).

lending, liquidity investment and fees for providing deposit accounts, credit cards, and other traditional banking services. Traditional banking activities continued to account for about three-quarters of Canadian banks' total gross income in the years before the global financial crisis. This explains why the Canadian banking system was able to avoid being swept away by the financial tsunami that hit, for instance, American and British shores in 2007–8.

If we now take a closer look at the Canadian banking industry's balance sheet, we see that loans on the asset side of the ledger have also remained dominant. For instance, Figure 9.2 shows that loans accounted for 53 per cent of total banking assets in Canada in 2006. This figure is almost the same as it was in 1997 (52 per cent). Examining Figure 9.2, we also observe that the share of mortgage loans has increased slightly between 1997 and 2006, from 16 per cent of total assets to 20 per cent (from 31 to 38 per cent of total loans). Finally, in line with the rise in income from trading activities, the percentage of total banking assets invested in securities issued by other entities than Canadian governments has grown significantly, from 9 per cent in 1997 to 22 per cent in 2006. In particular, Canadian banks increased their exposure to US securities between 1996 and 2006, from less than 5 per cent of total assets to 10 per cent between 1996 and 2006 (Bank of Canada 2008a, 22). There was therefore a significant increase in market-based banking on the asset side of Canadian banks' balance sheets, although still at a far lower level than in the United States, United Kingdom, and a range of European countries. Nevertheless, these market-based banking assets were the basis for

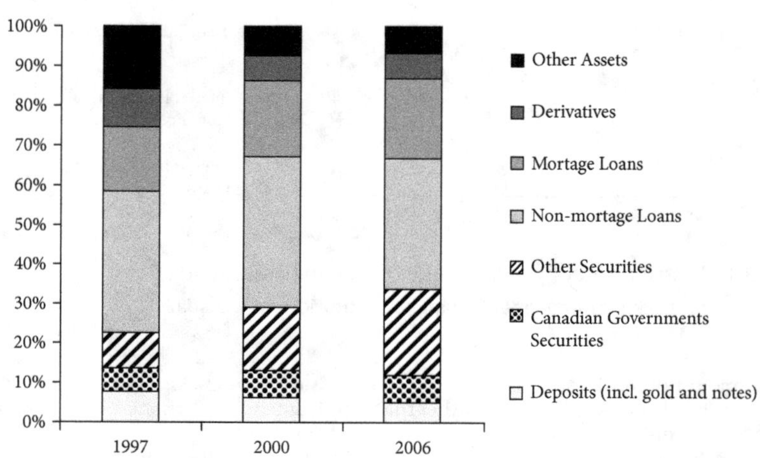

Figure 9.2. Distribution of assets of all banks in Canada
Source: Office of the Superintendent of Financial Institutions of Canada.

the significant write-downs (or impairment charges) that Canadian banks recorded in their financial accounts in 2008 and 2009.

How Do Canadian Banks Fund Themselves? The Credit Side of the Balance Sheet

As indicated in the introductory chapters of this volume, Canadian banks have a negative funding gap, which means that loans are more than fully financed by deposits. Put another way, about 80 per cent of deposits held by Canadian banks were extended as loans, the remainder was used to fund other assets (see also International Monetary Fund 2009, 38). Furthermore, unlike many other banking systems analysed in this volume, Canadian banks continue to finance their operations mainly from deposits. In Figure 9.3, we can observe that deposits have consistently accounted for more than 60 per cent of total liabilities (including shareholders' equity) between 1997 and 2006.[10] Of this figure, retail deposits, which are more stable than wholesale deposits, represent 40 per cent, which is twice the US level (International Monetary Fund 2009, 27).[11]

One of the reasons for the continued importance of retail deposits for Canadian banks is the fact that there is limited competition for household savings from non-banks (International Monetary Fund 2009, 2–3). This is because Canadian banks took over a large share of two other pillars of the Canadian financial system in the 1980s and 1990s as a result of changes in legislation: trusts[12] and securities dealers (i.e. investment banks).[13] They also expanded into mutual funds and wealth management services (Brean et al. 2011). For its part, financing from market-based sources has accounted for only about 20 per cent of total liabilities over the same period.

So when global liquidity dried up in the wake of Lehman Brothers' failure in the fall of 2008, Canadian banks were well shielded from such a systemic shock since the majority of their funding base was stable and not at the mercy of market sentiment. This explains why the cost of bank financing (both in the inter-banking and corporate bond markets) in Canada increased much

[10] Bordo et al. (2011) and Brean et al. (2011) argue that the removal of interest rate controls on deposits and loans in Canada in 1967 is a key reason why the banking system was able to continue relying on deposits for its financing (see also Freedman 1998). In the United States, because controls remained until the 1980s as a result of Regulation Q (in the Glass–Steagall Act), the high inflationary period of the 1970s saw savings move away from deposits in commercial and saving banks to unregulated money market mutual funds invested in the securities markets, which in turn led to the rise in securitization and the so-called shadow banking system.

[11] In the United States, retail deposits accounted for 20 per cent of total deposits in 2008 (International Monetary Fund 2009, 27).

[12] Trusts specialized in residential mortgages and term deposits.

[13] The fourth pillar of the Canadian financial system consists of life insurance companies.

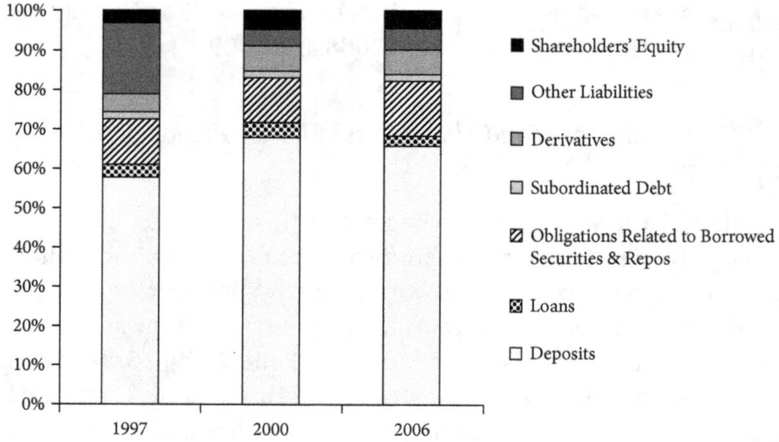

Figure 9.3. Distribution of liabilities of all banks in Canada
Source: Office of the Superintendent of Financial Institutions of Canada.

less than in the Euro area, United Kingdom, and United States during that period of intense uncertainty in global financial markets (Bank of Canada 2008b, charts 6 and 12).[14]

Canadian Banks and Securitization

Given that banks' activities have remained predominantly traditional in Canada, securitization has played a relatively minor role in Canadian capital markets. In spite of the fact that it tripled in size between 2000 and 2007, it represented only 5 per cent of the total securities market in Canada at the end of 2007 (Bank of Canada 2008a, 10). Outstanding asset-backed securities (ABSs) totalled C$328 billion at the end of 2007, 56 per cent of which was accounted for by residential mortgage-backed securities (RMBS) (Bank of Canada 2008a, 10). The remaining 44 per cent consisted of securities mainly backed by the following assets: credit cards, personal lines of credit (secured

[14] As a result of the global credit crunch that also affected Canadian banks in late 2008 and early 2009, the Government of Canada set up the Insured Mortgage Purchase Program (IMPP) as a temporary measure to inject liquidity in the banking system. The IMPP authorized the Canada Mortgage and Housing Corporation (see Footnote 17 for details) to purchase up to C$125 billion in National Housing Act mortgage-backed securities from Canadian financial institutions. This injection of liquidity into the banking system did not represent additional risk for the Canadian government since the securities purchased consisted of pools of mortgages already insured by the Government of Canada (through the CMHC or private sector insurers). When the IMPP was terminated at the end of March 2010, the CMHC had purchased C$69 billion of mortgage-backed securities through auctions. Essentially, the IMPP was meant to partially replace capital markets, which were not functioning properly as a result of the crisis (CMHC 2012). For more details on mortgage-backed securities in Canada, see the next section.

and unsecured), automobile leases and loans, commercial mortgages. Credit cards and personal lines of credit account for about one-third of this 'other' securitization market while the share pertaining to car leases and loans is approximately one-fifth (DBRS 2008, 4). The big six banks dominate the securitizaton market in Canada. In the case of the RMBS market, this is obvious as the big six banks account for the majority of mortgages outstanding. But this also true for the non-RMBS portion of the market, where the securities dealers belonging to the big six banks hold a market share of about 90 per cent (DBRS 2008).

In Canada, there are two different markets for ABS: asset-backed commercial papers (ABCPs) and term ABSs. ABCPs are short term in nature, with maturities of less than 365 days, while term ABSs are for periods of more than one year. Unlike term ABSs, ABCPs do not require prospectuses (if issued publicly) or offering memorandums (if placed privately); they are issued by special purpose vehicles called 'conduits'. Before 2008, conduits could be sponsored by either Canadian banks (also called 'bank-sponsored' ABCPs) or non-bank-affiliated (i.e. independent) financial firms (also called 'non-bank sponsored' ABCPs). In order to be rated by a credit rating agency, ABCP conduits must have liquidity support (or protection), which is normally provided through committed credit facilities (e.g. lines of credit) or asset purchase agreements. The sponsor normally provides this liquidity support. In the case of non-bank sponsored ABCPs, liquidity facilities were provided by so-called 'third-party' banks, most often foreign ones (Khami and Tuer 2007, 14). At the end of 2007, outstanding bank-sponsored ABCPs and non-bank sponsored ABPCs totalled C$76 billion and C$32 billion, respectively (Bank of Canada 2008a, 10). This means that the amount of outstanding term ABS was C$220 billion.

In August 2007, the Canadian ABCP market was caught up in the turmoil that hit the ABS market in Europe and the United States in the summer of 2007. At the time, the non-bank sponsored ABCP market was forced to shut down when fears emerged that the collateralized debt obligations (CDOs) that backed the ABCPs (77 per cent of all so-called 'affected' ABCPs) were themselves backed by US subprime mortgages (International Monetary Fund 2008a, 21).[15] In fact, most of the growth in the Canadian ABCP market between 2003 and 2007 came from programmes backed by CDOs (rather than by the underlying assets directly). And these CDOs originated largely from outside Canada, mostly the United States. The crisis occurred when the third-party banks that were responsible for the conduits' liquidity support refused to provide funding when the ABCP programmes could no longer be rolled over as a result of investor panic (Kahmi and Tuer 2007, 15). The

[15] According to DBRS (2008, 10), there were no CDOs backing bank-sponsored ABCP programmes.

liquidity providers argued that the conditions for a general market disruption had not been met and, therefore, they were not required to intervene (Khami and Tuer 2007, 15). Only one of the big six Canadian banks was involved in this collapse: National Bank (through its subsidiary, National Bank Financial) (DBRS 2008). A restructuring was agreed to in January 2009, whereby the frozen ABCPs were converted into term ABS notes that were more in line with the underlying assets' maturities (International Monetary Fund 2009, 6). The ABCP programmes sponsored by Canadian banks (two-thirds of the ABCP market at the end of 2007) were not caught up in the crisis and continued functioning relatively normally, although they saw their yields increase as a result of greater investor nervousness (Kamhi and Tuer 2007, 15). Since 2008, the bank-sponsored ABCP market is the only one available in Canada.

Between 2000 and 2007, the percentage of residential mortgages that Canadian banks securitized increased from 5 per cent to a little more than 20 per cent (Bank of Canada 2008a, 25).[16] This is much less than in the United States, where more than 50 per cent of residential mortgages were securitized during this same period (International Monetary Fund 2007, 17), reaching a level of 60 per cent by the time the crisis hit (International Monetary Fund 2009, 5). The large majority (over 80 per cent) of residential mortgages that are securitized by banks in Canada is guaranteed by the Canadian government through a mortgage-backed securities programme (under the National Housing Act) sponsored by the Canada Mortgage and Housing Corporation (Bank of Canada, 2007, 18).[17] Canada therefore shares with the Netherlands (see Chang and Jones, this volume) a situation where the extent of the reliance on market sources of financing overstates the exposure to the market, because the government guarantee means that the source of financing is relatively stable. Since by law in Canada mortgages with loan-to-value (LTV) ratios greater than 80 per cent must be insured, mortgages that end up securitized by Canadian banks are either insured privately or have LTV ratios of less than 80 per cent.

According to Freedman and Engert (2003), the securitization of mortgages in Canada has been much less important than in the United States because Canadian banks have generally not been faced with a mismatch between the long-term maturities of the mortgages and the short-term nature of their funding (i.e. deposits). In Canada, although amortized over 25–30 years, the duration of mortgage contracts is for the most part of five years or less because

[16] The securitization of consumer credit (e.g. credit cards) stood at 18 per cent in 2007. Overall, securitized credit represented only 13 per cent of all household and business credit in Canada in 2007 (Bank of Canada 2007, 18).

[17] The Canada Mortgage and Housing Corporation (CMHC) is an agency of the Government of Canada responsible, among other things, for insuring residential mortgages. As such, it is the Canadian equivalent of Fannie May and Freddie Mac in the United States. The CMHC also guarantees privately insured mortgages but at a maximum of 90 per cent of their value.

the Canadian Mortgage Housing Corporation (CMHC) will not guarantee mortgages with maturities longer than five years (see also Kiff 2009). This has made it a lot easier for banks to finance mortgages with deposits, many of which are five-year, fixed-term deposits. Nevertheless, with the increased attractiveness of mutual funds, banks have found it more difficult to attract term deposits, which is why the securitization of mortgages in Canada has become more important since the mid-1990s (Freedman and Engert 2003, 10).

As for subprime mortgages in Canada, they represented less than 5 per cent of mortgages in 2006 (same as in 2001), compared to 25 per cent in the United States (10 per cent in 2001) (International Monetary Fund 2008b, 15). The quality of subprime mortgages in Canada is generally much better than in the United States, because Canadian subprime lenders have been focusing on near-prime and Alt-A customers (good credit history but no income documentation (e.g. self-employed individuals)). This is why, between 1998 and 2006, Canadian banks had delinquency rates of about 1 per cent on average compared to about 8–9 per cent for the United States (Bank of Canada 2007, 8).

Thus, whether securitized or kept on the books, mortgages are for the most part a low-risk affair for Canadian banks. This explains why residential loan–loss provisions by Canadian banks stood at 0.01 per cent of outstanding mortgages between 2000 and 2005 (International Monetary Fund 2007, 17). Lately, there have been concerns about the rise of household indebtedness in Canada and its impact on residential mortgage and real estate markets (Crawford et al. 2012). Household indebtedness in Canada now surpasses UK and US levels (Crawford et al. 2012, 4). Although the ratio of debt to disposable income in Canada was slightly below that in the last two when the international financial crisis hit, it continued to increase—albeit at a slower rate as a result of a series of administrative measures introduced in recent years to restrict access to mortgages as well as consumer loans guaranteed by housing assets (see Appendix B in Toka et al. 2012). In spite of this increase in Canadian households' indebtedness, debt sustainability and banks' robustness are not in doubt (e.g. Onyett-Jeffries 2012; Toka et al. 2012).

Although the Canadian banking system has seen its share of market-based activities gradually increase over the last 20 years, it remains predominantly focused on traditional activities such as loans and deposits. Compared to their counterparts in the United States and in Europe, Canadian banks make relatively little use of capital markets for generating revenues as well as for funding their income-generating activities (i.e. they had low levels of market-based banking on both sides of the balance sheet). Furthermore, the market-based activities pursued by Canadian banks were low-risk ones in general. As a result, the Canadian banking system was able to withstand the financial tsunami that hit the North Atlantic shores in the fall of 2008. Why that was the case is the next section's focus.

Why Did Canada Have a Relatively Low Market-Based Banking System When the Crisis Hit?

In spite of the increasing role that market-based activities played in the Canadian banking system, the latter still relied mainly on traditional deposit-taking and loan-making activities for generating its profits. Bordo et al. (2011) argue that a 'grand bargain' stands at the heart of the Canadian banking system's conservatism:[18] restricted market entry in exchange for tight regulation.

The Canadian (federal) government already began restricting entry into the banking market in the late nineteenth century, by raising the amount of capital stock required to obtain a banking license (Bordo et al. 2011, 11).[19] In 1967, foreign banks were effectively prevented from entering the Canadian market when it was decided that no individual or group of associated individuals could own more than ten per cent of the shares of a bank, with aggregate foreign ownership limited to a maximum of 25 per cent (Freedman 1998, 5).[20] In 1980, foreign-owned banks were allowed to enter the Canadian market under the newly created Schedule II class, which imposed no ownership restrictions. For their part, existing banks (i.e. those with the 1967 ownership restrictions) became classified as Schedule I banks. Hence, Schedule I banks were de facto Canadian owned while Schedule II banks were foreign owned. However, Schedule II banks faced restrictions in terms of the share of the market that they could compete for: the total assets of all foreign-owned banking subsidiaries could not exceed 15 per cent of total financing by banks in Canada (Policy Research Branch 2003, 8). In 1999, foreign banks were allowed to set up operations in Canada without having to establish a subsidiary (or Schedule II bank); however, such branches were not allowed to accept deposits below C$150,000, effectively prohibiting them from offering retail banking services (Daniel 2003, 6). In 2001, the Canadian government introduced a size-based ownership regime. For large banks, then defined as having equity of C$5 billion or more,[21] any investor (domestic or foreign) could not own more than 20 per cent of outstanding voting shares and 30 per cent of non-voting shares.[22] For medium banks, then defined as having equity between C$1 and C$5 billion, there was a requirement that at least 35 per cent of their shares be publicly traded. Finally, for small banks, i.e. with

[18] The authors do not address the issue of market-based banking directly, however.

[19] The minimum was set at C$500,000.

[20] The 25 per cent limit on aggregate foreign ownership was eliminated in 1995 as a result of Canada signing onto the World Trade Organization's General Agreement on Trade in Services.

[21] The level was increased to C$8 billion in 2007 and C$12 billion in 2012.

[22] In addition, any person wanting to acquire 10 per cent of more of a large bank's equity was required to obtain the approval of the minister of finance.

equity below C$1 billion, there were no ownership restrictions. As a result of these legal restrictions on bank ownership, the Canadian banking system became dominated by an oligopoly of six banks, as indicated in the previous section. Moreover, according to Koeppl and MacGee (2007, 21), these restrictions 'help to account for the fact that foreign bank subsidiaries have chosen to restrict their scope of operation either geographically or to focus on specific market niches (such as credit cards or online banking).'

Ownership restrictions in Canada's banking sector have in fact served to limit competition for deposits, which helps explain why the large Canadian banks had less need to resort to capital markets to finance their activities. The deregulation of financial services in the 1980s and 1990s—whereby banks were allowed acquire trusts and securities dealers in order to offer securities brokerage and wealth management services as well as investment (mutual) funds—provided another means through which a large share of Canadian savings (i.e. deposits) could stay within the banking system instead of circulating through capital markets (Bordo et al. 2011; Brean et al. 2011).

The other side of the 'grand bargain' identified by Bordo et al. (2011) is that Canadian banks were faced with a tighter regulatory environment relative to the other countries considered in this volume (see Ratnovski and Huang 2009). First, Canada's financial regulator, the OSFI, set the thresholds for minimum capital requirements as a percentage of risk-weighted assets above those advised by the Basel Accord: 7 and 10 per cent for Tier 1 and total capital, respectively, compared to 4 and 8 per cent. In fact, Canadian banks had Tier 1 capital–adequacy ratios above 9 per cent prior to the crisis (Bank of Canada 2008b, 24). Second, Canadian banks had to satisfy a maximum assets-to-capital multiple of 20 (Bordeleau et al. 2009). This means that banks' total (i.e. non-risk weighted) assets could not be more than 20 times their total capital.[23] This measure was meant to limit the amount of leverage that Canadian banks could undertake. After all, credit booms are strongly associated with financial crises, which then lead to severe recessions (if not depressions) and slower recoveries (Jordà et al. 2011). Ideally, both on-balance sheet and off-balance sheet items would be included in the calculation of the multiple; however, in the Canadian context securitized assets were not included in the multiple's calculation while direct contractual obligations were (Crawford et al. 2009, 49). Nevertheless, given that securitization by Canadian banks remained limited, the augmented leverage multiple, which includes securitized assets, was still on average only 21 in 2007, compared to 19 for the regulatory measure (Crawford et al. 2009, 49). Prior to the crisis, Canada was the only country, with the United States, to impose leverage constraint on its banks, though the Canadian measure is more restrictive than

[23] This multiple corresponds to a minimum leverage ratio of 5 per cent.

the American one according to D'Hulster (2009, 2).[24] Third, OSFI applied its capital requirements on a consolidated basis, which means that it covered all financial activities falling under a bank's roof. This was also the case in the United States for bank holding companies, though no off-balance sheet items were included in the ratio's calculation (D'Hulster 2009, 2). As for the larger, independent investment banks, they faced no limits on leverage. This is why US investment banks had, on average, assets-to-capital multiples around 35 when the crisis hit, while US commercial banks had multiples around 10 (Bordo et al. 2011, 40). In the end, more stringent capital constraints also contributed to limiting the level of wholesale (i.e. market) funding by Canadian banks. As Ratnovski and Huang (2009, 16–17) point out: 'banks constrained in balance sheet size engage less in wholesale operations [i.e. securitization], as retail operations can satisfy a greater fraction of their investment needs.'

On the asset side of the balance sheet, one could think that constraints on leverage would create an incentive for banks to invest in riskier assets in order to try to boost profits. However, looking at US banks, Koudstaal and van Wijbergen (2012) find that this is not the case empirically. More leveraged banks tend to have riskier asset portfolios. In the Canadian case, we saw in the previous section that banks' assets and revenues were not significantly market based; however, even when assets were market based, like securitized residential mortgages, their riskiness was generally low. According to Laeven and Levine (2009), the reason for Canadian banks' low level of risk taking may be because the large banks' ownership is widely held, where managers have less incentive to take risks. Moreover, with a dominant position in the Canadian financial system, large banks face less competition and, therefore, have less need take on more risks in order to try to increase returns. Finally, according to Bordo et al. (2011), the fact that there is little maturity mismatch between a mortgage and its financing in Canada, contrary to the situation in the United States, means that Canadian banks have not had to resort as much to securitization as banks did in the United States. This is compounded by the presence of extensive national branch networks for the large Canadian banks, which makes financing mortgages and other loans through deposits easier than in the United States where generally smaller banks have to access capital markets using securitization in order to finance their lending (Bordo et al. 2011).

In sum, the relatively low level of market-based banking in Canada is a result of, on the one hand, a concentrated banking sector protected from

[24] Switzerland has since introduced such a leverage ratio requirement for its large multinational banks but the minimum ratio has been set at 3 per cent rather than 5 per cent (International Monetary Fund 2009, 17). The Basel III Accord, which sets the new standards for banking regulation in the world in response to the global financial crisis, recommends (after a review period) the adoption of a minimum leverage ratio, which might also be set at 3 per cent (corresponding to a multiple of 33).

competition and, on the other hand, a relatively tougher regulatory system in terms of capital and leverage requirements. In making stability in the banking system a policy priority, the Canadian government ended up, more by accident rather than by design, slowing the growth of volatile market-based banking in Canada in favour of traditional banking activities that tend to be less risky in nature.

Conclusion

Faced with the world's worst financial crisis since the Great Depression, Canada remained an oasis of relative financial stability while Europe and the United States succumbed to the pressures of rapidly depreciating assets, indebtedness and frozen credit markets. In the context of this volume's argument, the explanation for this admirable performance by the Canadian banking system rests squarely on its low exposure to market-based activities, both on the asset and liability sides of the balance sheet. Given that Canada is generally placed alongside its Anglo-Saxon brethren when it comes to characterizing its system of capitalism (see Hall and Soskice 2001), it may appear surprising to find its banking system categorized with Japan rather than with the United Kingdom and the United States. But such a finding only confirms the usefulness of the market-based banking approach developed in this volume. Without this new conceptualization, it would be difficult to explain why Canada did not experience a banking crisis in 2007–9 whereas the United Kingdom and the United States did.

References

Allen, D. E., R. R. Boffey, and R. J. Powell (2011) 'Peas in a pod: Canadian and Australian banks before and during a Global Financial Crisis.' Manuscript. Edith Cowan University. Available at <http://ssrn.com/abstract=1884084>.

Bank of Canada (2007) 'Financial System Review.' December. Ottawa. Available online at <http://www.bankofcanada.ca/wp-content/uploads/2010/04/fsr_1207.pdf>.

Bank of Canada (2008a) 'Financial System Review.' June. Ottawa. Available online at <http://www.bankofcanada.ca/wp-content/uploads/2010/04/fsr_0608.pdf>.

Bank of Canada (2008b) 'Financial System Review.' December. Ottawa. Available online at <http://www.bankofcanada.ca/2008/12/publications/periodicals/fsr/december-2008/>.

Bank of Canada (2011) 'Financial System Review.' June. Ottawa. Available online at <http://www.bankofcanada.ca/wp-content/uploads/2011/06/fsr_0611.pdf>.

Bologna, P. (20100 'Australian Banking System Resilience: What Should Be Expected Looking Forward? An International Perspective.' IMF Working Paper No. 10/228. Washington, DC: International Monetary Fund.

Bordeleau, E., A. Crawford, and C. Graham (2009) 'Regulatory Constraints on Bank Leverage: Issues and Lessons from the Canadian Experience.' Discussion Paper No. 2009–15. Ottawa: Bank of Canada.

Bordo, M. D., A. Redish, and H. Rockoff (2011) 'Why didn't Canada have a banking crisis in 2008 (or in 1930, or 1907, or …)?' NBER Working Paper No. 17312. Cambridge, MA: National Bureau of Economic Research.

Brean, D. J. S., L. Kryzanowski, and G. S. Roberts (2011) 'Canada and the United States: Different roots, different routes to financial sector regulation.' *Business History*, 53, 2, 249–269.

Calmès, C. and Y. Liu (2009) 'Financial structure change and banking income: A Canada-U.S. Comparison.' *International Financial Markets, Institutions and Money*, 19, 1, 128–139.

Canada Mortgage and Housing Corporation (2012) 'CMHC Insurance and Securitization Activities.' Available online at <http://www.cmhc-schl.gc.ca/en/corp/nero/jufa/jufa_007.cfm>.

Canadian Bankers Association (2012) 'Domestic Banks' Financial Results: Fiscal Year End for the years 2006–2011.' March. Toronto. Available online at <http://www.cba.ca/contents/files/statistics/stat_banksann_db251_en.pdf>.

Crawford, A., C. Graham, and É. Bordeleau (2009) 'Regulatory Constraints on Leverage: The Canadian Experience.' Financial System Review, June. Ottawa: Bank of Canada, 45–50.

Crawford, A. and U. Faruqui (2012) 'What Explains Trends in Household Debt in Canada?' *Bank of Canada Review*, Winter 2011–2012, 3–15.

Davis, E. P. (2001) 'Multiple Avenues of Intermediation, Corporate Finance and Financial Stability.' IMF Working Paper No. 01/115. Washington, DC: International Monetary Fund.

Daniel, F. (2003) 'Recent Changes to Canada's Financial Sector Legislation.' *Bank of Canada Review*, Winter 2002–2003, 3–16.

DBRS (2008) 'Canadian Securitization Market Overview.' August. Available online at <http://www.dbrs.com/research/223953/canadian-securitization-market-overview-august-2008.pdf>.

D'Hulster, K. (2009) 'The Leverage Ratio: A New Limit on Banks.' *Crisis Response*, Note No. 11, December. Washington: The World Bank Group. Available online at <http://www.worldbank.org/financialcrisis/pdf/levrage-ratio-web.pdf>.

Financial Stability Board (2012) 'Peer Review of Canada: Review Report.' 30 January. Basel. Available online at <http://www.financialstabilityboard.org/publications/r_120130.pdf>.

Freedman, C. (1998) 'The Canadian Banking System.' Technical Report No. 81. Ottawa: Bank of Canada.

Freedman, C. and W. Engert (2003) 'Financial Developments in Canada: Past Trends and Future Challenges.' *Bank of Canada Review*, Summer, 3–16.

Haldane, A. (2011) 'Control rights (and wrongs).' Speech, 24 October, Bank of England. Available online at <http://www.bankofengland.co.uk/publications/Documents/speeches/2011/speech525.pdf>.

Hall, P. A. and D. Soskice (2001) *Varieties of Capitalism: The Institutional Foundations of Comparative Advantage*. New York: Oxford University Press.

International Monetary Fund (2007) 'Canada: 2007 Article IV Consultation—Staff Report; and Public Information Notice on the Executive Board Discussion.' IMF Country Report No. 07/51. Washington, DC.

International Monetary Fund (2008a) 'Canada: Financial Stability Assessment—Update.' IMF Country Report No. 08/59. February. Washington, DC.

International Monetary Fund (2008b) 'Canada: Selected Issues.' IMF Country Report No. 08/70. February. Washington, DC.

International Monetary Fund (2009) 'Canada: 2009 Article IV Consultation—Staff Report; Staff Statement; and Public Information Notice on the Executive Board Discussion.' IMF Country Report No. 09/162. Washington, DC.

Jordà, Ò., M. H. P. Schularick, and A. M. Taylor (2011) 'When Credit Bites Back: Leverage, Business Cycles, and Crises.' NBER Working Paper No. 17621. Cambridge, MA: National Bureau of Economic Research.

Kamhi, N. and E. Tuer (2007) 'The market for Canadian asset-backed commercial paper revisited.' Financial System Review, December, 13–16. Ottawa: Bank of Canada.

Koeppl, T. V. and J. MacGee (2007) 'Branching Out: The Urgent Need to Transform Canada's Financial Landscape and How to Do It.' Commentary No. 251, June. Toronto: C.D. Howe Institute. Available online at <http://www.cdhowe.org/pdf/Commentary_251.pdf>.

Kiff, J. (2009) 'Canadian Residential Mortgage Markets: Boring But Effective?' IMF Working Paper No. 09/130. Washington, DC: International Monetary Fund.

Koudstaal, M. and S. van Wijnbergen (2012) 'On risk, Leverage and Banks: Do Highly Leveraged Banks Take On Excessive Risk?' Duisenberg School of Finance—Tinbergen Institute Discussion Paper No. TI 12–022/2/DSF31. Available online at <http://www.tinbergen.nl/discussionpapers/12022.pdf>.

Laeven, L. and R. Levine (2009) 'Bank governance, regulation and risk taking.' *Journal of Financial Economics*, 93, 259–275.

Létourneau, H. and P. Heidrich (2010) 'Canadian Banks Abroad. Expansion and Exposure to the 2008–2009 Financial Crisis.' Ottawa: The North-South Institute. Available online at www.nsi-ins.ca/publications/canadian-banks-financial-crisis/.

Onyett-Jeffries, D. (2012) 'Debt is not yet cracking households' foundation.' Current Analysis, February. Toronto: RBC Economics. Available at <http://www.rbc.com/economics/market/pdf/debt.pdf>.

Policy Research Branch (2003) 'Restrictions on Foreign Ownership in Canada.' TP14500E, August. Ottawa: Transport Canada. Available online at <http://www.tc.gc.ca/media/documents/policy/tp14500e.pdf>.

Ratnovski, L. and R. Huang (2009) 'Why Are Canadian Banks More Resilient?' IMF Working Paper 09/152. Washington, DC: International Monetary Fund.

Schmidt, R. H. and M. Tyrell (1997) 'Financial Systems, Corporate Finance and Corporate Governance.' *European Financial Management*, 3, 3, 333–361.

Toka, F., J. Scott and N. Flanders (2012) 'Evaluating Canadian Banks' Residential Mortgage Exposure.' Special Report. May 21. New York: Fitch Ratings.

Zysman, J. (1983) *Governments, Markets and Growth: Financial Systems and the Politics of Industrial Change*. Ithaca, NY: Cornell University Press.

10

Market-Based Banking in Japan: From the Avant-Garde to Europe's Future?

Ryunoshin Kamikawa[1]

Introduction

The banking sector of Japan was not damaged significantly by the financial crisis that erupted in 2008. In the fall of 2008 when the crisis reached its peak after the collapse of Lehman Brothers, most Japanese financial institutions had a sound financial base and the financial system was stable. Data on government support to the financial sector confirm that the Japanese banking sector was damaged less than those of other developed countries. The amount of capital injection was only 0.1 per cent of 2009 gross domestic product (GDP) and the amount of purchase of assets and lending by the treasury was also only 0.1 per cent of 2009 GDP (IMF 2010, 35–6). This state assistance to banks was much smaller than those in other developed countries owing principally to the limited development of 'market-based banking' in Japan (see Hardie and Howarth, Chapter 2, this volume, and Hardie, Howarth, Maxfield and Verdun, Chapter 1, this volume, for an explanation of the concept).

Nonetheless, Japan remains an interesting case in examining 'market-based banking'. Japan has been classified as a 'coordinated market economy' (CME), which features a 'bank-based' financial system offering patient capital, 'cross-shareholdings', and the corporate groups (sometimes called horizontal *keiretsu*) (Hall and Soskice 2001). In contrast with Germany, also normally categorized as a CME, the banking side of the Japanese CME has remained intact and banks have neither operated as 'universal banks' (engaged in both

[1] For helpful comments on earlier version of this chapter, I wish to thank David Howarth and Iain Hardie, as well as other participants in workshops at University of Victoria and the University of Edinburgh. This work was supported by the Ministry of Education, Culture, Sports, Science and Technology Grant-in-Aid for Science Research (22730115).

commercial and investment banking) nor relied on 'market-based' funding to support lending. This was partly because the segmentation between banking and securities businesses was maintained for a long time in Japan, as in the United States. In contrast to the United States, however, securities companies remained focused on intermediating equity and bond markets and did not engage in the large-scale expansion of their balance sheets, financed by short-term market borrowing, as the US investment banks did.

This chapter focuses on the limited development of 'market-based banking' in Japan which, at first glance, can be explained by institutional factors such the strict regulatory framework. However, in the 1980s, Japanese market-based banking was higher than that at the end of 2007. Japanese banks developed substantial overseas operations and launched investment banking business in overseas markets. Japanese banks were at the vanguard of market-based banking in the late 1980s. The distinctive character of Japan is that the extent of market-based banking and financial internationalization reversed in the 1990s, despite regulatory liberalization, even though market-based banking developed rapidly in many other developed countries. These facts indicate that the limited development of market-based banking in Japan results from not only the institutional factors but also macro-economic factors in the early 1990s. The factors stem from Japan's own financial crisis starting in the early 1990s and the banks' strategic responses to this crisis. In the face of this crisis, Japanese financial institutions moved to cut back international operations and reduce assets. Many European banks facing the crisis have followed a similar deleveraging trend accelerated by Basel III guidelines on capital requirements (*Financial Times*, 3 May 2012). The history of Japanese banking since the early 1990s may point the future of European banking.

This chapter is organized as follows. In the second section, the development of market-based banking in Japan is measured. In the third section, the impact of the international financial crisis on the Japanese financial system is considered. In the fourth section, the institutional factors which hindered the development of 'market-based banking' are examined. In the penultimate section, the impact of the Japanese financial crisis on the development of market-based banking is analysed.

The Limited Development of Market-Based Banking in Japan

Japan has been classified as a CME, which features a 'bank-based' financial system offering patient capital. 'Cross-shareholding' is another core element of the Japanese CME model. In Japan, as a defensive measure against hostile takeovers, a large proportion of shares of publicly traded corporations have been held by banks and companies within the same corporate groups (sometimes called horizontal *keiretsu*) which have been structured to centre on one major bank as in France in the 1990s. Non-financial companies (NFCs) held each other's shares as did banks and their client companies. Though cross-shareholdings declined in the 1990s and 2000s (Hoshi and Kashyap 2001, 322–3; Culpepper 2011, 116), banks and NFCs continued to be each other's major shareholders and many large corporations adopted defensive measures against hostile takeover attempts, such as a poison pill. The Japanese CME model remained intact.

As explained in the introduction to this volume, the traditional dichotomy between 'bank-based' and 'market-based' financial system has become insufficient to understand the financial systems in industrialized countries because of the appearance of market-based banking. Even in a country which has a largely bank-based financial system, such as Germany and Spain, the exposure of bank assets and liabilities to the market can be high (see Hardie and Howarth, Chapter 2, this volume; Royo, Chapter 7, this volume). Therefore, in this section, the degree of the development of market-based banking in Japan is measured.

Corporate Finance

Table 10.1 shows that the ratio of shares and other equities of total NFCs liabilities in Japan was as high as other countries and that of loans was not so high. However, this is because of cross-shareholding. In Japan, banks and NFCs held a huge amount of shares. At the end of 2007, NFCs held 34.1 per cent and banks held 7.5 per cent of all shares (Cabinet Office, Government of Japan. 2008).

The financial system in post-war Japan was bank centred. Most firms relied on bank borrowing for their external funding. Stock and bond financing were limited by strict regulations. In the late 1970s, the deregulation of corporate financing started. This encouraged the development of capital markets and large firms moved away from bank financing. However, small and medium-sized enterprises (SMEs) have mainly relied on bank financing.

Table 10.1. The component ratio of non-financial corporations' financial liabilities (at the end of 2007)

	Japan (%)	US (%)	UK (%)	Germany (%)	France (%)
Loans	25.2	17.1	33.0	31.5	21.5
Corporate debenture	5.9	10.5	9.2	2.9	4.7
Shares and other equities	48.4	54.7	53.8	50.9	62.7
Others	20.6	17.7	4.0	14.7	11.1

Source: Cabinet Office, Government of Japan (2008), Figure 2–5-1.

Table 10.2. The component ratio of household assets (at the end of 2007)

	Japan (%)	US (%)	UK (%)	Germany (%)	France (%)
Currency and deposits	50.4	13.3	26.8	35.5	29.4
Securities other than shares	4.4	8.5	0.7	7.2	1.6
Investment trust	4.5	14.2	5.5	11.9	9.2
Shares and other equities	11.0	29.4	8.4	13.1	17.6
Insurance and annuity reserve	25.3	30.8	55.1	31.3	37.8
Others	4.4	3.8	3.5	0.9	4.5

Source: Cabinet Office, Government of Japan (2008), Figure 2–5-3.

Table 10.3. The asset side of Japanese banks' balance sheets (at the end of 2007)

	(trillion yen)
Loans	469 (59.2%)
Industrial securities and shares	100 (12.7%)
Central government securities, etc.*	87 (11.0%)
External assets	58 (7.3%)
Others	79 (9.9%)
Total	792 (100.0%)

* This consists of Central government securities, Fiscal investment and loan programme (FILP) bonds, Treasury discount bills, and Public corporation securities.

Source: Cabinet Office, Government of Japan (2008), Figure 2–5-24.

Table 10.2 shows that about half of household financial assets were held as bank deposits, which included postal savings. Securities holdings were quite limited. Table 10.3 shows that the loans and central government securities (etc.) to assets ratio for the Japanese banks was 70.2 per cent, which was very high compared with other developed countries.[2] Therefore, the main flow of money in the Japanese economy was supplied by household deposits with banks which provided credit to firms (Cabinet Office, Government of Japan 2008, 142–5) and the government. Japanese banks mainly engaged in traditional banking.

At the end of 2007, the stock market capitalization to GDP ratio was 106.4 per cent, private debt securities to GDP ratio was 47.2 per cent, and bank assets to GDP ratio was 178.9 per cent (IMF 2008). These figures show that bank assets were larger than the sum of stock market capitalization and private debt securities (IMF 2008). There was a clear difference between Japan and the United States, the leading example of the market-based model (see Hardie and Maxfield, Chapter 3, this volume). In Japan, the role of bank loans was more important in corporate finance than that of bonds or equity.

[2] This loans to assets figure includes loans to other banks. However, the amount of loans to other banks was small. For example, the data in March 2008 show that the loans (including loans to other banks) to assets ratio was 57.1 per cent and call loans (accounting for most loans to other banks) to assets ratio was only 1.8 per cent (Zenkoku Ginko Kyokai 2008). We can say that Japanese banks had a very high loans plus holdings of government securities figure.

In many European countries including the supposed market-based United Kingdom, however, bank assets were much larger than in Japan and the role of bank loans was much more important than that of bonds or equity in corporate finance (see Hardie and Maxfield, Chapter 3, this volume). While the assets of traditional banking are loans to customers and their liabilities are deposits, market-based banking involves financing bank assets with market-based (notably wholesale and inter-bank) borrowing rather than predominantly through deposits. Therefore, it is necessary to look at the Japanese banks' balance sheets.

Assets

As far as bank assets are concerned, the development of market-based banking in Japan remained very low. The trading assets (central government securities, etc., industrial securities, and shares) to assets ratio was 23.7 per cent—thus comparatively high. However, this can be explained by the huge amount of shares held by banks, which were not likely to be sold because of cross-shareholdings, despite the use of the label 'trading asset'. They also held the huge amount of Japanese government bonds, which were more stable than other market-based assets.

The Japanese banking system had the lowest exposure to securitized financial products among the G7 countries and one of the lowest levels among the industrialized economies. At the end of 2008, the exposure of Japanese deposit-taking institutions (banks and cooperative financial institutions) to subprime-related products amounted to 565 billion yen, only about 1.1 per cent of Tier 1 capital. Their exposure to subprime-related products (including through asset backed commercial paper (ABCP) programmes), collateralized loan obligations (CLOs), collateralized debt obligations (CDOs), residential mortgage-backed securities (RMBS), commercial mortgage backed securities (CMBS), and leveraged loans amounted to 19,408 billion yen, only about 3.8 per cent of GDP (Financial Services Agency 2009). This figure was very low compared with other industrialized countries.

Liabilities

As far as bank liabilities are concerned, the development of market-based banking in Japan remained very low. Table 10.5 shows that deposits accounted for 75.7 per cent of total bank liabilities. This was very high compared with other industrialized countries. In Japan, however, commercial banking and securities businesses have been separated strictly since 1948, as in the United States prior to repeal of Glass–Steagall Act by the Clinton administration and unlike the universal banking model that is widespread in Europe. Therefore,

Table 10.4. The realized losses of Japanese deposit-taking institutions due to securitized products (from 1 April 2007 to 31 December 2008)

(Billion Yen)

Exposure to subprime-related products								CLO, CDO*		RMBS*		CMBS		Leveraged Loans		Total	
CDOs		RMBS		Others		Subtotal											
Book value	Realized profits/ losses	Book value	Realized profits/ losses	Book value	Realized profits/ losses	Book value	Realized profits/ losses	Book Value	Realized profits/ losses	Book Value	Realized profits/ losses	Book Value	Realized profits/ losses	Book Value	Realized profits/ losses	Book Value	Realized profits/ losses
119	–680	300	–159	145	–80	565	–919	6251	–905	5072	–248	2671	–19	4849	–76	19408	–2167

*Excluding subprime-related products.

Note 1: The above figures are based on interviews with individual institutions, and thus can be further revised in the process of examination by each institution.
Note 2: CDOs include the exposures to SIVs.
Note 3: RMBS does not include GSE MBS.
Note 4: While the definition of leveraged loans can vary depending on each financial institution, it generally refers to loans to low-rated companies, including loans made for mergers and acquisitions.
Note 5: Apart from above figures, losses on CDS transactions with monoline insurers (about 30.0 billion yen) have been reported.
Source: Financial Service Agency (2009).

we must consider the total liabilities of both deposit-taking institutions and other financial dealers and brokers (principally securities companies) (Table 10.5). Deposits, nonetheless, still represented 69.0 per cent of total funding: a very high figure.

Further data support the fact that the Japanese financial sector's reliance on wholesale funding was rather low. First, the loans to deposits ratio in Japan is very low among industrialized countries. It was 80.6 per cent at the end of 2007. Only Belgium, of the countries considered in this volume, had a larger surplus of deposits over loans as a percentage of GDP (Hardie and Howarth, Chapter 2, this volume). This shows that Japanese banks could lend by using only the deposits, without recourse to market-based funding, though this did not stop Belgian banks accessing a lot of wholesale market funding. Second, the amount of securitized paper issuance was rather small. In 2007, the total amount of securitized paper issuance was 6,811.9 billion yen, about 1.3 per cent of GDP (Table 10.6). This shows the low dependence of Japanese banks on securitization for lending. Furthermore, as of March 2011, covered bonds have not yet been issued in Japan.

Table 10.5. The liabilities side of Japanese banks' balance sheets and that of Japanese financial dealers' and brokers' balance sheets (at the end of 2007, 100 million yen)

	Banks (deposit-taking institutions)		Financial dealers and brokers		Total	
Deposits	11,183,076	75.7%	48,518	3.2%	11,231,594	69.0%
Wholesale	2,290,378	15.5%	1,175,152	78.1%	3,465,530	21.3%
Equity	1,072,162	7.3%	222,438	14.8%	1,294,600	8.0%
Other	221,801	1.5%	58,137	3.9%	279,938	1.7%
	14,767,417	100.0%	1,504,245	100.0%	16,271,662	100.0%

Source: Adapted from Bank of Japan, 'Flow of funds'. <http://www.stat-search.boj.or.jp/ssi/cgi-bin/famecgi2?cgi=$nme_a000_en&lstSelection=11>.

Table 10.6 The amount of securitized paper issuance (2007)

	Billion yen
Resident mortgage backed securities	3262.8
Commercial mortgage backed securities	1909.3
Collateralized debt obligations	350.8
Leasing receivables	649.3
Consumer loan receivable and credit card loan receivable	208.3
Shopping credit receivable and car loan receivable	295.5
Accounts receivable and bills receivable	39.3
Others	96.7
Total amount of securitized paper issuance	6811.9

Source: Japan Securities Dealers Association <http://www.jsda.or.jp/html/syoukenka/2/2007doukou2.pdf>.

Internationalization

The degree of internationalization of Japanese banks was very low. At the end of 2007, Japanese banks' external assets were US$ 2,401.8 billion, which were about 54.8 per cent of GDP, and their external liabilities were US$ 712.0 billion, which were about 16.2 per cent of GDP (BIS 2008). Both were rather low among industrialized countries. Moreover, at the end of 2007, Japanese banks' inter-bank borrowing from abroad was extremely low at only 3.4 per cent of GDP (BIS 2008). As discussed below, this is a reversal of the previous position. The degree of internationalization of Japanese banks was higher in the 1980s.

The Impact of the International Financial Crisis on Japan

The crisis has unfolded through four phases. Phase 1 started in August 2007, when BNP Paribas declared that it was banning investors from withdrawing money from three of its investment funds and the initial problem in the securitization and ABCP markets occurred (this is called 'Paribas Shock' in Japan). Phase 2 started in September 2008, when Lehman Brothers collapsed (this is called 'Lehman Shock' in Japan) and the financial market crisis spread internationally. Phase 3 was the period of slowdown in the real economy from fall 2008 to spring 2009. Phase 4 was the European sovereign debt crisis, which started in spring 2010.

Phase 1: Paribas Shock

With the Paribas Shock, it was widely acknowledged that the subprime loans problem was serious. In Japan, however, the problem was viewed as 'fire on the other side of the river'. The Japanese banking system held far less subprime-related products than the other national banking systems considered in this volume and did not suffer significant losses. Table 10.4 shows the realized losses of Japanese deposit-taking institutions due to subprime-related products from 1 April 2007 to 31 December 2008. They were 919 billion yen, only 0.17 per cent of GDP.

Phase 2: Lehman Shock

In Japan, the bankruptcy of Lehman Brothers was also viewed as 'fire on the other side of the river'. The Minister of State for Economic and Fiscal Policy, Kaoru Yosano, stated that it would have a 'bee-sting effect' on the Japanese economy and that Japanese financial institutions would not suffer from the fall (*Nihon Keizai Shimbun*, 17 September 2008). Yosano was broadly correct in his assessment that most Japanese financial institutions had a sound financial base and the financial system was stable. Japanese financial institutions took advantage of the crisis to expand overseas. Three major banks invested in financial institutions in the United States and the United Kingdom. Mizuho Corporate Bank invested in Merrill Lynch in January 2008 and Sumitomo Mitsui Bank decided to invest in Barclays in July 2008. In September 2008, Mitsubishi UFJ Financial Group invested US$9 billion for a 21 per cent stake in Morgan Stanley. In that month, one major securities company, Nomura Holdings acquired failed Lehman Brothers' operations in Asia-Pacific, Europe, and Middle-East.

The Japanese banking sector avoided losses linked to securitized products, including subprime-related products, and suffered no funding difficulties because of limited reliance on wholesale markets.

Phase 3: World Economic Crisis

Despite the limited impact of the financial crisis in Japan, the country's economy, however, was seriously damaged. The first impact of the crisis was that Japanese stock prices dropped sharply. This was because foreign investors sold the stocks of Japanese corporations in bulk. They had to compensate for losses incurred by the international financial crisis. The fall in stock prices had a significant negative impact on the financial condition of large banks. Through cross-shareholdings, they held a huge amount of stocks, valued at more than the value of their capital. Since the late 1980s, the United States and west European governments had pushed for the introduction of capital adequacy requirements. When Basel I was introduced in 1988, the Japanese government claimed that banks should be allowed to include the unrealized capital gains on their stocks in their capital. After the negotiations, they were allowed to include 45 per cent of unrealized capital gains on their securities in Tier 2 capital (which is composed of supplementary capital). This enabled Japanese banks whose ratios of capital to assets were low to meet the regulatory requirement. Because of this, however, their capital falls when stock prices fall, causing financial difficulty.

In 2001, in order to conform to the new Basel Capital Accord, the government decided to limit the total value of stocks which a bank could hold at less than the total value of its core capital by the end of September 2004. In 2003, the deadline was delayed until the end of September 2006. Then, banks started to sell their stocks, although they continued to hold a huge amount of stocks as cross-shareholdings.[3] Hence, the fall in stock prices had a negative impact on the banking sector and probably made banks reluctant to lend money in order to maintain capital adequacy ratios, as in the impact of 'market to market' assets (see Hardie and Howarth, Chapter 2, this volume). This worsened the real economy further.

The second impact of the crisis was that corporations became less able to finance from the capital market directly. Because of the Lehman Brothers default, investors avoided riskier assets. In Japan, from the late 1970s, the deregulation of corporate finance proceeded and large companies came to raise funds from stock and bond issues. By the 2000s, most large companies raised funds by issuing stocks, bonds, and commercial paper (CP). However, even large global corporations could not raise funds from the capital market directly at the end of 2008 (Nihon Keizai Shimbunsha 2009b, 132). They were compelled to rush to banks to borrow funds in order to manage cash flow. As banks increased lending to large corporations, they became reluctant to lend money to SMEs. They became indirect victims of financial market weakness, but were saved by the government, as noted below.

The third impact of the crisis was that Japanese exports fell sharply—as in Germany and many other export-reliant economies—causing a rapid deterioration in the real economy. This was due to the rapid slowdown in worldwide demand, especially in the United States, but also the sharp appreciation of the yen against both the dollar and the euro. Because the Japanese banking system was comparatively sound, investors bought yen and sold both the dollar and the euro. The large scale reversal of the 'carry trade' also pushed up the yen.[4]

The government and the Bank of Japan carried out several policy measures to respond to the crisis. In order to stimulate the economy, the Liberal Democratic Party's coalition government moved to reverse the fiscal restraint policies it had pursued since 2001. The government also took measures to support companies suffering funding problems. The main regulator and supervisor, the Financial Services Agency (FSA) urged financial institutions to apply for public capital to address banks' reluctance to lend and some banks accepted this funding to strengthen their capital base. The FSA also eased its inspection standards to a large degree and asked banks to lend money to SMEs more aggressively relaxing the Agency's treatment of bank lending.

The Bank of Japan decided to introduce outright purchases of CP and corporate bonds as temporary measures, as issuing conditions in the corporate bond and CP markets tightened. The Bank of Japan, responding to

[3] The major banks held stocks worth of more than 10 trillion yen (more than about US$104 billion at the June 2009 exchange rate) (Nihon Keizai Shimbunsha 2009b, 155).

[4] The 'carry trade' refers to investors borrowing the yen with a low interest rate and using the funds to purchase a different currency yielding a higher interest rate.

the appreciation of the yen, also decided to ease monetary policy (Nihon Keizai Shimbunsha 2009a, 247–72). Free from the need to financially assist the banking sector, the government and the Bank of Japan intervened in the market and increased spending.

Phase 4: Sovereign Crisis

The Greek sovereign debt crisis developed from the end of 2009 and spread to other European countries, including Ireland and Portugal in 2010 and Spain in 2011–12. Despite Japan's position as the most publicly indebted developed country, it avoided a sovereign debt crisis. At the end of 2007, Japanese public debt stood at 163.1 per cent of GDP (IMF 2008).[5] However, a huge amount of Japanese government bonds have been purchased in the market and the long-term interest rates have been low and stable. The long-term (10-year) Japanese government bond yield dropped to 0.79 per cent in June 2012 and has remained near historic lows.

Why has no sovereign debt crisis happened in Japan? The principal reason is that most Japanese government bonds are bought and held by domestic investors, as with Italy (see Pagoulatos and Quaglia, Chapter 8, this volume). Table 10.7 shows that only 7.3 per cent of Japanese public debt was held abroad.

This is related to the limited development of market-based banking in Japan. As noted above, bank deposits exceeded bank loans. Japanese banks

Table 10.7. The breakdown of Japanese government bond holders (at the end of 2007)

	Trillion yen	Percentage of total
General government (exclude public pensions)	2.3	0.4
Fiscal loan fund	16.5	2.4
Bank of Japan	65.1	9.5
Banks, etc.	270.7	39.6
Life and non-life insurance	125.9	18.4
Public pensions	75.2	11.0
Pension funds	26.9	3.9
Foreigners	49.9	7.3
Households	36.0	5.3
Others	15.9	2.3
Total	684.3	100.0

Note: From preliminary figures of the end of December 2007, Banks, etc., includes Japan Post Bank. Life and Non-life Insurance includes Japan Post Insurance.

Source: Ministry of Finance, Debt Management Policy Division (2008), 'Japanese Government Bonds—Recent Debt Management Policy Initiatives'. <http://www.mof.go.jp/english/bonds/ir/ir080527b.pdf>

[5] In 2010, the public debt amounted to 199.2 per cent of GDP and the budget deficit amounted to 8.0 per cent of GDP (Ministry of Finance 2010).

amassed a huge amount of deposits and purchased Japanese government bonds by using the surplus funds because they did not invest the deposits in high-risk, high-return financial assets. As a result, most Japanese government bonds were purchased in the domestic market, preventing a sovereign debt crisis.

Explaining Low Market-Based Banking: Institutional Factors

The banking sector of Japan was left only marginally scathed by the financial crisis because of the very low development of market-based banking. This section examines the institutional factors that undermined the development of Japanese market-based banking.

The Japanese Financial System

The first explanation focuses on the features of Japanese financial system, the banking side of the Japanese CME. About half of household financial assets were held as bank deposits and securities holdings were quite limited. Customer deposits exceeded customer loans by a substantial margin in Japan (see Hardie and Howarth, Chapter 2,this volume). Japanese banks did not need market-based funding to finance lending. In addition, banks did not invest customer deposits which were viewed as low-risk, low-return financial assets in high-risk, high-return financial assets and had a passive attitude toward market-based business (Sato 2010, 254–7). As a result, the Japanese banks' business model was that the deposit-loan business outweighed the market-related business. In Belgium, however, banks invested in high-risk, high-return financial assets, though it had a larger surplus of deposits over loans as a percentage of GDP, as noted above (Hardie and Howarth, Chapter 2, this volume). Then, the financial regulations should be examined.

The Financial Regulations

This bank-centred system was designed purposely by the government through a range of regulations. The Ministry of Finance (MOF), which was in charge of financial regulation and supervision, set its prime objective on maintaining the stability of the bank-centred system and restricted competition among financial institutions, lest a financial institution whose management was weak should fail.

In 1948, the Securities and Exchange Act was enacted. Patterned after Glass–Steagall, the act banned a single financial institution from conducting both banking and securities business. Most firms relied on bank borrowing for their funds because stock and bond financing were limited through strict regulation. As the stock market was undeveloped and the government encouraged savings, the primary household assets were held as bank deposits and postal savings. Securities holdings were also limited. Because of cross-shareholdings, share trading was low.

The way of supervising financial institutions by the MOF, which limited competition and protected weak financial institutions through regulation, is called the 'convoy system'. This term comes from the fact that in convoys, all ships have to match the speed of the slowest ship in order to protect it. The convoy system was maintained until the 1990s and deprived financial institutions of a spirit of competition and discouraged them from innovation.

Further, unlike universal banks in Europe, banks could not develop market-based banking in part because the government prohibited them from engaging in securities businesses. In the United States, investment banks developed highly 'market-based banking' (Hardie and Maxfield, Chapter 3, this volume). In Japan, however, the financial base of securities companies was undermined because the Japanese stock market remained undeveloped. Securities companies, therefore, were thought not to be capable of launching investment banking business. They remained focused on intermediating equity and bond markets. Because stock trading commissions were regulated by the MOF, they could earn a decent amount of revenue without launching new business areas.

The Partial Relaxation of Regulation

The MOF had advanced financial deregulation since the 1970s. However, it proceeded at a much slower pace than in the United States and the United Kingdom. Moreover, it did not proceed at the same pace in all financial areas. Regulation, as in Canada (Leblond, Chapter 9, this volume), is therefore an important part of the reason why Japan did not develop market-based assets in the same way as, for example, Belgium (Chang and Jones, Chapter 4, this volume) and Germany (Hardie and Howarth, Chapter 2, this volume).

The deregulation of corporate finance proceeded more smoothly. As a result, banks suffered from lost borrowers and narrowed profit margins. Large NFCs began to raise funds through issuing corporate bonds and new stocks, becoming less dependent on bank finance. This would contribute to the stock bubble in the late 1980s. Meanwhile, banks began selling high interest rate Negotiable Certificates of Deposit owing to interest rate deregulation and this decreased interest margins which were their prime source of earnings. Therefore, banks had to find new sources of earnings.

Facing this change of business environment, most major commercial banks, which are called 'city banks', and long-term credit banks aspired to become universal banks, modelling themselves on banks in western Europe which also managed securities businesses (Okazaki and Hoshi 2002).[6]

However, banks' strategy to launch securities businesses was derailed. The regulations on the segmentation of financial services had not been eased for a long time. It was not until 1993, when the 1992 Financial System Reform Law became effective, that banks were allowed to form subsidiaries that could partially operate in the securities businesses. Even with this change, the services that bank-owned security subsidiaries could offer were heavily restricted.

Three reasons explain why Japanese financial services were not deregulated evenly. First, securities companies strongly opposed city banks' entry into their business. They thought that they would be beaten by city banks because the latter had an extremely strong business base and close relationships with firms. It had been said that securities companies tipped influential politicians off on good stock purchases and brought about a price increase through concentrated sales efforts and told the politicians when to sell for a handsome capital gain before the stock dropped back down (Rosenbluth 1989, 38). Thus, securities companies had a strong influence on politicians who blocked banks from entering the securities business for many years. Second, the MOF was concerned that financial deregulation would increase competition among financial institutions and drive some of them into bankruptcy. In 1927, the bankruptcy of one bank triggered a run on others, resulting in financial crisis. Then, the MOF decided to avoid the bankruptcy of any banks by discouraging competition in the sector. Third, the MOF was concerned about the conflict of interest between the banking and securities businesses, specifically that banks might make companies in financial difficulty issue corporate bonds and equity in order to recover their loans. Because of this concern, some firewalls between banks and their securities subsidiaries were maintained even though financial deregulation was completed by the 'Big Bang' financial reforms at the end of 1990s (*Asahi Shimbun*, 4 June 2009).

Regulation prevented banks from entering the securities business in the domestic market. With the rise in land prices in the 1980s, banks, whose primary business remained lending to firms, found real estate financing as a new source of earnings. The regulations on segmentation of financial services were not eased as steadily as those on corporate finance and this 'distorted

[6] In particular, long-term credit banks which specialized in long-term lending to large firms were expected to be endangered in the future. This was because large firms became less dependent on bank finance and because city banks took away their customers by lengthening loan maturities.

financial deregulation' contributed to banks' huge real estate loans in the late 1980s (Hoshi and Kashyap 2001; Okazaki and Hoshi 2002).

Land Price Bubble

The land prices around Tokyo started to soar in the early 1980s. First, foreign financial institutions expanded into Tokyo facilitated by financial deregulation in Japan, resulting in a lack of office space in the capital. Occupancy rates in Tokyo exceeded 100 per cent by the early 1980s (Bank of Japan 1990). Second, the government deregulated land utilization and building standards, disposed of state-owned land, and advanced large-scale development projects in the capital (Otake 1994, 189–211). In May 1985, the National Land Agency published 'The Capital Reform Project' which made an over-inflated demand forecast for Tokyo office space (Kishi 1994, 169–93; Nihon Keizai Shimbunsha 2000, 40–4; Tahara 1993, 201–24). These government announcements sparked a further surge in land prices in business districts. These soaring land prices in commercial districts spread to residential areas. Residents of central Tokyo enjoyed very generous tax breaks when they sold their land and homes and transferred to the suburbs (Noguchi 1989, 54; Kawano 1995, 72).

Banks suffering from the decline in corporate lending and narrowing profit margins tried to increase their profits by increasing real estate lending because such loans were expected to bring in high profits thanks to rising land prices. In post-war Japan, moreover, the land prices had risen continually except for the year after the oil crisis in 1973 and, as in the US before 2007, 'the myth of ever-higher land prices' prevailed. Banks lent money as long as borrowers offered land as collateral. Therefore, banks made real estate loans on a massive scale without sufficiently considering the risk that land prices would fall (on Spain in this regard, see Royo, Chapter 7, this volume). This increased transactions and drove land prices up sharply (Aizawa 1995, 129–36; Yoshikawa 1999, 61–2). Interestingly, securitization was not necessary to fund this lending activity because of the large deposit base of Japanese banks.

Furthermore, a low interest rate policy was pursued for an extended period. In September 1985, the Plaza Accord was reached, in which G5 countries agreed to jointly intervene to appreciate non-dollar currencies against the dollar in order to lower the US trade deficit. This triggered a sharp appreciation of the yen and the Japanese economy weakened because much of its growth relied on exports to the United States. The US government also continued to demand that the Japanese government expand domestic demand, as it thought that exchange rate adjustment alone could not correct the trade imbalance. Hence, the Bank of Japan continued to lower interest rates from 1986 and left its official discount rate unchanged at 2.5 per cent, an extremely low rate for that time, from February 1987 to May 1989. Low rates increased speculative investments in stocks and real estate further and the stock and land bubble emerged.

In sum, thanks to the regulated segmentation of banking and securities businesses and the land bubble, banks could concentrate on traditional banking business in the domestic markets. This long-standing regulation has kept the 'bank-centred' financial system and the Japanese CME intact and contributed to the conservative management style of Japanese banks that avoided risk-taking and took a negative attitude toward financial innovation.

As noted below, however, Japanese banks developed substantial overseas operations and launched investment banking business in overseas markets in the 1980s. They were at the vanguard of market-based banking in the late 1980s. They cut back international operations rapidly after the Japanese bubble burst in the early 1990s. This suggests that Japanese financial institutions were constrained by not regulation but another factors. This is examined in the next section.

The Remuneration System

Another factor of the Japanese CME also restricted the development of Japanese market-based banking. The remuneration system that inspired bank employees to maximize short-term profits was not adopted widely in Japan which contributed to delayed financial innovation.

Whereas most continental European countries are classified as 'industry-based' CMEs, Japan is classified as a 'group-based' CME, where cooperation on sensitive matters takes place within the corporate groups operating in different sectors with one major bank at its centre and within the vertical *keiretsu* consisting of one parent company and many subsidiaries (Hall and Soskice 2001). In 'group-based' CMEs, workers are encouraged to acquire firm-specific skills through on-the-job training within their firms. In order to persuade them to invest in skills of this specificity, the large firms have customarily offered many of them life-time employment and adopted the remuneration system which encouraged them to work for the same firm until retirement age. Thus, the seniority-based personnel system, with salary and job position rising with age and length of service, has been widely adopted.

Japanese financial institutions adopted the seniority-based pay system, rather than a pay system that offers generous bonuses to bank employees who contribute significantly to bank profits. Therefore, bank employees tended not to try to make huge profits in a short time through high-risk, high-return investments but to achieve small but secure profits through low-risk, low-return traditional banking business.

This character of the remuneration system prevented the development of new financial services and products. European and US financial institutions, especially those in 'liberal market economies' which have a flexible remuneration system, can secure advanced technical experts who develop new financial services and products through giving huge rewards or poaching staff from other financial institutions by offering huge rewards. However, because of the seniority-based pay system, it was very hard for Japanese financial institutions to secure such experts. Many young talented bank clerks and securities company employees who were experts in investment banking switched to foreign financial institutions which could offer huge rewards. In Japan, as a result, foreign financial institutions maintained near-monopolies on investment banking until the late 2000s.

In the late 1980s, however, Japanese banks and securities companies were most 'avant-garde' of market-based banking, as noted later in this chapter. They expanded overseas operations and launched investment banking in overseas markets very aggressively. Though the seniority-based remuneration system was adopted, the salary of bank and securities company employees rose sharply because they earned higher profits in this period. Therefore, they could secure talented foreign experts in the international business.

After the bubble burst, however, they cut back international operations rapidly. Their employees' salaries plunged sharply in the late 1990s. They could not sufficiently secure talented experts in the international business. Among securities companies, only Nomura Securities, the largest securities company, expanded overseas operations again from the late 1990s. However, it continued to make huge losses from the East Asia financial crisis in 1997, the Russian financial crisis in 1998, and the investment in commercial mortgage-backed securities in the United States in 1998. Because of a shortage of talented experts in the international business, it has been difficult for Nomura Securities to succeed in international operations and the investment banking business. As noted above, Nomura Holdings acquired the operations of the failed Lehman Brothers with the aim of securing talented experts in investment banking business (*Nihon Keizai Shimbun*, 24 October 2008).

Impact of the Previous Crisis

There remain questions which an examination of these institutional-regulatory factors cannot explain. First, the financial regulations that segmented

Japanese financial services were eased rapidly in the late 1990s, but Japanese financial institutions still failed to expand investment banking business until the late 2000s. This suggests that Japanese investment banking was limited by another factor. Second, in the late 1980s, in fact, Japanese banks and securities companies became more market based, especially in the international markets. However, the Japanese financial crisis and non-performing loan problem from the early 1990s to the early 2000s hindered the development.

Financial Deregulation in the 1990s

As noted above, the regulations that segmented Japanese financial services were gradually eased in the 1990s. In 1993, banks were allowed to form subsidiaries that could partially operate in the securities business. The services that bank-owned security subsidiaries could offer were heavily restricted. They were not allowed to underwrite stock issues or deal in the secondary market for corporate bonds and stocks (Hoshi and Kashyap 2001, 252).

In 1997, then Prime Minister Ryutaro Hashimoto launched the 'Japanese Financial Big Bang', which eliminated a range of financial regulations and liberalized financial markets comprehensively. The 'Big Bang' liberalized regulations applying to international capital transactions, brokerage commissions, securities derivatives, and so on. More importantly, the long-maintained segmentation of financial services was rapidly relaxed. That is, banks were allowed to sell investment trusts and issue non-structured bonds; the scope of business services of banks' securities subsidiaries was liberalized; banks and securities companies were allowed to sell insurance products; insurance companies were allowed to enter the banking business; financial holding companies that included a bank, a securities dealer, an investment trust company, an insurance company, and a financial services firm were allowed, and so on (Hoshi and Kashyap 2001, 290–5).

After the Big Bang, the regulations on segmentation between banking and securities businesses still remained. Banks continued to concentrate on traditional banking business. Investment banking activities, such as mergers and acquisitions, securitization of real estate and loan assets, and financial advice, continued to be undertaken by securities companies, but banks were allowed to launch into it through their security subsidiaries. It was expected that the Big Bang contributed to the development of market-based banking in Japan in the 2000s. However, Japanese securities companies remained focused on intermediating equity and bond markets. They delayed expanding investment banking activities and fell further behind the US and European financial institutions.

The style of financial administration also was transformed. In the late 1990s, the MOF was blamed for the Japanese financial crisis and was stripped of its financial divisions. The FSA, founded in July 2000, was given control over financial regulation and supervision. The style of financial administration was transformed from the MOF's discretionary administration, which took precautions in advance, into the FSA's rule-based administration, which reviewed ex post facto. The FSA respected the initiative and autonomy of the market players and kept arm's length from financial institutions. It was expected that the move to lighter touch regulation contributed to the gradual development of market-based banking in Japan in the 2000s. Nevertheless, Japanese financial institutions did not expand fully into new business areas such as investment banking and other international activities.

Market-Based Banking in the 1980s

Despite the various regulatory and institutional constraints, the Japanese banking system was becoming more market based in the late 1980s. First, Japanese banks' assets in the late 1980s are examined. From the late 1970s, financial deregulation regarding corporate finance proceeded. Large NFCs started to raise funds on the capital markets and moved away from bank financing. In the 1980s, there was a boom among firms in making speculative investment on the stock exchange (so-called, *'Zai-Tech'* boom) and the scale of investment in stocks expanded. As the low interest rate policy was implemented when speculative money flowed into the market, stock prices soared sharply in the late 1980s. Thanks to rising share prices, companies could obtain huge amounts of funds through issuing new shares, convertible bonds, and bonds with equity warrants. As a result, stock markets and bond markets expanded rapidly.[7]

Banks were afraid that the relationship with their client companies might break up when they repaid their loans. In order to keep the relationship with them, banks purchased the shares they issued and helped them to issue new shares (Kawano 1995, 112–15). Table 10.8 shows that the amount of shares that Japanese banks held increased sharply in the late 1980s. Table 10.9 shows, however, that the loans to assets ratio at the end of 1990 was 67.9 per cent, which is higher than at the end of 2007. This suggests, as far as bank assets are concerned, that Japanese banks in 1990 were more 'traditional' than those in 2007. While this was in line with the experience of other countries in this volume, in the case of Japan, this was because banks increased real estate loans rapidly in the late 1980s.

[7] The Japanese stock market bubble parallels the collapse of the German 'Neuer Markt', which listed young German companies and opened up equity financing in a bank-based system. It collapsed after the dot-com bubble burst, undermining government efforts to develop it (Hardie and Howarth, Chapter 5, this volume).

Table 10.8. The amount of domestically licensed banks' shareholdings (at the end of year)

	Billion yen
1984	11060.6
1985	12238.1
1986	13620.5
1987	16671.9
1988	21570.4
1989	27843.5
1990	34278.4
1991	36729.6
1992	37102.7
1993	37364.8

Source: Adapted from Bank of Japan, 'Financial Institutions Accounts'. <http://www.stat-search.boj.or.jp/ssi/cgi-bin/famecgi2?cgi=$nme_a000&lstSelection=3>.

Table 10.9. The asset side of Japanese banks' balance sheets (trillion yen and percentage of total in brackets)

	At the end of 1990	At the end of 2007
Loans	538 (67.9)	469 (59.2)
Industrial securities and shares	96 (12.1)	100 (12.7)
Central government securities etc.*	43 (5.4)	87 (11.0)
External assets	33 (4.2)	58 (7.3)
Others	82 (10.4)	79 (9.9)
Total	792 (100.0)	792 (100.0)

*This consists of Central government securities, Fiscal investment and loan programme (FILP) bonds, Treasury discount bills, and Public corporation securities.

Source: Cabinet Office, Government of Japan (2008), Figure 2–5–24.

Second, Japanese banks' liabilities in the late 1980s are examined. At the end of 1990, deposits accounted for 60.5 per cent of total banks' liabilities. This was lower than that at the end of 2007. Moreover, the loans to deposits ratio at the end of 1990 was 112.3 per cent, which is higher than 80.6 per cent at the end of 2007, and indicates some need for market financing of lending in the earlier period. As far as bank liabilities are concerned, in Japan, market-based banking in 1990 was more developed than that in 2007, a notable difference on other countries in this volume.

Third, and connected to the more market-based liabilities above, the stock price bubble influenced household selection of financial assets, as Table 10.10 shows. The rise in stock prices, especially the soaring of the Nippon Telegraph and Telephone Corporation stock, which was privatized in 1985 and the equity of which started to be sold in 1986, triggered a *Zai-Tech* boom among ordinary people who had not previously invested in the stock market. The number of households who started to invest in stocks increased.

Table 10.10. The component ratio of Japanese household assets (percentage of total)

	At the end of March 1991	At the end of 2007
Currency and deposits	47.4	50.4
Securities other than shares	6.3	4.4
Investment trust	3.4	4.5
Shares and other equities	16.9	11.0
Insurance and annuity reserve	20.8	25.3
Others	5.2	4.4

Source: Adapted from Bank of Japan, 'Flow of funds'. <http://www.stat-search.boj.or.jp/ssi/cgi-bin/famecgi2?cgi=$nme_a000_en&lstSelection=11>.

Financial Internationalization in the late 1980s

In the late 1980s, Japanese banks became more market based in the international markets than in the domestic markets. Japanese banks developed international operations and launched investment banking in overseas markets. In the early 1970s, Japanese banks and securities companies launched overseas operations and the number of Japanese large firms which raised funds in the Euro market increased. Unlike at home, the Euro market had no regulations on segmentation of financial services. Most of the large banks either established wholly owned investment bank subsidiaries or entered into joint ventures with British merchant banks. They participated in underwriting syndicates for Eurodollar issuance by Japanese corporations, despite Japanese securities companies complaining that Japanese bank participation in underwriting syndicates for Japanese corporate bonds ran counter to the regulations on segmentation between banking and securities businesses (Rosenbluth 1989, 150–1).

Before the bursting of the Japanese bubble in the early 1990s, the internationalization of Japanese financial institutions proceeded rapidly. Japanese banks aggressively expanded overseas operations, particularly in lending, but also in some securities businesses (especially participating in the Eurobond market as lead underwriters). The Japanese Big Four securities companies (Nomura, Daiwa, Nikko, and Yamaichi) also expanded their international business and obtained banking licenses abroad. They could also avoid the domestic regulations on segmentation of financial services.

Japanese banks increased their presence in overseas markets dramatically, subsidized by very high profits in the domestic markets thanks to the bubble, meaning they could afford to lend huge amounts of money at very low interest rates. The BIS 59th annual report (1989) argues that Japanese banks played the dominant role in the international market at that time. It argues that Japanese banks were the only net lenders to the non-bank sector among the larger banking systems during 1988, and that the increase in their loans to non-bank entities exceeded that of their deposit liabilities by nearly US$21 billion. The Japanese banks funded this net lending largely in the inter-bank market and through securities issues (BIS 1989, 117–19).

In sum, Japanese banks developed market-based banking in the international market on the liabilities side of their balance sheets. At this point, Japanese banks made up seven of the top ten largest banks globally (in 1990). Japanese securities companies also dominated the league tables for arrangers of Eurobond issuance. However, their presence declined rapidly after the Japanese bubble burst in the early 1990s (see Tables 10.11, 10.12, 10.13).

The Collapse of the Stock Market Bubble

If this bubble economy had continued to expand, the Japanese 'bank-based' financial system might have transformed into a market-based one and Japanese banks and securities companies might have developed their international businesses even further. However, the bubble economy burst in

Table 10.11. International bank assets and liabilities, by nationality of banks

	At the end of the year (billions of US dollars)								
	1985	1986	1987	1988	1989	1990	1991	1992	1993
Japanese banks									
Assets	707.0	1,120.1	1,552.1	1,756.4	1,967.2	2,120.4	1,931.5	1,677.7	1,683.4
Liabilities	672.5	no data	no data	1,706.3	1,924.7	2,059.8	1,824.5	1,512.7	no data
US banks									
Assets	593.3	599.2	647.6	675.2	727.4	712.4	711.6	656.3	693.4
Liabilities	555.2	no data	no data	688.9	742.4	741.6	743.7	678.7	no data
French banks									
Assets	245.2	289.6	375.5	384.1	432.1	555.2	542.6	657.0	688.4
Liabilities	248.9	no data	no data	400.4	458.0	610.9	613.8	693.0	no data
German banks									
Assets	191.0	270.1	347.9	353.8	435.8	601.8	636.6	683.1	786.6
Liabilities	157.4	no data	no data	275.0	329.3	459.3	485.5	571.6	no data
UK banks									
Assets	191.0	211.5	253.9	238.6	247.3	272.3	260.2	293.9	332.2
Liabilities	200.8	no data	no data	266.8	308.7	321.6	312.0	340.3	no data
Other									
Assets	786.2	963.5	1,204.3	1,190.1	1,329.4	1,707.2	2,064.3	2,072.0	2,075.9
Liabilities	780.0	no data	no data	1,226.8	1,336.8	1,774.8	2,104.2	2,141.1	no data
Total									
Assets	2,713.7	3,454.0	4,381.3	4,598.2	5,139.2	5,969.3	6,146.8	6,040.0	6,260.0
Liabilities	2,614.8	no data	no data	4,564.2	5,099.9	5,968.0	6,083.7	5,937.4	no data

Note: Cross-border positions in all currencies plus the foreign currency vis-à -vis residents of banks in the following countries: Austria, Belgium, Luxembourg, Canada, Denmark, Finland, France, Germany, Ireland, Italy, Japan, the Netherlands, Norway (from 1992 only), Spain, Sweden, Switzerland, the United Kingdom and the United States (cross-border positions in domestic currency only); the figures for US banks also include the cross-border positions reported by US banks' branches in the Bahamas, the Cayman Islands, Panama, Hong Kong and Singapore. Positions are classified according to the nationality of ownership of banks. Non-bank positions include official monetary institutions and, on the liabilities side, banks' issues of CDs and other securities.

Source: BIS Annual Report (various years).

Table 10.12. Nationality of international bond issuers

Issuers		New issues (billions of US dollars)						Stocks (billions of US dollars)					
		1985	1986	1987	1988	1989	1990	1982	1985	1987	1988	1989	1990
Japan	A	20.2	31.8	42.4	50.8	96.7	57.9						
	B		27.0	36.5	40.3	83.8	38.5	17.7	64.1	153.5	183.6	265.3	317.7
US	A	40.2	41.6	22.5	17.2	16.9	21.9						
	B		32.6	11.4	6.1	-0.3	1.5	36.0	102.7	163.6	165.5	162.5	170.3
Canada	A	8.8	17.9	9.0	12.9	13.3	13.0						
	B		13.6	2.1	5.8	4.1	4.2	41.4	68.6	92.6	97.1	100.6	107.9
UK	A	14.4	20.2	11.1	26.4	24.8	23.2						
	B		17.5	9.4	20.1	21.6	16.8	11.1	29.8	64.3	82.8	98.4	127.8
France	A	11.9	13.4	8.4	16.4	13.4	18.1						
	B		5.7	3.2	10.0	9.2	10.8	18.4	39.0	58.3	65.3	74.0	90.8
Total	A	163.8	222.4	175.9	226.3	261.8	241.7						
	B	123.0	159.7	107.0	138.1	174.3	131.0	259.1	572.5	1,006.6	1,098.2	1,252.3	1,472.5

Note: A: announced gross new issues; B: completed new issues, net of repayments.
Source: BIS Annual Report (various years).

Table 10.13. Issuing activity in the international securities markets

Country of residence	New issues (billions of US dollars)				Amounts outstanding at end-1993 (billions of US dollars)
	1990	1991	1992	1993	
All countries	128.6	142.2	82.5	128.6	1,433.9
Japan	28.7	36.1	–5.0	–43.8	261.1
US	3.3	12.4	14.6	25.1	210.5
Canada	–0.2	0.8	–1.7	1.4	48.8
UK	27.9	24.7	13.1	20.5	174.7
France	12.2	22.4	19.6	24.1	145.6
Germany	1.7	3.7	9.4	20.7	43.8

Note 1: All bonds, notes, and other debt securities issued by the private sector.
Note 2: Changes in amounts outstanding at constant exchange rates, except for data on international bonds, which are on a flow basis.
Source: BIS Annual Report (various years).

the early 1990s. Ordinary people who had invested in the stock market for the first time during the bubble period made heavy losses. Moreover, it was revealed that large securities companies had compensated only their largest clients for losses sustained in the stock markets. Then, ordinary people rapidly withdrew from the stock market.

Securities companies, which grew rapidly in the bubble period, suffered great losses because stock prices dropped rapidly and their turnover decreased. Moreover, large securities companies were severely condemned because it was revealed that in 1991, they had assisted a 'Yakuza gang' (Japanese mafia gang) in buying up the shares of a railroad company and that in 1997, they had granted corporate racketeers huge, illegal payoffs. They lost people's confidence, further denting equity market investment.

The low stock prices in the 1990s meant that securities companies could not afford to participate in the investment banking business. Among securities companies, only Nomura Securities has expanded overseas operations since 1997, but not succeeded because of a shortage of talented experts in investment banking, as noted above. Other securities companies could not afford to expand overseas operations. Yamaichi Securities went bankrupt in 1997 because of the burden of huge off-the-book debts. Nikko Securities managed to survive by forming an alliance with Citigroup in 1998. Daiwa Securities also managed to survive by cooperating with Sumitomo Bank in 1998. Japanese securities companies remained focused on intermediating equity and bond markets and did not expand the fixed income and balance sheet-expanding business of international investment banking.

Non-performing Loan Problem

Japanese banks cut back international operations rapidly after the Japanese bubble burst in the early 1990s because they had to focus on dealing with domestic non-performing loans. They faced decreasing capital adequacy ratios after the collapse of the bubble. Borrowers became unable to pay back their debts because business conditions worsened sharply and the value of lands offered as collateral fell drastically. Banks had to set aside reserves to cover the expected loss from selling of property held as collateral. Moreover, the fall in stock prices had a significant negative impact on the financial conditions of large banks, which held very significant amounts of equity as cross-shareholdings. They had to reduce assets in order to meet the capital adequacy ratio requirements, as European banks have done recently (*Financial Times*, 3 May 2012). Interestingly, however, Tables 10.14 and 10.15 show that their loans and bills discounted increased until 1997, while their overseas branches' assets declined from 1991, increased again from 1995 and then declined once more from 1997. This was partly because many NFCs could not raise funds through the financial markets directly and became dependent on bank finance after the bubble burst. And another reason is 'ever-greening' ('*oikashi*').

When loans become non-performing, banks have to set aside reserves to cover the expected losses. However, banks did not like to post losses in order to write off bad loans rapidly because they were afraid of losing face. Besides, some banks' non-performing loans were so large that they could not write them all off at once. If they had done so, they could not have maintained their capital adequacy ratios above the regulatory requirement or could even have become insolvent. As a result, many banks underestimated the amount of non-performing loans and did not set aside adequate reserves

Table 10.14. Trends in lending by domestically licensed banks (outstanding loans and bills discounted)

	Amounts outstanding loans and bills discounted (at the end of the year) (billion yen)
1989	384,625
1990	408,791
1991	421,083
1992	427,972
1993	511,018
1994	508,850
1995	512,747
1996	512,060
1997	513,748
1998	502,902
1999	493,035
2000	475,265
2001	454,020
2002	432,326
2003	409,875
2004	398,531
2005	398,932
2006	406,977
2007	410,686
2008	427,160

Source: Adapted from Bank of Japan, 'Deposits and Loans Market'. <http://www.stat-search.boj.or.jp/ssi/cgi-bin/famecgi2?cgi=$nme_a000_en&lstSelection=4>.

Table 10.15. Principal assets and liabilities of overseas branches of domestically licensed banks

	Loans and bills discounted (billion yen)	Investment securities (billion yen)
1989	59,226.9	9,812.7
1990	76,037.8	10,320.7
1991	74,043.1	8,555.6
1992	72,765.8	7,617.9
1993	65,011.3	6,944.7
1994	62,808.2	6,715.9
1995	74,951.4	6,793.9
1996	81,836.0	7,110.7
1997	81,087.8	7,100.7
1998	49,678.0	4,449.4
1999	32,499.0	3,566.1
2000	29,217.1	4,708.1
2001	27,966.2	6,249.2
2002	20,266.4	5,893.2
2003	13,951.9	5,092.3
2004	14,547.4	4,324.7
2005	19,443.7	5,852.4
2006	24,524.6	7,393.3
2007	32,509.9	7,687.4
2008	33,163.0	6,143.4

Source: Adapted from Bank of Japan, 'Financial Institutions Accounts'. <http://www.stat-search.boj.or.jp/ssi/cgi-bin/famecgi2?cgi=$nme_a000&lstSelection=3>.

to cover them. Banks therefore extended fresh loans to corporations that could not pay back their loans in order to allow them to make the interest payments, allowing banks to classify the loans as performing. This is called 'ever-greening' (*'oikashi'*). Financial institutions also hid their losses through shifting non-performing assets to their affiliated companies. This off-balance sheet liability is called *'tobashi'*. (Tanaka 2005).

Many banks could conceal non-performing loans by extending additional loans to almost insolvent firms. In November 1997, however, Sanyo Securities, a mid-sized securities company, and Hokkaido Takushoku Bank, a big city bank, went bankrupt. Moreover, Yamaichi Securities Company, one of Big Four securities companies, was forced to close down voluntarily because about 260 billion yen (US$2.1 billion at the November 1997 exchange rate) off-the-book liabilities (*tobashi*) were uncovered. The Japanese financial crisis erupted and most Japanese at last became aware of the depth of the financial problems (Svensson, Mabuchi and Kamikawa 2006). As the public and politicians blamed the MOF for its failure in financial supervision, the financial regulators had to supervise and inspect financial institutions more strictly and it became difficult for banks to postpone the disposal of their bad loans.[8] Therefore, they had to reduce assets sharply from the autumn of 1997 in order to meet capital adequacy ratio requirements. As a result, banks became reluctant to lend money to SMEs whose lending risk was regarded as high. This is called *'kashi-shiburi'* and made it difficult for SMEs to raise funds.

Meanwhile, many companies also lost their motivation to invest in new plant and equipment. In the bubble period, most companies expected the economy to grow and increased investment in new plant and equipment on a large scale, by borrowing money from banks or by issuing corporate bonds. However, the bubble economy collapsed and there remained a surplus of manufacturing capacity. Many companies were burdened by a huge debt and had to pay back their debt over a long period instead of borrowing money from banks. Most of them also expected the economy to worsen over future years. As a result, except for companies which suffered a severe cash-flow shortage, they became very careful about borrowing money from banks. Therefore, the total amount of loans from domestic banks continued to decrease from 1998 to 2004 (Table 10.14) and banks did not need market-based finance. Bank lending decreased even as banks became more traditional in their liabilities. The non-performing loans were so large that it was not until 2004 that the problem was resolved. In 2005, bank lending started to rise because the

[8] Until 2001, when new accounting standards were introduced, if a controlling entity did not hold more than 50 per cent stocks, entities that it controlled (subsidiaries) were not consolidated. Hence, a financial institution could shift their non-performing assets to subsidiaries that it controlled substantially but of which it did not hold more than 50 per cent of equity (Tanaka 2005).

non-performing loan problem was solved and the Japanese economy started to recover thanks to growing exports to China and the United States.

Japanese banks concentrated on the disposal of bad loans and increased financial strength took priority over increased profitability in the early 2000s, when the securitization business and the originate-to-distribute model spread worldwide. Unlike the US and European banks, therefore, they could not take any increased risk (Sato 2010, 254–7) and the development of market-based banking was prevented.

In addition, Japanese banks improved the quality of risk management in the process of the disposal of non-performing loans. From the end of 1990s to the early 2000s, the financial regulators enhanced the effectiveness of financial supervision and inspection because they established the assessment standards for assets and the standards of loan-loss reserves as trustworthy and developed the framework for disclosure. The Japanese government adopted Basel II in the fiscal year ending March 2007, ahead of the United States and Europe. Following the strengthening of bank supervision and inspection, the quality of banks' risk management was improved. Thus, they became more careful about producing and selling financial products whose risk characteristics were too complicated and investing in securitized products whose risk was unclear (Sato 2010, 254–7). Although Japanese financial authorities came to respect the initiative and autonomy of market players from the end of 1990s, they became eager to severely punish market players for their acts against the rules at the same time. Some financial institutions called the FSA the 'Financial Punishment Agency' (Kamikawa 2012). Thanks to the strict financial authorities, unlike some European banks, Japanese banks did not get involved in off-balance sheet activities, such as ABCP, in order to get around capital adequacy rules and improve capital ratios (Hardie and Howarth, Chapter 2, this volume).

The Financial Regulations or the Financial Crisis?

As noted above, in the bubble period, Japanese banks expanded international operations and launched securities businesses in overseas markets, avoiding the domestic regulations, and securities companies similarly expanded aggressively. After the bubble burst, financial deregulation continued, but the pre-crisis expansion reversed. This suggests that Japanese financial institutions were constrained less by regulation than the impact of the bubble bursting. Even though there were the domestic regulations on segmentation of financial services, they could launch new business areas in overseas markets. If the Japanese bubble had not burst and Japanese banks had expanded international operations further, they might have raised money in foreign capital markets and become more 'market based'. However, the Japanese bubble burst and they cut back international operations rapidly because they had to reduce assets in order to meet the capital adequacy ratio requirements. Similarly, Japanese securities firms might have become more like the US investment banks whose activities they had increasingly been trying to emulate before the Japanese bubble burst.

This interpretation is confirmed by the fact that Japanese banks started to prepare for becoming more market based, as the non-performing loan problem was being resolved. In the early 2000s, large financial institutions were reorganized into financial groups centring on three megabanks. In a financial group, a holding company holds stocks issued by a city bank, a trust bank, and a securities company. In the mid-2000s, Mitsubishi UFJ Securities and Mizuho Securities, which are securities subsidiaries of banks, and Daiwa Securities SMBC, the joint venture between Daiwa Securities and Sumitomo Mitsui Financial Group, launched investment banking business.[9] Megabanks pushed forward with this reorganization of the financial sector aggressively in order to enter the securities business, though this had not had a significant impact by the time of the international financial crisis.

The Japanese Crisis Strengthened the 'Bank-Centred' Financial System

The Japanese financial crisis reinforced the preference of most Japanese households for low-risk, low-return bank deposits over high-risk, high-return financial assets, such as securities. This was because they learned from the collapse of the bubble that stock investment was dangerous. The primary household saving vehicle still remained bank deposits and the character of Japanese bank-centred financial system did not change (see Table 10.16).

Banks decreased lending, but amassed a huge amount of deposits. They invested the funds in the safest assets, or Japanese government bonds to maintain capital adequacy ratios. This stemmed partly from their previous post-bubble experiences that they had struggled to maintain capital adequacy ratios above the regulatory requirement. Therefore, most Japanese government bonds were purchased in the domestic market and the sovereign debt crisis did not happen in Japan despite the government issuing an enormous volume of bonds. To sum up, the cause of the absence of a sovereign debt crisis in Japan can also be traced to the Japanese financial crisis.

[9] In 2009, Sumitomo Mitsui Banking Corporation acquired Nikko Cordial Securities from Citigroup and made it a wholly-owned subsidiary. The joint venture between Daiwa Securities and Sumitomo Mitsui Financial Group was dissolved and Daiwa Securities acquired all of the shares of Daiwa Securities SMBC.

Table 10.16. Trends in the component ratio of household assets

(percentage of total at the end of March in the year)

	Currency and deposits	Securities other than shares	Investment trust	Shares and other equities	Insurance and annuity reserve
1991	47.4	6.3	3.4	16.9	20.8
1992	50.4	6.9	2.8	12.3	22.3
1993	50.3	7.3	2.5	11.0	23.4
1994	50.0	6.9	2.5	10.9	24.2
1995	50.1	6.8	1.9	10.1	25.0
1996	50.1	5.9	2.3	11.5	25.4
1997	52.2	5.5	2.2	8.2	26.6
1998	53.9	4.9	1.9	7.0	27.1
1999	54.5	4.1	2.0	7.3	27.0
2000	53.2	3.6	2.3	9.9	26.4
2001	54.1	3.5	2.4	7.7	27.2
2002	54.2	2.9	2.2	6.0	29.7
2003	54.5	2.5	2.0	5.1	30.3
2004	53.4	2.2	2.3	8.1	28.7
2005	53.1	2.5	2.5	9.0	28.3
2006	50.2	2.6	3.4	12.6	26.8
2007	49.5	2.8	4.1	12.4	26.9
2008	52.3	3.0	4.2	7.6	28.7
2009	54.7	2.9	3.3	5.7	29.5
2010	54.2	2.8	3.8	6.8	28.3

Source: Adapted from Bank of Japan, 'Flow of funds'. <http://www.stat-search.boj.or.jp/ssi/cgi-bin/famecgi2?cgi=$nme_a000_en&lstSelection=11>.

Conclusion

To begin with, this chapter confirms that the development of market-based banking in Japan remained very low and the Japanese banking sector was much less damaged by the international financial crisis than those of other developed countries. Then, this chapter examines why it remained very low in Japan.

The distinctive character of the Japanese financial system was that the CME model remained intact. The main flow of money in the Japanese economy continued to be that households deposited money with banks and banks lent money to firms and the government. Most households chose bank deposits as their main investment vehicle and banks did not need to depend on market-based finance because bank deposits exceeded bank loans. Banks invested the surplus of deposits in Japanese government bonds and a sovereign debt crisis did not happen because banks held such a high proportion of government bonds. In addition, the remuneration system adopted by Japanese financial institutions was the seniority-based personnel system, which was a suitable system for the Japanese 'group-based' CME. Because of this system, bank employees did not try to maximize short-term profits through high-risk, high-return investment and financial institutions did not secure talented foreign experts in the investment banking business.

What then kept this system intact? At first glance, financial regulation seems to be the reason. However, it is argued here that the financial crisis after the collapse of the Japanese bubble economy was more important. Because of this earlier financial crisis, Japanese banks had to focus on dealing with non-performing loans and could not afford to expand securities businesses and international activities from the early 1990s to the early 2000s when financial innovation developed rapidly in the United States and Europe. After the late 1970s, banks had expanded international operations and launched securities businesses in overseas markets, avoiding the domestic regulations on the segmentation of financial services. After the bubble burst, however, they cut back international operations rapidly and reduced their assets in order to meet the capital adequacy ratio requirements. Even after the deregulation of the 'Japanese Financial Big Bang', they did not expand fully into investment banking business until 2004 when the financial crisis was resolved. Moreover, thanks to the financial crisis, the financial authorities became much stricter in supervising and auditing Japanese banks. They improved their risk management and became much more careful about producing and selling financial products whose risk characteristics were too complicated, and investing in securitized products whose risk was unclear.

On the other hand, securities companies could also not afford to participate in the investment banking business with the continuing sluggish Japanese stock prices in the 1990s. Only Nomura Securities expanded its overseas operations, but could not succeed because of a shortage of talented experts in the international businesses. Individual investors who made huge losses due to the bubble bursting withdrew from the stock market. As a result of the experiences of the last crisis, the primary household saving vehicle still remained bank deposits. The financial crisis made banks keep concentrating on the traditional banking business and securities companies keep concentrating on intermediating equity and bond markets. It prevented the development of market-based banking.

Not in the late 1990s, when the financial deregulation proceeded rapidly but in the mid-2000s, when the Japanese financial crisis was resolved, did three financial groups centred on megabanks expand their investment banking business through their securities subsidiaries. Their remuneration systems, however, did not change fully and they fell behind foreign financial institutions in investment banking because of a shortage of experts.

With regards to the absence of a sovereign debt crisis in Japan, the financial crisis was again the primary reason. Because of the last crisis, most households preferred low-risk, low-return bank deposits. Banks amassed deposits significantly in excess of loans and purchased Japanese government bonds because they preferred low-risk, low-return financial assets. This is because they struggled to meet capital adequacy requirements in the period after the Japanese crisis. As a result, most Japanese government bonds were held by domestic investors and there was no sovereign credit crisis in Japan, though the highest debt to GDP ratio of any developed country.

References

Aizawa, K. (1995) *Nichigin-Ho Nijugo-Jo Hatsudo: Heisei Kin'yu Kyoko kara Manabu mono* [Exercising the Article 25 of the Bank of Japan Law: Things to Learn from Heisei-Era Financial Crisis]. Tokyo: Chuo Koronsha.

Bank of Japan (1990) 'Waga Kuni ni okeru Kin-nen no Chika Josho no Haikei to Eikyo ni tsuite'. [About the Background and Influence of Surging Land Prices Recently in Our Country]. *Chosa Geppo*, April 1990: 34–85.

BIS (Bank for International Settlements). various years. *Annual Report*. Available online at <http://www.bis.org/publ/arpdf/archive/index.htm>

BIS (2008) *Statistical Annex*. Available online at <http://www.bis.org/publ/qtrpdf/r_qa0806.pdf>

Cabinet Office, Government of Japan (2008) *Annual Report on the Japanese Economy and Public Finance 2008*. Available online at <http://www5.cao.go.jp/j-j/wp/wp-je08/08.html>

Culpepper, P. D. (2011) *Quiet Politics and Business Power: Corporate Control in Europe and Japan*. New York: Cambridge University Press.

Financial Services Agency (2009) 'Exposures of Japanese Deposit-Taking Institutions to Securitized Products Based on the Leading Practices Summarized in the FSF Report'. Available online at <http://www.fsa.go.jp/en/news/2009/20090306-2/02.pdf>

Hall, P. A. and D. Soskice (2001) 'An Introduction to Varieties of Capitalism'. In *Varieties of Capitalism: The Institutional Foundations of Comparative Advantage* (eds P. A. Hall and D. Soskice). New York: Oxford University Press.

Hoshi, T., and A. Kashyap (2001) *Corporate Financing and Governance in Japan: The Road to the Future*. Cambridge: The MIT Press.

IMF (2008) *Global Financial Stability Report: Financial Stress and Deleveraging Macro-Financial Implications and Policy*. October. Available online at <www.imf.org/external/pubs/ft/gfsr/2008/02/index.htm>

IMF (2010) *Global Financial Stability Report: Sovereigns, Funding, and Systemic Liquidity*. October. Available online at <www.imf.org/external/pubs/ft/gfsr/2010/02/index.htm>

Kamikawa, R. (2012) 'The Interaction between Financial Regulation and Financial Crisis in Japan: Change in Financial Administration and Two Financial Crises from 1980 to 2010'. *Osaka University Law Review*, No. 59: 1–26.

Kawano, K. (1995) *Kin-yu Jiyuka Senryaku no Kiketsu: Ginko no Obahangu to Hanguoba* [Consequence of Financial Liberalization Strategy: Overhang and Hangover of Banks]. Tokyo: Yuhikaku.

Kishi, N. (1994) *Kenjin Tachi no Gosan: Kensho Baburu Keizai* [Miscalculations by the Sages: Examining the Bubble Economy]. Tokyo: Nihon Keizai Shimbunsha.

Ministry of Finance (2010) *Waga Kuni Zeisei no Genjo Zempan ni Kansuru Shiryo (Heisei 22 nen 10 gatsu genzai)*. [General Information on Our Country's Current Conditions of Tax System and Budget (As of October 2010)]. Available online at <http://www.mof.go.jp/jouhou/syuzei/siryou/genjo.htm>

Nihon Keizai Shimbunsha (ed.) (2000) *Kensho Baburu: Han'i naki Ayamachi* [Examining Heisei-Era Bubble: Mistake without Malice]. Tokyo: Nihon Keizai Shimbunsha.

Nihon Keizai Shimbunsha (ed.) (2009a) *Jitsuroku Sekai Kin'yu Kiki* [The Record of the World Financial Crisis]. Tokyo: Nihon Keizai Shimbun Shuppansha.

Nihon Keizai Shimbunsha (ed.) (2009b) *Dai Shushuku: Kensho Gurobaru Kiki* [The Great Contraction: Examination of the Global Crisis]. Tokyo: Nihon Keizai Shimbun Shuppansha.

Noguchi, Y. (1989) *Tochi no Keizaigkau* [Economics of Land]. Tokyo: Nihon Keizai Shimbunsha.

Okazaki, T., and T. Hoshi (2002) '1980 nendai no Ginko Keiei: Senryaku, Soshiki, and Gabanansu' [Management of Banks in the 1980s: Strategies, Organizations, and Governance]. In *Heisei Baburu no Kenkyu (Jo): Baburu no Hassei to sono Haikei Kozo* [The Study of the Babble of the Heisei Era (vol. 1): The Outbreak of Bubble Economy and Background Structures] (eds M. Muramatsu and M. Okuno). Tokyo: Toyo Keizai Shimposha.

Otake, H. (1994) *Jiyushugi teki Kaikaku no Jidai: 1980 nendai zenki no Nihon Seiji* [The Era of Liberal Reforms: Japanese Politics in the early of 1980s]. Tokyo: Chuo Koronsha.

Rosenbluth, F. M. (1989) *Financial Politics in Contemporary Japan*. Ithaca: Cornell University Press.

Sato, T. (2010) *Kin'yu Gyosei no Zahyojiku: Heiji to Yuji wo Koete* [Coordinate Axes of Financial Administration: Beyond Peacetime and Emergency Situations]. Tokyo: Toyo Keizai Shimposha.

Svensson, T., M. Mabuchi and R. Kamikawa (2006) 'Managing the Bank-System Crisis in Coordinated Market Economies: Institutions and Blame Avoidance Strategies in Sweden and Japan'. *Governance*, 19 (1): 43–74.

Tahara, S. (1993) *Heisei Nihon no Kanryo* [Bureaucracy in Japan in Heisei Era]. Tokyo: Bungei Shunju.

Tanaka, T. (2005) 'Nihon ni okeru Furyo Saiken Mondai no "Sakiokuri": Kin'yu Kikan ni yoru Furyo Saiken Shori no "Sakiokuri" to Seifu ni yoru Kin'yu Kikan Shori no "Sakiokuri"' [Postponement of the Non-performing Loan Problem in Japan: Postponement of the Disposal of Non-performing Loans by Financial Institutions and of Resolution of Financial Institutions by the Government]. In *Heisei Baburu Sakiokuri no Kenkyu* (ed. M. Muramatsu) [The Study of Postponement about the Babble of the Heisei Era]. Tokyo: Toyo Keizai Shimposha.

Yoshikawa, H. (1999) *Tenkan-ki no Nihon Keizai* [Turning Point of Japanese Economy]. Tokyo: Iwanami Shoten.

Zenkoku Ginko Kyokai [Japanese Bankers Association] (2008) 'Heisei 19 nendo Zenkoku Ginko Sogo Zaimu Shohyo' [Financial Statements of All Banks in Fiscal 2007]. Available online at <http://www.zenginkyo.or.jp/stats/year2_02/details/account2007_terminal/index.html>

Index

The manufacturer's authorised representative in the EU for product safety is Oxford University Press España S.A. of el Parque Empresarial San Fernando de Henares, Avenida de Castilla, 2 – 28830 Madrid (www.oup.es/en or product.safety@oup.com). OUP España S.A. also acts as importer into Spain of products made by the manufacturer.

www.ingramcontent.com/pod-product-compliance
Lightning Source LLC
LaVergne TN
LVHW011751200926
848484LV00003B/676
9780199662289